ORESTES A. BROWNSON'S
ROAD TO
CATHOLICISM

PUBLICATIONS OF

THE AMERICAN INSTITUTE

UNIVERSITY OF OSLO

ORESTES A. BROWNSON'S ROAD TO CATHOLICISM

By

PER SVEINO

UNIVERSITETSFORLAGET, OSLO
HUMANITIES PRESS, NEW YORK

Section: A.60.04-4T

PUBLISHED IN NORWAY
BY UNIVERSITETSFORLAGET

PUBLISHED IN THE UNITED STATES OF
AMERICA AND CANADA
BY HUMANITIES PRESS

Cover design by
ODDVAR WOLD

Printed in Norway
HESTHOLMS BOKTRYKKERI

Were we not trained in Boston, 'the Hub of the Universe,' at a time when it was really the focus of all sorts of modern ideas, good, bad, and indifferent? What have any of you to teach one who participated in the Boston intellectual movement from 1830 to 1844? We Bostonians were a generation ahead of you.

Orestes A. Brownson in 1875 (*Works*, IX, 551).

One divine thought runs through the whole, and nothing does or can stand alone. We study things too much in their analysis, not enough in their synthesis.

Orestes A. Brownson in 1869 (*Works*, IX, 332).

There is a Power whose care
Teaches thy way along that pathless coast—
The desert and illimitable air—
Lone wandering, but not lost.

William Cullen Bryant ("To a Waterfowl").

Preface

While at Harvard University 1952–1953 on a Fulbright/Smith-Mundt scholarship, I was encouraged by my advisers Professor Perry Miller and Professor Kenneth B. Murdock to undertake a study of Orestes A. Brownson. In 1953 and 1954, during shorter stays at Notre Dame University, Indiana and Sorbonne University, Paris, I gathered additional material.

Throughout the following years I have been working on my treatise in leisure hours. But my regular work as teacher in secondary schools tended to give my study a rather fragmentary character.

Yet an award for 1968–1969 from Norges almenvitenskapelige forskningsråd (the Norwegian Research Council for Science and the Humanities) enabled me to finish my treatise and also make it more coherent in tone and composition than otherwise would have been possible. I want to express my gratitude to the Research Council for this excellent opportunity given me to concentrate solely on my project.

My thanks are due to the late Professor Perry Miller and Professor Kenneth Murdock of Harvard University, and to Archivist Thomas McAvoy, C.S.C., who kindly gave me access to the valuable, still unpublished collection of Brownson material at Notre Dame University. Grateful acknowledgment is also made to the Sorbonne University authorities for admittance to the University library.

But first of all, I want to express my heartiest thanks to Professor Sigmund Skard, leader of the American Institute at the University of Oslo. Throughout the years he has steadily encouraged me in my work and given me valuable suggestions and criticisms, both regarding subject matter and composition. In practical matters related to my work he has given me invaluable help.

I also want to thank the teaching staff at the American Institute, Oslo, and my colleagues at Ålesund Gymnas for their encouragement and interest in my work.

Finally, I express my best thanks to my wife for suggestions and criticisms and, perhaps no less, for her patience.

Part of the treatise, Chapter VIII: "New Views," has been printed in *Americana Norvegica: Norwegian Contributions to American Studies*, I, ed. Sigmund Skard and Henry H. Wasser (Philadelphia, 1966).

Ålesund, October 1970

Per Sveino

Contents

Introduction

The first part of the nineteenth century was in the United States a period of hectic restlessness. Obviously, the young nation tried to ascertain its potentialities and build its foundation for the future.

During the first years, the Federalists and the Democrats were in heated disagreement on the division of power between the Federal Government and the state governments, and this controversy was not a matter of theory only. The Federalists, representing the trading and manufacturing interests of the North-East, wanted a strong central or Federal Government for the benefit of those interests, while the Democrats, representing the plantation owners of the South, the farmers throughout the Union, and the growing working population of the Northern cities, advocated the rights and even the sovereignty of the single states.

Throughout the period in question, the Democratic Party dominated the political scene, first through the half rustic, half aristocratic Jeffersonian democracy, then through the more grass-roots, Western-influenced democracy of Andrew Jackson. Characteristically, during that period almost all presidents came from the Democratic Party. Yet in 1840 the Whigs, mainly descending from the old Federalist Party, came into office. Basic issues between the Whigs and the Democrats were the questions of tariffs and a national bank. The overriding issue: the division of power between the Federal Government and the state governments was gaining increasing momentum due to the growing sectional differences between the South and the North. Slavery was brought more and more sharply into focus, both through the ardent debates in Congress on the extension of slavery into the new territories, and through the well-meant, but often fanatical zeal of the Abolitionists.

Yet the religious scene during that period of American history offered a picture even more many-sided and heterogeneous. The so-called disestablishment, i.e. the rupture of any administrative links between the churches and the Government, whether local or federal, was completed by the end of the Jacksonian period, placing all denominations on an equal footing before the secular authorities. The descendants of the old Puritans: the Congregationalists and the Presbyterians, had some difficulty in holding their own against the Baptists and the Methodists, who were in the ascendancy. Above all in the West, but also to a great extent in the East the latter churches were gaining a strong foothold. But a far more serious problem facing the old churches was an increasing general skepticism as to the stern Calvinistic dogmas. This skepticism paved the way for so-called liberal forms of Christianity like Universalism and Unitarianism.

To the younger generation of Unitarian ministers growing to adulthood in the 1830's and 1840's, even Unitarianism in its half-dogmatic form was not liberal or radical enough. Consequently, they planted themselves on their own instincts, only trusting "the inner light." Thus, Unitarianism developed into Transcendentalism.

But even if Boston (with surroundings?) has been called "the Hub of the Universe," Unitarianism and its offshoot Transcendentalism were, after all, typically New England phenomena. In the other parts of the Union orthodox Christianity was dominant.

As for the Episcopal Church, its influence was on the increase during the first part of the nineteenth century. Its emphasis on High Church principles and sacramentalism appealed to those who did not favor the strongly individualistic and even revivalistic forms of Christianity. Indeed, toward the middle of the century, as a parallel to similar contemporary tendencies in England and Europe, an increasing belief in Christian and churchly tradition made itself manifest in different American denominations.

At the beginning of the century the Roman Catholic Church was a tiny minority with a center in Baltimore, Maryland; but with the growing influx of Catholic immigrants from Europe, it became, already in the 1840's, one of the largest single denominations in the United States. Protestant Americans, and especially "Native Americans," fearful of Popish hegemony, witnessed the growth of this church with uneasiness and even alarm.

Finally, it should be mentioned that throughout the whole period in question, there was a widespread, though often vaguely defined desire for Christian unity.

To round out the picture, the representatives of "freethought" should be taken into account. Continuing the tradition from the Era of Enlightenment, this group represented a wide spectrum of thought, ranging from deism to atheism, from vague beliefs in Providence to downright infidelity. Yet the "freethinkers" were united in their rejection of traditional Christian dogma, and most of them were wedded to the cause of educational, social, and political reform. Much on their initiative, the so-called "community system" was introduced, often on a socialist or even communist basis, with the view of eventually changing the large society outside.

In this country and in this period, the United States of 1800–1850, Orestes Augustus Brownson was born and grew to manhood. His character and intellectual development reflect in many ways the impatience and restlessness, but also the drive and energy of the young nation. Born 1803 into a poor Vermont family, he was, like his countrymen, influenced by diverse political and religious ideas of his time, but he responded much more actively and intensely to these ideas than did most of his compatriots. Politically, he espoused the cause of the Democratic Party, urging the adoption of radical social reforms, above all the abolition of the hereditary right of property; then, from 1840 onward, he was verging toward conservatism. Yet his religious experience was more spectacular. He went through the different stages of Presbyterianism, Universalism, "freethought," Unitarianism and finally, in 1844, became a convert to Catholicism. Though far from living a calm, peaceful life after his conversion, he remained a Catholic until his death in 1876.

Although for the most part a self-made scholar, Brownson became a Universalist and a Unitarian minister, but first of all, he was a lifelong contributor to and editor of a great many journals and periodicals. In a direct and forceful manner and with a terse and robust style he dealt with current political, religious, and philosophical problems. A keen logician, he loved to push first principles to extremes. Certainly, he often made too hasty and too long strides from his premises to his conclusions. This was due partly to the lack of a regular formal education, partly to the very nature of journalistic work.

But the real reason lay deeper. Above all, Brownson was a man of feelings, a man completely absorbed by the issues which for the time occupied his mind. Indeed, neutrality, disengagement, cool objectivity were not his characteristics. Consequently, like his contemporaries, modern readers will sometimes find his arguments shockingly one-sided, but seldom or never uninteresting. His good friend and fellow Catholic Isaac T. Hecker was undoubtedly right when he said about him: "He was routine in nothing" (*Catholic World*, XLV [July 1887], 466).

Yet his power of logic and his strong feelings were not the only contrasting features in Brownson's mental make-up. His tendency to extremism was counterbalanced by a desire of harmonizing opposing principles. Sometimes the former tendency was more manifest, at other times the latter. However, his strong personal involvement also gave his craving for synthesis a flavor of "extremism." After all, it is an interesting paradox that this logician with his love of analytical extremes was proud of calling himself an Eclectic, and formulated a "synthetic philosophy."

A charge often brought against Brownson was his alleged frequent changes of opinion, and not a few of his contemporaries considered him a weather-vane. In his amusing *A Fable for Critics* (1848), James Russell Lowell, besides stressing Brownson's strong logic, which might turn white into jet-black, pointed to his supposed proneness to change:

> He shifts quite about, then proceeds to expound
> That't is merely the earth, not himself, that turns round,
> And wishes it clearly expressed on your mind
> That the weathercock rules and not follows the wind...

(*The Complete Writings of James Russell Lowell*, XII [Boston and New York, 1904], pp. 42–43).

Far less humorious, however, was Octavius Brooks Frothingham, who attributed Brownson's presumed variability to a "mental baselessness" (*Transcendentalism in New England* [New York, 1876], p. 132). This, to say the least, is definitely an exaggeration.

Yet even if there really was some grain of truth in the charge as to his frequent changes of views, these changes very often only concerned details or the surface of things, whereas, by a closer analysis, a basic consistency is traceable in his intellectual development. In the heated atmosphere of journalistic debate his supposed inconstancy often only represented shifts of emphasis, necessitated by the changing situations. The deepest layers of his thought, however, were mostly undisturbed by the fluctuations on the surface. In any case, opponents and sympathizers alike agreed that he was honest through and through, and was motivated by a never failing love of truth.

But his downright honesty and much more his categoric, sometimes aggressive manner of stating his convictions tended to make him a rather lonely figure in the very midst of controversy. Doubtless, the cause of truth would not have fared any worse if he had chosen a more moderate form of expression. On the other hand, it was just this overweening assurance of the truth of his opinions that made him the lonely, but also the strong-willed and fascinating person he really was.

Nevertheless, there is no evidence that he ever sought loneliness or isolation. On the contrary, this independent, truculent, and lonely man not only yearned for human contact; he also—though perhaps without being aware of it—made his own psychological need of fellowship an integrating part of his views on philosophy and religion. Highly individualistic though he was, he believed more firmly than most others in the solidarity of mankind and in the significance of mutual influence in human relationships. The lonely man believed in the divine instincts of the masses, and when he thought they deceived him, he believed in the influence of "Providential Men" and the church. Of course, Brownson's philosophical and religious thought cannot be reduced to a matter of personal psychology; but on the other hand, it seems evident that his emphasis on the solidarity of the human race, at least to some extent, was a compensation for his feeling of loneliness. In any case, the man who in his own words considered himself standing "very much apart" (*Works*, XIX, 581) fervently believed in a doctrine of "life by communion."

At the turn of the twentieth century a speaker—M. J. Harson—in the Catholic Club of New York City called Brownson "a man of courage and a great American," but he also had to admit that this extraordinary convert "was almost forgotten by American Catholics" (*Catholic World*, LXXIX [April 1904], 1–21, esp. 19).

He was hardly any more remembered by his non-Catholic countrymen, who had difficulty in understanding and accepting his adoption of the Catholic cause. Already by 1882, only six years after Brownson's death, Joseph Henry Allen complained that "the strong, stormful, rude, yet tender-hearted man passes away, leaving hardly a ripple in our memory to remind us what his influence had been" (*Our Liberal Movement in Theology* [Boston, 1882], pp. 87–88).

True, Henry F. Brownson's edition of *Brownson's Works* in twenty volumes (Detroit, 1882–1887) and his own three-volume biography on his father (Detroit, 1898–1900) did not go unheeded, but did not reawaken any widespread interest in Orestes A. Brownson and his writings.

The most obvious reason for this lack of interest or even neglect was the journalistic character of Brownson's work. He mostly dealt with problems of the day, and the current significance of the topics was easily reduced with the change of events. Thus the writer himself, too, might be—and was—easily forgotten.

Yet, in the long run a man like Brownson simply refuses to be forgotten. When the journalistic dust was removed from his writings, later generations more clearly than his contemporaries saw—and see—the lasting value of his work. Thus, the 1930's and 1940's witnessed a real renewal of interest in Brownson, above all with the biography of Arthur M. Schlesinger, Jr., *Orestes A. Brownson: A Pilgrim's Progress* (Boston, 1939) and that of Theodore Maynard, *Orestes Brownson: Yankee, Radical, Catholic* (New York, 1943). In addition to these works, from which I have drawn much benefit, I will also mention two informative periodical articles from the same time: Helen S. Mims, "Early American Democratic Theory and Orestes Brownson," *Science and Society*, III, No. 2 (Spring, 1939), 166–198, and A. Robert Caponigri, "Brownson and Emerson: Nature and History," *New England Quarterly*, XVIII (September, 1945), 368–390. Then, in 1965, appeared Americo D. Lapati's book *Orestes A. Brownson*, which is a good introduction to Brownson's thought, and something more than "a primer," which the author modestly calls it.

It may seem presumptious that someone—and a foreigner at that—should undertake a study of Orestes Brownson in addition to those mentioned above. My only justification for so doing is a matter of emphasis. Schlesinger was primarily concerned with Brownson's social and political ideas, and Maynard first of all intended to draw a "portrait of a very remarkable man" (Introduction, p. x). My purpose is to give a detailed treatment of Brownson's views, above all his religious and philosophical views, before his conversion to Catholicism, and my thesis is to prove a basic consistency in his intellectual development toward his conversion. Although mainly dealing with his ideas and not intending to give any biographical portrait of Brownson, I want to treat his intellectual development in the light of his highly interesting character, briefly sketched in the foregoing lines. Finally, and still from the viewpoint of the thesis, his development after his conversion will be given a short treatment.

Some readers will perhaps think there are too many repetitions in my work. It should be borne in mind, however, that my genetic, chronological method, the very purpose or argument of the dissertation, and, above all, Brownson's own recurrent preoccupation with certain main themes make it extremely difficult to completely avoid repetitions.

While at Harvard, I collected material concerning Brownson's pre-Catholic period, above all his own writings scattered about in different journals and reviews. This material has not, in my opinion, been treated in sufficient detail by other writers, and makes it possible to give a more rounded and detailed picture of his "internal" biography prior to his conversion. In addition, I want to give a more extensive treatment of European influences on and counterparts to Brownson's thought than has, so far, been given.

However, the fact that Brownson himself in his autobiography *The Convert* (1857) wrote about his road to Catholicism seems to make my own treatment of the same theme quite superfluous. Yet once more the question of emphasis comes up. Although not writing an avowedly controversial or polemical book, Brownson focused his interest on certain trains of thought, while treating slightly or excluding others. Thus, for instance, he seems to have underrated the impact of Transcendentalism on his mind.

With all due respect paid to *The Convert*, to which frequent references will be made throughout my exposition, I express the hope that my book will be something more than a mere paraphrase of Brownson's autobiography. In any case, my intention to write an "internal" or intellectual biography is justified by Brownson's own words in his semiautobiographical work *Charles Elwood* from 1840: "The man lies beneath his deeds, and is but slightly revealed by the outward events of his life. Would you become acquainted with the man you must read the history of his soul—make yourself familiar with his spiritual experience, his inward struggles, defeats, victories, doubts, convictions, ends and aims" (*Works*, IV, 174).

Remains the final question, the answer to which, in the last analysis, justifies or not justifies a study as this one: Which are the lasting values of Brownson's writings? To the present writer, Brownson's importance in American intellectual history lies in his responsiveness to new ideas, an exceptional ability to expose the diverse ideologies of his time, combined with an ingrained sense of tradition, and great emotional and intellectual force in the presentation of his views. His vigorous and fluent style seems surprisingly "modern" and has kept its freshness and lucidity up to the present time. Also, his power of composition should be emphasized.

All in all, one cannot—and should not—forget a man who, in Van Wyck Brooks's words, was "something more than a journalist, something less than a sage..." (*The Flowering of New England* [New and revised edition; New York, 1941], p. 249).

I

A Youth in Quest of Himself

Already from early childhood Orestes Brownson took an almost unusual interest in religious subjects. He seized every opportunity to listen to others talking about religion, and even took active part himself in such conversations. Once, during a muster of the local militia in a neighboring town, the nine-year-old Orestes got into a hot argument with two old men, who were discussing free will and election. Completely forgetting the soldiers and what was going on around him, young Orestes took intense delight in the theological dispute, bravely defending free will against an authority like Jonathan Edwards.[1]

A boy discussing theological problems with old people: this episode not only shows his early religious interests, but also illustrates his childhood in general. About half a century later Brownson, in his autobiography, *The Convert,* regretted that "properly speaking I had no childhood, and have more of the child in my feelings now than at eight or ten years of age."[2] Obviously, it was his own childhood he had in mind in 1863 when admonishing the readers of his review to "keep the child a child as long as you can, and let the child to the last moment revel in the poetry, the sunlight of childhood."[3]

Born at Stockbridge, Vermont, September 16, 1803, he had to leave his home already at the age of six and was placed with an old couple at Royalton to be brought up. His widowed mother was not able to support her five children, and the youngest ones, Orestes and his twin sister Daphne, were temporarily "adopted" by other families. Later, though not disguising the fact that he had been "debarred from all the sports, plays, and amusements of children," he paid due credit to his former adoptive parents for their great kindness and affection.[4] Being themselves brought up in New England Congregationalism, they taught him the good, though somewhat stern Puritan rules of conduct and also gave him some religious knowledge by teaching him the Shorter Catechism, the Apostles' Creed, and the Lord's Prayer.

With the aid of *The Franklin Primer* he learned to read early, and he had soon read through the books of the scanty family library. Its collection of profane literature was limited to a history of the Indian wars and a work of fiction similar to *Robinson Crusoe*. Religious literature was somewhat more ample, consisting of psalms and sermons, Edwards's *History of Redemption*—which, by the way, must have provided the young disputant with material for debate—and, above all, a Bible, which he had read through before he was eight, and a great portion of which he knew by heart before he was fourteen.[5] Especially toward the end of his life he repeatedly stressed the importance of Bible-reading and the great benefit he had himself drawn from his early reading and studies of Holy Writ: "Whatever strong and manly culture we have ourselves received, or whatever merits our writings may have been thought to have, we owe chiefly to our early study of the Holy Scriptures, however imperfect our understanding of them till our conversion, and which, we hope we may be permitted to say, are not sufficiently studied by our Catholic laity."[6]

The Passion of the Lord particularly impressed the young Bible-reader, and according to *The Convert* (page 5), he held spiritual communion with Jesus, the Virgin, and even with the Angel Gabriel, who had announced to her that she was to be the mother of the Redeemer. It seems a little strange, though, that a child brought up in typically Protestant surroundings held mysterious "communion" with the Virgin Mary and the angels. At any rate, the young "hero" of his semiautobiographical book *Charles Elwood* (1840) seemed to remember from his childhood none but his "sweet and mysterious communion with the Father of men."[7] What really matters, however, is that such spiritual intercourse indicated a strong religious disposition, accentuated by his loneliness. Yet he was no weak, sentimental youth with no or little interest for practical matters. According to Henry F. Brownson, his father "had more than ordinary dexterity of hand, and suffered no one of his age to surpass him in any kind of manual labor; but," he continued, his father "was not a favorite sought after by his companions. He was not wholly insensible to this fact, but happily it did not disturb him much."[8]

No wonder, after all, that this youngster with his marked religious disposition very early wanted to become a minister of religion. But—

like his younger contemporary Theodore Parker, who also from early childhood felt that he would be a minister[9]– he would hardly become one of the very peaceful sort, since, as he himself readily admitted, he had "an irritable temper, and was subject to violent outbreaks of passion."[10]

Yet even if he read much about religion, he felt the need of a more thoroughgoing instruction in religious matters. No one taught him the real sense of the Apostles' Creed; nor did those who taught him, require him to believe it. Nonetheless, he did believe most of the Creed, except for the articles on the Holy Catholic Church and the Communion of Saints, which he did not understand at all.[11] But perhaps one of the churches in the town could lead him to truth?

At Royalton there were a lot of denominations, like Congregationalists, Methodists, Baptists, Universalists, and a sect whose members called themselves by the sweeping name of Christians, though pronouncing the word *Christ-yans*.[12] Orestes attended especially the meetings of the Methodists and the Christians, but he thought the Methodists the better, because they spoke in a louder, almost noisy tone and gave more picturesque descriptions of hell and brimstone. For fear of hell and not for love of God he was on the point of submitting to the Methodists. But then an elderly Congregationalist woman admonished him not to go with the Methodists or other "New Lights;" instead, before joining any body calling itself a Christian body, he should "find out and join one that began with Christ and his apostles, and has continued to subsist the same without change of doctrine or worship down to our own times."

According to *The Convert* (page 8), these words had a strong and lasting impression on the twelve-year-old boy and really prevented him from becoming a genuine Protestant or even a thoroughgoing radical. Belonging to the Congregationalists or, as they were still called at that time, "The Standing Order," the woman had retained the old Puritan idea of a strong church founded and directed by Christ himself. Obviously, then, she believed her own church to be the true church, but, more important to young Brownson, she gave him glimpses of a higher conception of the church as such, i.e. as a means of salvation, and made him skeptical about the strongly individualistic religion he witnessed around him.[13]

In 1843, while still a Unitarian, but heading toward Catholicism, he emphasized the old Puritan conception of the church. He complained that Unitarians like other Protestants, both of the liberal and orthodox kind, had passed "from high churchism to low churchism, and finally to almost *no* churchism." But, he continued, "our Puritan fathers, while opposing with great force and obstinacy all prelatical and hierarchical forms of church government, which they were authorized by the New Testament to do, still believed, as firmly as any Catholic, in the Church as the living body of our Lord, in its existence as a Divine Institution, and in its necessity, as the medium of communion with Christ our Saviour, and therefore its necessity as the medium of salvation."[14]

At the age of fourteen he moved together with his mother, brothers, and sisters to Ballston Spa, New York. There Orestes attended an academy and also worked for some time in a printing office.[15] It is uncertain how long he attended this academy, but the instruction he got there was the only formal education he ever received. Though at that time apparently sufficient for becoming a school teacher, such an education was hardly adequate to an intellectual youth like Brownson. Despite his delight and perhaps even pride in being a self-made scholar, he stressed, especially in later years, the importance of a regular academic training, indirectly regretting his own lack of it. In 1867 he wrote in the *Catholic World:* "The studies and discipline of the college and the seminary may seem to impatient and inexperienced youth wearisome and unnecessary, but they are prescribed by wisdom and experience, and he who has never submitted to them or had their advantage feels the want of them through his whole life, to whatever degree of eminence he may have risen without them."[16]

But Ballston Spa was something more than the academy and the printing office. At this new place he was exposed to many diverse and —in his own words in *The Convert* (page 9)—"corrupting" influences. While at Royalton the orthodox Protestants, though split in many churches, seemed to dominate the scene as a rather homogeneous mass, Ballston Spa offered a much more pluralistic picture, made up not only of orthodox Christians and half-orthodox Universalists, but also of deists, atheists, and so-called "nothingarians," i.e. those who did not profess any particular religion. Orestes came into contact with these groups and got more bewildered than before. He felt to be "in a labyrinth of doubt, with no Ariadne's thread to guide me out to the light of day."[17] Sometimes he was almost sure that all religion was a delusion, sometimes he distrusted his own reason as a means of leading him to truth.

When he was about nineteen years of age, he happened to pass a Presbyterian meetinghouse at Malta, Saratoga County, New York. On this quiet, beautiful Sunday morning he felt an almost imperious need to go in and "join with" the people gathering for the service. He was soothed and even touched to tears by the singing of psalms, and he listened respectfully to the reading of the Scriptures and the sermon. The thought struck him that he might join this church and do what she commanded him. Had his own reason not failed him? Now he would abnegate his reason and submit himself to the authority of this church. In a strong and convincing paragraph in *The Convert* (page 10), he described his own "existential" situation just before he joined the Presbyterian Church:

I have, said I, in my self-communing, done my best to find the truth, to experience religion, and to lead a religious life, yet here I am without faith, without hope, without love. I know not what to believe. I know not what to do. I know not whence I came, why I am here, or whither I go. My life is a stream that flows out of darkness into darkness. The world is dark to me, and not a ray of light even for one instant relieves it. My heart is sad, and I see nothing to hope for, or to live for. For me heaven is dispeopled, and the earth is a desert, a barren waste. Why is this so? Why does my heart rebel against the speculations of my mind? If doubt is all there is for me, why cannot I discipline my feelings into submission to it? Why this craving to believe when there is nothing to be believed? Why this longing for sympathy, when there is nothing to respond to my heart? Why this thirst for an unbounded good, when there is no good, when all is a mere show, an illusion, and nothing is real? Have I not mistaken my way?

Not only his desire for an authority, but also his "longing for sympathy" or fellowship motivated his decision to join the Presbyterian Church. He wanted to "join with" the members of the church and not "stand alone," continuing his unavailing "self-communing."[18]

In fact, his intense craving for fellowship was already manifest on this early occasion. Brownson, who more than once was to alienate and even offend other people through his convictions and especially through the manner in which he put them forth, also spoke gentle words of human relationships: "Who of us has ever conversed for one half-hour with a really great and good man, but has felt that a virtue has come out of him to us, and that we ourselves are lifted up, and are no longer, and never can be again, what we were before?"[19]

Some days later, Orestes told about his decision to the Presbyterian minister of Ballston Spa. After being accepted by the Session of the church, he was, on the following Sunday, in October 1822, baptized and received into the Presbyterian communion.[20]

However, his Presbyterian experience proved to be an unhappy one. Almost at once he seemed to be disgusted with the alleged Presbyterian practice of drawing sharp lines between "the elect" and "the sinners." Worse still, "the elect" were even admonished not to have any social or personal relationships with "the sinners" and to restrict their business relations with them to the absolute minimum. He felt ill at ease about the supposed espionage between the church members and their constant fear of being reported by one another to the Session. He soon understood that he had made a mistake in becoming a Presbyterian, that he had "no sympathy with the Presbyterian spirit, and should need a long and severe training to sour and elongate my visage sufficiently to enjoy the full confidence of my new brethren."[21]

The fifty-four-year-old Catholic controversialist, when looking back to his Presbyterian experience, wrote that the most rigid Catholic ascetic could never imagine a discipline a thousandth part as rigid as the one to which he himself had been subjected; he even found the Presbyterian discipline infinitely worse than the contemporary political system of espionage in Europe.[22]

In *Charles Elwood* there is an interesting description of a so-called "Inquiry meeting," a description which, partly at least, seems based on personal experience. These meetings were held with the view of stating the spiritual condition of those who had "obtained a hope" of salvation. Those who had "found religion," were led to "the saints' apartment," while the others were ushered into a crowded room—much crowded, indeed, as "sinners' apartments always are."[23] It should be added, however, that Brownson in *Charles Elwood* also stressed the benefits of what is commonly called "revivalism" or, as he called it, "revival measures." Despite the fanaticism and bigotry often attached to it, revivalism meant a reaction against the materialism of the times, and a serious attempt—which also seemed to succeed—at "shaking the dry bones, . . ." and "preparing . . . a more advanced state of the church and of society."[24]

Yet, although the neophyte had difficulty in adapting himself to the Presbyterian milieu, he seems to have had more difficulty in accepting the Presbyterian view of authority and reason. Even if the church did not claim infallibility for her doctrines, but told each member to look for the truths in the Bible, the church nevertheless had the right to excommunicate those who did not comply with her doctrines. At the same time, his brethren expressed a lack of confidence in the human mind to grasp spiritual truths. Gradually he came to the conclusion that he should not have abnegated his reason, which, after all, was the only guide to truth he had. His joining the Presbyterian Church was, as he later saw it, "the act of an intellectual desperado."[25] After a couple of years he felt assured that the Presbyterian Church was only a self-created body with no authority from God.

Once having rejected the authority of the church, he also rejected the Calvinist doctrine of unconditional election and reprobation, "and the doctrine that God foreordains the wicked to sin necessarily, that he may damn them justly."[26] It is a question, however, if the problem of church authority, let alone church infallibility, had such a crucial importance to young Brownson, as stated in *The Convert.* At any rate, in *Charles Elwood,* in which Brownson gave a "novellistic" version of his Presbyterian period, his young protagonist sees religious dogmas in the light of reason, and not in relation to the authority of a church.[27] Most probably, Brownson's Presbyterian experience gave him more or less conscious ideas of church authority and human reason. Later, he gave these ideas coherence and distinctness when seeing them in the light of his intellectual development.

Brownson's retrospective appraisal of Presbyterian life and manners, especially the church discipline, sounds exaggerated. He pointed out some latent or open defects, but to his restless, sensitive mind they had assumed too great dimensions. Judging from the diary he kept at that time, the adolescent was often prey to conflicting sentiments. On New Year's Eve, 1822, he confessed his great sinfulness, and in January, 1823, he wrote despondently that he felt no life in religion at all; but immediately after he was convinced that Christ saved him in spite of his wickedness.[28] His exclamation in the diary, "Dead is every sense of pleasure,"[29] might have a double significance: his desire for a deeper religious life and a growing dissatisfaction with a rigid church discipline.

His diary also revealed an increasing doubt as to the truth of certain dogmas. In the entry for May 30, 1823, he was enthusiastic about missionary activities among the heathen, but already by June 6 the same year there was, indeed, little left of his enthusiasm: "That system of religion which is taught them must certainly be productive of no good consequences. What are its fruits at home? What sober reflecting man can view the divisions, the discordant views disseminated by the disciples of Calvin and Arminius and not feel his bosom glow with honest indignation at their baneful effect? Can he, then, wish it to be carried to those who are deplorable enough already?"[30]

However, other Presbyterians, too, seemed to question the truth of Calvinistic doctrines. In *The Convert* (page 19) Brownson even maintained that his "honest pastor" had tried in the General Assembly of the Presbyterian Church in 1821 to get modified or even rescinded altogether the doctrine of unconditional election and reprobation, but that his motion failed by one or two votes.

In a long review of Brownson's *The Convert* in the worthy Presbyterian periodical the *Biblical Repertory and Princeton Review*, the writer–probably the well-known editor and theologian Charles Hodge –found "the possibility of any such vote in the General Assembly in favor of any material modification of that article in any stage of its history, . . . extremely questionable."[31] More important, the pastor in question, Reuben Smith, stated in the same number of the review that no vote concerning "foreordination" was taken at all in the General Assembly of 1821.[32]

But it should be remembered that already in the late 1820's a long doctrinal controversy broke out between "the Old" and "the New School" Presbyterians.[33] Nathaniel W. Taylor (1786–1858), First Professor of Theology at Yale Divinity School, advocated a somewhat modified Calvinism by maintaining that the free will of the sinners is the reason for God's punishment.[34] Although Taylor did not consciously deviate from Calvinist dogma, the church historian William Warren Sweet concludes that "the two main departures of Taylorism from orthodox Calvinism were its denial that God is the author of sin, and the virtual repudiation of the doctrine of election."[35] Even in the early 1820's, therefore, Presbyterian congregations and their pastors could not have been completely waterproof to similar doctrinal influences.

Brownson's Presbyterian experience was his only encounter with evangelical Christianity, and it must have utterly disappointed him. In 1849 he labeled Presbyterianism "the most odious of all the forms of Protestantism,"[36] and as is evident from *The Convert*, not even thirty-five years had softened very much his bitterness. Indeed, even as late as 1875, and perhaps more vehemently than ever, he thundered against Calvinism as "the most thoroughly satanic form of Protestantism," and above all against the Calvinistic sects Presbyterianism and Methodism, which required extraordinary grace for conversion to Catholicism![37] One cannot help feeling that Brownson suffered from a lifelong Presbyterian complex. In any case, his Presbyterian experience determined his consistent view of orthodox Protestantism until the end of his life. Symptomatically, the following were some of the last lines he wrote: "We, after brief experience, while still in our nonage, rejected Presbyterianism as a sham..." and "ever since our twentieth year, we have looked upon Protestantism as a humbug or something worse."[38]

The above-mentioned statements must have been colored by his memories of the Presbyterian milieu in Ballston Spa. In his essay "What Human Reason Can Do" in *Brownson's Quarterly Review* for April, 1855, he gave a balanced and well-defined view of his own attitude toward Calvinism, and thereby Presbyterianism: "Calvinism, by its exaggerated supernaturalism, by its doctrine of total depravity, and its annihilation of nature for anything good, declaring our best acts done without grace sinful and deserving eternal damnation, drove us into infidelity, into a denial of the proper supernatural, and the assertion of an exaggerated rationalism. Catholicity has redeemed us, and taught us that the supernatural presupposes the natural."[39]

When leaving Presbyterianism, he took reason for his guide and criterion of truth, and made it even a rule for the Scriptures. He passed from orthodox to liberal Christianity, and from being a supernaturalist he became a rationalist. Yet he did not believe in the sufficiency of natural reason to reach all truth or to avoid all error.[40] Already from his Presbyterian prelude he seems to have got a more or less conscious feeling of human reason as something not hostile to the supernatural, but as something serving as a means to receive spiritual truths. In his Transcendentalist or Eclectic period he believed in an idealized "Reason" or "the inner light," and before his conversion to Catholicism he believed in a correspondence or harmony between reason and the supernatural as two halves of one whole.

But for the immediate future, the twenty-one-year-old Brownson would be concerned primarily with the realm and capacity of reason, while paying comparatively little attention to the other half of the circle.

[1] *The Convert (Works,* V; Detroit, 1884), p. 5.
[2] *Ibid.*, p. 4.
[3] *Brownson's Quarterly Review,* 3rd New York Series, IV (January 1863), 122–123. Hereafter referred to as *BrQR.*
[4] *The Convert,* pp. 4, 6.
[5] *Ibid.*, pp. 4–5.
[6] *BrQR,* Last Series, II (July 1874), 417. See also *BrQr,* Last Series, III (April 1875), 290–291, and *BrQR,* Last Series, III (July 1875), 413.
[7] *Works,* IV, 197.
[8] Henry F. Brownson, *Orestes A. Brownson's Early Life* (Detroit, 1898), p. 8. Hereafter referred to as *Early Life.*
[9] Theodore Parker, *Experience as a Minister.* In *Works. Centenary Edition,* ed. Rufus Leighton (Boston, 1910), 209.
[10] *The Convert,* p. 6.
[11] *Ibid.*, pp. 6–7.
[12] *Ibid.*, p. 7.
[13] *Ibid.*, pp. 8–9.
[14] "The Mission of Jesus," *Christian World* (Boston), January 14, 1843.
[15] *Early Life,* p. 10.
[16] *Works,* VIII, 476.
[17] *The Convert,* p. 9.
[18] *Ibid.*, pp. 9, 10.
[19] "The Philosophy of History" *(Democratic Review,* 1843), *Works,* IV, 408.
[20] *The Convert,* p. 11.
[21] *Ibid.*, 12.
[22] *Ibid.*, pp. 12–13.
[23] *Works,* IV, 192.
[24] *Ibid.*, 191–192. Brownson probably thought of the Presbyterian revivalist preacher Charles G. Finney (1792–1875), who was preaching in the later 1820's in New York State. Through his "New measures" Evangelism he stressed the need of combining revivalism and reform with the view of "remaking society" (See *American Christianity: An Historical Interpretation with Representative Documents,* ed. H. Shelton Smith et al., II [New York, 1963], pp. 12–15).
[25] *The Convert,* p. 18.
[26] *Ibid.*, p. 19.
[27] See, for instance, Chapter VII on "Authority" *(Works,* IV, 198–201).
[28] *Early Life,* pp. 11–12.
[29] *Ibid.*, p. 12.
[30] *Ibid.*, pp. 14–15, 16.
[31] "Brownson's Exposition of Himself," *Princeton Review,* XXX (Philadelphia, 1858), 134.
[32] Reuben Smith, "Brownson's Development of Himself," *Princeton Review,* XXX (1858), 390–392. Smith also refuted Brownson's statement in *The Convert* that he was received into the Presbyterian Church on the basis of his views of reason and authority. Also, Smith objected to Brownson's description of the Presbyterian attitude toward "sinners."
[33] See William Warren Sweet, *Religion in the Development of American Culture: 1765–1840* (New York, 1952), p. 207: "The years from 1828 to 1837 in American Presbyterianism were filled with continuous controversy and more heresy trials took place within that ten-year period than in any other similar period on record."
[34] See, for example, Sidney E. Ahlstrom, "Nathaniel William Taylor and the

New Haven Theology," *Religion in American Life: The Shaping of American Religion*, ed. James Ward Smith and A. Leland Jamison, I (Princeton, 1961), pp. 254–260; and *American Christianity: An Historical Interpretation with Representative Documents*, ed. H. Shelton Smith et al., II (New York, 1963), pp. 28–36.

35 Sweet, *op.cit.*, p. 200.

36 *BrQR* (July 1849), 403.

37 *BrQR* (Oct. 1875), 567.

38 *Ibid.*, p. 577.

39 *Works*, I, 322.

40 *The Convert*, p. 19.

II
A Universalist Interlude

One might expect that Brownson, after his unhappy Presbyterian experience, would have kept far away from any religious body or, if his need of an authoritative and infallible church had been so acute as presented in *The Convert,* would have immediately sought for a church claiming absolute authority and infallibility. But after all, since he "was unwilling to be an unbeliever, and felt deeply the need of having a religion of some sort,"[1] so-called liberal Christianity, stressing the role of reason in matters of faith without stating any definite, positive doctrines, presented itself to him as the best solution under the circumstances. And among the forms of liberal Christianity, Universalism was the one with which he was most acquainted. Already before he became a Presbyterian, an aunt of his, obviously herself a Universalist, enthusiastically told him about the eloquent preacher Elhanan Winchester, whom she had listened to in her youth, and whom Brownson considered "the founder of American Universalism."[2]

From a general point of view Universalism was an offshoot of the rationalism which in both Europe and America so strongly influenced theology, especially Protestant, in the latter part of the eighteenth and the first part of the nineteenth century. In the United States, where Calvinism was still dominant, Universalism was primarily a reaction against the Calvinistic doctrine of unconditional election and reprobation. The Universalists believed, as their name itself signifies, in universal salvation or the final salvation of all men. The earlier Universalists, however, were on the whole orthodox Protestants with the exception of their view of salvation and their more or less strong emphasis on reason in matters of faith.

The first who avowedly preached Universalism in the United States was John Murray, who came from Great Britain in 1770. He became minister of the First Universalist Congregation at Gloucester, Mass., and later became minister of the First Universalist Society in Boston.[3] At about the same time the itinerant preacher Elhanan Winchester, originally a Calvinistic Baptist minister who had rejected the doctrine of endless punishment, began to preach the doctrine of universal salvation or restoration.

Both as a preacher and a writer Elhanan Winchester seems to have wielded a far greater influence than John Murray. Already when Brownson was between fourteen and fifteen years of age, his well-meaning aunt gave him some of Winchester's books to read, among which was a lengthy versified exposition of Universalist doctrine. Although later he came to regard Winchester as a poor theologian and poet, his books had shaken young Brownson's early belief in future rewards and punishments.[4]

Yet also within more distinctly Congregationalist churches Universalist sentiments became more and more manifest. One of the most outstanding and learned representatives of early American Universalism was Charles Chauncy, pastor of the First Congregational Church in Boston. It was perhaps symptomatic of the uncertain position of Universalism that his book *Salvation for All Men Illustrated and Vindicated as a Scripture Doctrine* was published anonymously—in London (1782, 1784). In this book, which young Brownson came to read,[5] the author, in order to prove his thesis of universal salvation, first appealed to reason: Is it really possible, he asked, to think that God, as First Cause of Creation, did not intend from the beginning to make all His creatures finally happy? But his chief arguments Chauncy allegedly drew from the Bible, which, as he understood it, postulated a stage of trial—except, possibly, for the very good and very pious—before the final and universal beatitude. He considered God's punishment purgative or reformative and not vindictive, but his very belief in a divine punishment, though limited or temporary, after death, made him avoid sheer fatalism, and motivated encouragement to good works.[6]

However, another of the earlier Universalists, Joseph Huntington, pastor of the Congregational Church in Coventry, Conn., did not seem to avoid the pit of fatalism. In his book *Calvinism Improved*, which also fell into teen-ager Brownson's hands, he reasoned on Calvinistic lines, though with one important difference: while Calvinism considered the vicarious sacrifice of Christ valid for the elect only, Huntington confidently stated that the atonement automatically saved all men, will they or nill they. Thus, his "Calvinism improved" might as well be called "Calvinism enlarged" or even "Calvinism attenuated."[7]

Yet, despite their doctrinal differences, the earlier Universalists kept within the orthodox system of faith or at least within an orthodox frame of reference. In more or less marked contrast to these, the later Universalists adopted an independent attitude toward the Scriptures, while stressing the important role of reason. Some of them even thought reason supreme in matters of faith.

The most prominent and perhaps also the most radical of the later Universalists was Hosea Ballou, by Brownson called "the patriarch of American Universalism."[8] In his book *A Treatise on Atonement*, which was first published in 1805 and reappeared in many editions, the author tried to demolish the whole body of orthodox doctrines. On the basis of human reason he rejected the doctrines of the Trinity and the divinity of Christ, and the whole traditional scheme of salvation. Accordingly, he did not interpret the death of Christ as a vicarious, expiatory sacrifice, since God as the original author of sin did not need to be reconciled. Instead, this death was to serve as an example for man to live a life in "universal submission to Christ, in holiness and happiness." Moreover, he repudiated not only endless punishment like other Universalists, but also limited punishment after death, believing that sin was punished only in this life, and always with a reformative purpose.[9]

An optimistic fatalism—if the term may be permitted—was a dominating feature of Hosea Ballou's thought. God, in the last analysis, intended man to sin; consequently, sin had a good purpose. Yet he seemed to admit a kind of dualism, insofar as he considered man's carnal mind in opposition to God. As might be expected, Ballou did not believe in the existence of the Devil, though the reasons he gave for his non-existence were somewhat strange: a created being could only be in one place at a time, and besides, there would be nothing for a devil to do![10]

However, Hosea Ballou could also write words like these: "But when we speak of *God*, abstractedly, our words ought to be few and chosen."[11] And stressing man's direct encounter with God without the medium of any "hireling priesthood," he asked his readers this probing question: "Are we not right, in judging of the nature and character of God, from the dictates of his spirit in us? If so, does this spirit teach us the necessity of endless transgression and misery?"[12]

Though he did not accept all its doctrines and arguments, this book made a deep impression on young Brownson. From his later, Catholic position he expressed his conviction that a more heretical book than this one had probably never issued from the American press. But even if Ballou's heresies were old, Brownson added, they were nearly all original with the author. He once told Brownson that his only aids in writing his book were the Bible, Ethan Allen's *Reason: The Only Oracle of Man* (which Ballou called "a deistical work") and his own reflections. And Brownson, the Catholic controversialist, triumphantly declared that this was an excellent example of the Protestant rule of faith: the Bible without the proper notes and comments! But he also gave Hosea Ballou credit for being one of "the most original thinkers of our times."[13]

In any case, Ballou's rejection of the doctrine of the Trinity made him approach Unitarianism, the other important form of American liberal Christianity at that time. William Warren Sweet states in epigrammatical terms the basic similarity between these two trends: "The Unitarians and Universalists were in fundamental agreement, the Universalists holding that God was too good to damn man; the Unitarians insisting that man was too good to be damned."[14] Sociologically, however, there was in general a marked difference between them. While Unitarianism was primarily an urban, *bourgeois* phenomenon, led by academically educated ministers, Universalism was mostly a rural, grassroots movement, making extensive use of lay preachers, the so-called "farmer-preachers."[15] This sociological difference between rustic Universalism and urban Unitarianism is reflected in Brownson's amusing description in *The Convert* (page 30) of a Universalist brother minister and also, indirectly, of his own ambitions: "He was a tall, majestic person, of grave and venerable aspect, a chaste and dignified speaker, and the best sermonizer I ever knew among Universalists. But he had too refined and cultivated a taste to be a popular Universalist preacher, and finally, I believe, followed my example, and associated with the Unitarians."

Since Brownson already before he joined the Presbyterian Church had become rather well acquainted with Universalism, this knowledge must have colored his views of Presbyterianism. While a Presbyterian, he also seems to have attended Universalist meetings, a fact which strongly displeased his coreligionists.[16]

On the whole, his thoughts and sentiments seem to have been very much unsettled at that time. Like Ralph Waldo Emerson, who also in those years tried to come to grips with the problem of evil,[17] Brownson asked himself in the diary without getting any answer: If God existed, where did evil come from? And evil, at least, existed: "Call you this God's world? To me it seems more like the devil's world, in which Ahriman, the prince of darkness, is supreme." Being utterly depressed by the "cant," mammon worship, and social inequality he saw around him, he broke out in youthful self-pity, feeling completely unable to convince others: "I am nobody, and if I venture to say anything, the only answer is, he is a poor devil, has not a red cent in his pocket,–heed not his sayings."[18]

However, he soon got the chance of earning some cents: he was employed as a school teacher at Stillwater in upstate New York (1823), then at Springwells, eleven miles from Detroit, Mich. (1824), and finally at Elbridge, New York (1825). In 1824 he declared himself a Universalist, and already the next year the General Convention of Universalists gave him permission to preach. During the following year he stayed in his native Vermont, studying and preaching alternately. Then, in the summer of 1826, he was solemnly ordained a Universalist minister at Jaffrey, N. H. While a Universalist minister, he stayed at different places in New York State, particularly at Litchfield, Ithaca, and Auburn.

In 1849, when paying due tribute to the "metropolis" Boston, he epitomized his wandering past life: "We speak without prejudice, for, though we were born in Vermont, we were brought up in the Middle States, and it has been our lot to love the South, to reside in the West, and to find a home in old Massachusetts."[19]

In 1827 he married Sally Healy, a former pupil, whom he had come to know at Elbridge. Generally speaking, she was a modest, pious woman, who preferred to stay in the background, and her husband appreciated her gentle, unobtrusive influence. Virtually, if not actually, she seems to have converted to Catholicism before him.[20] According to Henry F. Brownson, his father "often read his articles to his wife before publication, and attached great importance to her judgment; indeed, he often said that intellectually she was his superior." And it was to comply with her last wish that he resumed the publication of his review.[21]

Perhaps one might briefly characterize Brownson's attitude toward his wife as reflected in his often repeated view of love between man and woman: love should be idealized, not sentimentalized.[22] They had eight children: six sons and two daughters. Two of their sons died at the very early ages of six and nine, and two other sons were killed during the Civil War. The Brownsons had their due share of griefs and sorrows.

In 1857, Brownson, when looking back on his Universalist phase, described this period, which lasted till 1830, as a steady development toward downright infidelity. Realizing that he could not harmonize the Bible with the doctrine of universal salvation, he was forced, at least theoretically, to give up the Bible altogether as a reliable source of truth. This doctrine also made moral accountability and, in the last resort, Jesus as Savior and God as father superfluous. On Universalist principles, which Brownson in theory pushed to extremes, God was hidden behind fixed, inexorable natural laws, and was unmoved by human prayer and devotion. Although he did not accept in his heart "all these frightful conclusions," he did not hesitate to call the last two years of his Universalist phase "the most anti-Christian period of my life."[23]

However interesting the summary of his intellectual development given in *The Convert,* his writings in the biweekly Universalist magazine the *Gospel Advocate and Impartial Investigator* give a more representative picture of his thoughts and sentiments as a Universalist. To this journal he was attached as a contributor and, from the beginning of 1829, as its editor. When Brownson became its editor, it was "the most widely circulated and the most influential" Universalist periodical in the United States.[24] About thirty years later he said about his writings in the *Gospel Advocate:* "In it is a confused medley of thoughts, and the germs of nearly all I subsequently held or published till my conversion to the Catholic Church."[25] From this statement may be concluded that a study of Brownson's writings in this magazine will give a better understanding of the different views he held prior to his conversion to Catholicism.

Already in his first article he struck the note of a theme which he often repeated. The young Universalist minister, who even as a Presbyterian had despaired of the strifes between Calvinists and Arminians, maintained that religion, whose chief aim was to give help and consolation, had actually become the reverse: a bitter controversy about dogmas and opinions. Yet this strife was quite unnecessary, since morality was the only thing that mattered.[26]

He asked: Who is responsible for these dogmatic divisions and, consequently, the deterioration of true religion? His answer came promptly: the priests. The organized priesthood had defiled and distorted original Christianity, as it was taught by Christ. Upon his simple doctrines of morality the priests, in the course of centuries, had heaped a lot of unintelligible dogmas, which helped them secure their power over the people. For this purpose the priests had also made alliances with despotic rulers, and for the same purpose the contemporary orthodox Protestants tried to dominate the political institutions of the United States.[27] It was above all against the orthodox Protestants of the day that Brownson waged his war. Despite his general denunciations of priesthood or priestcraft, he seldom touched the subject of Catholicism proper in his articles for the *Gospel Advocate.*

But when he did touch the subject, he was surprisingly tolerant of the Catholic Church. True, he underscored "the great corruption of christianity [sic] known by the name of the great papal apostasy," and he was not blind to the horrors of the Inquisition. But, the former Presbyterian continued almost in the same breath: the Protestants—from Calvin to the modern orthodox—were indeed no better![28] Elsewhere, Brownson even defended Catholicism: "In my opinion, it would be better for you not to speak disrespectfully of the Roman Catholick [sic]. His church may have failings, but children should not devulge [sic] them."[29] Perhaps they even had something to learn: "The church which was not improperly styled the 'mother of harlots' has begun her reformation and bids fair to outstrip her daughters in this laudable work."[30]

However, Brownson was not yet any "churchman," either on the Catholic or the Protestant side. On the contrary, he maintained that, in order to destroy the allegedly pernicious influence of priestcraft, it was necessary to abolish the prevailing church system.[31] Also, baptism and the Lord's Supper, both characteristic of the common church system, he rejected as vain ceremonies.[32] Churches should be turned into "temples of science," Brownson argued, and the priests, instead of being mediators between God and men, should become mere instructors of the people. His criterion of a true church was "free enquiry," which was also its only legitimate right of existence.[33]

Evidently, Hosea Ballou's book *A Treatise on Atonement* influenced Brownson's view of the priesthood and the church systems. In his book Ballou thundered against vain forms of worship and the "hireling priesthood." But also William Godwin's work *An Enquiry Concerning the Principles of Political Justice* (1793), which Brownson read more thoroughly later, must have influenced him in the same direction.[34]

The first duty of the instructors of the people, he continued, was to state the facts of man and nature. These facts should be studied diligently and comprehensively, because they alone could be known and ascertained by human beings. What lay beyond our sense perception could not be grasped by our minds; our primary concern, therefore, was to know the world of the senses. Observation and experiment were the foundation of true philosophy, which, again, was more important than faith, Brownson concluded.[35]

True religion must be rational, that is, it must conform to reason, or to science; in fact, it was dependent on science. Religion, as he defined it, was itself a science, "the science of living well."[36] The test of every religious doctrine, then, was whether it promoted the wellbeing of the individual. A doctrine, therefore, must be judged according to its utility, so much the more because the objective reality of a religious doctrine could not be proved.[37] However, every doctrine must be reasonable; what was not reasonable, could not exist at all.[38] Such a doctrine was, at best, useless; at worst, mischievous. On this ground Brownson rejected the dogmas of the Trinity, the vicarious atonement of Christ, predestination, and eternal punishment.[39]

On the other hand, the dogmas of God's goodness and of a future life did not contradict reason, and, as their practical utility was obvious, they ought to be cherished by everyone.[40] Despite all its faults and imperfections, it was the Bible that revealed these two dogmas.[41] From nature alone the existence of God as God, or as He really is, could not be concluded.[42] However, "nature with one voice proclaims the existence of a Supreme Power or Intelligence," or "some great vivifying Power" behind the phenomena, though the specific character or the attributes of such a being were "matters of faith."[43] On this point, then, Brownson maintained that revelation was necessary, but, he added, nature proved or asserted the validity of revelation.[44] As far as the doctrine of a future life was concerned, it corresponded neatly to the "natural" belief in perfectibility, which demanded for its realization a future existence.[45]

The dogma of universal salvation Brownson defended on common Universalist grounds, but, despite Universalist logic, he also stressed man's own responsibility.[46] Obviously, he had great difficulty in adopting a purely fatalistic system. About the problem of evil he said that it did not originate–directly–in God, but in man, and was a result of man's special "constitution." Thus God as creator indirectly introduced evil as part of His "ulterior design," which, in short, was the universal happiness of mankind.[47] But elsewhere Brownson maintained that vice or evil originated, quite simply, in human ignorance. Knowledge, on the other hand, led to virtue.[48] Yet, evil and goodness, vice and virtue, were not to be determined on the basis of absolute moral standards, but simply in view of their tendency. What was good was good because it involved pleasure; what was evil was evil because it involved pain.[49]

More or less in connection with evil, Brownson pointed out the negative role of habit. Ignorance and habit he considered the two great obstacles to the intellectual and moral progress of the human race. Nevertheless, as man possessed the "power of improvement," his progress could not for any long time be arrested.[50]

Thus Brownson's views at that time were to a great extent an afterthought of deistic and utilitaristic ideas from the Era of Enlightenment. Typically enough, people said about him that he wrote in the spirit of Hume, Paine, and Voltaire.[51] But even if he reduced religion to a matter of "subordinate rank" and sometimes expressed a doubt as to God as father,[52] he could scarcely reconcile himself with the thought of an impersonal "Great First Cause," a Jehovah in distant, utter darkness.[53] In certain moments he wished "rather to *feel* than to *reason*–to indulge a silent communion with the God of nature rather than to pursue the track of demonstration... There is something sublime... in feeling ourselves in the kind embrace of an affectionate Father who knows all our wants, and is ever ready to relieve them."[54] He also assured his readers that he had not become so "enlightened" that he might be satisfied with universal skepticism and the cold and unfeeling dreams of the deist and the materialist. The world would have lost its beauty and charm if blind necessity were behind everything.[55]

After all, logic was not only cool reasoning. Surprisingly enough, Brownson, the logician *par excellence,* already realized that "the logick [sic] of the heart" was stronger than "the mere logick of the head."[56] The young Universalist minister even seemed to anticipate his later Transcendentalist position. Developing Hosea Ballou's thesis of "the dictates of his [i.e. God's] spirit in us," Brownson expressed his nascent belief in a "God within the mind" or "the internal evidence" by which to determine the truth of the Scriptures.[57] And already in the *Gospel*

Advocate he heralded his later concern with the problem of intuition which was an integrating part of his philosophy in both his Transcendentalist and Catholic periods. "All faith," he wrote, "must arise from intuitive perception, experience, or from testimony. Intuition is undoubtedly the strongest evidence we can have. This is what irresistably [sic] compels us to believe our own existence, to trust the intelligence of our senses and which at first thought, without any process of reasoning, leads us to admit it is impossible for the same thing to be and not to be, that a whole is greater than a part, etc."[58] In any case, his "logick of the heart" and his ideas of a "God within the mind" and intuition assured him of the integrity of the individual and saved him from deistic determinism.

However, already in his Universalist period the individualist Brownson called attention to the fact that man was also a social being: "Society is his element, out of which he sickens and dies."[59] But what he saw around him in contemporary society was far from encouraging. Social inequality exasperated him. The luxury of the rich was based on the blood and sweat of the poor! he blurted out indignantly.[60] But he could also be more sober and reflective. "It will be found," he wrote in an essay on "Equality," that "the more the laborer produces the poorer he grows. This seems a hard case, that plenty should increase poverty, a surplus should produce want. Yet so it is. The inequality which exists tends to perpetuate and increase itself." In the keen competition for wealth, he continued, all good feelings between men were almost forgotten. If this tendency were not counteracted, individual crimes and bitter class wars would be the inevitable result.

He suggested the solution that "every man should produce for himself or every one should be engaged in some branch of productive industry. This would secure to each one a competence." For those branches of industry which the individual could not master alone, Brownson would introduce the principle of coöperation. If every man were secured the products of his own labor, he held, the worst aspects of social inequality would soon disappear, and the unhappy distinction between the laboring class and the consuming class would be broken down.[61]

Despite his pessimistic statements about the evils of society, however, the young Universalist was full of confidence in man's power to do away with all evils—whether social, political, or moral—in the future. Patriotic feelings increased his optimism: in his own country, with the best form of government possible, man's progress would be accelerated.[62]

Many of Brownson's views made his fellow Universalists consider him a heretic, and, in fact, he emphasized more and more in his writings the matters of the earth, while reducing at the same time the positive role of religion. "Half in mockery, but at bottom in sober earnest,"[63] he published some months before he left Universalism a so-called "creed," consisting of five points, which enjoined honesty, kindness to all, family obligations, and a sweeping duty to "improve the condition of the human race, and to increase the sum of human happiness."[64]

Just before he ended his Universalist career, he drew up "A Gospel Creed," but, apparently, with no great enthusiasm. After stating his belief in God "as the prime mover of all things," and his belief in Jesus as "the greatest and best reformer ever vouchsafed us by Heaven," he said he considered the problem of universal salvation unsettled. He was even more blunt: "And though my heaven has not as much immediate felicity as the Universalist supposes, neither has it the misery of the orthodox hell. I do not like the notion of teaching men they may sin all their lives and be equally happy at death with the most virtuous..."[65]

Obviously, Brownson did not regard himself as a Universalist any longer, and at last, when openly supporting the cause of the avowed unbelievers Frances Wright and Robert Dale Owen, he left—or even was asked or told to do so—his post as editor of the *Gospel Advocate*.[66]

Let us now briefly consider Brownson's statement in *The Convert* that his articles in the *Gospel Advocate* contained the germs of nearly all the views he held or published until his conversion to Catholicism.

His general rationalistic, unorthodox view of religion remained basically the same until 1842 when he began to verge toward Catholicism. Yet his embryonic thoughts of intuition and "a God within the mind" heralded his spiritual or Transcendentalist emphases of the 1830's. Moreover, his glimpses of "the logick of the heart" and his desire to believe in God as father made him discard his deistic and utilitaristic notions and develop deeper and more positive feelings about religion.

Further, even if Brownson for a long time considered the idea of a heavenly paradise a matter of little interest, already from the early

1830's he no longer considered religion as such a matter of "subordinate rank." Instead, he adopted what he called a "religion of humanity," a sort of spiritualized natural or rationalistic religion which he believed to be a powerful instrument for individual and social reform.[67] And although his conception of the church until the early 1840's remained essentially the same, already in the middle 1830's he adopted broader and more positive views of the historical importance of the church.[68]

Above all, his two essays on "The Laboring Classes" published in 1840 strongly re-echoed his sentiments of his Universalist period about priestcraft and churches, while also showing his increased belief in *the spirit* of religion, or "the Christianity of Christ." Also, for the abolition or leveling out of social inequality he proposed, in part, the same measures to be adopted as he did in the *Gospel Advocate*, i.e. the breaking up of the industrial system into small, independent units.[69]

Since his acquaintance with Universalism dated back to his childhood and youth, one might be justified in calling his Universalist period the starting-point of Brownson's intellectual career.[70] True, by way of contrast, his short Presbyterian experience made him emphasize the role of reason more strongly than he would otherwise have done. But although of "secondary rank" in his Universalist period, Christian revelation was not quite superfluous to him. And it was just in his Universalist phase that he formulated the idea that was to lead him to Catholicism and even to dominate his thinking until the end of his life: revelation and reason, he told his readers, are two parts of one whole.[71]

1 *The Convert*, p. 20.
2 *Ibid.*, pp. 20–21.
3 Brownson referred to him as "that eccentric Irishman" (*The Convert*, p. 20).
4 *Ibid.*, p. 21.
5 *The Convert*, p. 22.
6 See excerpts from Chauncy's work in *American Christianity: An Historical Interpretation with Representative Documents*, ed. H. Shelton Smith et al., I (New York, 1960), pp. 489–492.
7 *The Convert*, pp. 22–23.
8 *Ibid.*, p. 24.
9 Hosea Ballou, *A Treatise on Atonement* (6th ed.; Utica, New York, 1839), pp. 6, 12, 53, 205.
10 *Ibid.*, p. 35.
11 *Ibid.*, p. 180.
12 *Ibid.*, pp. 123, 179.
13 *The Convert*, p. 26.
14 Sweet, *op.cit.*, p. 197.
15 *Ibid.*

[16] See his article on "Intolerance" in the Universalist magazine the *Gospel Advocate and Impartial Investigator* (Auburn, New York), VI (Aug. 30, 1828), 279: Once having attended a Universalist meeting, he was admitted to the Lord's Supper in his own church only after due apologizing and without even having the chance of explaining and defending himself. In another place he told the readers of his magazine that a Presbyterian woman had been excommunicated because she had accompanied her husband to Universalist meetings (VI, 395). The magazine will hereafter be referred to as *G. A.*

[17] *The Journals and Miscellaneous Notebooks of Ralph Waldo Emerson*, ed. William H. Gilman et al., I (Cambridge, Mass., 1960), p. 92.

[18] *Early Life*, p. 18.

[19] *BrQR* (July 1849), 403.

[20] *Works*, XIX, 581–582.

[21] Henry F. Brownson, *Orestes A. Brownson's Latter Life* (Detroit, 1900), pp. 579–580. Hereafter referred to as *Latter Life*.

[22] *BrQR* (Jan. 1859), 140–144.

[23] *The Convert*, p. 39.

[24] *Ibid.*, p. 31.

[25] *Ibid.*, p. 32.

[26] *G. A.*, V (Nov. 10, 1827), 355–356.

[27] *G. A.*, V (Dec. 15, 1827), 393–394; VII (July 25, 1829), 240–241; VII (Sept. 19, 1829), 299.

[28] *G. A.*, VI (March 29, 1828), 98.

[29] *G. A.*, VI (March 1, 1828), 72.

[30] *G. A.*, VI (March 15, 1828), 88.

[31] According to a report from a Universalist meeting, Brownson objected to "the organization of churches and church government adopted by our order and Christian churches generally" (*G. A.*, V [Nov. 10, 1827], 357–358).

[32] *G. A.*, V (Nov. 24, 1827), 374; VII (March 21, 1829, 90–91.

[33] *G. A.*, VI (June 7, 1828), 180–181, 187–188; VII (Feb. 21, 1829), 49–54.

[34] *The Convert*, p. 51.

[35] *G. A.*, VI (April 26, 1828) 133–134; VI (Aug. 16, 1828), 262–264; VI (Aug. 30, 1828), 278–279; VI (Sept. 13, 1828), 289–294.

[36] *G. A.*,VI (March 1. 1828), 69; VI (March 29, 1828), 101.

[37] *G. A.*, VI (June 7, 1828), 181; VI (Sept. 13, 1828), 295–296.

[38] *G. A.*, VI (Aug. 16, 1828), 262–264.

[39] *G. A.*, VI (April 12, 1828), 118; VI (Nov. 22, 1828), 375; VII (Nov. 28, 1829), 377.

[40] *G. A.*, VI (Aug. 16, 1828), 264–265.

[41] *G. A.*, VI (May 10, 1828), 151–152; VI (Aug. 30, 1828), 273–279; VII (Feb. 21, 1829), 54–56.

[42] *G. A.*, VII (Jan. 24, 1829), 21; VII (April 18, 1829), 121–123.

[43] *G. A.*, VI (Aug. 16, 1828), 264–265; VII (Aug. 22, 1829), 274.

[44] *G. A.*, VII (April 18, 1829), 121–123.

[45] *G. A.*, VI (Aug. 30, 1828), 273–278.

[46] Sometimes he made use of Scriptural arguments to defend the doctrine of universal salvation (VI, 273–278), at other times he stressed the alleged moral tendency of Universalism (VI, 6). But toward the end of his Universalist period he stated openly that both Calvinism and Universalism could be defended on Scriptural gounds (VII, 367–368). As for his view of man's moral responsibility, see *G. A.*, VI (April 12, 1828), 113.

47 *G. A.*, VII (April 18, 1829), 127–128. But he also stated that God could not possibly make evil good (VI, 295–296). He even doubted if evil existed at all in God's original design (VI, 273–278).

48 *G. A.*, VI (Sept. 13, 1828), 289–294.

49 *G. A.*, VI (July 19, 1828), 230–231.

50 *G. A.*, VII (Jan. 24, 1829), 19; VII (May 2, 1829), 136. "We are as yet in the infancy of the world" (VII, 52). See also *G. A.*, VII (Jan. 10, 1829), 9.

51 *G. A.*, VII (June 27, 1829), 205.

52 *G. A.*, VI (Sept. 13, 1828), 295–296.

53 *G. A.*, V (Dec. 15, 1827), 394–395. Therefore, he identified "the Great First Cause" with "the all-benignant Parent of the Universe."

54 *G. A.*, VI (Aug. 16, 1828), 264–265.

55 *G. A.*, VII (March 21, 1829), 91.

56 *G. A.*, VI (Sept. 13, 1828), 289–294.

57 *G. A.*, VII (March 21, 1829), 8 ff.; VII (June 27, 1829), 205.

58 *G. A.*, VII (Feb. 7, 1829), 37

59 *G. A.*, VII (Jan. 10, 1829), 9.

60 *G. A.*, V (Nov. 17, 1827), 361–362.

61 *G. A.*, VII (Sept. 5, 1829), 282–283.

62 *G. A.*, VII (May 2, 1829), 137.

63 *The Convert*, p. 43.

64 *G. A.*, VII (June 27, 1829), 199–201. "My Creed" also quoted inThe Convert, pp. 43–44.

65 *G. A.*, VII (Oct. 3, 1829), 310–311. Also quoted in *Early Life*, pp. 30–34.

66 Ulysses F. Doubleday, the publisher of the *G. A.*, sharply criticized Brownson's "course" toward "atheism," a course that the good Universalist labeled inconsistent with the plan of the *G. A.*" (VII, 369), So at Bronwson's request "mental aberration." In any case, Brownson's views were consideres "widely whether he might continue as editor of the *G. A.*, Doubleday's successor "felt unwilling to engage him. This was on *Monday*. The same evening," Doubleday continued, Brownson "attended Miss Wright's lecture, and on *Tuesday*, the next day, 'held out to her the hand of fellowship and became attached to the *Free Enquirer*'" (VII, 396–397). In 1845, Brownson wrote: "We ourselves, many years ago, were excommunicated, and without even a hearing or a notice, by the Universalists, for having embraced views not quite in harmony with theirs" (*Works*, VI, 528). According to *The Convert* (page 39), however, he seems to have left Universalism quite voluntarily, even at a time when he "was beginning to acquire a prominent position in the denomination."

67 See, for example, his articles in the *Unitarian* (Cambridge and Boston, 1834). As for the term, see *The Convert*, pp. 66–74.

68 See especially his book *New Views of Christianity, Society, and the Church*, *Works*, IV, 1–56.

69 *Boston Quarterly Review*, III, 358–395, 420–512. For a brief extract of these articles, see *The Convert*, pp. 104–108.

70 *The Convert*, p. 19.

71 *G. A.*, VI (May 10, 1828), 151–152.

III

Brief Rendezvous with "Wright" Reason

It was toward the end of the year 1829 that Brownson was "discharged" as editor of the *Gospel Advocate.*[1] What caused the definitive rupture was his hearty, almost enthusiastic welcome to the so-called "Free Enquirers," whose leaders were Frances Wright and Robert Dale Owen.

Frances Wright was a Scotswoman who had come to the United States some years before. Like many other contemporary immigrants from Great Britain she was disposed to social and political radicalism and, like them, but much more intensely, she believed America to be the place where her ideas might be carried into practice.[2] These words which she wrote in 1819, at the age of twenty-four, reveal her trust in the United States as well as her early developed self-assurance: "I shall feel that I have not wholly labored in vain and merit perhaps to leave my name in remembrance with the people of this great country which in its infancy has brought the art of government to perfection and is destined I would fondly hope, in its mature age, to foster and advance every other art and be at once the land of liberty and of genius."[3]

This was the golden age of the "community system." Among the initiators of the system in the United States was the English social reformer Robert Owen, who in 1825 bought a piece of land in Indiana and established a coöperative society, "New Harmony," there. During the following generation some forty more or less similar communities were founded. These associations were meant to be economically self-dependent, and their number was supposed to increase so that, finally, the whole society or nation would consist of coöperative colonies. For different reasons, however, most of these communities proved to be rather short lived. "New Harmony" itself became a failure, and Owen, having contracted great debts, had already left it in 1827.

Frances Wright, too, tried her hand at a community experiment. Robert Owen, seemingly indifferent to the Negro question, did not even admit Negroes to "New Harmony." Frances Wright looked differently upon this matter. In a pamphlet, published 1825, she proposed a "plan for the gradual abolition of slavery in the United States without danger or loss to the citizens of the South."[4] She suggested that Congress grant land for experiment farms in the South. This plan was a result of her deliberations with influential men like Jefferson and Lafayette, whose adopted daughter she was proud to be.

In the same year her own community was founded at Nashoba in Tennessee, some fifteen miles from Memphis. After about fifteen years' work the Negro slaves whom she had bought were to obtain their freedom and then emigrate to Haiti, Mexico, or Liberia. However, her coöperative colony was no more successful than "New Harmony," and Frances Wright left Nashoba three years after it had come into existence. Although the experiment caused her no small financial losses, she nonetheless fulfilled her pledge to her Negro workers by giving them their freedom.

By now she seemed to realize that the community system was of little use if people were not disposed to it. Nor could slavery be abolished until Americans radically changed their views on the Negro question. How could this change–a change of mind and heart–be brought about? She had her answer ready: Education.

And then she set about "educating" the people. She did so in several ways: giving lectures, publishing booklets, and editing the *Free Enquirer*. In New York she helped to establish the "Hall of Science," a former religious meetinghouse transformed into a bastion of "freethought." Her speech at the inauguration of the "Hall," May 28, 1829, is representative of her basic attitude, which gave the trend to all her work as a lecturer and a publicist: "Let us, instead of speculating and disputing where we can discover nothing, observe and inquire where we can discover everything." Accordingly, religious sermons should not be delivered in the "Hall of Science," but allowance was made for discussions on religious subjects, since the world was "overrun with conflicting religious superstitions."[5]

Her attitude was motivated by a Lockian, sensist view of knowledge. "All real knowledge is derived from positive sensations," she declared at about the same time.[6] And these "positive sensations," if they did not indicate the existence of God, made her at least keenly aware of the evils of contemporary society, such as race and class barriers and social inequality of sex. In her pamphlet *Fanny Wright Unmasked, by Her Own Pen* (N. Y., 1830), written mainly in defense of the Nashoba colony, she tried to "unmask" a vicious principle (page 5): "Need we hesitate to denounce the principle as vicious, which places the interests of each individual in continual opposition to those of his fellows;... And must we be told that this is in the nature of things?" she asked indignantly. No, she answered with assurance, "it certainly is in the nature of our anti-social institutions, and need we seek any stronger argument to urge against them?"

Even in the United States, the only country where political freedom existed, prejudices were extremely strong, preventing individuals from obtaining "moral freedom," which she thought indispensable to the happiness of man.[7] Hence the necessity of education: "Let us teach the young mind to reason, and the young heart to feel,... and show, that acquaintance with our own nature can alone guide us to judicious practice."[8]

Education of the young, then, was her primary concern. In the *Free Enquirer*, a weekly paper of which she was an editor from 1829 to 1834, Frances Wright advocated an educational system which contrasted sharply with that in use. She proposed that children from two years upward should leave their parents and, as wards of the State, live in boarding schools until the age of sixteen. The parents should be allowed to visit their children, but in no way to interfere with their instruction. Through such a forced separation the children, according to Frances Wright, might escape the destructive influence of society. As might be expected, religion, and especially in any dogmatic form, was not to be taught in these schools.

Yet, even if this educational scheme looked rather "revolutionary," Frances Wright did not at all intend any grand-scale, sweeping abolition of the "anti-social institutions" overnight. Her very emphasis on education and the state of "the public mind" clearly indicated her typically reformist attitude: "Reform ought never to travel faster than the public mind; whenever it does so it produces alarm and with alarm, confusion."[9]

Her program of social reform, which she set forth in her journal, included, among other things, the abrogation of imprisonment for debt, the abolition of capital punishment, a ten-hour working-day for artisans, and women's rights. Apart from her educational scheme, her reform program seems quite reasonable to people of today. Even many contemporaries, and not only those belonging to the lower classes, might have tolerated several of her proposed reforms. What shocked them and made her suspect in their eyes were her denunciations of Christianity and the clergy. It is "by our credulity or our hypocrisy" that the priests have gained their strong position, the "Priestess of Beelzebub" exclaimed.[10] It should be added, however, that her attacks on Christianity were primarily directed against dogmatism. At least, some years later, she made a distinction between Christian theology, which to her was only "prattle," and religion, which she regarded as some undefined power binding and obliging individuals.[11]

But what shocked people even more than her sarcasms on religious beliefs and practices were her servere criticisms of the existing marriage law and her supposed championship of "free love." On hearing the very name of Nashoba, many people conjured up a picture of a real "free-love" colony, partly because James Richardson, the overseer, admittedly lived together with a mulatto woman without marrying her, partly because Frances Wright herself seemed to approve of such a state of affairs in the colony: "The marriage law existing without the pale of the institution, is of no force within that pale."[12] But, in any case, outside that pale or for society at large, Frances Wright and her fellow workers cherished "free love" only as a principle, which could not safely be put into practice until the general tone of feeling among individuals had been much more elevated.[13]

Chief among her fellow workers at that time was Robert Dale Owen, the eldest son of Robert Owen. After his arrival in the United States, in 1825, he and Frances Wright became coeditors, first of the *New Harmony, Indiana Gazette*, then of the *Free Enquirer* in New York. Later in life, he was to become a member of Congress and a U. S. minister to Italy. As an editor of the *Free Enquirer*, however, he seems to have been outshone by his six years older and more powerful female associate. Another of her companions was the Frenchman William Phiquepal D'Arusmont, who suggested parts of her educational plans, and who also was in charge of business during her lecturing tours. Some time after, while staying in France, they were married.

Toward the end of his Universalist period, Brownson's views to a large extent coincided with those of Frances Wright and her fellow workers. Generally speaking, he was at that time a Lockian, sensist, and materialist,[14] but more particularly, two well-known reformers had contributed very much to form his opinion and to arouse his interest in the "Free Enquirers."

In his work *An Enquiry Concerning the Principles of Political Justice*, which wielded a tremendous influence on the young people of the contemporary and following generations, William Godwin stated his belief in human reason and its capability of creating a new and better world. But reason was thwarted and hindered in its activity by the evils of government, whether political or ecclesiastical. Godwin, therefore, declared an unflinching war upon kingcraft and priestcraft. Once the human mind had been liberated from all external authority, reason was omnipotent. The author, writing under the mighty impact of the French Revolution, stressed the revolutionary force of mere ideas. To Brownson, this book was itself a revolution. In *The Convert* (page 51) he stated plainly that it "has had more influence on my mind than any other book, except the Scriptures, I have ever read." And he praised the author for his "merciless logic, and a chasteness, vigor, grace, and elegance of language, which I have never seen surpassed."

Robert Owen, too, wanted to do away with the existing society and introduce a new one. This aim of his was implied in the very title of his most important book, *A New View of Society* (1813), which Brownson certainly must have read, though without mentioning it explicitly.[15]

Like Godwin, Owen maintained that the individual was hindered in his free development by the existing institutions of property, marriage, and religion. But instead of loathing all institutions and all government as such, he wished to destroy the old institutions in order to make place for new and better ones. To Owen, then, neither ideas nor the wills of scattered individuals were in themselves strong enough to carry through a real change of society. Individuals must be united and induced to act harmoniously together. To achieve this, the principle of association was necessary. Environment and association formed the individual.[16]

To Brownson, Frances Wright seemed to have "hit upon a just medium between the individualism of Godwin and the communism of Owen." Therefore, Brownson, being favorably disposed to a similar view, very easily found himself a fellow worker of Frances Wright.[17]

The first time Brownson drew the attention of his readers to Frances Wright and her companions was in the *Gospel Advocate* of March 21, 1829. He paid compliments to this class of "Deists, Scepticks, Free Enquirers, and Materialists," who made "some noise in our little world." He said Frances Wright was not only a talented woman, but she also possessed philosophical knowledge in no small degree. In fact, she seemed to be a new Epicurus, a philosopher whom the youthful Brownson held in very high esteem.[18] Probably he had read Frances Wright's book *A Few Days in Athens* (1822), in which she showed her admiration of Epicurus and expressed her belief in "the Epicurean doctrine that the desire for pleasure and the avoidance of pain are the underlying motives beneath all human action."[19] Perhaps this book even helped shape his utilitaristic conception of morality, which he held at that time.

Yet he was skeptical as to Frances Wright's view of religion and written laws, which she—as far as he understood her—wanted to abolish. Far from destroying it, the "religion of Jesus" ennobled human nature, and Brownson doubted whether man would ever be so just as to make religion and all written laws superfluous. He complained that some papers, among them the *Free Enquirer*, did not make any distinction between religion and superstition.[20]

While he had read only two lectures by Frances Wright, Brownson had become more acquainted with the thoughts of Robert Dale Owen. Brownson appreciated that "he always keeps his temper and manifests a truly catholick spirit." Yet, his vast toleration of religious creeds might indicate a philosophical indifference and lack of energy to carry out an "extensive revolution." No doubt, the young Universalist minister, beginning to dream about world reform, cherished more Frances Wright's "visionary notions," made sweet by her "feminine graces."[21]

In August, Brownson reprinted an article by Frances Wright, who maintained that morality was based not on any system of belief, but on the knowledge of nature and of ourselves. The reprint was preceded by Brownson's defense of the woman publicist:

> We are ashamed of our countrymen that they should exhibit such enmity towards a woman who, whatever may be the correctness of her conclusions, has given no mean proofs of an enlightened mind and a truly philanthropick heart. And we regret to see the female part of the community so severe upon one who adorns their sex and seems anxious to give woman her proper rank in society, the high rank she ought to fill. Miss Wright may err, and who may not? But, abating her views on matrimony, which probably are more censured than understood, and censured by more than believe them ill-founded, we have seen nothing in her *ethicks* that should be discarded.[22]

Some weeks later he told a subscriber to the *Gospel Advocate* that, if Miss Wright were a "freethinker," he would hope that there were more such "freethinkers" in the world. Brownson now felt assured that she was not against Christ and Christianity.[23]

Some time after, Brownson, during a trip in eastern New York, met for the first time Frances Wright at Utica, where she was giving a lecture.[24] And just as he did a little later at Auburn, he found "her manner peculiarly fascinating."[25]

She was fascinating, indeed. Not even twenty-five years could obscure his vivid memory of her: "Her lectures were eminently popular. Her free, flowing, and ornate style,–French rather than English,–her fine, rich, musical voice, highly cultivated and possessing great power, her graceful manner, her tall, commanding figure, her wit and sarcasm, her apparent honesty of purpose, and deep and glowing enthusiasm, made her one of the most pleasing and effective orators, man or woman, that I have ever heard."[26]

Also on Walt Whitman did Frances Wright make a deep impression. His father was a subscriber to the *Free Enquirer*, and as a boy or a young man Whitman himself often attended Frances Wright's lectures in New York. Brownson's description of her seems fairly modest compared with Whitman's panegyric praise: "She has always been to me one of the sweetest of sweet memories: we all loved her and fell down before her: her very appearance seemed to enthrall us." And if this was not enough, he declared that he "never felt so glowingly toward any other woman."[27]

As a result of Brownson's encounter with Frances Wright, he "held out... the hand of fellowship" to the "Free Enquirers" by becoming corresponding editor to their magazine.[28]

Frances Wright, on her part, had already discovered the writings of the young editor of the *Gospel Advocate*, and had even reprinted many "interesting" extracts from the Universalist journal. But, she added, "with that individual, until a few weeks since, we had no personal intercourse whatever." However, she had already recognized him as "an honest laborer in the same vineyard with ourselves," who, though nominally attached to a sect, was no sectarian either in thought or feeling: "We saw that he had dropped from the clouds upon the solid earth, and that he had renounced the chair of dogmatism to pursue enquiry in the field of nature and of human life." Therefore, it was more to her pleasure than to her surprise that Brownson offered direct assistance to the "Free Enquirers."[29]

Then, in November, 1829, Brownson took leave as editor of the

Gospel Advocate, though "with no pleasant emotions."[30] The publisher of the magazine, Ulysses F. Doubleday, was both angry and disappointed with Brownson. After all, Brownson, while touring eastern New York, had sent him friendly letters, witnessing a lively interest in the cause of Universalism.[31] But then his young editor made common cause with Frances Wright, this "enthusiastick female," who not only denied God's existence and all natural and supernatural religion, but also defended "community of goods"—the contemporary term of communism—and sexual promiscuity. The brave Universalist had nothing but contempt for all these "visionary projects" and "wild chimeras of foreigners." But judging from the tendency of Brownson's writings Doubleday had understood that his editor's open support of the "Free Enquirers" was no "sudden conversion."[32]

In his defense of Frances Wright and her associates, Brownson stated that they did not advocate communism. True, they maintained that marriage in its traditional form was immoral, since love and hatred—so their argument ran—were dependent on their object and not controlled by the will. Divorce, therefore, was sometimes necessary, but the children of divorced parents should be educated by the State.[33] He was assured that Frances Wright did not want to abolish marriage, but to improve it. In any case, according to Frances Wright as understood by her new colleague, "the organization of society should be such that the parties may separate without injury to themselves or their children."[34]

As for Doubleday's charge of communism, Frances Wright was far from adopting the extreme radicalism of Thomas Skidmore, who wanted to abolish the existing property system.[35] Robert Dale Owen, too, was against the "equalization of property," at least "among the adults of the present generation."[36] Strangely, it was Brownson who ten years later and well advanced in his Unitarian-Transcendentalist period voiced similar radical doctrines on the bequest and equalization of property.[37]

Brownson's contributions to the *Free Enquirer* were not numerous. Nor were they such inflammatory messages as might have been expected of a man who, quite recently, had criticized Robert Dale Owen for lack of zeal. In fact, his articles in the *Free Enquirer* were written in such a gentle, moderate form that one might really doubt whether he was a strong and wholehearted "Free Enquirer." Albert Post suggests one reason: "Brownson . . . failed to speak out boldly and loudly against religious superstition, in part because of extreme youthfulness."[38]

But this is hardly correct, because when Brownson was editor of the *Gospel Advocate*, his "extreme youthfulness" did not seem to put any check on his mode of utterance. Rather, the real reason will be found in *The Convert:* "The moment I broke off my connection with the Universalists, and took my position openly and aboveboard, not as a disbeliever, but as an unbeliever, I felt restored to my manhood—I felt like a new man. My irritation ceased, and almost instantly the tone of my feelings changed towards Christianity. I was no longer obliged to profess, or to seem to profess, more than I believed; and from that moment my mind began to recover its balance . . ."[39] Or, as he expressed his position in a conciliatory "letter" to his former coreligionists: He was "too honest to preach that which I do not know." And his "creed" was brief, but clear: "I wish to be simply an observer of nature for my creed, and a benefactor of my brethren for my religion."[40] According to this view, he stressed the importance of paying due attention to the wrongs of this world and trying to remove them, instead of wasting one's time by meditating on unseen worlds and imaginary beings.[41]

Indeed, what cooled his enthusiasm for the Universalists was their lack of tolerance. Their eternal quarrels about creeds tired him out. After all, it was a man's disposition that made him choose his creed; his creed would not change his disposition. Yet he had found his former "brethren" more benevolent and forbearing than any adherents of other churches. More significantly, he assured his readers that truth might be sought and found everywhere, among the orthodox as well as among the "reputed" heterodox.[42] Obviously, the new "Free Enquirer" was no extremist. In politics, he was trying to find "a just medium" between individualism and communism; in religion, too, he seemed already to anticipate his later Eclecticism.

Did Brownson already feel a bit ill at ease among the "Free Enquirers?" He really wondered if infidels had treated Christians better than Christians had treated infidels. On the background of his recent controversies with the Universalists, and his Presbyterian experience, his attitude seemed surprising. And Frances Wright's fellow worker even declared that he was no more an "anti-religionist" than a "religionist."[43] After all, he had his "most anti-Christian period" of his life behind him.[44]

As for his basic views, his few articles in the *Free Enquirer* did not mark any new approach to religion. Just as he did when he was a Universalist, Brownson considered religion on the basis of the Benthamite theory of utility. And his general position at that time as during the latter part of his Universalist phase was that of agnosticism. Since nobody could ascertain the truth of religious doctrines, it was useless to be concerned with them.[45]

The agnostic often has a sharp sense of the visible world and its evils. If he also believes in social and political action, he tries to abolish these evils. And this is what Brownson did. In his case, there was also a craving need for "a positive belief" after his Universalism had worn off.[46] Turning from unseen worlds to this world, Brownson–in the words of his *alter ego* Charles Elwood–discovered everywhere "injustice, oppression, inequality in wealth, social position, moral and intellectual culture,–the many everywhere toiling for the few." Society was "all wrong," and Charles Elwood–alias Brownson–wanted to set it right: "Now I had found a purpose, an end, an aim,–a future . . ."[47]

But for the real reform of society, education was of primary importance. At that time there seemed to be a universal, almost naive belief in education as a–or even *the*–great panacea of all evils of society. This belief drew its support from the still reigning Lockian theory of knowledge, according to which the mind of every newborn child was a blank sheet to be filled out and formed by all the impressions received. Quite naturally, Brownson became interested in the educational scheme of Frances Wright and her fellow workers.

Perhaps more than other contemporary educators, the "Free Enquirers" thought education to be the farreaching means by which to create a new and better society. Most of their energies, therefore, were concentrated on their school program. As their schools were meant to be supported by the State, public opinion had to be aroused in their favor. Moreover, such men had to be elected to the state legislatures as were friendly to this educational system. According to Brownson, a secret society, presumably modeled after the *carbonari* in Italy, was organized, and Brownson was one of its organizers. Yet he soon "tired of the work, and abandoned it after a few months."[48]

In fact, the intended educational scheme, which presupposed the removal of two-year-old children from their parents, could not but lose its appeal to a man who had recently become the father of two sons: "I was a husband and a father, and did not altogether relish the idea of breaking up the family and regarding my children as belonging to the state rather than to me. Parents might not be in all cases well qualified to bring up their children properly, but where was the state to get its army of nurses, teachers, governors &c. better qualified?"[49]

However, the organization of this allegedly secret society was not the only measure adopted by Frances Wright and her coworkers to get their educational program introduced. They also helped start and organize the Workingmen's Party, first in Philadelphia in 1827, then in New York two years later. Its chief founders were Frances Wright, Robert Dale Owen, Robert L. Jennings, and George Henry Evans. Jennings belonged to the editorial staff of the *Free Enquirer*, and Evans was editor of the *Workingman's Advocate* (1829–1837, 1844–1847), the first important labor paper in the United States.

Brownson seemed to think that the only purpose of founding this party was to get control of the State with the view of carrying through the new system of schools.[50] This was hardly correct. Henry F. Brownson was probably more right when stating that the new party met a general demand for social reform among the increasing working population in the cities, because the two great political parties were primarily wedded to political causes.[51] One should not forget, however, that the Jackson administration as such inspired social reform movements.[52] More immediate motives for founding this party were a strike in the building trades in Philadelphia and Mathew Carey's published letters about the deplorable working conditions of the seamstresses in the great cities.[53]

The formation of this party, then, was primarily a result of the reaction among workers in the great Eastern cities against their conditions of work and living. From the start, therefore, the party did not have any fixed ideological basis. Hardly contemplating any revolutionary change of society, the Workingmen's Party only demanded some reforms, the most important of which were a ten-hour day and the abolition of imprisonment for debt. The only radical theorist among its leaders seems to have been Thomas Skidmore, who advocated an equal distribution of property. Together with Alexander Ming he edited the *Friend of Equal Rights*, but exerted little influence, and his faction within the party had died out already in 1830–1831.[54]

However, as the Workingmen's Party was only a local phenomenon and as its leaders were "freethinkers," the party as such declined during the 1830's. Yet many of its members easily found a new platform for their ideas in the Equal Rights Party or the so-called Locofocos, which came into existence in New York City in 1834–1835.[55] In his biography of Andrew Jackson, Professor William Graham Sumner referred to a correspondent, who in the middle of the 1830's declared—and "correctly," Sumner added—that "the workingmen's party and the equal rights party have operated as causes, producing effects that will shape the course of the two great parties of the United States, and consequently the destinies of this great republic."[56] Thus, from a broader point of view, the Workingmen's Party was something more than a local phenomenon. And Frances Wright herself, though strongly devoted to her far-flung educational plans, also realized the immediate needs of the workingman. Typically, Frances Wright also joined hands with the Locofocos in the later 1830's.[57]

Brownson, who had already shown his sympathy with the working classes and even suggested plans of reforms, entered the Workingmen's Party "with enthusiasm." He established in western New York a paper in its support, the *Genesee Republican and Herald of Reform*, and helped conduct another, the *Daily Sentinel*, in New York City. But he "soon tired of the party," and instead gave his influence and that of his paper to the Jackson candidate, E. T. Throop, against Frank Granger, the candidate of the Anti-Masons, for Governor. A few days after the election in the autumn of 1830, Brownson disposed of his journal to his partner and was no longer its editor.

The constellation Masons versus Anti-Masons, which often crossed party lines, was due to the disappearance of William Morgan, allegedly murdered by Masons, because Morgan, a very poor bricklayer living at Batavia, New York, had written about the secrets of freemasonry, he being himself a Mason. In 1830, three years after the incident, the Anti-Masons came out as an anti-Jacksonian party, particularly in New York, Pennsylvania, Massachusetts, and Brownson's native Vermont.

In any case, Brownson seems, at least for the time being, to have had enough of party politics, as he had tired of his work for the educational schemes. As he himself put it: "The truth is, I never was and never could be a party man, or work in the traces of a party." But, he continued, he had not abandoned "the workingmen's cause, and to that cause I have been faithful according to my light and ability."[58]

No doubt, his dislike of party work as such induced him to break with the Workingmen's Party; but he had another reason, too, perhaps equally strong, for leaving it. He soon realized that the workingmen were not numerous enough to form an efficient political party. Moreover, he was convinced that the workers, as a class, could do but little, if anything, against the moneyed classes. In a conflict between man and money, man was utterly helpless. The only reasonable thing to do was to present the workers' conditions in a true light, so that the other classes of society might be induced to look more favorably on the underdog. Only in this way might the workers have any chance of improving their lot.

So there is no reason to believe that Brownson deceived himself—and others—when declaring that he remained loyal to the cause of the workers, even if he left their party. Throughout the 1830's the lot of the lower classes was always in his thought. As he himself stated his consistent position from 1828 to 1842: "The various systems I embraced or defended, whether social or political, ethical or aesthetical, philosophical or theological, were all subordinated to this end [i.e. "to secure all men a paradise on earth"], as means by which man's earthly condition was to be meliorated."[59] And it was, above all, "the poorest and most numerous class" he had in mind.[60]

Toward the "Free Enquirers" Brownson felt a growing resentment. He could not in the long run accept their basic views of man and religion: man seemed to be reduced to a mere animal, and religion was mostly regarded as superstition. If man were nothing else than an animal, which, when it dies, is no more, all that he could do for him, Brownson concluded, had no importance whatever. His self-sacrifice and disinterestedness for man would have been completely wasted. If, on the other hand, man has an eternal existence, one's sacrifice and love for him would be amply justified. It is religion that tells us that man is immortal, and through this very doctrine it emphasizes the immense value of man.

Gradually, religion was beginning to appear in a new light to him. For a long time he was not to consider it *per se*, but as a means to achieve man's happiness on earth. His view of religion remained for many years ahead oriented toward this life, and not the hereafter. But he was now beginning to turn away from the crass utilitaristic view of religion. In any case, his skeptical attitude toward the "Free Enquirers" made it difficult for him to remain their companion. For the immediate future he preferred complete independence, and established himself as an independent preacher.[61]

After all, as Brownson concluded about this period of his many years later, "my honest avowal of unbelief was, under the circumstances, a step that brought me nearer the kingdom of God."[62]

1 *Free Enquirer* (New York), Dec. 12, 1829; I, 55–56.
2 See Albert Post, *Popular Freethought in America: 1825–1850* (New York, 1943), pp. 32–33.
3 From the preface to her play *Altorf* (1819). Quoted in A. J. G. Perkins and Theresa Wolfson, *Frances Wright, Free Enquirer* (New York and London, 1939), p. 43.
4 Perkins and Wolfson, *op.cit.*, p. 138.
5 *Ibid.*, pp. 237–238.
6 Frances Wright, *Course of Popular Lectures*, 3rd ed. (New York, 1830), p. 25 (quoted in Post, *op.cit.*, p. 144).
7 Frances Wright, *Fanny Wright Unmasked*, p. 4.
8 *Ibid.*, p. 8.
9 *Free Enquirer*, I (Nov. 21, 1829), 31. See also *Political Letters of Frances Wright D'Arusmont* (New York, 1844), p. 30, where she stated plainly that reformation and not revolution was in the true interest of the people. Perkins and Wolfson suggest influence from Auguste Comte, who was skeptical about sudden and violent changes of society (p. 337).
10 *Fanny Wright Unmasked*, p. 5.
11 *Political Letters of Frances Wright D'Arusmont* (New York, 1844), p. 11. Her general attitude was that of agnosticism (Post, *op.cit.*, p. 144).
12 *Fanny Wright Unmasked*, p. 7. "Physical amalgation" between the two races was intended by the Nashoba colony, but it should be accompanied by "a moral approximation" (p. 11). In any case, Frances Wright regretted the publication of the diary of Nashoba, especially because of Richardson's "confessions" (Perkins and Wolfson, *op.cit.*, p. 173).
13 *The Convert*, p. 61.
14 *BrQR* (July 1874), 412.
15 *The Convert*, pp. 40–43.
16 The title of Owen's book was not very much unlike the title of Brownson's work, published in 1836: *New Views of Chritianity, Society, and the Church.* But apart from the title and the utopian vision of a social millennium on earth the two books had very little in common.
17 *The Convert*, p. 56. Brownson's terms "individualism" and "communism" do not seem inadequate. By comparison, a modern scholar, Professor Crane Brinton, prefers the not very dissimilar terms "anarchism" and "environmentalism" *(The Shape of the Modern Mind* [Mentor Books; New York, 1953], pp. 127, 132.
18 "Free Enquirers," *G. A.*, VII (March 21, 1829), 91 ff.
19 Perkins and Wolfson, *op.cit.*, p. 60.
20 *G. A.*, VII, 91 ff.
21 *Ibid.*, pp. 91 ff.
22 *G. A.*, VII (Aug. 8, 1829), 253–255; his defense: pp. 253–254. His defense of Frances Wright also quoted in *Early Life*, p. 42.
23 *G. A.*, VII (Sept. 19, 1829), 300.
24 *Early Life*, p. 41.
25 *G. A.*, VII (Nov. 14, 1829), 364–365.
26 *The Convert*, p. 58.
27 Horace L. Traubel, *Walt Whitman in Camden*, II (New York, 1908) pp. 204–205, 500.
28 *Free Enquirer*, I (Nov. 7, 1829), 16. See also *G. A.*, VII (Dec. 12, 1829), 396–397.
29 *Free Enquirer*, I, 16.

[30] *G. A.*, VII (Nov. 14, 1829), 362.

[31] *Early Life*, pp. 35–39. His information about the different views of Universalists as to the Lord's Supper clearly indicated the lack of defined dogma and practice of their denomination. For his own part, he did not see much "practical benefit" to be derived from this ordinance, but, the later sacramentalist and "churchman" continued, "mankind must have some outward ordinance." In any case, the Universalists did not seem to be more traditional in their views of baptism and the Lord's Supper than the Unitarians.

[32] *G. A.*, VII (Dec. 12, 1829), 396–397.

[33] *G.. A.*, VII (Dec. 26, 1829), 409 ff.

[34] *G. A.*, VII (Nov. 28, 1829), 378–379.

[35] Perkins and Wolfson, *op.cit.*, p. 252.

[36] *Free Enquirer*, I (Dec. 29, 1829), 71.

[37] "The Laboring Classes," *BQR*, III (1840), 358–395, 420–512.

[38] Post, *op.cit.*, p. 40.

[39] *The Convert*, p. 39. To Brownson, "disbeliever" seemed to be identical with "atheist," while "unbeliever" signified "agnostic." See also *The Convert*, p. 43: "I neither asserted nor denied the existence of God."

[40] *Free Enquirer*, I (Nov. 28, 1829), 38.

[41] *Free Enquirer*, I (Dec. 12, 1829), 55–56.

[42] *Free Enquirer*, II (Jan. 2, 1820, yet written already Nov. 27, 1829). "And this liberty to embrace truth wherever found, is the mental independence I prize so highly."

[43] *Free Enquirer*, II (Jan. 16, 1830), 95–96.

[44] *The Convert*, p. 39. From the perusal of the *G. A.* one gets the impression that Brownson's own term "anti-Christian" was too strong for his attitude in the Universalist period. "Irreligious" seems a more appropriate term, so much the more as Brownson himself described his position as unbeliever and not disbeliever (*The Convert*, p. 39).

[45] *Free Enquirer*, I, 38, 55–56; II, 95–96.

[46] *The Convert*, p. 40.

[47] *Works*, IV, 223, 224, 225.

[48] *The Convert*, p. 62. See also "Liberal Studies" (Oration delivered at Mount St. Mary's College, Emmitsburg, 1853), *Works*, XIX, 442.

[49] *The Convert*, p. 65.

[50] *Ibid.*, p. 63.

[51] *Early Life*, p. 47. Helen L. Sumner, "Citizenship (1827–1833)." In John R. Commons's *History of Labour in the United States*, I (New York, 1926), pp. 212, 223, 231, 246, 253, 274.

[52] Allan Nevins and Henry Steele Commager, *The Pocket History of the United States* (Overseas Editions; New York, 1942), p. 145.

[53] *Early Life*, p. 45. Helen L. Sumner, *op.sit.*, p. 169.

[54] *Free Enquirer*, I (Dec. 29, 1829), 71. *Early Life*, p. 45. Helen L. Sumner, *op.cit.*, pp. 211, 234.

[55] On October 29, 1835, at a nomination meeting in Tammany Hall, New York, the left-wing Democrats used locofoco matches and candles after the right-wing Democrats, being forced to leave the Hall, had turned off the gas. The next day the *Courier and Enquirer* labeled the Equal Rights Party the Locofocos.

[56] *American Statesmen*, ed. John T. Morse, Jr., Vol. XVII of 32 vols. (Boston and New York, 1899), p. 436.

[57] *Ibid.*, p. 449.

[58] *The Convert*, p. 63.
[59] *Ibid.*, p. 48.
[60] Brownson often repeated this term, which he had borrowed from Claude Henri, Comte de Saint-Simon. See, for example, his article "Church of the Future" (*BQR*, 1842), *Works*, IV, 73.
[61] *The Convert*, pp. 65–66. It is somewhat of a paradox that the hope of immortality should motivate one's work for creating a paradise on earth or "securing to man his earthly felicity," while the thought of the future existence as such is of no or little interest. To Brownson, the belief in immortality, apart from stressing the worth of the individual, "secured" the continuance and completion of his work begun in this world: "The rough sketch shall hereafter become the finished picture ..." (*Charles Elwood*, *Works*, IV, 223).
[62] *Ibid.*, p. 47.

IV

A Seeker after Truth

In more than one respect Brownson's decision of resuming his work as a minister marked a change in his early life. After his preoccupation with political problems, both as an organizer for the Workingmen's Party and as a champion for one of the candidates for the governorship of New York State, he now turned his back on politics. Moreover, during the last years he had been more or less linked with others in the work for a common cause or common causes; now he declared himself completely independent of any political party as well as of any religious denomination.

And truly, Orestes Brownson loved independence, not only at twenty-eight, but throughout his life. Twenty-five years after his death, a writer in the *Nation* hit the mark when calling him "an irrepressible individualist," one "who was born to be a free lance, and was unhappy when obliged to hold his lance at rest."[1] At about the same time the worthy *Dublin Review* described him as "self-valiant,"[2] emphasizing that his character and "upbringing" had made him independent.[3] Strangely, this love of independence was counteracted by a craving for fellowship and authority, evidenced by his attitude toward the Presbyterian Church and, later, toward the Catholic Church. No wonder, after all, that such contrasting features of character have made some people regard him as a psychological enigma.[4]

This fervent individualist, once having been converted to Catholicism, waged war against the principle of individualism, which he looked upon as the keystone of Protestantism. Yet his own individualistic disposition was useless to fight against and, in fact, he did not want to fight it either. Instead, he was proud of this dominant feature of his character:

I am no saint, never was, and never shall be a saint. I am not, and never shall be, a great man, but I always had, and I trust I always shall have, the honor of being regarded by my friends and associates as impolitic, as rash, imprudent, and impracticable. I was and am, in my natural disposition, frank, truthful, straightforward, and earnest; and therefore have had, and, I doubt not, shall carry to the grave with me, the reputation of being reckless, ultra, a well-meaning man, perhaps an able man, but so fond of paradoxes and extremes, that he cannot be relied on, and more likely to injure than serve the cause he espouses. So, wise and prudent men shake their heads when my name is mentioned, and disclaim all solidarity with me.[5]

Such a person was not well fitted for the work of organizing political parties, nor could he relish the idea of being a hard-core partisan. Moreover, his strong individualism had run counter to the strict Presbyterian discipline and had found a too narrow scope even in Universalism.[6] Finally, his individualistic disposition made him revolt against the emphasis that the Owen-inspired "Free Enquirers" placed on the environment, more particularly on its collective and materialistic aspects.[7]

Instead, he had begun to realize that other influences were needed to give meaning to life in general and his own life in particular. Briefly, he needed "religion of some sort."[8]

He settled down at Ithaca, N.Y., a place not unknown to him, because he had been there for about one year as a Universalist minister. In the beginning of February, 1831, he delivered his first sermon as an independent preacher. Though stating his independence of all sects and creeds, he showed, nonetheless, where his sympathies were tending: "Should I assume the name of any party, it should be Unitarian, as that denomination approximates nearer, in my estimation, to the spirit of Christianity, than any other." To the young minister, the spirit of Christianity was not to be found in dogmatic teaching; in fact, Brownson was yet miles away from any defined system of creed and even farther from Rome. No, the spirit of Christianity, or "the power of godliness," was to him something eminently "practical;" therefore, he paid tribute to Unitarianism, whose ministers enjoined "charity, a refined moral feeling, and universal benevolence."

However, he was not inclined to join any particular denomination, not even the Unitarians. His reasons were two-fold. First, he was convinced that the whole truth was not contained in any specific church; second, the churches, which were often only stale organizations, might present a real obstacle to the moral and intellectual development of the individual. The truth might be sought in many different places, and the task of every honest seeker was to collect fragments of truth wherever he might find them. In contrast to a lifeless church organization Brownson presented the picture of a living association of men and women who spontaneously and with one mind and heart pursued the same objects.[9]

This inauguration sermon contained in a nutshell Brownson's position during this period, which lasted until the summer of 1832 when he became a Unitarian minister. Yet his sermon was and could be nothing but a sketch of his views during his "independence;" later he was to state more fully and clearly his thoughts on different questions.

He did so from the pulpit, but perhaps more efficiently through his own biweekly journal, the *Philanthropist*, which was started already in the autumn of 1830. It might seem somewhat curious that a minister, in addition to his ordinary work, had any time and energy to publish a paper of his own. In Brownson's case, however, it must be remembered that he had already some years' experience as a journalist and editor. Also, this grim and lanky Vermonter might not always feel as much at ease in a pulpit before a scrutinizing congregation as in his lonely study or printing office. Even more important, he probably felt the study to be the place which fitted him best in the circumstances. He regarded himself only as a student, a seeker after truth, not as an authoritative preacher. This he did not forget to tell both his congregation and the readers of his journal.[10]

In a way, then, the former disciple of Frances Wright was still a sort of "Free Enquirer," which was manifest in the very motto of the *Philanthropist:* "Let us enquire.–Reason," and in the whole tenor of his writings. Nevertheless, his scope had widened, which was evident from the sequence of the editor's program: "Devoted to the dissemination of rational and liberal Christianity."

Through these epigraphs: "rational" and "liberal," Brownson wanted to make clear that he rejected Christianity in its traditional, orthodox sense. Stripped of all its irrational dogmas, such as the divinity of Christ and justification by faith, "Christianity itself is nothing less than a system of moral righteousness."[11]

Jesus was the great example, or great "model man,"[12] but as such he was different from men only in degree, not in kind. By consequence, Christ, instead of being our "imputed righteousness," was "the moving cause of our righteousness."[13] Every individual, therefore, had to work out his own salvation, a term which, too, was given an unorthodox interpretation: "The salvation the Christian receives is only that happiness which flows from a good heart and the consciousness we have done our duty."[14]

To the young, independent preacher this was rational and liberal Christianity. Yet, when Brownson a quarter of a century later looked back upon this time, he probably thought "religion of humanity"[15] to be a more appropriate term.

Let us briefly consider this term in the light of Brownson's views as presented in his journal and in his autobiography. First, his was a religion of humanity because Jesus himself, in his essence, was considered to be no more than a human being. Second, it was a religion of humanity, because it was regarded only as a means by which to create human happiness, individually and socially, on earth. For man as an individual: "The Gospel is but another term for those great and all comprehending principles which are necessary to perfect the human character, to make all feel and act as they should, to produce the greatest sum of human happiness."[16] For man as a social being: "My great aim was, not to serve God, but to serve man; the love of my race, not the love of my Maker, moved me. I was still bent on social reform, and regarded religion and all things else solely in relation to that end."[17]

True, Brownson believed in the doctrine of a future life. But he thought future existence would be a state not much unlike this life. He believed future life to be the great possibility of every human being to perfect himself, not only individually, but socially, or as a member of the human family: "I view this doctrine only as connected with the fact we shall all rise from the dead, all live hereafter in a social state, which will be happy or miserable in proportion as we are fitted for each other's society and have a just cultivation of the inner man."[18] Even in future life, therefore, the center of interest would be man, whether in his individual or collective capacity.

Third, it was a religion of humanity because, according to Brownson, all elements of religion were furnished by the human mind itself. Far from being a "mysterious affair," "it is, in fact, nothing more or less than the right exercise of all our faculties. It is nothing above, foreign to, nor different from, our ordinary powers and what we may every day feel, know and perform."[19] Or, as he said in *The Convert* (page 68): "I found in me certain religious sentiments that I could not efface; certain religious beliefs or tendencies of which I could not divest myself. I regarded them as a law of my nature, as natural to man, as the noblest part of our nature, and as such I cherished them; but as the expression in me of an objective world I seldom pondered them."

In the light of this basic view might be seen his strong insistence on religion being "an individual concern." Religion was not a matter to be determined by "a plurality of voices," which many orthodox Protestants seemed to think, nor had "the pretended successor of St. Peter" any right whatever to decide what the individual should think about religion. On the contrary, every one had the right to interpret the Bible for himself, only guided by his own reason.[20]

Such a heavy emphasis on religious individualism easily brings about a skeptical attitude toward tradition. Indeed, the young, independent minister was no great lover of historical Christianity. His tones were almost Emersonian when he attacked the uncritical worship of everything traditional, especially in the field of religion.[21]

The elements of the Christian tradition which Brownson thought to be of dubious value, were not only the orthodox interpretations of the Bible, but also much of the church ritual, whether Catholic or orthodox Protestant. To Brownson, the churches should, primarily, have a social function. Although no "temples of science" as he had wanted them to be earlier, they should be convenient places where people might meet and learn to know one another. No wonder, therefore, that Brownson interpreted the Lord's Supper along the following lines: "The act should be deemed commemorative of exalted worth and the pledge of common brotherhood and mutual friendship; and when thus viewed it becomes a source of rational joy and strong encouragement." Since baptism, however, did not seem to have any such similar social purpose, he considered it "of too positive and artificial a cast to comport well with a purely spiritual religion."[22]

Interestingly enough, only some months after Brownson wrote this, Emerson delivered his famous farewell sermon on the Lord's Supper before the Second Church in Boston. Like Brownson, Emerson pointed out that Christianity was "a moral system" and not at all "a formal religion." But, strangely indicative of a basic difference between them, Emerson did not even stress the Lord's Supper as "the pledge of common brotherhood and mutual friendship." Instead, the pure individualist in Boston, finding nothing of value in this commemorative meal, declared bluntly from the pulpit that he was "not interested in it."[23]

As a rationalist Brownson was not only opposed to aged orthodox tradition; in no less degree he reacted against the phenomenon commonly called "revivalism," which, by the way, had become part of the more recent orthodox tradition. He considered revivalism from the historical point of view: "The staid and drab-colored religion of the Puritans, which consisted in suppressing all emotions and resigning up all intellectual sovereignty, was giving way to a religion of impulse, fanaticism, and mere boisterous rant."[24] But first of all, he looked upon this phenomenon from a social point of view. Revivalist meetings, the rationalistic preacher warned, threatened to destroy familiy life by the "unnatural" and "artificial" atmosphere they tended to create.[25]

Brownson, then, maintained that religion was an individual concern, but he also, in different contexts, stressed its social function. How to reconcile these apparent contradictions? Evidently, his statements were not contradictory. As for doctrines, creeds, opinions on religious matters, it was up to the individual to decide for himself what to believe or not believe, but as far as morality was concerned, religion was eminently a social affair. Religion determined, or should determine, the character of relations, not only those between man and man, but those between man and society at large.

When a fellow worker of Frances Wright, Brownson began to realize, or rather feel, the importance of Christianity as a lever for social reform. The only efficient means by which to improve the lot of the poor would be an appeal, on the basis of Christian morality, to the individuals making up all classes of society. Though no longer nominally attached to the Workingmen's Party, he had by no means failed in his allegiance to the workingmen's cause. "The whole weight of our laws is against the poor man," the independent preacher thundered in his journal, and perhaps also from his pulpit. "Law is an instrument of oppression in the hands of the rich; very seldom of defence in the hands of the poor." Not only the laws, but also taxation unduly favored the rich, and even if the fathers of the republic sympathized with the workingmen, franchise was still of little help to those who wore "a black coat."[26] He had nothing but scorn for a Unitarian who wrote in the periodical *Christian Examiner* that poverty was "the beneficent appointment of God." No, Brownson exclaimed with assurance, the reason of poverty was not to be found in God, but in man himself, in his folly and wickedness.[27]

The implicit conclusion was: man must improve himself and then carry through the needed reforms, "without invoking the genius of revolutions, or departing from the spirit of our present form of government." After all, the security and prosperity of the country were based on individual excellence of character rather than on legislative enactments or the resolutions of public meetings.[28] In the same reformist spirit he encouraged the workingmen: "Verily the Workingmen are arousing. We are glad of it. We hope they will be temperate, and labor to elevate themselves, not to pull others down."[29] And he certainly hoped for active support from other classes of society in "elevating" the workingmen, not primarily for the sake of charity, but for the sake of justice.

In his Universalist period Brownson, strongly inclined to deism and utilitarianism, was mostly indifferent to religion. Partly then and in his "freethought" period he was an agnostic or as his son Henry put it: "He never was an atheist, in the sense that he denied God; but he was so near to atheism that if he refused to say, 'There is no God,' he did say, 'I do not believe a God.' "[30] Some time before he became an independent preacher and till about the end of the year 1831, his position was that of a typical religious rationalist. His former indifference and even more his unbelief had been replaced by a vague belief in religion as a motivating force for creating man's individual and social happiness on earth.

But especially from the beginning of 1832, his rationalism was assuming a more spiritual character. As far as the grounds of morality were concerned, he had already in his phase of unbelief begun to question the value of self-interest—enlightened or not—as a motive for action.[31] While a Universalist, he adhered to the Benthamite and Epicurean notions of morality: an action was good insofar as it involved pleasure, bad insofar as it involved pain. And as late as toward the end of 1831, he seemed to hold the same utilitaristic view, by stressing the "usefulness"—presumably in a narrower sense—of religion.[32] Yet by June in the next year he dissented clearly from strict utilitarianism. Quoting the statement of Epicurus that "gratitude is a virtue that has commonly profit annext [sic] to it," Brownson asked: "And where is the virtue, say I, that has not? But," he added significantly, "still the virtue is to be valued for itself, and not for the profit that attends it."[33]

As for the belief in God's existence, Brownson so far seems to have shared, though with some doubts, William Paley's views of design and harmony as a more or less valid "proof," if not of the existence of God as such, at least of a "Supreme Power or Intelligence." Also as a religious rationalist he adhered, for some time, to this deistic conception of the universe, regarding it as an indirect proof of God's existence and his "oneness."[34] But early in the year 1832 he openly disavowed Paley, who, in fact, through this very doctrine of harmony and design, had made young Brownson doubt the existence of God and led him deeper and deeper into skepticism:... "my doubts were first awakened by reading Paley's *Natural Theology*." An atheist, he continued, would not be induced to religious belief through the theory of design, but simply ask if there was any designer or creator at all.

Brownson, therefore, discarded the idea of proving God's existence from external nature. Instead of looking outward, he concluded, one should turn inward, to one's own "spiritual nature," and then one would hear "the still, small, but clear and convincing, voice of God speaking to his soul. My own faith rests on this internal revelation from God to the inner man. I have thus a witness within; and, having this witness, I can find its testimony corroborated by the whole of external nature. I forgot the spirit, looked only at the flesh, and this witness was unheeded. It was therefore I doubted. I turned my voice inward. I heard the voice of God, I believed–felt myself again locked in the embrace of my Father."[35]

No doubt, these were new tones. As Brownson wrote in *The Convert* (page 69): "I was willing to agree with the Christian world as far as I could, and no longer wished to fight it. But I found myself gradually, I hardly know how or wherefore, cherishing views and feelings more and more in accordance, I will not say with Christianity, but with natural religion. I began to approximate to a belief in God as a creator and moral governor, not so much from any reasoning on the subject, as from the silent operations of my natural religious sentiments."

Yet it is abundantly clear that the celebrated Unitarian minister William Ellery Channing (1780–1842) was the one who at that time wielded the greatest influence on him. According to *The Convert* (page 69), he one day "fell in with" Channing's sermon on the "Dignity of Human Nature." More correctly, the sermon was called "Likeness to God," which Brownson also expressly stated in his "letter" to Channing in 1842 on *The Mediatorial Life of Jesus:*

I had lost, not my unbelief, but my hostility to religion, and had even to a certain extent recovered my early religious feelings, when a friend, no more, read me one day your sermon on *Likeness to God*, preached... 1828... I listened as one enchanted. A thrill of indescribable delight ran through my whole soul. I could have leaped for joy. I seemed suddenly to have found a Father. To me this was much. I had never known an earthly father, and often had I wept when I had heard, in my boyhood, my playmates, one after another, say "my father."[36]

The impact of Channing's sermon on his mind was also reflected in his book *New Views of Christianity, Society, and the Church* (1836). Brownson especially stressed Channing's words: "In ourselves are the elements of Divinity. God, then, does not sustain a figurative resemblance to man. It is the resemblance of a parent to a child, . . ." And on the basis of this–to Brownson–"sublime declaration," the author of *New Views* concluded: "Humanity, after so many years of vain search for a Father, finds itself here openly proclaimed the true child of God."[37]

Channing's words made him think and feel highly of the human soul and, thereby, of man's real, inner worth: "Where do we derive our knowledge of the attributes and perfections which constitute the Supreme Being? I answer, we derive them from our own souls. The divine attributes are first developed in ourselves, and thence transferred to our Creator."[38] In the same sermon Channing termed the divine elements in man "the voice of God," "the Divinity within us" and the "inward law."[39] With almost explosive force this sermon opened up to the young independent preacher at Ithaca bright vistas of the infinite capabilities of the human soul, so that he became "almost a worshipper of man."[40]

Above all, he became a "worshipper" of William Ellery Channing: "As a writer he stands at the head of the brightest geniuses of our country; as a Divine, the lofty and ennobling views he presents of Christianity are only surpassed by the purity of his life and the unaffected character of his piety."[41]

Channing's elevated views of man and man's soul strengthened Brownson's belief in immortality:

Perhaps it is not unreasonable to infer a future state from the capacities of the human soul itself. Few who have contemplated the soul, its mighty powers, its sublimity of feeling, its moral grandeur, its continual aspirations after something it has not, its wish to stretch beyond the narrow circumference of the earth, beyond the stars, beyond the farthest limits of space, to rise and hold communion with the Mysterious Power it feels but sees not,–few have taken this view of the human soul, and have not deemed it destined to survive the frail tenement of clay in which it is lodged.[42]

Some time later the rationalistic preacher admitted that he could not define "spirit;" it was something too "subtile for the external senses." Then, with apparent confidence, he told his readers that the "Image of God" in every individual enabled him to form his concepts of "the spirituality of the Divine Being."[43]

A loftier view of the human soul and the conception of God as father marked such a change in his outlook that he did not hesitate to call it "conversion." Although Brownson in his autobiography did not mention any particular "conversion" occurring at that time, the "conversion" referred to in his journal was obviously the result of the mighty impact of Channing's writings on his mind.[44] Rather than a sudden change of position, however, the "conversion" mentioned was a slow process. According to Henry F. Brownson, his father was influenced by Channing's writings as early as 1829,[45] and in Orestes Brownson's above-mentioned letter to Channing (1842), the author wrote as follows: "The train of thought then suggested [i.e. by Channing's sermon on "Likeness to God"], pursued with fidelity, led me to believe myself a Christian, and to resume my profession as a Christian preacher."[46] Yet the effects of Channing's ideas on Brownson are clearly manifest in his journal only during the last half year of its existence.

What, then, did this "small voice" reveal to Brownson, and reveal so convincingly? First, the inner voice was "the living witness" of God's existence.[47] In fact, it was the only witness, since God's existence could be proved from neither written nor oral records of the past,[48] nor from the "design" or "mechanism of nature." Second, and this was the more important point: the inner voice was the living witness of God as father or "moral governor" of the world.[49]

Brownson's idea of God as father was clearly presented in his article on "Unitarians not Deists," an article which marked a more spiritual approach to Christianity than his rationalism. The deists imagined God to be only the creator of the universe and the prime mover of the laws of nature. After setting the great clock in motion, the creator had disappeared from the scene, keeping solemnly aloof from His work of creation. The Unitarians, on the contrary, believed in an omnipresent God. To them, God was actively present both as the governor of the universe and, more important, as the ever-present upholder of individual man. God governed the physical universe by means of the laws of gravity, attraction and electricity, etc. Man, however, endowed with free will, was upheld primarily by God's special Providence.[50]

At first sight, it may be questioned if Brownson meant this inner voice to be quite identical with the human soul or to be something different from it. In one place God spoke *to* the soul, in another place, *in* the soul and, in a third place, the soul itself "images forth the Deity."[51] In case Brownson had any clear thoughts on the subject, he considered the small, still voice or "inward light" a constitutive element of the soul itself, a 'something' which was not merely reason or conscience, but that which illumined reason and conscience.[52] After all, although no longer plain rationalism, this was still "religion of humanity."

Also, it was a religion of humanity because the "inward light" was common to all men, wherever and whenever they lived. Brownson emphasized that the "inward light" was not a privilege reserved for the chosen few. Traces of this universal "revelation" could be found not only in the Bible—no particular revelation had been given to the half-barbarous Jews, indeed!—but also in the sacred books of the Chinese, Japanese, Hindus, Persians, etc.[53]

Thus Christianity lost its supposed unique character among the religions of the world. Since God speaks in the soul, every individual had all the religion he needed. In fact, a redskin, whose lot was so much lamented by the Orthodox, did not need the Gospel at all! He had the Law of the Great Spirit written in his heart.[54]

To Brownson, therefore, the essence of Christianity was nothing but the teachings of the inner voice, i.e. Christianity and natural religion were identical. Since this "Christianity" consisted of a minimum of tenets: God as father and the immortality of the soul, and since the core of any religion was considered to be morality, Brownson safely concluded that all "good" men had been Christians, "in spirit, if not in letter, and of course accepted with God."[55]

However, the teachings of the inner voice did not make "model men" superfluous. By their example they helped other men lead better lives. Our supreme "model man," Jesus, repeatedly enjoined and carried out in his own life the "moral propositions" of Christianity.[56]

This belief in a God speaking in the soul seems to have satisfied, at least for some time, the psychological needs of the young seeker after truth. Torn and bewildered by many conflicting creeds and opinions, Brownson retired from the bustling scene to consider things calmly and at a distance. Deep in the heart he felt a need of being alone to clarify his views and become aware of his position. Gradually he came to realize that man is easily exposed to and carried away by contradictory influences from without, because he has neglected to create the necessary counterpoise in himself. In an interesting essay on "Creeds," which was printed in the *Christian Register* of Boston, Brownson stated that a religious belief must be formed, not borrowed, because: "A borrowed faith, which is all most people can boast, is constantly directing us to some external source; carrying us away from ourselves, and constantly urging us to fix upon some one else. There is no abiding principle within; no ever ready monitor in the breast whose voice may be consulted and whose decisions obeyed."

Without, perhaps, being fully aware of it, Brownson, in the following lines, gave a lucid characterization of himself. Throughout his life, he was strongly, although mostly temporarily, influenced by certain people he met and certain authors whose books he read. In turn, persons like William Godwin, Frances Wright, William Ellery Channing, Victor Cousin, Pierre Leroux, and Vincenzo Gioberti held the sway over his mind. Brownson's intellect was not cool, "academic," calmly appreciative; his intellect was eruptive, it was brought to play and sparkle only in the light of one great, dominating thought or feeling. Here are his own words: "There is a constant struggle between what passes in our own minds and the opinions we have borrowed; we obey first one and then the other; rise or fall as one or the other predominates; consequently our life is made up of contradictions, of conduct constantly varying, and shifting from one direction to another; arising now from one motive and now from another. From this we should learn that a creed can never be beneficial to any person unless he be fully, and rationally, convinced it is true."[57]

His Presbyterian experience taught Brownson that to believe must be a rational act, and that human reason and revelation, the natural and the supernatural were not antagonistic to each other, but two parts of one whole. In his Universalist period he stressed this harmony, although revelation and the supernatural at that time were of little interest to him. While an independent preacher, he restated this idea of harmony between reason and revelation. At that time he interpreted revelation as the inner light or God's internal witness. Later, he also kept steadfastly to the same principle of harmony between the two halves of one whole, although his understanding of revelation and the supernatural was gradually changing as he approached nearer to Christian beliefs. Brownson's view of reason and revelation furnishes a good example of a basic consistency on central issues, or "what passes in our own minds." On the other hand, his shifts of emphasis were generally caused by the change of events and "the opinions we have borrowed." In 1885, a reviewer in the *Month* pointed at this characteristic feature in Brownson: "They [i.e. all his works] are the record of a life of thought and action. At the same time, from the outset he had grasped very clearly certain great principles to which he was loyal throughout. Indeed, his change of views was often only apparent, for changing circumstances seemed to him to call for different applications of principles that remained the same."[58]

Amid "the hurry and bustle of the times," which were "extremely unfavorable to sober reflection, to calm thought," at a time when parties tyrannized the individual, who was easily lost in the masses,[59] the young seeker was in quest of stable values in his own self. And for some time, he seemed convinced that he had found these values.

The belief in an inner light was no new doctrine. In the American intellectual tradition it can be traced back to Quakerism, and even to the so-called Antinomianism of the early seventeenth century. More recently, this doctrine of an inner light had been strengthened and renewed by the powerful, but elusive "movement" commonly called Romanticism, whose spokesmen talked of "das religiöse Bewusstsein" (Schleiermacher) and "der innere Gott der Wahrheit" (Herder).

Undoubtedly, the belief in the inner light was "in the air." Channing, who expressed his belief in an internal witness,[60] strongly influenced his younger contemporaries of liberal ministers. One of them, Convers Francis (1795–1863), Unitarian minister at Watertown, Mass., and later Professor at Harvard Divinity School, in 1832 wrote an article on "Natural Theology" in the worthy periodical *Christian Examiner*, stating his belief in "the light of nature" or "that image of God within us" that indicates the existence of God.[61] Four years later Francis published a little book, whose very title brilliantly epitomized this view of religion based on the inner-light doctrine: *Christianity as a Purely Internal Principle*.

In a broader perspective, Brownson in his writings in the *Philanthropist* reflected tendencies of Romanticism, whereas his articles in the *Gospel Advocate* indicated a later stage of the Enlightenment. The gradual transition from one trend of thought to the other is traceable in Brownson's intellectual development. In morality, he gradually turned away from utilitaristic relativism to a belief in absolute standards of right and wrong. From a mechanistic conception of the universe as an external indication of God's existence, he turned inward, finding an internal witness to vouchsafe both the existence of God and the immortality of the soul. His belief in God as a prime mover was gradually changed into a firm belief in God as father; his more or less confirmed belief in inexorable natural laws was changed into a belief in God's special Providence. Also, his worship of man and his deathless energies, his romanticizing theories about natives like the Red Indians, and his emphasis on "the spirit of Christianity," reminiscent of Chateaubriand's *Génie du Christianisme,* which he also read with benefit in his phase of unbelief[62]—indicated the influence of Romanticism.

To people of today, some of Brownson's ideas in his journal seem rather strange. Modern readers will not easily understand that a so-called "inward light" furnishes a better "proof" of God's existence than a so-called theory of "design." Not only the "problems" of then and now may be different, but, more important, the approach to them is different.

Nor is it to be expected that a modern reader of the *Philanthropist* will feel himself familiar with the language of the young editor. Sometimes the reader finds it too high-flown, sometimes he thinks it contains too strong doses of sentimentality; too often, it seems to him, the language of the journal is stuffed with "romantic" clichés.

And yet! However "romantic"—in a two-fold sense—the idea of an inner light may be, Brownson wanted to emphasize, through this very doctrine, the intrinsic worth of the individual. To Brownson, the doctrine of or the belief in the dignity of the human soul and the inner light was by no means an abstract notion to be used only to embellish his sermons and to give a pathetic touch to his essays.

The best proof of the contrary was his earnest plea for G. C. Clark, who had been sentenced to death for murder. Brownson was against capital punishment, because, in his view, society had no right to take the life of a "human being, bearing the image of the Deity—a man—a brother, . . ."[63] After all, Brownson's "religion of humanity" had practical applications—indeed so "practical" that he was not permitted to deliver his speech in defense of the murderer.[64]

Although Brownson's paper attracted some attention, not only in the neighborhood, but even as far away as in the cultural metropolis of Boston,[65] he was forced, in the summer of 1832, to stop publication of the *Philanthropist.* He complained that the subscribers had failed him, and, worse still, he was accused of dishonesty, unstability, and hypocrisy. A rather dubious compliment to a man who called himself and wanted to be a seeker after truth!

His words of leave-taking, though marred by self-praise and self-pity, were no doubt genuinely felt: "The banner of truth may then be furled, ourself ruined, and the friends of a mild and rational religion be compelled to wait yet longer for the day of redemption." With a pathetic sigh, the young seeker after truth, the independent preacher, retired to "obscurity."[66]

A Norwegian cannot help being struck by certain parallels between Brownson's "religion of humanity" and the spiritualized rationalistic religion of the poet Henrik Wergeland (1808–1845). Generally speaking, although Wergeland primarily reminds one of Walt Whitman, the impetuosity and the frequent "impolitic" behavior of the Norwegian poet easily conjure up the picture of Brownson. Perhaps even Wergeland's following "self-portrayal" might be applied to the American publicist as well (my own abortive attempt at translation in parenthesis):

For koldt jeg selv jo finder alt,
de Andres Blod er mig for svalt.
Mit eget maa jeg derfor øde.
I Verdens Frost jeg ellers døde.[67]

(Alas! wherever I behold,
The blood of others is too cold.
My own blood, therefore, I must shed,
Or in the world frost I were dead.)

1 "Orestes A. Brownson's Latter Life, from 1856 to 1867," *Nation*, LXXIII (July 4, 1901), 16.
2 "Brownson's Latter Life," *Dublin Review*, CXXIX (1901), 189–190.
3 "Orestes A. Brownson's Middle Life, from 1845 to 1855," *Dublin Review*, CXXVII (1900), 196–198.
4 Wilfred Parsons, S. J., "Brownson, Hecker and Hewit," *Catholic World*, CLIII (1941), 397.
5 *The Convert*, pp. 45–46.
6 *Free Enquirer*, I (Jan. 2, 1830).
7 *The Convert*, p. 65.
8 *Ibid.*, p. 66.
9 *The Philanthropist*, II (Jan. 14, 1832), 85–94. Hereafter referred to as *Ph*. The sermon is also printed in *Early Life*, pp. 52–55.
10 *The Convert*, p. 68; *Ph.*, II (Dec. 17, 1831), 53–54.
11 *Ph.*, I (July 23, 1831), 138.
12 *The Convert*, p. 69.

13 "Justification," *Ph.*, II (Dec. 3, 1831), 35–37.
14 *Ph.*, I(July 23, 1831), 138.
15 Title of Chapter VIII in *The Convert*, pp. 64–74.
16 *Ph.*, II (Dec. 17, 1831), 51.
17 *The Convert*, p. 68.
18 *Ph.*, II (June 12, 1832), 233. As he pointed out, this view contrasted both with the Calvinistic dogma of "election and reprobation" and the dogma of his "quondam Universalist friends."
19 *Ph.*, II (Jan. 14, 1832), 81.
20 *Ph.*, II (Nov. 19, 1831), 21; *Ph.*, II (Nov. 5, 1831), 11–14.
21 *Ph.*, II (Dec. 17, 1831), 53–54.
22 *Ph.*, II (June 26, 1832), 244–245.
23 *The Complete Works of Ralph Waldo Emerson, Concord Edition*, XI (Boston and New York, 1904), pp. 1–25, esp. 20–24.
24 *Ph.*, I (July 23, 1831), 141.
25 *Ph.*, II (Dec. 17, 1831), 62–63; II (March 13, 1832), 154–155.
26 *Ph.*, II (March 13, 1832), 156. He added that he had the same political views as when he edited the *Herald of Reform.*
27 *Ph.*, II (March 27, 1832), 160–162.
28 O. A. Brownson, *An Address, on the Fifty-Fifth Anniversary of American Independence, Delivered at Ovid, Seneca Co., New York, July 4, 1831* (Ithaca, 1831), pp. 11–12.
29 *Ph.*, II (May 29, 1832), 224.
30 *Early Life*, p. 58.
31 *The Convert*, p. 66.
32 *Ph.*, II (Nov. 5, 1831), 9–10.
33 *Ph.*, II (June 12, 1832), 240.
34 *Ph.*, II (Dec. 17, 1831), 56.
35 *Ph.*, II (Feb. 14, 1832), 113–115.
36 *Works*, IV, 141.
37 *Ibid.*, 46.
38 "Likeness to God," *The Works of William E. Channing, D. D., Eighth Complete Edition*, III (Boston and New York, 1848), p. 233.
39 *Ibid.*, p. 234.
40 *The Convert*, p. 70.
41 *Ph.*, II (April 10, 1832), 190.
42 *Ph.*, II (Nov. 19, 1831), 19.
43 *Ph.*, II (Dec. 17, 1831), 55.
44 *Ph.*, II (Feb. 14, 1832), 113–114. His "conversion"meant, as he himself put it, a transition from "that eclipse of the soul, that midnight of reason" to "an unwavering and joyful belief in our God–my Father" (pp. 114–115). Interestingly, Brownson already mentioned his intention to write a book about his "conversion," a plan which later materialized in this semiautobiographical novel *Charles Elwood; or, The Infidel Converted*, written for the most part in 1834, but not published until 1840 (see *Ph.*, II, 115, and *Works*, IV, 316).
45 *Early Life*, p. 88.
46 *Works*, IV, 141.
47 *Ph.*, II (Feb. 28, 1832), 134.
48 *Ph.*, II (March 13, 1832), 145–150.
49 *Ph.*, II, 145–150; *The Convert*, p. 69.
50 *Ph.*, II (May 15, 1832), 193–195.
51 *Ph.*, II, 115; II, 134; II, 145–150.

[52] *Ph.*, II, 193–195.
[53] *Ph.*, II, 134.
[54] *Ph.*, II (March 13, 1832), 153–154.
[55] *Ph.*, II (Feb. 28, 1832), 143.
[56] *Ph.*, II (Feb. 28, 1832), 132.
[57] *Christian Register*, II (July 30, 1831), 121.
[58] "Brownson's Political and Literary Essyas," *Month*, LV, 440.
[59] *Ph.*, II (June 12, 1832), 246–247.
[60] See, for example, *A Discourse on the Evidences of Revealed Religion*, 3rd ed., American Unitarian Association (Boston, 1826).
[61] *Christian Examiner*, XII, New series, VII (May, 1832), 196, 198.
[62] In 1857, when reviewing this book, Brownson wrote that it was the first book that defended Christianity on a purely human basis, and although as a Catholic he did not find Chateaubriand's arguments absolutely satisfactory, the work had, he said, a good influence on mind and heart. He expressed his deep gratitude to the author, whose book fell into his hands when he was an avowed infidel and helped remove his hostility to Christianity (*BrQR*, 1857, pp. 142–144).
[63] *An Address, Prepared at the Request of Guy C. Clark, with the Intention of Having It Delivered to the Assembly on the Day of his Execution, February 3, 1832*. By O. A. Brownson (Printed for the author; Ithaca, 1832), p. 3.
[64] *Early Life*, p. 77.
[65] George Ripley, the editor of the *Christian Register* and Brownson's later friend, repeatedly drew attention to the *Philanthropist* (Oct. 1831, p. 166, and Jan. 7, 1832).
[66] *Ph.*, II (June 26, 1832), 256.
[67] From "Den første Sommerfugl" ("The First Butterfly;" 1837), in *Henrik Wergelands skrifter, folkeutgaven*, ed. L. Amundsen and D. A. Seip, III (Oslo, 1960), p. 26.

V

The Religious Sentiment

Most probably, Brownson did not believe fully in his own declaration that he was retiring to "obscurity." In any case, not long after the last number of the *Philanthropist* had been issued, he offered his service as minister to the Unitarian congregation at Walpole, a pleasant town only ninety miles from Boston.

Although he had not formally become a Unitarian, his views and sentiments largely coincided with those of the Unitarians. Moreover, he had, on repeated occasions, clearly expressed his sympathy for Unitarianism and its adherents. On the other hand, his attitude toward his former coreligionists, the Universalists, seems to have deteriorated as compared with his favorable treatment of them in the *Free Enquirer*. Thus, in his very first sermon as an independent preacher, after duly praising the Unitarians for their "charity, a refined moral feeling, and universal benevolence," he characterized the Universalists as those who "excommunicated me and published me from one end of the country to the other as a rejector of Christianity, as an unprincipled villain!"[1] And in the very last number of the *Philanthropist*, after commenting upon the variations and contradictions of Universalist dogmas, the editor concluded: "We think upon examination that it will be found that unitarians have all that there is really good connected with the system, without its revolting and mischievous errors."[2]

Like Universalism, American Unitarianism was primarily a revolt against Calvinism with its conception of God as a stern Jehovah and its doctrines of election and reprobation. Features of Unitarianism can be traced already in the sermons of Jonathan Mayhew (1720–1766), pastor of West Church in Boston. With his rejection of Trinitarianism and his advocacy of free will and private judgment, he was an early herald of American Unitarianism. Yet, strangely enough, it was an

Episcopal church, King's Chapel in Boston, which, in 1785, after leaving out the Trinitarian formulas in the Prayer Book, became the first avowed Unitarian congregation in the United States. However, the change did not take place unheeded. The minister of the church wrote a series of letters to a Unitarian leader in Britain about the religious situation in Boston, and these letters, subsequently inserted in a biography, were later published, separately, by the Orthodox in Massachusetts under the incendiary title: *Unitarians Caught and Convicted! Systematic Hypocrites! Let Christian Fellowship Be Wholly Denied Them!*[3]

Toward the close of the century, Unitarianism also gained a foothold in Philadelphia. In 1794, the British physicist and educator Joseph Priestley (1733–1804), being forced to leave his home country because of his liberal ideas, settled in Philadelphia and founded there, in 1796, the second Unitarian church in the country. In the same year, he published his book *Unitarianism Explained and Defended.*

Although met with continuous opposition from orthodox quarters, "the progressive tendencies went quietly on, step by step the old beliefs were discarded; but"–George Willis Cooke continues in his history of American Unitarianism–"it was by individuals, and not in any form as a sectarian movement."[4] From the very beginning, then, American Unitarianism was a cast of thought rather than a fixed dogmatic system. The local autonomy of the Congregational churches and the old Puritan theory of a "covenant" between God and man, a theory which in the course of time was to lay increasing stress on man's role in the covenant, helped promote, at least indirectly, the disintegrating process of Calvinism and make way for liberal tendencies.[5]

A strong impetus to the cause of Unitarianism was the appointment, in 1805, of Henry Ware (1764–1845) as the first Unitarian Professor of Divinity at Harvard College. In 1819 he founded the Divinity School at Harvard, though at that time he could hardly imagine that only two decades later he would be obliged to defend his Unitarianism against Transcendentalism or, more particularly, the influence of a certain Divinity School address. At any rate, Henry Ware's description of Emerson's Address as "a denial of the personality of God"[6] clearly indicated both the Transcendentalist position and his own, the so-called "Old School" Unitarianism, which had retained some basic elements of traditional Christian faith.

Another and even more erudite Unitarian theologian was Andrews

Norton (1786–1853), who was attached to Harvard from 1811 to 1840. His principal work was his three-volume *The Evidences of the Genuineness of the Gospels* (1837, 1844), and, like Henry Ware, though more intensively, he was engaged in controversy both with Trinitarians and, later, with Transcendentalists.

By far the most influential of all American Unitarians was William Ellery Channing. His discourse on "Unitarian Christianity," delivered in 1819 in Baltimore at the ordination of the Rev. Jared Sparks, was the programmatic sermon of Unitarianism. In distinct opposition to the Calvinist conception of Deity, he stressed the "Parental character" of God, expressing his belief that God's "almighty power is entirely submitted to his perceptions of rectitude." Not only did Channing reject typically Calvinist dogmas, but also the common, traditional belief in the vicarious atonement. He was convinced that God did not need to be reconciled with man through the sacrifice of Christ,[7] but, as he tried to explain his position somewhat later, "that his death is an important means of our salvation, we gratefully acknowledge; but ascribe its efficacy to the merciful disposition of God towards the human race."[8] At any rate, the mission of Jesus was, according to Channing, to "communicate holiness" through his own example.[9] Like many Unitarians of the earlier generation,[10] Channing seemed to hold Arian views on the person of Christ, but what he emphasized most strongly were his beliefs in God as father and the dignity of human nature. On the whole, Unitarianism, especially as exposed by Channing, was, as he himself put it, "a rational and amiable system, against which no man's understanding or conscience, or charity, or piety revolts."[11]

Channing's Baltimore sermon contained the quintessence of American Unitarianism. Channing, however, was no typical theologian. As Joseph Henry Allen said: "Religious truth with him was more a matter of contemplation than of study and clear definition."[12] But first of all, religion was to him the means of "self-culture" or "self-elevation,"[13] the formation of character. Despite his deficiency and, perhaps, superficiality as a theologian, Channing's personal piety and integrity of character were undisputed, and to his own statement: "Men can be wrought upon by generous influences,"[14] one may safely add that he was himself one of those "generous influences." No wonder that Channing was called "the apostle of Unitarianism," and Emerson remembered him as "our bishop" and even as "the star of the American Church."[15] With his insistence on the capacities of the human soul and the "inner witness," Channing served as a link between "Old School" Unitarianism and Transcendentalism, or "the New School."

All in all, Unitarians rejected the Calvinist dogmas of God's arbitrary power, and election and reprobation; also, they discarded the traditional Christian beliefs in Trinitarianism and the atonement. On the affirmative side, Unitarians believed in God's benevolence and the divinity of man. Moreover, in contrast to the orthodox emphasis on conversion, Unitarians stressed the gradual formation of character. In contrast to Universalism, Unitarianism at an earlier stage disputed the whole orthodox system, especially its Christology, and not only the typically Calvinist dogmas. On the other hand, Unitarians, at least in the early period, seemed more observant of church ordinances than Universalists. As for the belief in a future existence, Unitarians did not have any definite doctrine, but seemed to think of the hereafter as a continuation of life on earth, while rejecting the extreme views of Calvinism and Universalism.

Brownson's favorable attitude toward Unitarianism and his expressed sympathy with its adherents probably made it rather easy for him to be accepted by the congregation at Walpole as their minister. From Petersham, Brownson wrote his wife, then at Elbridge, what had happened to him on his travel, and he did so with a pride not too well concealed: "Walpole suits me." The Unitarian ministers he had met were "all respectable, but with rather narrow views." At Walpole he had even been pronounced superior to any one! Although he thought this to be exaggeration, he felt convinced that he had not met any other clergyman who possessed so much "practical knowledge" as he did. Admitting that he was inferior to all he had met in "mere useless browsing," he gave himself credit for taking thorough and comprehensive views of man and religion. Then he said something which, for better or for worse, was genuinely characteristic of himself: "I believe it is in my power to impart two ideas where I may receive one."[16]

The negative side of this "power," Brownson's fondness for logical hairsplitting, was humorously presented by James Russell Lowell in his *Fable for Critics* (1848):

> The worst of it is, that his logic's so strong,
> That of two sides he commonly chooses the wrong;
> If there *is* only one, why, he'll split it in two,
> And first pummel this half, then that, black and blue.[17]

On the other hand, the positive aspect of this characteristic feature, that is, his mental alertness and his capacity of grasping and developing some main ideas, is reflected in the following words of Joseph Henry Allen: "With a curiously slender stock of erudition, he showed an equally extraordinary arrogance and fertility in abstract argument. For example, having toiled with much ado (as he told me) through some fourteen pages of Kant's *Introduction*,–having got the idea of it to his own satisfaction,–he proceeded to write more than fifty pages of what, I am told by those more competent to judge than I, is really instructive exposition."[18]

Once settled in Walpole, Brownson fell in with a society which was quite new to him. People talked about authors and books that he had not heard anything about before. What was more, he had access to a whole body of literature–English, French, and German–whose existence had been quite unknown to him.

Now the young Unitarian minister could not help feeling a bit uneasy: knowledge by reading, was it nothing but "mere useless browsing?" In any case, he made up his mind to learn to know the writings of some European authors and philosophers and, for this reason, began to study French and a little German.[19] He set to work with unrelenting energy, sleeping little and often working in his study until two or three o'clock in the morning.[20] But after some time he had taught himself so much French that he possessed a sufficient reading knowledge of the language.

Brownson was to read many books in French, and some of them he perused with the greatest zeal and attention. Indeed, throughout his life he maintained a vivid interest in all things French, whether in the political, literary, or philosophical field. Not only his numerous articles dealing with French matters bear witness to this interest, but also his correspondence with prominent Frenchmen, like the philosopher Victor Cousin, whose works he helped introduce in the United States, and the Catholic writer and statesman Charles Forbes de Tryon, Comte de Montalembert (1810–1870), leader of the "liberal" Catholic party in France.

In 1851, in an essay on the French Republic, Brownson crystallized his general view of France and French civilization, and his personal indebtedness to French literature: "She is as it were the missionary station of the world, and it is not a matter of indifference to other nations whether she preaches the true gospel, or another. Her doctrines have immense weight in England; they reign supreme in this country; Germany reaches us only through France, and from France we import not only our fashions, but our tastes, our principles, our ideas, our philosophy, and our literature." In fact, this "literature has had more to do in forming our mind and taste than that of our own mother tongue."[21]

The influence of French thought on Brownson's mind is not too difficult to account for. A much more complicated task would be to determine possible influences of French language on the style and composition of his writings. Even if he primarily modeled his language after the pattern of classical English, his lucid, easy-flowing style, which sometimes seems to flow a bit too easily, his clear-cut presentation of argument, sometimes strengthened by the effects of oratory, might indicate influences from his reading of French literature.

But Benjamin Constant (1767–1830), the first French author he read in the original language, gave him more than enough to do. In fact, Constant's five-volume work *De la Religion, considérée dans sa source, ses formes, et ses développements* (1824–1831) was a remarkably serious and earnest production of an author who had become famous for his frivolous novel *Adolphe* (1816). It is possible that Brownson's attention had been drawn to this work through the above-mentioned article by Convers Francis in the *Christian Examiner*.[22] At any rate, he vigorously studied Constant's work, and to his delight, the diligent reader, plodding his way through strange words and idioms, found that the thoughts themselves were not strange to him. He had felt and thought almost the same, but rather in an abstract manner, without giving due notice to history to confirm his views.

Constant's leading doctrine was that religion originated in a sentiment natural to man. This religious sentiment, whether an instinct or a revelation from God, was universal. Yet this did not mean that the sentiment manifested itself always and everywhere in exactly the same way. In fact, there was an enormous difference between fetishism and monotheism. The forms of worship, widely divergent as they were, depended on the degree of intelligence of the worshipper. The sentiment itself, however, was invariable. This doctrine of the religious sentiment and its changing forms was closely linked with another, the doctrine of religious progress. Each new form of religion, then, was considered an improvement upon the previous form.

In Constant's theory of the religious sentiment Brownson recognized his own idea of the inner light. In the Frenchman's theory of religious progress he discovered his own long cherished idea of the progress of mankind. The part of Constant's thought that proved most fruitful to the attentive reader was the thesis that man always sought to embody his thoughts and feelings in institutions, which, in their day and circumstances, served as means of progress. However, when these institutions no longer satisfied the wants and intelligence of the times, they had to be replaced by new and better institutions.

The young reader asked himself: Do not my age and my country need such a religious institution, an organization, a church, which will satisfy the wants and cravings even of the most advanced minds of the age? He could not help thinking–and dreaming–of such a church, and of the part he himself might play in its establishment. True, a couple of years later, in 1836, he made preparations for such an organization, by establishing the Society for Christian Union and Progress, he himself serving as its minister. Although this was by no means an abortive attempt: in fact, the society lasted until 1843–its results certainly fell short of the idealistic and, perhaps, somewhat vainglorious hopes of its founder. The society did not become what it was meant to be: the initial stage of the "Church of the Future."[23]

Later, in his Catholic phase, and even partly before, Brownson rejected most of Benjamin Constant's theories. The latter's doctrine of the religious sentiment as "a fundamental law of human nature"[24] Brownson repudiated as sheer subjectivism. Likewise, he discarded Constant's theory of religious progress. What Brownson had thought to be progress, he later came to consider a decline. As truth is older than error, he postulated, monotheism is older than polytheism and fetishism.[25] Finally, the "Church of the Future," based on the "religion of humanity," dwindled into insignificance, whereas the Catholic Church: the Church of the Past, became to him the Church of all times.

Nevertheless, the influence of Constant's book on his mind should by no means be underrated. It was probably the first book of its kind which he studied methodically. He did so not only because the book was written in a foreign language, but also because he began to realize that "practical knowledge" did not necessarily reduce reading to "mere useless browsing."

Also in another respect Constant's book meant something to him. When a Universalist and an unbeliever, he waged war against the common church system which he looked upon as priest-ridden and pernicious. Constant taught him that these institutions, though dominated by the priests, had not always been pernicious. On the contrary, they might have been good and useful in their own time and circumstances. Catholicism, for example, though today a superannuated form of religion, had at least historical importance. During the thousand years from the fall of the Western Roman Empire to the Reformation, the Catholic Church had its grand mission. Indirectly, Brownson seemed to derive from Constant's work the conception of Protestantism as something "simply critical, destructive, and without the slightest organic character or tendency, or the least power to erect a temple of concord and peace, of union and progress."[26] These views of Catholicism and Protestantism Brownson was to develop and systematize in his book *New Views of Christanity, Society, and the Church* (1836). It would be too much to say that Constant led Brownson to Catholicism. But through Constant's theories Brownson became dimly aware of the Catholic tradition.

Brownson was well received by his Unitarian congregation at Walpole. Reported the *Christian Register* of Boston: "Rev. Mr. Brownson was installed at Walpole in May under very favorable auspices; his congregation having nearly doubled the past year."[27] His youthful energy and his not too much "priest-like" manners probably had a kind of appeal to people who were no regular churchgoers. Moreover, the young pastor did not demand that they believe in a fixed set of dogmas in order to become Christians. On the contrary, he told his listeners that they should not make any attempt at all to "believe." Why? The religious sentiment which God had "incorporated ... into our very natures," revealed to them God's existence, the immortality of the soul and their moral accountability. Who denied this, did not deny the right belief, but his own nature.[28]

Indeed, doctrinal requirements must have been extremely light for those wanting membership in the Unitarian congregation at Walpole. From the pulpit it was repeatedly stated that religion should be "attractive, simple, lovely, sweet."[29] Theological systems and confessions were nothing but "opinions of opinions," "beliefs in beliefs." Only the religious sentiment, teaching us principles instead of opinions, had real, unchangeable value.[30]

Brownson, for his part, was well at ease in his new environment. He paid his due share of credit to the Unitarian Association,[31] although on another occasion he stated that his "party" was neither Unitarianism nor

Trinitarianism, but God and humanity; and his only belief was love of truth.[32] This statement, which did not seem to evoke any protest, showed not only Brownson's essentially non-denominational position, but also the extreme toleration of many Unitarians as to matters of doctrine. As he said about the Unitarians in *The Convert* (page 70): "I found that they were liberal, that they eschewed all creeds and confessions, allowed the unrestrained exercise of reason, and left their ministers each to stand on his own private convictions, and to arrange matters each as best he could with his own congregation." Even William Ellery Channing, the founder of the American Unitarian Association (1825), did not advocate any definite system of belief and, according to *The Convert* (page 78), "inclined strongly to individualism, and distrusted all associated action, though sometimes tolerating, and even encouraging it."

The young pastor of the Unitarian congregation at Walpole was busy telling his audience about the unchangeable religious sentiment, assuring them that forms of religion depended on varying circumstances. After all, uniformity of belief was no desirable aim, since Christianity consisted in doing, not in believing.[33]

Yet, sermonizing alone could not satisfy a man who had been used to address a larger audience through journals, and as he had no paper of his own, he became a regular contributor to the *Christian Register* of Boston. In three series of "letters" he communicated his thoughts on different religious subjects.

In the first series: "Treatment of Unbelievers," he attacked the supposedly prevalent notion among Christians that bad morals lay at the bottom of infidelity. Indeed, doubters and infidels, the former unbeliever stated, should not be denied the right of having their own opinions. After thus clearing the way, Brownson gave the following advice of "treatment" of unbelievers: "We have in ourselves the means of determining whether Christianity be true or false. When I propose Christianity to an unbeliever, I refer him to the workings of his own soul, to what passes in his own mind, for proofs of its truth."[34] The unbeliever should learn to know the Christian concepts of morality in their purest form, their harmony with his own nature being clearly shown. "Ancient records" should not be trusted too much: spirit and life must replace letter and death![35]

In his next series: "Faith and Works," Brownson tried to give a summary of his theology. He rejected both the Calvinist dogma of election and reprobation, and the dogma of universal salvation, on the ground that neither of them recognized man's freedom of will. But, to Brownson, not even the dogma of justice by faith or "imputed righteousness" fully recognized this freedom. In fact, Brownson found that this dogma was "a paralytic shock upon man's powers, and makes him believe that it matters not what he does."[36] According to Brownson, St. Paul did not contrast "faith" to "works" in the traditional sense of those terms. As the Unitarian minister interpreted it, "faith" meant faith in Jesus as the great model man, and the righteousness of Jesus could not save us unless we became "righteous in the same sense in which he was."[37] As for "works," Brownson was convinced that the apostle only meant the old Jewish ceremonial law, and as this law enjoined only an external kind of worship, it could not justify any one. St. Paul's great aim, then, was to contrast the "spiritual religion of Jesus" to the ceremonial Jewish religion. Brownson saw this contrast between "faith" and "works" in a larger perspective. Thus the Reformation was a reaction against the vain ceremonies of Catholicism, not against its charity work; the rationale of Quakerism was its opposition to the "external worship" of Protestantism. In either case, power of godliness against form![38] Religion, Brownson proclaimed, was "a sentiment of the heart."[39]

In his third series: "Letters to an Unbeliever," Brownson dealt particularly with the idea of the religious sentiment. He pointed out that he had arrived at the same thoughts about the religious sentiment long before he read Constant's work: "I may be considered, then, as an independent witness to the same truths." Obviously, Brownson had a wonderful knack for catching ideas and sentiments that were "in the air." Thus, already as a Universalist he had written about intuition and even a "God within the mind."[40] Generally speaking, although he was greatly enthusiastic about certain books and authors, none of them was "a paralytic shock upon" him; he was intellectually and even emotionally prepared for their message. This was true of his attitude toward Channing and Constant, whose works he thought to be brilliantly suited to win unbelievers for Christianity.[41]

According to Constant and Brownson, religion was something "instinctive," a matter of consciousness rather than a matter of belief: "We are religious because we were made to be religious, because religion is as much a want of the soul as food or drink is of the body." The only difference, then, between a Christian and an unbeliever was that the latter denied the existence of the religious sentiment. Brownson, therefore, tried to "prove" its existence: the sentiment is natural to man; if it is not quite universal, it is almost so. Could anyone deny that "men love to adore," and that "they look around for some object of worship?" Indeed, "even when we doubt the existence of God, we feel this propensity." *Ergo*, the religious sentiment exists.[42] And since the religious sentiment is universal, or almost so, and since "It is not from abroad, but from within, that we obtain the proofs of religion,"[43] Brownson concluded with complete assurance, or almost so, that God exists.[44] Perhaps the seeker after truth was already beginning to feel the dilemma: Did–or could–the religious sentiment as "a fundamental law of human nature" reveal or correspond to objective reality?

Anyhow, Brownson, suppressing for the time being similar doubts, confidently developed the ideas supposed to be inherent in the religious sentiment. "The idea of God" created "love of unbounded greatness" and "reverence for the highest wisdom."[45] The idea of immortality removed the feeling of hopelessness, creating instead a positive attitude to life.[46] Finally, the idea of moral accountability, or "the sentiment of moral justice," was not based upon any motives of "usefulness:" "On this idea of the just as independent of the useful, is founded the whole fabric of morality." A knife was good or bad according to its usefulness; a human action, however, could not be judged according to this standard.[47]

Obviously, Brownson had by now discarded his utilitaristic view of morality and religion which he maintained when he was a Universalist: "Whatever produces agreeable sensations, we call good; and we call ourselves happy in proportion as these sensations are predominant. –Evil and misery are the reverse ... Pain is an evil." And: "God did not make us, that we might be religious beings, but he made us religious beings that we might be happy."[48] But now he wrote lines as these: "They [that is, men] should never propose happiness either here or hereafter as the end of our exertions, but always the growth and perfection of mind, the purification of the soul and its exaltation to God. He who makes his own happiness his object, the end of his existence, whether it be happiness on earth, or in heaven, is selfish, has, in my estimation, no conception of true virtue."[49]

This profounder view of religion and morality enabled him even more to make sacrifices for his fellow man. If, Brownson continued, one took away the truths disclosed by religion, i.e. the religious sentiment, one could see nothing in one's fellow man worth any sacrifice. To the skeptic or the unbeliever, who did not recognize these truths, who did not see God's image in every human being, man was reduced to a brute. And who wishes to fight or die for a brute? This, Brownson concluded, was the attitude that the skeptic, the unbeliever was eventually bound to take.[50]

However, Brownson's enlarged view of the grounds of ethics, signalized already in the *Philanthropist,* was no unique phenomenon of the time. At Harvard University, Levi Frisbie, Professor of Moral Philosophy from 1817 to 1822, advocated the idea of justice as something absolute and independent of any utilitaristic notions.[51] At the same University, the increasing importance of the Scottish School of philosophy with its emphasis on internal ideas of ethics[52] could not but influence more or less the students, among whom were Ralph Waldo Emerson and Brownson's later friend George Ripley (1802–1880).

Already in 1821 young Emerson wrote in his diary: "Dr Price says that right & wrong are not determined by any reasoning or deduction but by an ultimate perception of the human mind. It is to be desired that this were capable of satisfactory proof but as it is in direct opposition to the sceptical philosophy it cannot stand unsupported by strong and sufficient evidence. I will however read more & see if it is proved or no."[53]

And at least by 1831 Emerson seems to have found the desired "satisfactory proof." His statement in his journal at that time that God "is most present" in the soul, and that "the Soul rules over matter" clearly indicated his rejection of utilitarian morality.[54]

No less convincingly George Ripley had discarded "the sceptical philosophy" when, in 1833, he reviewed Sir James Mackintosh's book on *Ethical Philosophy* (1832). Ripley maintained that there is an "Idea of Right" in the human mind, a moral faculty that perceives truth intuitively. Stressing the difference between obligation and motive, duty and interest, he wanted to make clear that a strictly "useful" action is not necessarily a virtuous one.[55]

Obviously, the Puritan moral heritage, recently strengthened by other influences, was still manifesting itself. And more particularly, a certain Unitarian minister at Walpole found in the religious sentiment "motives to beneficent action."[56]

1 *Ph.*, II (Jan. 14, 1832), 86; *Early Life*, p. 52.
2 *Ph.*, II (June 26, 1832), 255.
3 William C. Gannett, *A Hundred Years of the Unitarian Movement in America, 1815–1915; a Sermon Preached on Nov. 28, 1915, at the Fiftieth Anniversary of the Unitarian Church in Germantown, Pa.* (1915), p. 13. The pamphlet referred to was published in 1815.
4 Cooke, *Unitarianism in America. A History of its Origin and Development* (Boston, 1902), p. 48.
5 *Ibid.*, p. 26. As for the "Covenant Theology" and its tendency, see Perry Miller and Thomas H. Johnson, *The Puritans* (New York, 1938), pp. 57–58, 191–194.
6 Gannett, *op.cit.*, p. 21.
7 *The Works of William E. Channing, D. D., Eighth Complete Edition,* III (Boston and New York, 1848), pp. 84–85, 89.
8 "Objections to Unitarian Christianity Considered" (1819), *Ibid.*, p. 394.
9 *Ibid.*, p. 92.
10 Frederic Henry Hedge, *Theological Progress during the Last Half Century; a Sermon* (Providence, 1878), p. 6. However, according to Samuel J. May, *What do Unitarians Believe?* (2nd ed.; Syracuse, N. Y., 1865), many Unitarians held Arian views as late as in the 1860's (p. 5).
11 *Channing's Works,* V, p. 408. Yet twentieth-century Unitarians seem somewhat skeptical about Channing's principles, which, to them, may tend toward "feeble, unwise tenderness" and even soften "the sinews of a social conscience" (Paul Revere Frothingham, *Our Heritage of Faith: A Sermon Preached at Sanders Theatre, Cambridge, Mass., May 10, 1925, in Celebration of the One Hundredth Anniversary of the Foundation of the American Unitarian Association* [Boston, 1925], p. 21).
12 Allen, *Our Liberal Movement in Theology* (Boston, 1882), p. 58.
13 "Lectures on the Elevation of the Laboring Portion of the Community" (1840), *Channing's Works*, p. 187.
14 "Likeness to God:" Discourse at the ordination of the Rev. F. A. Farley. Providence, R. I., 1828, *Channing's Works,* III p. 253.
15 Ralph Waldo Emerson, "Historic Notes of Life and Letters in New England." *The Complete Works, Concord Edition,* X (Boston and New York, 1904), pp. 339, 576.
16 Letter of Oct. 15, 1832: *The Brownson Papers* at Notre Dame University.
17 *The Complete Writings of James Russell Lowell, Elmwood Edition,* XII (Boston and New York, 1904), p. 43.
18 Allen, *op. cit.*, p. 86.
19 *The Convert*, p. 70.
20 *Early Life*, p. 70.
21 *Works*, XVI, 271–272.
22 Convers Francis, "Natural Theology," *Christian Examiner,* XII, New series, VII (1832), 193–220, esp. 205 ff.
23 Title of an essay in the *Boston Quarterly Review* (1842), *Works,* IV, 57–78. See also *The Convert,* p. 76.
24 *Christian Register,* No. 48, XII (Nov. 30, 1833), 190. Hereafter referred to as *Chr. Reg.*
25 *The Convert,* p. 73. See also his articles on "Origin of Civilization" *(Catholic World,* 1871), *Works,* IX, 418–434, esp. 424; "Primeval Man" *(Catholic World,* 1869), *Works,* IX, 318–332, esp. 319; and "The Primeval Man Not a Savage" (1873), *Works,* IX, 457–485, esp. 472.
26 *The Convert,* p. 74.

[27] *Chr. Reg.*, No. 30, XII (July 27, 1833), 118. According to the *Chr. Reg.*, No. 23, XII (June 8, 1833), he was installed as pastor for the First Congregational Church and Society in Walpole on May 30, 1833 (p. 90). He had been serving as minister of the church before the official installation.

[28] *Chr. Reg.*, No. 31, XII (Aug. 3, 1833), 121–122.

[29] Report of Brownson's speech at a meeting of the American Unitarian Association at Concord, N. H., on June 6, 1833 (*Chr. Reg.*, No. 26, XII [June 29, 1833], 102).

[30] *Chr. Reg.*, No. 31, XII (Aug. 3, 1833), 122.

[31] "If he is now a believer in Christianity, if he now no longer feels himself a friendless child without a father," he owed this to the form of Christianity represented by the American Unitarian Association (Report of Brownson's speech at a meeting of the A. U. A. at Concord, N. H. on June 6, 1833 [n. 29]).

[32] *Chr. Reg.*, No. 24, XII (June 15, 1833), 94–95: Report of a speech at a meeting at Keene, N. H., for the friends of Religious Liberty and Free Enquiry, May 21, 1833.

[33] *Ibid.*, pp. 94–95. The thought that Christianity consisted in doing, not in believing, was common among Unitarians. See, for example, John Pierpont, *On Substitutes for Religion,* Tract of A. U. A., 1st series, No. 56, V (Boston, 1832) and Henry Ware, Jr., *Three Important Questions Answered,* Tract of A. U. A., 1st series, No. 82, VII (Boston, 1834).

[34] *Chr. Reg.*, No. 5, XII (Feb. 2, 1833), 18.

[35] "Treatment of Unbelievers," *Chr. Reg.* (Dec. 8, 1832), 194; No. 2, XII (Jan. 12, 1833), 6, and No. 8, XII (Feb. 23, 1833), 30.

[36] *Chr. Reg.*, No. 19, XII (May 11, 1833), 73.

[37] *Chr. Reg.*, No. 24, XII (June 15, 1833), 93–94.

[38] *Chr. Reg.*, No. 22, XII (June 1, 1833), 85–86.

[39] *Chr. Reg.*, No. 48, XII (Nov. 30, 1833), 190.

[40] *G. A.*, VII, 37, 87 ff., 205.

[41] *Chr. Reg.*, No. 48, XII (Nov. 30, 1833), 190.

[42] *Chr. Reg.*, No. 49, XII (Dec. 7, 1833), 194.

[43] *Chr. Reg.*, No. 50, XII (Dec. 14, 1833), 198.

[44] *Chr. Reg.*, No. 48, XII (Nov. 30, 1833), 190.

[45] *Chr. Reg.*, No. 46, XII (Nov. 16, 1833), 182.

[46] *Chr. Reg.*, No. 47, XII (Nov. 23, 1833), 186.

[47] *Chr. Reg.*, No. 50, XII (Dec. 14, 1833), 198.

[48] *G. A.*, VI (1828), 230–231, 181.

[49] "Motives to Beneficent Action," *Chr. Reg.*, No. 18, XIII (May 3, 1834), 71.

[50] *Ibid.*: "Man, go look at thy brother enslaved, enslaved by vice, by crime, by ignorance, or by his fellow man; look at him, see in him a being of immortality, of infinite worth, see a child of God there ruined, canst thou look and see this, and not feel thy soul burn to be his deliverer?"

[51] George Ripley and George P. Bradford, "Philosophic Thought in Boston," *The Memorial History of Boston,* ed. Justin Winsor, IV (Boston, 1881), pp. 296 ff.

[52] Edgeley Woodman Todd, "Philosophic Ideas at Harvard College, 1817–1837," *New England Quarterly,* XVI (1943), 63–90, esp. 76.

[53] *The Journals and Miscellaneous Notebooks of Ralph Waldo Emerson,* ed. William H. Gilman et al., I (Cambridge, Mass., 1960), p. 51.

[54] *The Complete Works of Ralph Waldo Emerson,* XI, pp. 549–550.

[55] *Christian Examiner,* XIII, New series, VIII (1833), 311–332, esp. 320, 327, 330.

[56] *Chr. Reg.*, No. 18, XIII (May 3, 1834), 71.

VI

"Reformed" Individuals: A Reformed Society

Brownson's "letters" to the *Christian Register* attracted attention. Already at the beginning of 1833 George Ripley, its editor, wrote him a letter, in which he gave him credit for his "valuable communications" to the journal. And he continued: "We wish to give it some point, energy, and actual effect. Nothing can be better than your articles." The editor found that "their style is pithy, lucid, and direct—just what is needed for a religious newspaper." And perhaps even more important: "You have had an uncommon and interesting experience—let us be benefitted [sic] by the results of it."[1]

At the end of the same year Bernard Whitman, editor of the new periodical the *Unitarian*, wrote to Brownson that his "letters" to the *Christan Register* had been "much liked and generally read. I was however surprised yesterday to find that many in Boston did not know their author. ... Mr. Francis spoke in high terms of the letters, and wished to know if you would not collect them into a volume. Mr. Emerson of Boston did not know the author."[2]

However, after his three series of "letters" Brownson made rather few contributions to the *Christian Register.* Instead he began writing articles—longer and more substantial ones—for the *Unitarian.* This periodical was meant to appeal to a larger group of readers than did most of the religious journals, and among its contributors were Noah Worcester, James Freeman Clarke, and Brownson.[3]

The chief editor, Bernard Whitman, seems to have been a well-meaning man, whose great concern was the conversion of "infidels" to Unitarian Christianity. His zeal, however, sometimes carried him a bit too far, when, for example, he asked his readers to provide information, not only about the conversion of "infidels," but also about the practical consequences of unbelief, even suicide.[4]

On the whole, as Albert Post points out, one of the most used arguments against the unbelievers was their supposed immorality.[5] Also the contemporary controversy between orthodox and liberal Christians was very much concerned with the alleged practical tendency of doctrines. Thus the Orthodox maintained that Unitarianism finally led to infidelity. To this the Unitarians retorted that their "rational and amiable" religion led to piety, while Calvinism with its irrational dogmas inevitably drove people into unbelief.[6] Brownson, however, seemed to take a larger view on this issue. He repeatedly stated the difficulty of determining such an elusive question as possible tendencies of belief or non-belief, and though he assumed such "results," they were to him more the effects of a basic attitude than of certain opinions or beliefs.[7] Like Emerson, who had a "passion for 'First Truths,' "[8] Brownson wanted to make clear that he was primarily concerned with "first principles."[9]

Yet, Bernard Whitman, in contrast to many contemporary Unitarians, was keenly aware of social problems, and this was probably one of the reasons why he wanted Brownson, the former "Free Enquirer" and ex-disciple of Frances Wright, to write for his monthly. In the above-mentioned letter to Brownson, Whitman, asking him to write an article on the Workingmen's Party, assured him: "You can do more than any one else to produce the right result." But, Whitman cautioned, —when trying to convince the rich, one must avoid irritating them. He felt confident that Brownson had "seen enough of the business to avoid those absurdities of which some *ten hour* men are guilty."[10]

In his "letters" to the *Christian Register* Brownson had not treated Christianity from a social point of view, but considered the doctrine of the religious sentiment primarily in its individual aspect. True, he regarded his "religion of humanity" or "spirit of Christianity" as a means of introducing an earthly paradise. But for some time, while pursuing his theological and philosophical studies, he did not pay immediate attention to the thought of this social millennium. Now he developed his cherished idea of Christianity as a lever for social reform, and dreamed daring dreams of a heaven realizable on earth.[11] He put forth his views in the *Unitarian* and in speeches, particularly a Fourth of July address, on which two sources most of the following in the present chapter is based.[12]

Symptomatic of this shift of emphasis was the very title of Brownson's first articles in the *Unitarian:* "Christianity and Reform."[13] Yet he was careful to point out that the first stage of this reform concerned the individual, because only through individual "reform" could real reforms of society be effected. If the contrary method was adopted, the new laws and institutions, however excellent they might be in themselves, would not correspond to the ethical standard of the members of society. In the course of history, such a discrepancy between newly established institutions and the individuals, not yet mature enough to accept them, had had disastrous results, as, for example, in France in the 1790's.

Yet another and even greater revolution was perhaps at hand, threatening to sweep away the existing social order and everything held sacred. In these circumstances the great task of everyone should be to lead this revolutionary spirit into the right channels, i.e. to combine it with religion and not with atheism. Arguing on the basis of "first principles," Brownson maintained that the very principle of atheistic morality was expediency.[14]

Admittedly, atheistic reformers might have good reasons for distrusting the Christian church. During the Middle Ages and later the secular interests of the clergy were often identical with those of the leaders of the State. Yet abuses of the church and the clergy could not justify attacks on religion itself. The essence of religion, or the spirit of Christianity, was always the same, though the forms of religion were constantly changing and had to change, "as mind advances and there is felt the want of something more liberal and more refined." With firm conviction Brownson stated that incessant progress–intellectual and moral –was a law of human nature and a necessary condition of human society.[15]

Brownson then tried to show how the spirit of Christianity had influenced man and, thereby, society in their endless progress. The spirit of Christianity, though always and everywhere the same, was identical with "the spirit of reform." Since Jesus, the founder of Christianity, instilled in men "a deeper sense of duty and of individual responsibility," the Gospel had all the time operated as a leaven in the different societies, gradually changing the outlook and the habits of individuals and the character of the State. To effect this gradual change was the grand mission of Jesus, whose prime concern was not to make men happy in a future life, but to introduce the kingdom of God on earth.

Thanks to the influence of Christianity, men had learned to know that peace, in principle, was preferable to war; owing to the same influence, the focus of interest had gradually shifted from the authority of the State to the rights of the individual. Yet, what had been achieved during the past nineteen centuries was only a feeble beginning of what was expected to come: "changes of almost inconceivable magnitude are yet to be effected in man's moral and social condition."[16]

To Brownson, Christianity had not only forwarded the moral progress of man. In his Fourth of July Address at Dedham he pointed out that even man's intellectual progress, manifesting itself, e.g. in the art of printing and in the art of governing, was more or less due to the influence of Christianity.[17]

At first sight, Brownson's emphasis on the role of Jesus might indicate a view of Christianity as an objective power or reality distinctly apart from man. True, in an article on Benjamin Constant in the *Christian Examiner* of 1834 he wrote: "A great excellence of Christianity, and one of the most striking proofs of its divine origin, is the fact, that it is wedded to no form, but can unite with all forms, and exist in all stages of civilization." But he continued: "Indeed, in the last analysis, it is little else than the religious sentiment itself, detached from all forms, exhibiting itself in its divine purity and simplicity."[18] He thought Christianity to be "a naked idea,"[19] and according to *The Convert* (page 76), he supposed at that time that "ideas themselves were potent, but, hard pressed, I probably should have said, they are potent by the potency of the human mind, or the divinity in man." After all, the religious sentiment was "a fundamental law of human nature," and Christianity was considered identical with this sentiment in man, or almost so...

Yet his words "little else" indicated that his mind was not completely settled and, possibly, that he vaguely felt Christianity to be something more than "a sentiment of the heart." And a couple of years before his conversion to Catholicism Brownson realized that he had never built so exclusively on the doctrine of the religious sentiment as something fundamentally human or purely subjective as his "mental confusion" on the subject might have led others and even himself to believe.[20]

Generally speaking, in the middle 1830's Brownson's thoughts on the religious sentiment and the influence of Christianity were by no means unique. Thus in an article in the *Christian Examiner* (1834) Frederic Henry Hedge, considering institutions stationary and, more audaciously than Brownson, applying Constant's thesis even to the American government, stressed the idea of progress and the importance of Christianity in individual and social life. Yet Hedge's idea of Christianity seemed even more "naked" than Brownson's. To Hedge,

Christianity seemed synonymous with truth in general.[21] Apparently, both men were heading for Transcendentalism.

Brownson was undoubtedly pleased when he received a letter from William Ellery Channing, whom he also met for the first time while he was Unitarian minister at Walpole. Brownson had already written two letters to Channing, in order to thank "the apostle of Unitarianism" for the inspiration he had given him. In his reply of January 11, 1834, Channing called Brownson "a gifted spirit," but added cautiously: "I know that a man's writings are not sure tests of his character, and that a stranger, like yourself, not brought up among us, and who has made important changes of religion, cannot be regarded immediately with that entire reliance which we place in a long known and tried friend."

According to this letter, Channing took particular delight in Brownson's article in the January issue of the *Unitarian*, in which the author regarded Christianity as a principle of reform. Also, Channing wrote that he shared Brownson's view of the artificial division between the classes of society.[22] On the whole, Brownson's views of Christianity and reform largely coincided with Channing's conception of "self-culture."

Yet in the following articles he wrote for the *Unitarian* Brownson dealt more particularly with social problems. In an essay he characterized the Workingmen's Party as an American counterpart to similar movements in England and France. He declared that the party was not founded only with the view of abolishing temporary and local evils; its coming into existence marked a discontent with "the whole framework and texture of society as it is."

But the former champion of the Workingmen's Party now believed that this alleged revolutionary discontent had been exaggerated and could hardly be justified. He even now regarded the party as an "anomaly in the history of parties," since, in his view, the conditions of the workers had already been improved at the time when the party was started.

After thus distancing himself from the Workingmen's Party and above all its supposed revolutionary aspect, Brownson hastened to admit that there were still reasons for social discontent. He declared that "a rich man, who has obtained his wealth by means which would have sent a poorer man to the penitentiary, is welcome, go where he will, . . ." And Brownson added significantly that such reasoning of the individual worker was "a proof of his progress."[23]

Somewhat later, when reviewing a book by a clergyman, Brownson objected violently to the author's idea that the social evils were God's foreordination. Just as he wrote in the *Philanthropist*, Brownson stated that the social evils were due to man. Consequently, they could and ought to be abolished. And "the remedy is in Christianity–in Christianity, not as a dogma, not as a system of belief, but as a grand, all-comprehending principle of moral and social action." This remedy should be applied, because "the gospel is emphatically the working-man's religion."[24]

In his Fourth of July Speech at Dedham, Brownson leveled an even stronger and a more specified attack on social evils. The gulf between the workers and their employers, between those who produced and those who reaped the fruits, was steadily increasing. Moreover, the laws which were destined to protect all citizens in an equal manner, expressly favored the rich at the expense of the poor. Not only equality before the laws, but "equal laws" were in demand, i.e. laws which had "the same practical effect upon all." Oppression, fraud, over-reaching, etc., crimes mostly committed by employers and well-to-do people, involved rather small fines, whereas theft, to which the poor might be easily induced, resulted in heavy penalties, such as long imprisonment or even death. In education, too, there was a glaring inequality, since "all our higher seminaries of learning are virtually closed to all except the rich."[25]

Though the social inequality was "an evil of immense magnitude,"[26] so that even a great social revolution was perhaps on the way, Brownson did not propose any particular, immediate measures–by way of legislative enactments–to be taken in order to remove, or reduce, this evil. Consistent with his view of individual "reform" as the basis of social reform, he proposed a general measure: education, or the "formation of character."[27] And it was on religion, "the principle of perfectibility," that the education of man's whole nature–physical, intellectual, and moral–had to be based.[28]

But in some quarters Brownson's Fourth of July Address was considered something more than an appeal to individual reform. A writer in the *Christian Register*, admitting that the speech contained matter for very serious examination, complained of its alleged uncalled-for "criminations against our social and political state." The lawmakers, whom Brownson attacked, had been elected by the people "by universal suffrage, a suffrage from which only paupers, who make themselves pauper, are excluded." Fearing that Brownson's inflammatory address might create dissension and hatred between the classes, the writer confidently stated the supposed advantage of the existing social conditions; further, Providence–always benign–had ordained that not even despotism could exist without the right of property being protected, and where this right was protected, there would always be riches and poverty; finally, at least in New England, there was no great difference in economic status between the classes.[29]

In his reply Brownson said that the social evils would not be abolished through legislation, "not by any change begun in external circumstances, but by enlightening, and training the whole community to be moral and truly religious. I wish for more equality than I find existing, and I hope to effect it, by rendering education, (by which term I understand the 'formation of character,') more equal." And: "Increase of knowledge and virtue in all classes" would, of necessity, be followed by reforms "in the external circumstances."[30]

The opponent, still unconvinced as to Brownson's real intentions, quoted a statement in the latter's speech, which might indicate that Brownson did want to change the laws themselves: "I not only ask for equality before the laws, but for equal laws,–for laws which shall not only speak the same language to all, but which shall have the same meaning for all, the same practical effect for all."[31] By way of reply, Brownson cited statements in his speech in order to strengthen his argument. Talking about the nature and function of government, he stressed its "negative" character: "In its best state, its mission is mostly negative." Accordingly, "its nature is never to lead, but to follow. The people must precede it, opinion must go before it. If the people go right, government cannot go wrong." He concluded: "We must leave . . ., to a certain degree, legislative enactments."[32]

"To a certain degree" probably meant the legislative measures which could not be avoided if education should be "more equal."[33] Yet Brownson did not present any complete program for educational reform. He only suggested some general ideas or principles, accompanied by attacks on the prevailing system of education. The common schools and especially the higher seminaries "educate us to be fond of distinctions, to be fond of popularity, and to look with contempt on the people."[34] Instead, children and young people should learn to understand that all individuals, whether rich or poor, belonged to the same brotherhood of man. They should learn that every man and woman must be judged according to their inner worth, not to any other criterion. This should be the real aim of education; the acquisition of factual knowledge was, after all, of secondary importance. The essential task of the educator was not to stuff masses of knowledge into the pupil's head, but to "unfold" his inner capabilities.[35]

There is little reason to believe that Brownson in his concept of education was directly influenced by the contemporary "educator," the highly eccentric, but sometimes genuinely original Amos Bronson Alcott (1799–1888), who perhaps was a distant relative of his.[36] As the leader of the Temple School in Boston from 1834 to 1837, Alcott stated and—with changing success—practiced the tenet that children when born knew everything and needed only have their thought "opened out of the soul."[37] In fact, this expression was very similar to the one used by Brownson: "unfold." Obviously, such expressions and their underlying thoughts, sure forebodings of Transcendentalism, were beginning to manifest themselves. In any case, terms like "unfold" and "open out of the soul" both signified the very opposite of the prevailing Lockian view of *tabula rasa.*

True, in Brownson's case there was no strong desire, as yet, to challenge Locke or other authorities held in esteem by leading Unitarians. But his idea of the internal light or the religious sentiment would, sooner or later, make such a challenge unavoidable.

For the time being Brownson simply wanted "republican education." By the word "republican" he wanted to state that education should be equal, that is, for all, and not "aristocratic," or for the privileged few.[38]

Though contested as to its "purity," Brownson's belief in individual "reform" as the basis of social reform was shared by most Unitarians. On one important point, however, Brownson differed from many of his brother ministers. He could not accept the thesis that poverty was "the express appointment of God."[39] Nor could he accept fully the supposed benefit of almsgiving. To him, it was only something "falsely called charity." Really constructive solutions had to be sought and applied. Without giving any definite suggestions, Brownson encouraged the rich to help the poor in such a way that the poor would be able to help themselves.[40]

In any case, Brownson, whose life, at least until the late 1830's, was "a continual struggle with poverty,"[41] strongly dissented from the idea of poverty as something in the natural order of things, let alone God's own will. Unitarianism as an essentially *bourgeois* movement with its emphasis on individual "reform" or "self-culture" was, after all, socially conservative, or as William W. Fenn puts it: "There was about it [i.e. Unitarianism] a square-toed solidity and integrity—sixteen ounces to a pound and one hundred cents to a dollar—which commands respect but fails to kindle the imagination."[42]

However, at least one Unitarian minister went even farther than Brownson. In a letter to Brownson (August 18, 1834), Samuel C. Allen of Northfield, the Workingmen's candidate for governor of Massachusetts, said bluntly that individual improvement would not be sufficient to improve, generally, the lot of the poor: "Individual character is very much formed by social institutions, and among these that of property in all its aspects is of chief influence. It bases itself upon a supposed moral right, however immoral may be the methods of its acquisition, under the present order of things." Allen complained that, though "all wealth is the product of labor and belongs of right to him who produces it," only a little part of the product of labor fell on the laboring class. It was high time for the workingmen to "recover what belongs to them." First, knowledge of political economy was important, for "the history of the tenure of land and the state of labor everywhere and in all past time would answer this question": Why was government in the hands of the rich? But insight, knowledge only, was not enough. "Common counsels and joint efforts" of the workers were necessary. Only through legislative action could a change for the better be brought about. Allen felt sure that, "thanks to our free political forms, the people can now do it without violence or wrong," so much the more because the workingmen had a true champion in President Jackson. But Allen was also convinced that those Christians, whether ministers or not, who profited by the existing economic system, would do nothing to effect any social improvement.[43]

No doubt, this letter disclosed both insight and firm conviction on the part of the writer. But at that time Brownson did not draw the same conclusion, though his diagnosis of the social situation was pretty much the same as Allen's. Why, then, did Brownson stop halfway?

There were two main reasons. First, he was strongly influenced by the dominating doctrine of "self-culture." In an article in the January issue of the *Christian Examiner*, 1835, Brownson steadfastly held to this doctrine. "The real work for the Reformer," he wrote, "is to put into the hands" of all "not equal wealth,—but the means of spiritual cultivation and growth." For, after all: "Poverty is not itself an evil, it is only the symptom of an evil." The real evil was "the injury done to the mind."[44]

At that time, he was not aware of possible fallacies of this doctrine. For example, who could warrant that the moral conscience of the upper classes would ever reach such a level that all necessary social reforms might easily be carried through? And who could deny, even if one did not accept Robert Owen's "environmentalism," that individuals in their views and attitudes were more or less influenced by their economic and social conditions? Finally, why should not social reforms, like higher wages and reduction of working hours, be a stimulus, at least indirectly, to "self-culture" for the workingman?

Second, Brownson, like many contemporaries, believed ideas themselves to be almost omnipotent, endowed with a half-mystic force that was changing the world:

> No word can drop idly to the ground. A word, little heeded when spoken, may kindle up a virtuous energy in some bosom, which shall pass from that to another, from that to still another, till there be collected a moral force sufficient to shake the empire of evil and then to create an entire [sic] new order of things. Every man may, in consequence of this law of our social development, be contributing something to the knowledge and virtue and happiness of the most distant generations... This is the grand secret of human improvement, the action of man upon man and of generation upon generation.

"This law of our social development," coupled with the doctrine of "the endless progress of human reason,"[45] was basically optimistic. Within a loose teleological frame, individuals of the various epochs were, according to this view, given free scope to make their own wills manifest. While influencing the course of events, individuals helped accelerate the intellectual and social development of mankind. Although, in this view, the present and the future were preferable to the past, such an attitude involved a respect for or, at least, a sense of tradition and continuity. By consequence, social reforms suddenly introduced, not to talk about social revolutions, might do more harm than good if the members of society had not reached the "right" level of morality and intelligence. The "progress of society," then, was a result of individual "progress."[46]

Obviously, such a view, however optimistic it might be as to a distant future, did not and could not offer an immediate solution to the social problems. So, even if Brownson was much concerned with the social aspect of Christianity, he regarded at that time social reform more as a general principle than a series of definite practical measures to better the conditions of the workingmen.

Yet it should be taken into account that the industrial revolution in the United States was still only in its beginning, so that the labor problem was far less acute than it was going to be. In the 1830's the country had still a typically rural character with less than ten per cent of the population living in towns of more than 8000 inhabitants.[47] So, if allowance is made for 1837, the year of a grave financial crisis, Arthur M. Schlesinger, Jr., is probably right in his pointed remark that individual "reform" would almost have been enough in the uncomplicated American society of the 1830's.[48]

However, from a more general point of view, Brownson's "law of our social development" is of great interest. First, it foreshadows his doctrine of life and communion, which led him to the Catholic Church; second, it indicates his growing awareness of the importance of tradition, and third, this "law" crystallized the Romantic thought of organic harmony and coherence between all members of mankind.

And as Benjamin Constant strengthened Brownson's belief in the individual through his doctrine of the religious sentiment, another Frenchman, Saint-Simon, stressing the social aspect of religion, strengthened his belief in the universal brotherhood of man. To Brownson, "reformed" individuals meant, in the last analysis, a "reformed" humanity, governed and hallowed by Saint-Simon's "universal church,"[49] or his own "Church of the Future."

1 Letter of Jan. 15, 1833: *Early Life*, p. 104.
2 Letter of Dec. 26, 1833: *Early Life*, p. 101.
3 *Early Life*, p. 96.
4 *Unitarian*, I (Cambridge and Boston, 1834), 50.
5 *Popular Freethought in America: 1825–1850* (New York, 1943), p. 200.
6 C. H. Faust, "The Background of the Unitarian Opposition to Transcendentalism," *Modern Philology*, XXXV (February 1938), 297–324.
7 *Chr. Reg.*, No. 2, XII (Jan. 12, 1833), 6; and No. 24, XII (June 15, 1833), 94–95.
8 Octavius Brooks Frothingham, *Recollections and Impressions 1822–1890* (New York, 1891), p. 171.
9 *Unitarian*, I (May 1834), 240.
10 *Early Life*, pp. 100–102.
11 *The Convert*, p. 74.
12 The *Unitarian* lasted no longer than one year, probably owing to Bernard Whitman's death ("Obituary," *Unitarian*, I, 579–582). *An Address, Delivered at Dedham, on the Fifty-Eighth Anniversary of American Independence, July 4, 1834.* By O. A. Brownson. Published by request (Dedham, 1834). Hereafter referred to as *Dedham Address*.

13 *Unitarian*, I (Jan. and Feb. 1834), 30–39, 51–58.
14 *Ibid.*, p. 33.
15 *Ibid.*, p. 38.
16 *Ibid.*, pp. 39, 52, 58.
17 *Dedham Address*, pp. 13–14.
18 XVII, New series, XII (Sept. 1834), 69–70.
19 *BrQR* (July 1875), 577.
20 *The Convert*, p. 154.
21 XVI, New series, XI (March 1834), 1–21, esp. 13, 16, 19 ff.
22 *Early Life*, pp. 88, 106–107.
23 *Unitarian*, I (April 1834), 170–177, esp. 172, 175–176.
24 *Unitarian*, I (May 1834), 238–244, esp. 238, 240.
25 *Dedham Address*, p. 9.
26 *Ibid.*, p. 9. "We have equality in scarcely any sense worth naming."
27 *Ibid.*, p. 19.
28 *Unitarian*, I (May 1834), 240–241.
29 *Chr. Reg.*, No. 2, XIV (Aug. 23, 1834), 6.
30 *Chr. Reg.*, No. 3, XIV (Aug. 30, 1834), 10.
31 *Ibid.*, p. 10 (The preposition "upon" in the published address was incidentally replaced by "for" by the writer in the *Chr. Reg.)*.
32 *Chr. Reg.*, No. 5, XIV (Sept. 13, 1834), 18.
33 *Chr. Reg.*, No. 3, XIV (Aug. 30, 1834), 10.
34 *Dedham Address*, p. 19.
35 *Unitarian*, I, 241–242; *Dedham Address*, pp. 19–20.
36 Theodore Maynard, *Orestes Brownson* (New York, 1943), p. 23, n. 8.
37 *The American Transcendentalists*, ed. Perry Miller (Doubleday Anchor Books; New York, 1957), p. 86.
38 *Dedham Address*, p. 19.
39 *Ibid.*, pp. 20–21.
40 Excerpts from Brownson's speech in Young Men's Bible Society in Boston, April 20, 1834; *Chr. Reg.*, Nos. 26 and 27, XIII (June 28 and July 5, 1834), 101, 105–106.
41 Letter of Sept. 6, 1839, to Victor Cousin: *The Brownson Papers* at Notre Dame University.
42 *The Religious History of New England* (King Chapel Lectures; Cambridge, Mass. and London, 1917), p. 125.
43 *Early Life*, pp. 114–118.
44 XVII, New series, XII (Jan. 1835), 283–301, esp. 298.
45 *Unitarian*, I, 91, 243–244.
46 "Progress of Society," *Christian Examiner*, XVIII, New series, XIII (July 1835), 345–368.
47 Merle Curti, *The Growth of American Thought* (2nd ed.; New York, 1951), p. 297.
48 *Orestes A. Brownson* (Boston, 1939), p. 39.
49 "Memoir of Saint-Simon," *Unitarian*, I (June 1834), 279–289, esp. 286.

VII

Approaching "The Centre of Indifference"

Brownson, having received a unanimous invitation from the Unitarian congregation at Canton, Massachusetts, accepted the offer and resolved to leave Walpole, where he had stayed for about two years.[1] But he had no strong wish to leave. The still rustic Vermonter had felt well at ease in that small, cozy town with its not too urbanized population. In a letter to his wife (Feb. 19, 1834) he wrote: "But, I shall stay at Walpole if they make me out five hundred dollars, let who will call—I see no place so pleasant, no people I like so well as Walpole and my own congregation."[2] His congregation, for their part, bore testimony to the ability and high moral character of their minister.[3] What made him, finally, prefer Canton to Walpole was the opportunity of getting easy access to the Boston and Cambridge libraries[4] and, one might add, of coming in closer contact with the leading Unitarians.

On May 14, 1834, Brownson was installed as minister of the First Congregational Parish at Canton. The preacher was George Ripley, who was then Unitarian minister of the Purchase Street Church in Boston.[5] As editor of the *Christian Register*, Ripley had reprinted some of Brownson's articles in the *Philanthropist* and, later, asked him to write for his journal. George Ripley became one of Brownson's closest friends, and at least until Brownson's conversion to Catholicism they stimulated and encouraged each other in many ways. Though Ripley's mild and cautious behavior presented a singular contrast to Brownson's irascible temper, they were both downright earnest and honest in all their undertakings. To a large extent they shared the same views and sentiments, and their intellectual development, particularly in the 1830's, followed the same main line.

Both men were strongly moved by William Ellery Channing's sermons, and increasingly stressed the spirit of Christianity while depreciating its orthodox dogmas. Already in a letter of November 24, 1824, the young student at Harvard wrote to his mother: "In short, true religion is in the heart, and is not connected with any form or any language."[6] And in the later 1820's the Universalist Brownson, despite his deistic tendencies, had a vague feeling of "a God within the mind,"[7] —a feeling which some years later developed into his conviction of religion as "a sentiment of the heart."[8] From this common point of departure, both men were to play a predominant role in the so-called "New School," or Transcendentalism.

More particularly, both Ripley and Brownson stressed the social aspect of Christianity. Feeling more and more ill at ease in his congregation of well-to-do, "respectable" members, who seemed quite indifferent to the social evils around them, Ripley in 1840 took leave of his church in Purchase Street in a long, pathetic letter to its elders. "Blame me for it if you will," he wrote, "but I cannot behold the degradation, the ignorance, the poverty, the vice, the ruin of the soul, which is everywhere displayed in the very bosom of Christian society in our own city, while men look idly on, without a shudder." Declaring that all his sympathies were with "the down-trodden and suffering poor," he concluded his remarkable letter with the statement that "the purpose of Christianity, as I firmly believe, is to redeem society as well as the individual from all sin."[9]

In the same manner, but more fervently, Brownson throughout the 1830's preached a social Christianity, proclaiming that "the gospel is emphatically the workingman's religion."[10] Symptomatically, Ripley, already in 1834, encouraged Brownson to start a Christian reform society with the view of saving the working population from unbelief.[11] And two years later this wish of Ripley's materialized in Brownson's Society for Christian Union and Progress. About the preparations for this society, Brownson wrote as follows, and there is almost universal agreement that George Ripley was the person in question: "One man, and one man only, shared my entire confidence, and knew my most secret thought. Him, from motives of delicacy, I do not name; but, in the formation of my mind, in systematizing my ideas, and in general development and culture, I owe more to him than to any other man among Protestants. We have since taken divergent courses, but I loved him as I have loved no other man, and shall so love and esteem him as long as I live. He encouraged me, and through him chiefly I was enabled to remove to Boston and commence operations."[12]

On the other hand, Brownson directly or indirectly stimulated

Ripley to undertake the Brook Farm experiment. In a letter of December 18, 1842, Ripley wrote these acknowledging and affectionate words to his friend: "We have truly sympathized as few men have done; you have always quickened my love for humanity; and for no small share of what mental clearness I may have, am I indebted to the hours of genial, pleasant intercourse I have enjoyed with you." And more particularly: "If I had never known you, I should never have been engaged in this enterprise. I consider it as the incarnation of these transcendental truths which we have held in common, and which you have done much to make me love."[13]

In fact, their increasing belief in the value of institutions, i.e. as living organisms, reflected their dissatisfaction with "naked" ideas and their growing realization that ideas had to be "clothed" or "incarnated." George Ripley became wedded to Fourierism, which, according to the strong individualist Emerson, was "coherent and comprehensive of facts to a wonderful degree," and satisfied the longing of many for "society, concert, coöperation."[14] And Brownson turned to a grander and more stable institution than Fourierite phalansteries. Typically, when, in 1875, looking back to his early manhood, he wrote that he "had only to be convinced that Jesus Christ did embody his religion in an institution, in a living organism, to be a Catholic at once."[15]

At Canton Brownson seems to have been very busy. Apart from his ministerial work he founded an association for young men, a "Lyceum," intended for their "literary and general mental improvement," and for this purpose he established a little library and even invited the celebrated orator Edward Everett (1794–1865) to come and give a lecture.[16] As for his own "mental improvement," Brownson continued to study European authors and philosophers, especially French. By the middle of 1834 he even asked James Walker, who was to become Professor of Philosophy at Harvard and later President of the same university, about a possible publication of some philosophical writings of Constant, Cousin, and Jouffroy in English translation. In his letter of September 12, 1834, Walker wrote that Dr. Charles Follen had planned a complete translation of Benjamin Constant's work, but for lack of encouragement, he had to give up the enterprise. And Walker continued: "I ought to say the other French authors mentioned by you I only know by hearsay."[17] Such a remark indicates that Brownson, the self-made scholar from without, was no more provincial in thought and outlook than many a Bostonian clergyman.

In fact, this gruff, self-confident Vermonter had already begun to slough off his awe-stricken respect—if he had ever had any—for Bostonian or New England Unitarianism. In an article on "the coldness of New England preaching" Brownson contrasted the stiff, formal tone of that preaching to the spontaneity and vividness of "the West." Strangely enough, he who could never be classed among orthodox Protestants, safe for his brief Presbyterian experience, here used and recommended evangelical or even revivalistic terms, like "the awful condition of the sinner," "the magnitude of the evil of sin," "but Christ and Him crucified." A minister seeing the reality behind these terms, Brownson wrote, could not "stop to select his words, to round and polish his periods, and cull the flowers of elocution, which will fade ere a soul can feel their beauty. No, he will speak right on."[18]

At a glance, such remarkable statements might indicate even a speedy return to traditional Christian beliefs. As Brownson wrote only some months before, he had been one of those who "reasoned themselves into unbelief, but the heart retains recollections of religion."[19] Perhaps he remembered vividly from his youth the Methodist ministers who preached about the sinner, the sin and Christ crucified, while urging him to "get religion," "experience religion."[20] But even if traditional, orthodox Christianity was from early childhood a substratum of his mind, making occasional sudden outbursts, Brownson's skeptical attitude toward Unitarianism signaled the coming of "the New School" or Transcendentalism rather than a positive re-evaluation of orthodox Christianity. As Clarence L. F. Gohdes points out, "transcendentalism was not primarily a philosophy or a reform movement: it was a mental and spiritual attitude." And he continues: "The chief manifestation of transcendentalism was in the sphere of religion. Indeed, transcendentalism in the narrower sense might be defined as Unitarianism in the process of 'getting religion.' "[21]

Unitarianism, which originally was a reaction against rigid Calvinistic dogmatism, was itself gradually developing into a dogmatically fixed system. The man who, above all others, represented dogmatic Unitarianism, was Andrews Norton, Professor of Sacred Literature in the Harvard Divinity School. In his book *Statement of Reasons for Not Believing the Doctrines of Trinitarians, Concerning the Nature of God, and the Person of Christ* (1819) Norton tried to formulate the chief doctrines of Unitarianism. Rejecting on a rationalistic basis the Trinitarian dogma, he had recourse to irrationalistic events, i.e. the biblical miracles, to prove the truth of Christianity: "The whole proof of the doctrines of religion, as taught by Christ, consists solely in the fact that he was a teacher from God. He did not reason; he affirmed. He adduced no arguments but his miracles. Considered as a self-taught philosopher, he did nothing to advance human knowledge, for he brought no new evidence for any opinion. But considered as a teacher from God, he has provided the authority of God for the foundation of our faith."[22]

In fact, there was a strange mixture of rationalistic and irrationalistic elements of thought in Norton's reasoning. First, it seems remarkable that miracles were necessary to prove that Christ was only an emissary from God and not the very Son of God. Although to Norton Jesus was not a "merely human teacher," but one whom "God had given his spirit without measure," he was essentially a man only.[23] Second, Norton, when arguing against Trinitarianism, emphasized the low intellectual standard of those Jews whom Jesus mostly addressed. For this very reason, Norton concluded, Jesus had to use metaphorical language in order to make them understand the relationship between God and himself.[24] According to this way of thinking, one might be entitled to ask why the miracles related in the Bible could not be regarded as crude, primitive means only to influence the supposedly ignorant Jews of that time in favor of Christianity. Third, Norton, staunch Unitarian dogmatist though he was, believed in the theory of the intellectual progress of man.[25] Since, according to this theory, the Christians of the nineteenth century were more advanced in knowledge than the first Christians, why, then, cling so obstinately to the biblical miracles, a definitely first-century phenomenon, as the final proof of the truth of Christ's teachings?

By way of answer, Norton would have drawn his arguments from the Lockian philosophy, which was still dominant at Harvard University.[26] In Unitarian circles John Locke (1632–1714) was still considered the great authority in philosophy and even, to a great extent, in theology. To Norton, at least, there seemed to be no sharp distinction between philosophy and theology: "Its [i.e. religion's] exposition and defence must become the study of philosophers, as being the highest philosophy."[27] Obviously, Norton was himself a close follower of Locke, whom he declared to be "the most enlightened theologian of his age and nation."[28] Locke maintained that "we have 'demonstrative knowledge' of the existence of God. But of anything other than God, we have no knowledge except such as is derived from and limited by the senses."[29] The Harvard Professor of Divinity reasoned along the same lines as the British empirical philosopher when writing as follows: "But if we except the case of miraculous operations exerted directly upon the minds of men, the power of God must be manifested by means of sensible objects."[30] And, according to Norton, the privilege of receiving this "divine illumination" was restricted to the apostles only.[31]

On the basis of Lockian empiricism, then, "the Unitarian Pope" labored to prove the "genuineness" of the biblical miracles as a prerequisite to belief in the authority of Jesus as a teacher from God.

To the Unitarian ministers of the younger generation Andrews Norton's arguments had no strong appeal. Becoming acquainted with the idealistic philosophy and theology of Germany and France and of the English Romanticists, they felt a growing resentment to Lockian empiricism or sensism, particularly when applied to religion. To them, Norton's argument for the Christian faith would make religion something outward and impersonal, even something arbitrary, since the truth of Christianity should finally depend on the alleged miracles performed by its founder nearly two thousand years ago.

Among these young Unitarian ministers, Frederic Henry Hedge (1805–1890), having enjoyed the privilege of studying in Germany, was the one most acquainted with the new philosophical and theological literature of that country. In a sermon delivered about fifty years later he made certain reflections on the fermenting 1830's when the two generations of Unitarians were gradually drifting apart from one another: "They [i.e. most Unitarians of the older generation] did not consider that every soul is heaven-born, that human nature has no moral limits, that God, as spirit, is in man as well as out of him. Unconsciously biased by the sensuous philosophy of Locke, himself a Unitarian, they conceived of God as wholly external–an individual in space; of heaven as topographically distinct from earth, of the human mind as receiving all its impressions from without."[32]

In contrast to Andrews Norton's theology, Hedge and other Unitarian ministers of the younger generation maintained that religion was something inward, something eminently of the heart. Contrary to Locke's theory that the human mind was only a blank sheet, they contended, more and more vigorously, that the inner light or the religious sentiment in man revealed intuitively the great truths of religion. By consequence, they reacted against the alleged crucial importance of the biblical miracles as proof of the truth of Christianity.

Thus in 1833, Hedge, in an article on Coleridge and German idealistic philosophy, regretted that the "supersensual" was neglected owing to the still dominating empiricist or sensist philosophy.[33] And two years later George Ripley, writing about Herder, stressed the view of the German philosopher that theology should serve "the interests and feelings of human nature, ... as created in the Image of God."[34] Shortly afterward Ripley, in a book review of Herder's works, pointed to Herder's insistence on "the inward divinity of truth" and his objection to resting "the divine authority of Christianity upon the evidence of miracles."[35] So far, however, Ripley did not openly dissent from the "official" Unitarian view of miracles. But in 1836, in his review of James Martineau's work *The Rationale of Religious Enquiry* (1836), he declared frankly and in his own right: "We deem it an error, under any circumstances, to rest a system of spiritual truth addressed to the soul, upon the evidence of miracles addressed to the senses."[36] And as for Jesus himself: "In the final appeal, he rested the claim of his truth on its intrinsic divinity and power."[37] In the same year Ripley presented similar views in his *Discourses on the Philosophy of Religion Addressed to Doubters Who Wish to Believe*, a collection of six sermons, of which the fifth one was, characteristically, called "On the Coincidence of Christianity with the Higher Nature of Man."

In Theodore Parker's words, "the genius of Emerson soon moved from the clerical constellation, and stood forth alone, a fixed and solitary star."[38] Thus already in 1826, in a sermon before the Middlesex Association of Ministers, Emerson underscored the primacy of spirit over matter and the immediacy of God to the human soul.[39] And in his sermon on "The Lord's Supper," in 1832, he declared that the doctrines in themselves and not the miracles were the evidences of the truth of Christianity.[40]

As Octavius Brooks Frothingham points out, in the 1830's "the great issue was the credibility of the miracles of the Old and New Testaments."[41] But in 1838 Emerson, in his famous "Divinity School Address," broadened the controversy into an open conflict between "Old School" Unitarianism and "the New School" or Transcendentalism. And Andrews Norton, who had stated his reasons for not believing the orthodox Christian dogma of the Trinity, had now to apply the orthodoxy he had left against "the latest form of infidelity."[42] But what could Norton's half-orthodox Unitarianism do against words like these: "One man was true to what is in you and me. He saw that God incarnates himself in man, and evermore goes forth anew to take possession of his world." And after stating this unorthodox view of the doctrine of Incarnation, Emerson proved no less unorthodox in his conception of "miracles:" "He [i.e. Jesus] spoke of miracles; for he felt that man's life was a miracle, and all that man doth, and he knew that this daily miracle shines as the character ascends. But the word Miracle, as pronounced by Christian churches, gives a false impression; it is Monster. It is not one with the blowing clover and the falling rain."[43]

At first sight, it is easy to smile at Andrews Norton's vigorous and voluminous attempts to prove the "genuineness" of the biblical miracles, while at the same time he considered Jesus only a human teacher. But his real motive was praiseworthy: he wanted to save Christianity —though in its half-dogmatic Unitarian form—as a unique, revealed religion. By contrast, to the Transcendentalists Christianity lost its character of uniqueness and became synonymous with natural religion. In any case, Joseph Henry Allen admitted that the Transcendentalists had, probably, not tried to really understand the traditional proofs of the truth of Christianity,[44] and Brownson, just after his conversion to Catholicism, actually approved of Norton's definition of Transcendentalism: "the latest form of infidelity."[45]

But in the 1830's Brownson, longing for a deeper religion than the cold, half-dogmatic Unitarianism then in vogue, did his share in ushering in "the New School." And influences from Transcendentalism are traceable throughout his later life.

One should almost think that Brownson had Andrews Norton's book *Statement of Reasons* in mind when in 1834 he wrote his article on "Spirituality of Religion" for the *Unitarian*. This essay, though signifying no open revolt against "official" Unitarianism or its great English philosopher, was an unmistakable harbinger of Transcendentalism.[46]

Brownson strongly complained of the "coldness in our religious and philosophical speculations." This masked materialism, fatal because not openly avowed, was a legitimate child of the eighteenth and the first quarter of the nineteenth century, when the physical sciences held the ground. The basic outlook typical of these sciences had, unfortunately, invaded "the moral, religious, and intellectual sciences" as well, so that even "our spiritualism is only a less gross materialism." The heart, the symbol of deep feelings and undefinable instincts, had recklessly been thrown aside. The mind, as seen in contrast to the senses, had likewise been shamefully neglected. In the reigning philosophy, adopting the same basic notions as the physical sciences, it was only the five senses plus the purely external layer of mind: "the understanding" that accounted for something. Therefore, "philosophy, which should be full of life, warm with a glowing enthusiasm and a generous love, is dwindled down into freezing dialectics."

In religion, "all is outward, objective; nothing inward, subjective. God is placed at an infinite distance from the human soul," a God "deprived of spirituality, or at least clothed with a materiality that prevents him from reaching men's hearts, but by the aid of the understanding, or through the medium of the cumbrous machinery of a formal revelation made by one man to be by him communicated to others." Since, especially according to Protestantism, faith should be founded on the written word, mostly quite literally interpreted, "faith is in something foreign to the soul; in something arbitrary, in that which has no necessary relation to consciousness." The "still small voice," however, establishes "an intercourse between God and the human soul." While we *assent* to the truth of the written word–an act of the understanding, in which the heart has nothing to do, we *confide* in the inspirations of the Almighty, made to our own souls. The great problems concerning God and mankind can only be perceived in this way, i.e. intuitively. For "religion is no deduction of reason; it is no calculation of interest; it is a sentiment, an inspiration. It is the poetry of the soul."[47]

In this essay Brownson stated the essential difference between "the Old School" Unitarianism and "the New School," or Transcendentalism. But as shown earlier, Transcendentalist tendencies were beginning to manifest themselves already in his later writings in the *Philanthropist*. For our present purpose it is sufficient to mention his changing attitude to Locke, as revealed in this journal. By the end of 1831 Brownson described Locke as one "who opened the vast storehouse of the human understanding, taught man to turn his mind within and learn the vast treasure he possessed in the intellectual world."[48] But in the issue of May 15, 1832, Brownson inserted an extract of Rousseau, who, stressing the sublimity of the soul, attacked "Locke and the materialists."[49]

No less interesting is that Brownson already in 1829 anticipated the Transcendentalist attitude toward biblical miracles. In the *Gospel Advocate* he declared that miracles could not prove the truth of Christianity or other moral and religious truths. Although Brownson did not doubt that "the events were performed," he regarded them as "isolated facts," used to convince ignorant people. Moreover, he asked, do we know all the laws of nature? In any case, the evidence of Christianity must be sought elsewhere, he concluded.[50] And as pointed out earlier, Brownson already in his Universalist period touched the idea of a "monitor within," "a God within the mind"[51] and "the internal evidence."[52]

True, Brownson was all his life fond of new things and "new views." As he wrote while a Universalist: "Any object, no matter how good or how useful in itself considered, loses its value in our estimation, the moment the charms of novelty have faded and it becomes generally known and generally received."[53] Yet, as the above-mentioned instances indicate, his intellectual development was gradual and consistent and was not characterized by leaps and bounds or sudden, unmotivated changes.

In *The Convert* (page 76) Brownson wrote that not only himself, but even leading Unitarians of the Boston area were dissatisfied with Unitarianism. They thought it cold, lifeless, uninspiring. They were longing for a new and better church or religious institution to take its place. This ardent desire for a real spiritual religion was no particular Boston phenomenon, nor was it any particular Unitarian phenomenon; the cry for a profounder religion—or religiosity—came from different quarters: "Carlyle, in his *Sartor Resartus*, seemed to lay his finger on the plague-spot of the age. Men had reached the centre of indifference; under a broiling sun in the *Rue d'Enfer*, had pronounced the everlasting 'No.' Were they never to be able to pronounce the everlasting 'Yes'?"

Brownson, like many others, considered William Ellery Channing to be *the* man who could lead them away from "the centre of indifference" into real spirituality. From the writings of Constant and Saint-Simon Brownson had got the idea that a religious organization of some kind was necessary in order to channel and give shelter to this fervent longing for a meaningful, spiritual life. For some time Brownson was convinced that Channing would be eminently suited to usher in and become the powerful leader of such a religious institution. Yet Channing, whose personality and sermons had so deeply influenced Brownson, was gradually, in the eyes of his "disciple," reduced to more moderate dimensions. Admitting Channing's affection for the poor and the outcasts, his genuine friendliness and warmheartedness, Brownson soon found out–or thought to have found out–that Channing was not the "representative man" the age called for. Though he was an eloquent preacher, he seemed to lack drive, vigor, and originality. When operating within a narrow range, he could sum up ably the points in question; but when he reasoned on broader principles and issues, his thoughts seemed rather feeble, if not confused.[54] Besides, since his outlook was essentially individualistic, Channing would not be well fitted to be the head of an organization, which called for strong, associated action.[55] Brownson admitted, humorously or not, that the idea flashed through his mind that he himself might be *the* man to found "the new order." However, he soon satisfied himself with the thought of becoming a sort of nineteenth-century St. John the Baptist, a precursor of the Messiah to come.[56]

No doubt, Saint-Simon's idea of the Universal Church was constantly present to his mind. Likewise, the Frenchman's emphasis on the universal brotherhood of man and, more particularly, his sympathy for the poor and more numerous classes of society could not fail to impress Brownson. In a sermon to the young people of his congregation at Canton, he underscored the interdependence and solidarity of all men: "God has made you social beings. He has linked, all over the earth, man with man, society with society, and made the good of each consist in the good of the whole." Therefore, the kingdom of God or "the reign of love" did not merely belong to the realm of imagination; it was something realizable on earth.[57]

To introduce this "reign of love" Brownson felt sure that a new, comprehensive religious organization of mankind was needed. In order to convince others of the necessity of such an organization, Brownson decided to found an association himself, based on the same principles as the Universal Church supposed to come, the Church of the Future.

But before he left Canton, an episode occurred which should not go by unnoticed. Late in 1835 Henry David Thoreau (1817–1862) arrived at Brownson's house in Canton. As a poor student, the later "poet-naturalist"[58] had to earn some money as a school teacher in order to finance his studies at Harvard. Brownson interviewed and recommended him to the local school board. For some weeks during the following spring, young Henry, who was living with the Brownsons, taught school at Canton, and Brownson's sons were among his pupils.[59]

Then, late in 1837, Thoreau wrote to his former benefactor, asking him for help to get another school job. He expressed his gratitude to

Brownson in these words: "I have never ceased to look back with interest, not to say satisfaction, upon the short six weeks which I passed with you. They were an era in my life—the morning of a new *Lebenstag*. They are to me a dream that is dreamt, but which returns from time to time in all its original freshness. Such a one as I would dream a second and a third time, and then tell before breakfast."[60]

How much this "morning of a new *Lebenstag*" really meant to Thoreau is difficult to ascertain. According to M. J. Harson, who had his information from Amos Perry, then American consul to Tunisia and former class comrade and even intimate friend of Thoreau at Harvard, —"during their college career Thoreau's thought was almost entirely dominated by Brownson, and ... he spoke of him with greater admiration than of any other writer." More particularly, "Thoreau told him that his profound love of nature was inspired by Brownson, not by Emerson, as is generally supposed."[61]

That Brownson's influence upon young Thoreau should have been of such a magnitude, sounds surprising, above all as far as Thoreau's love of nature was concerned. In fact, Brownson's own attitude toward external nature is difficult to account for, since his writings do not contain any descriptions of scenery. But indirectly the reader gets the impression that Brownson was no great lover of nature. True, in 1869, as an old local patriot he declared, though in very general terms, that a Vermonter loved his Home State with its green hills and fertile valleys.[62] Yet, in 1864, he wrote these strange words about the landscape of his country in general: "We have rich, varied, and magnificent natural scenery, though rarely equalling that of Europe, Mexico, or South America." But, he added with assurance, we—meaning his compatriots in general, but obviously himself in particular—do not love natural scenery, because we are too much used to it. External nature, in order to have any real importance, must be related to human life, he concluded.[63] Consequently, when reviewing books of fiction, he objected—as, for instance, in 1846—to "wearisome descriptions of natural scenery and external objects, which are uncalled for, and only interrupt the narrative."[64] After all, one cannot help feeling that to Brownson "the blowing clover and the falling rain" was hardly any "miracle."

Thoreau's biographer Henry Seidel Canby also attributed great importance to the meeting with Brownson at Canton: "Brownson was his first personal contact with the free world in which move the dynamic and liberated minds of the great and the near-great." Canby believes that Thoreau might have derived his distrust of Abolitionism from Brownson, and even his idea that self-reform should lead to passive resistance.[65] What Canby says about Abolitionism may be true, but I have not been able to find any indication in Brownson's writings to sustain the biographer's latter assumption. But at any rate, "Brownson invited him into the society of active minds where age and position are no factors,"[66] and as a more recent biographer on Thoreau points out, "Brownson was Thoreau's first stimulating encounter outside Harvard."[67]

Early in the year 1836 Brownson moved to Chelsea, a suburb of Boston, although he remained pastor of the First Congregational Parish at Canton until about the middle of the year. Reported the *Christian Register* for June 25, 1836: a new religious society, "The Society for Christian Union and Progress" has been recently started in Boston. The Society, which is "without any *denominational* distinction," will hold its meetings at the Masonic Temple; and the Minister of the Society is Mr. Brownson, late Pastor of the First Congregational Church in Canton.[68] In *The Convert* (page 82) Brownson wrote that the society was organized on the first Sunday in July.

It had a double aim. First, all Christians, whether orthodox or liberal, Trinitarians or Unitarians, were to rally under the broad banner of Christian unity. But however broad the banner might be: atheists, Jews, pagans, and Mohammedans could not be members.[69]

Brownson's ambition, however, went farther than that of starting a new Christian sect. As will be remembered, already in 1833 he had called for Christian unity and, although himself a Unitarian, apparently intended to place Unitarianism and Trinitarianism on an equal footing.[70] In fact, according to a letter from the Rev. Joseph Henry Allen to Brownson, it was manifest that the latter would not make the Unity of God, the chief Unitarian dogma, "a rallying point, a principle of organization." His reason, which Allen, too, fully accepted, was the very interesting one that "all sects are nominally Unitarian."[71]

Yet Brownson and Allen were not the only ones who were worried about contemporary sectarianism. Not only in liberal, but also in orthodox circles there was a more or less articulate belief in the final unity of all Christians. The journal *Cumberland Presbyterian* thus expressed this general longing for unity: "We believe that all true Christians will yet be united. The present generation may not witness a consummation so glorious; but so sure as the Bible is the word of God, so surely will all who are in Christ Jesus be encircled in the embraces of brotherly love. Sectarianism and separatism and every other ism is [sic] destined to an early grave, whilst the whole Church of Christ shall yet constitute one harmonious brotherhood."[72]

Second, the new society should labor for the intellectual and moral progress of its members. In his most sanguine moments Brownson certainly thought that this association, in contrast to all religious institutions past and present, would never come to a standstill in its development, but always contain and carry into practice "the principle of its own progress."[73] In order to assure the intellectual progress of its members, a wide scope should be given to "free enquiry and practice of it." To assure their moral progress, the social side of Christianity should be particularly emphasized so as to awaken and sharpen the moral sense and the social responsibility of the members.[74] Typically enough, Brownson originally intended to call his association "Social Reform Society."[75] That name was soon dropped, however, because he felt it too narrow to correspond to his proper purpose.

But his organization developed into a "social reform society" rather than a "society for Christian union and progress." Though some well-to-do people supported the congregation, most of its members were poor; and their minister increasingly stressed the need of social reform. In all probability, Brownson's defense of the poorest and most numerous class could not, in the long run, enlist general sympathy among the middle and upper classes, which mainly constituted the Unitarian movement. Although some leading Unitarians were pleased with Brownson's initiative to gather the anticlerical and religiously indifferent people, others were skeptical as to his undertaking. "Respectable" Bostonians felt a growing uneasiness about this "Mr. Brownson," especially so when they learned that the minister of this new society began to address even Trade Unionists, "the most odious part of the workingmen."[76]

Brownson remained, except for the period 1839–1842, minister of that society to the latter part of 1843. Though his society at times seemed to be successful, it did not become what its founder had intended it to be: the first steppingstone to the Church of the Future. And Brownson, who, full of confidence, had come to "the centre of indifference" in order to usher in his spiritualized "religion of humanity" and prepare men's hearts for the coming Universal Church, admitted that man–and himself included–was "an indifferent church-builder."[77]

[1] *Chr. Reg.*, No. 18, XIII (May 3, 1834), 71.
[2] *The Brownson Papers,* Notre Dame University.
[3] *Early Life,* p. 109.
[4] Letter to his wife: *The Brownson Papers,* Notre Dame University.
[5] *Chr. Reg.*, No. 20, XIII (May 17, 1834).
[6] Octavius Brooks Frothingham, *George Ripley (American Men of Letters,* ed. Charles Dudley Warner; Boston, 1883), p. 29.
[7] *G. A.*, VII (March 21, 1829), 87 ff.
[8] *Chr. Reg.*, No. 48, XII (Nov. 30, 1833), 190.
[9] Frothingham, *op. cit.*, pp. 74, 75, 87. Ripley's letter is printed *in extenso* in Frothingham's biography: pp. 63—91.
[10] *Unitarian,* I (May 1834), 238.
[11] *Early Life,* pp. 104—106.
[12] *The Convert,* pp. 81—82. Brownson's "secret thought" concerned the preparation for the Church of the Future.
[13] *Early Life,* p. 313.
[14] *The Complete Works, Concord Edition,* X (Boston and New York, 1904), p. 349.
[15] *BrQR,* Oct., 1875, 577.
[16] *Early Life,* pp. 124—125. But (in a letter of Sept. 14, 1835) Everett wrote that he had no opportunity to come.
[17] *Ibid.*, p. 122.
[18] *Unitarian,* I (March 1834), 153—154.
[19] *Chr. Reg.*, No. 45, XII (Nov. 9, 1833), 177—178.
[20] *The Convert,* p. 7.
[21] *The Periodicals of American Transcendentalism* (Durham, N. C., 1931), p. 10.
[22] Norton, *Statement of Reasons* (Cambridge, Boston, 1833 ed.), preface, p. xvi.
[23] *Ibid.*, pp. 32, 327.
[24] *Ibid.*, p. 106. Norton maintained that biblical passages indicating the doctrine of the Trinity must be understood figuratively; otherwise they would contradict "common sense" (p. 106) or "that reason which God gave us" (p. 122).
[25] *Ibid.*, p. 313.
[26] After suffering a temporary setback in the 1820's, Locke's philosophy in the next decade seems to have regained much of its former position at Harvard University (See Edgeley Woodman Todd, "Philosophical Ideas at Harvard College, 1817—1837," *New England Quarterly,* XVI [1943], 63—90, esp. 64—65).
[27] Norton, *op. cit.*, preface, p. xxxv.
[28] *Ibid.*, p. xxx.
[29] B. A. G. Fuller on John Locke in *The Dictionary of Philosophy,* ed. Dagobert D. Runes (New York, *s. a.)*, p. 170.
[30] Norton, *op. cit.*, p. 186.
[31] *Ibid.*, p. 314.
[32] *Theological Progress during the Last Half Century* (Providence, 1878), p. 7.
[33] *Christian Examiner,* XIV, New series, IX (March 1833), 108—129, esp. 116 ff.
[34] *Christian Examiner,* XVIII, New series, XIII (May 1835), 167—221, esp. 191—192.
[35] *Christian Examiner,* XIX, 3rd series, I (Nov. 1835), 172—204, esp. 194—195. In the following spring Ripley wrote in the same periodical an essay on the German theologian and philosopher Schleiermacher, who both stressed the religious consciousness and distinguished between religion itself and its outward manifestation (XX, 3rd series, II [March 1836], 1—46, esp. 4).
[36] *Christian Examiner,* XXI, 3rd series, III (Nov. 1836), 225—254, esp. 250—251.

[37] *Ibid.*, p. 252.

[38] *Experience as a Minister*, p. 294.

[39] Ch. XIV: "The Transcendental Pattern of Religious Liberalism," *American Christianity: An Historical Interpretation with Representative Documents*, ed. H. Shelton Smith et al., II (New York, 1963), p. 120.

[40] *The Complete Works of Ralph Waldo Emersen, Concord Edition*, XI (Boston and New York, 1904), pp. 20–21.

[41] *Recollections and Impressions: 1822–1890* (New York, 1891), p. 29.

[42] *A Discourse on the Latest Form of Infidelity; Delivered at the Request of the "Association of the Alumni of the Cambridge Theological School," on the 19th of July, 1839.* With Notes. By Andrews Norton (Cambridge, 1839).

[43] "An Address Delivered before the Senior Class in Divinity College, Cambridge, Sunday Evening, July 15, 1838," *The Complete Works of Ralph Waldo Emerson, Concord Edition*, I (Boston and New York, 1903), pp. 128–129.

[44] *Our Liberal Movement in Theology* (Boston, 1882), p. 73.

[45] "Transcendentalism" *(BrQR* for 1845 and 1846), *Works*, VI, 1, 111.

[46] *Unitarian*, I (Sept. 1834), 405–413.

[47] *Ibid.*, pp. 406–408, 410. "The understanding," as interpreted in this article, seemed to correspond to Kant's term "Verstand," i.e. the faculty of thinking sensible objects and disposing them in such a way as to form concepts, judgments, and principles. Though Brownson as yet had hardly studied *Kritik der reinen Vernunft*, he had most probably read Coleridge's writings on German philosophers. "Reason" as Brownson interpreted it in his statement "Religion is no deduction of reason" seemed to cover his idea of "the understanding" and did not suggest any conception of "reason" as "Vernuft"–i. e. *a priori* principles of the mind – as in Kant's philosophy. Yet in the same article Brownson wanted to make clear that he by no means discarded human reason as the "mystics" do. Though "inspiration" imparted to the soul an impulse and "an inward sentiment of moral truth" which reason could not give, Brownson stressed that God inspired men as rational, not as irrational beings (pp. 412–413).

[48] *Ph.*, II (Nov. 5, 1832), 4.

[49] *Ph.*, II (May 15, 1832), 195–198.

[50] *G. A.*, VII (April 4, 1829), 102–103.

[51] *G. A.*, VII (March 21, 1829), 87 ff.

[52] *G. A.*, VII (June 27, 1829), 205.

[53] *G. A.*, VII (Jan. 10, 1829), 8.

[54] *The Convert*, pp. 77–78. The "representative man": p. 81.

[55] *Ibid.*, p. 78.

[56] *Ibid.*, p. 79.

[57] O. A. Brownson, *Sermon Delivered to the Young People of the First Congregational Society in Canton, on Sunday, March 24th, 1835.* Published by request of the young men of the society (Dedham, 1835), pp. 6–10, esp. 6, 10.

[58] The felicitous characterization of Thoreau given in the very title of William Ellery Channing's book *Thoreau, the Poet Naturalist* (rev. ed.; Boston, 1902). The author, himself a poet, was the nephew of the celebrated Unitarian minister.

[59] *The Correspondence of Henry David Thoreau*, ed. Walter Harding and Carl Bode (New York, 1958), p. 19.

[60] Letter of Dec. 30, 1837: *Early Life*, pp. 204–206.

[61] "Orestes A. Brownson, LL. D., 'A Man of Courage and a Great American,'" *Catholic World*, LXXIX (April 1904), 6.

[62] "Beecher's Norwood" *(Catholic World*, Dec. 1869), *Works*, XIX, 537.

[63] "Literature, Love, and Marriage" (*BrQR*, July, 1864), *Works*, XIX, 498.

64 "Thornberry Abbey" (*BrQR*, Oct. 1846), *Works*, XIX, 137.
65 *Thoreau* (Boston, 1939), pp. 57, 59.
66 *Ibid.*, p. 60.
67 August Derleth, *Concord Rebel: A Life of Henry D. Thoreau* (New York, 1962), p. 8.
68 *Chr. Reg.*, XV (June 25, 1836). According to a report in the *Boston Daily Advertiser* and which was reprinted in the *Christian Register* for March 25, 1836, Brownson seems to have prepared the ground for his society with a series of discourses, "Free Lectures on Christianity." Brownson, stating that religious and social feelings were natural to man, argued "in a masterly manner" against the thesis of the unbelievers that religion was only imaginary ideas, a result of the intrigues of priests and politicians. And the reporter continued: "The mode of handling the subject must have been new to most of those who listened to it, and could not fail to suggest a solution of many difficulties, which are perhaps oftener felt than expressed. It is rarely that the philosophy of religion is presented before a popular audience with more clearness of expression, strength of argument, or discrimination of thought, than were exhibited on this occasion."
69 *Early Life*, p. 139.
70 *Chr. Reg.*, No. 26, XII (June 29, 1833), 102.
71 Letter of April 25, 1835: *Early Life*, p. 132.
72 *Chr. Reg.*, XV (Feb. 27, 1836).
73 *The Convert*, p. 74.
74 *Early Life*, p. 145.
75 *Ibid.*, p. 138.
76 *Early Life*, p. 146.
77 *The Convert*, p. 82.

VIII
"New Views"

Just after organizing the Society for Christian Union and Progress, Brownson wrote a small book, *New Views of Christianity, Society, and the Church* (1836).[1]

The author intended to state the principles on which his own association was based and on which a new church—the "Church of the Future"[2]—might be organized. However, he was concerned with the general ideas, not with the precise form of organization.

The views set forth in his book were, as the author himself admitted, to a large extent derived from the writings of Benjamin Constant, Victor Cousin, Heinrich Heine, and the Saint-Simonians.[3] Properly speaking, then, his ideas were not original. But in New England of the 1830's they doubtless had about them an air of newness and originality. Said a reviewer in the *Christian Examiner:* Brownson's book really contained new views, or, at any rate, old terms were given a "novel application," which had "the effect to give to the whole discussion a strange and foreign air." But the reviewer also wanted to make clear that "those even who are most convinced of the unsoundness or fancifulness of his general doctrine, will be as ready as any to acknowledge the ability, eloquence, and earnest feeling expended in its exposition and defence."[4]

Brownson opened his book with the thesis of Benjamin Constant that religion is natural to man, and stated that "Christianity, as it existed in the mind of Jesus, was the type of the most perfect religious institution to which the human race will, probably, ever attain."[5] To Brownson, however, neither the Catholic Church nor the Protestant churches had succeeded in realizing the perfect religious institution.

As for Catholicism, it fulfilled in its time an important historical mission. The Catholic Church met the wants and needs of the people and even aided the growth of the human mind. But Catholicism was founded on an exclusive principle: spiritualism. This principle was no doubt well fitted to prepare men for heaven, but hardly fitted to prepare them for life on earth. For this very reason Catholicism had not been able to keep pace with the progress of mankind.

The historical task of Protestantism was to demolish this system of pure spiritualism. However, Protestantism went more and more to the other extreme of exclusive materialism, while denying or depressing the spiritual. Protestantism recommended the acquisition of material wealth, rehabilitated the flesh, elevated humanity at the expense of divinity, and in principle presented a revival of the ancient civilizations of Greece and Rome. This revival of ancient paganism reached its climax in the great French Revolution of 1789, when churches were changed into pantheons and prostitutes were adored as goddesses of reason. To Brownson, Protestantism thus ended its work of destruction.

True, Protestantism stood for civil and political liberty, and also had a distinct democratic tendency from a social point of view. Yet these qualities, however valuable they may be in themselves, are not essentially religious. Within Protestantism even the traditional, central dogmas were being sloughed off: "The vicarious Atonement has hardly a friend left. The Deity of Jesus is questioned, his simple humanity is asserted and is gaining credence."[6]

To Brownson, German rationalism and English-American Unitarianism represented the last stage of Protestantism before complete infidelity. However logical this development might be, logic and consistency were not enough to outweigh the loss of true religion. For this very reason Protestantism was retrograding, whereas Catholicism, or spiritualism, was recovering lost ground: "Catholicism has revived, offered some able apologies for itself, made some eminent proselytes, and alarmed many Protestants, even among ourselves."[7] Loathing the "dead body" of Protestantism, men were beginning to look out for something else which might satisfy their longings for a really religious life.[8]

Yet a complete return to spiritualism was to Brownson not only undesirable, but altogether impossible. During its progress mankind had definitely passed by and discarded the exclusive principle of spiritualism. What was now needed was a combination and reconciliation of these two principles of spiritualism and materialism. Such a reconciliation, or atonement, was possible, since both principles were inherent in man's own nature. All through history the great mistake of all the religious sects was their attempt to form human nature according to their particular creeds instead of doing just the opposite. For "human nature is well made, its laws are just and holy, its elements are true and divine."[9]

On the basis of human nature, then, all opposites would be reconciled: the spiritual and the material, the eternal and the temporal, the heavenly and the earthly. The Christian dogma of the God-Man symbolizes the truth of this doctrine of atonement. Brownson was convinced that the second coming of Christ, as foretold in the Bible, meant the complete realization of this doctrine among men on earth.

True, the author did not believe in a speedy realization. However, the idea of human perfectibility and the idea of the essential holiness of all things warranted the establishment of this new civilization, when Church and State would be a holy unity. What really mattered for the present was to believe in these great ideas themselves, for "ideas, if they are true, are omnipotent."[10]

Obviously, Brownson rejected extreme spiritualism as well as extreme materialism. What he wanted to reconcile was "the affirmative or positive" principles of both systems.[11] This presupposed an eclectic method of reasoning, and the very term "eclectic" at once leads us to Victor Cousin, whose philosophy was called Eclecticism.

According to *The Convert* (page 85), Brownson became acquainted with Cousin's philosophy in 1833. One year before, Henning G. Linberg's English translation of Cousin's lectures on the history of philosophy had appeared in Boston. Brownson, then, was not the first one to introduce Cousin and his philosophy in the United States. But as long as his enthusiasm lasted he was one of his most ardent admirers and strongest supporters in the country.

Cousin's main thesis is that all philosophical systems are true in what they affirm. They err only to the extent that they are exclusive, that is, strictly narrow or one-sided.[12] He maintains that the history of philosophy shows the interplay of four great systems: sensualism, idealism, skepticism, and mysticism, which, taken together, are supposed to cover all the phenomena of human consciousness. There will never be more philosophical systems than those four. When regarded separately, each of them is only a fragment of the truth. But in its constant progress the human mind will increasingly be able to combine them into one harmonious whole. Cousin's object, therefore, was to mold these philosophical systems into a higher unity, called Eclecticism.[13]

But in Cousin's writing this term also meant the method by which to arrive at this comprehensive philosophy, or, as Paul Janet put it: the eclectic method is the history of philosophy given as the instrument of philosophy itself.[14] And it was, above all, this method that caught Brownson's attention. He concluded that if Cousin's method could be applied to philosophy, it could be used in religion as well. By means of the eclectic principle he set about analyzing spiritualism and materialism with the view of breaking their isolation and combining them in a higher unity.

In Brownson's little book Cousin's eclectic method thus offered the framework of ideas. But much of their substance he borrowed from the German author Heinrich Heine. The latter's work *Zur Geschichte der Religion und Philosophie in Deutschland* was published in 1834, and a French translation of the book with the brief title *De l'Allemagne* appeared in the following year.

Heine's immediate purpose was to inform the French of German religious and intellectual history, particularly after the Reformation. Despite his pessimistic mood and ironic temper Heine shared the general belief of the age in constant human progress, which he considered in the light of a conflict between "sensualism" and "spiritualism." Brownson replaced Heine's term "sensualism" by "materialism." Thus he did not fully adopt the German's terminology; but the two words as used by the two writers cover the same idea.[15]

Heine maintained that the real idea of Christianity was the mortification of the flesh. More particularly, this idea was to him the core of Catholic Christianity. However, since this idea conflicted too sharply with human nature, it never was fully realized. Instead, the Catholic Church was forced to make concessions to human nature. Unlike Brownson, Heine contended that the Reformation initially was a revolt of spiritualism against the glaringly materialistic tendencies of sixteenth-century Catholicism. Not long afterward, however, sensualism again raised its head. Monasteries were closed, and monks and nuns, together with the clergy, were allowed to marry. Luther's historic statement that the Bible and conscience should be the sole judges in matters of faith inaugurated a new era. This statement, stressing the importance of reason and individualism, reduced the power of the hierarchy and made way for "religiöse Demokratien."[16] A skeptical attitude made itself felt more and more in philosophy, literature, and science, and even fundamental Christian dogma was questioned.

Obviously, neither Heine nor Brownson intended to give any detailed historical treatment of their subject. They simply intended to present certain main ideas. To both of them the Reformation had a marked democratic tendency, furthering civil and political liberty; Brownson even regarded the French Revolution as a direct consequence of the Reformation. Yet he did not give any answer to the question of why the Protestant Reformation should have had so strong an impact on a basically Catholic country. Probably Protestantism to him was a general principle, an idea, more than a particular historical phenomenon.

They also agreed that both in religion and philosophy the work begun by the Reformation had ended in rationalism. Certainly, they knew that rationalism met with opposition from Protestant orthodoxy. But neither of them thought this opposition to be of any great importance. To Heine, "die protestantischen Orthodoxen sind Dogmatiker ohne Geist,"[17] and to Brownson, Protestant orthodoxy in the form of Calvinism was only Catholicism continued, though with some Protestant modifications. Accordingly, he regarded the adherents of Calvinism, this "decidedly spiritualistic" religion, as far behind the times. After all: "Every consistent Protestant Christian must be a Unitarian."[18] So Brownson as well as Heine emphasized the rationalistic and materialistic tendencies latent in the Protestant Reformation. In so doing they doubtless went too far in identifying Protestantism with Renaissance and Humanism, and seemed to overlook the specifically religious import of Protestantism.[19]

But although Brownson thus borrowed much from Heine, the two men differed widely in their basic attitudes, and they did not arrive at the same conclusions. Heine, for his part, was far from regretting the socio-religious development of mankind from spiritualism to sensualism. On the contrary, he apparently did not want to retain any element of spiritualism as a religion, much less revive it. What made the religion of spiritualism particularly suspect in Heine's eyes, was that its representatives so often in history had made common cause with authoritarian regimes and moneyed interests. To Heine this alliance was formed in order to suppress the popular demand of freedom, a demand which, in principle, originated in Protestantism, as "die wahre Religion des judäisch-deistischen Evangeliums."[20] Through this form of religion, matter had been greatly rehabilitated.

Brownson, on the other hand, reacted just as strongly against exclusive materialism as against exclusive spiritualism. In distinct contrast to

Heine he stressed the strong anti-rationalistic tendencies of the age, indicating that pure materialism had reached its end. Heine, in his work, had a social-political aim; Brownson, in his work, was particularly concerned with the religious aspect.

While Brownson derived his two terms "spiritualism" and "materialism" from Heine, it was the Saint-Simonian school that provided him with the doctrine with which to justify their synthesis.

To Saint-Simon and his followers there is no essential antagonism between the spiritual and the temporal, the holy and the profane. In fact, there is no basic dualism: all things are holy. By virtue of this idea the Saint-Simonians wanted to erect the Universal Church, which was to comprise and hallow all human activities.[21] Brownson reasoned along the same lines when he argued for the reconciliation of the spiritual and the material: "But the new doctrine of the atonement reconciles these two warring systems. This doctrine teaches us that spirit is real and holy, that matter is real and holy, that God is holy and that man is holy . . ."[22]

In his book *Nouveau Christianisme* (1825) Saint-Simon maintained that at any rate contemporary Catholicism tyrannizes the people and keeps them in ignorance, since it is building its organization on external power. Protestantism, on the other hand, is wrong in giving the Church an inferior position as compared to the State. Saint-Simon called for *one* religion and *one* organization, comprising State as well as Church. Brownson, too, wanted to put an end to the separation between Church and State. He visualized a future when "both [i.e. Church and State] will aim at the same thing, and the existence of one as separate from the other will not be needed. The church will not be then an outward visible power, coexisting with the state, sometimes controlling it and at other times controlled by it; but it will be within, a true spiritual—not spiritualistic—church, regulating the heart, conscience, and the life."[23]

The great purpose of the Universal Church based on Saint-Simonian principles was the speedy and continuous amelioration, moral, intellectual, and physical, of the poor and more numerous classes. Thus the intended new church had a social aim. Brownson's "Church of the Future" was to be devoted to the same end. Inspired by the utopian vision of Saint-Simonism he pictured a future when the idea of the holiness of all things had been carried into practice. In this social millennium men were to be "personally holy," governments "sacred," industry and agriculture "the worship of God." Slavery and wars should cease. Briefly: "The universe will be God's temple, and its service will be the doing of good to mankind, relieving suffering and promoting joy, virtue, and well-being."[24]

In contrast to Saint-Simon Brownson emphasized that he did not want to introduce a new Christianity, only a new church.[25] Thus he made the nice though somewhat debatable distinction between "the Christianity of Christ" and "the Christianity of the church."[26] The former is permanent; the latter is temporary.

What, then, is "the Christianity of Christ?" Brownson willingly conceded that the church has always regarded Jesus as making an atonement. But the church misunderstood the real character of this atonement. Instead of asserting the holiness of both spirit and matter, the church, by a false interpretation of the sayings of Jesus, stated that only spirit is holy. To the church, therefore, the mission of Jesus was not to effect the union of spirit and matter, but to redeem spirit from matter. Hence the symbol of the cross, hence spiritualism. On the other hand, "the Christianity of Christ"—or the Christianity of Brownson's *New Views*—"declares as its great doctrine that there is no essential, ... original antithesis between God and man ... Neither spirit nor matter is unholy in its nature ... All things, spirit, matter, God, man, soul, body, heaven, earth, time, eternity, with all their duties and interests, are in themselves holy."[27]

Brownson, then, put forth a rather unorthodox view of the central Christian dogma of the atonement. His theory is so unorthodox that his criticism of the Saint-Simonians for advocating a new Christianity, and not only a new church, might be directed against himself. After all, since both the Saint-Simonians and Brownson reject outright Christian dualism, it matters little what the new thing is called: "nouveau Christianisme" or, simply, "new views of Christianity."

Evidently, Brownson was wide of the mark in his attack on the alleged exclusive spiritualism of the church. Although the church has never declared that matter is in itself holy, she has not fallen into the other extreme of declaring matter to be "essentially unholy."[28] The very Christian dogmas of Incarnation and the Resurrection refute Brownson's sweeping view of churchly Christianity being an exclusively spiritualistic religion. Yet this implicit Christian approval of "matter" or "the body" does not invalidate the other traditional Christian idea of the conflict between "the flesh" and "the spirit" or—in

St. Paul's words in Rom. vii: 23—between the "law in my members" and "the law of my mind." Brownson seems to have overlooked that the churchly tradition, despite strong temporary tendencies to asceticism, has never considered "the flesh"—as interpreted above—synonymous with "matter" in general.

However, the very principle of synthesis or reconciliation of extremes proved very fruitful to him and motivated much of his intellectual development. Indeed, already from his Universalist period he had stated the necessity of harmonizing faith and reason, the supernatural and the natural; and although he did not, as yet, attach much definite meaning to terms like "faith" and "the supernatural," he had at any rate early discovered a principle, which he had made and even more was going to make consistent use of. The following statement in his *New Views* indicates Brownson's quest of synthesis or "union:" "Where there is but one term there is no union. There is no harmony with but one note."[29] Before his conversion to Catholicism he applied the principle of synthesis to his so-called synthetic philosophy and his doctrine of life and communion, and later, when describing Catholicism—or "Catholicity" as he preferred to call it[30]—he stated that "the type of Catholicity is the God-man," and that the Catholic religion always harmonizes opposites.[31]

More particularly, the Catholic Brownson, when viewing "matter" or "the natural" as an expression of cultural or civilizational work and thus reflecting St. Paul's emphasis on things "true," "lovely," and "of good report" (Phil. iv: 8), could with some right maintain, as he did in 1862, that there is "no contradiction, taken in their real relation, between earth and heaven, time and eternity, the terrestrial destiny of man and his celestial destiny, between the goods of this life, and the goods of the life to come."[32] He had in mind not only creation, but also "the development or effects of the incarnation."[33]

Yet in 1871 Brownson gave a more qualified and comprehensive statement, stressing not only the harmony between earth and heaven, but also the "moral antagonism" between good and evil: "Undoubtedly, all the works of the Creator are dialectic, and considered physically, as the works of the Creator, there is no antagonism between earth and heaven. Both are parts of one stupendous and harmonious whole. But it does not follow from this that there is no moral antagonism between a life lived for the world and a life lived for God." Not surprisingly, therefore, Brownson, who had long ago ceased to believe in his "religion of humanity" of the 1830's, now pointed to Saint Augustine's *De Civitate Dei* as his ideal.[34]

However, already in 1836 Brownson differed from the Saint-Simonians in one important respect. He could not accept their bold declaration about Saint-Simon, that he was giving reality to the brotherhood that was preached by Moses and prepared by Jesus. To Brownson Jesus, though only a man, but the representative "God-Man," occupied a unique position in history.

At the time when *New Views* was written, Transcendentalism or "the New School" had begun to make itself manifest among New England Unitarians. In the same year—1836—the Transcendental Club held its first meetings, which were attended by Emerson, George Ripley, Frederic Henry Hedge, James Freeman Clarke, Convers Francis, William H. Channing, Brownson, and others. Emerson, though admitting a common "sympathy of studies and of aspiration," said that "there was no concert" between the members,[35] and James Freeman Clarke, with a touch of humor, put it in this way: "We called ourselves the club of the like-minded, I suppose because no two of us thought alike."[36] Yet the truculent debater Brownson was too much to bear even for this loosely knit group of thinkers and poets. According to Hedge, "Brownson met with us once or twice, but became unbearable, and was not afterward invited."[37] Also, unlike some members of the Club, Brownson was probably too practical or earth-bound to be willing to go "to heaven in a swing,"[38] and not surprisingly, Amos Bronson Alcott, one of the most ethereal of the Transcendentalists, labeled Brownson "the proud Philistine."[39]

However, although Transcendentalism was a philosophical trend more than a fixed and clearly defined system of thought, the Transcendentalists shared some common beliefs or, at least, some common attitudes. They joined hands in their opposition against Calvinism. And more and more conspicuously they stood up against "the Old School" Unitarianism.

In fact, the very year 1836, when *New Views* was published, was ripe in books more or less Transcendentalist in outlook. Thus Convers Francis wrote in his journal for the same year: "I find that George Ripley is publishing *Discourses on the Philosophy of Religion*; besides, Brownson is out with his *New Views*, and Alcott with *Questions on the Gospels*, for Children. Then there is Furness' book, *Remarks on the Gospel*, so that it seems the spiritualists are taking the field in force. I have long seen that the Unitarians must break into two schools —the old one, or English School, belonging to the sensual and empiric philosophy, and the new one, or the German School (perhaps it may be called), belonging to the spiritual philosophy."[40] Francis might have added his own book that appeared in the same year, and whose title was typical of "the New School," *Christianity as a Purely Internal Principle*. But the literary and philosophical highlight of the year was Emerson's *Nature*.

Even if Brownson's *New Views* is not exactly a Transcendentalist manifesto,[41] the book contains some ideas that were characteristic of "the New School."

First, Brownson stressed that religion is "natural to man." The religious sentiment in us is "universal, permanent, and indestructible;" it makes us think and feel the holy and prompts us to revere it.[42] By his insistence on the innate religious sentiment, Brownson reacted against the Lockian view held in esteem by "the Old School" Unitarians, that the human mind is originally a blank sheet, a *tabula rasa*, regarding religion as well as everything else.

Second, in *New Views*, religion is above all presented as springing from the heart. Neither outdated orthodoxy nor barren rationalism can offer a suitable outlet for this deep emotion. Brownson, then, takes his stand both against Calvinism, and Unitarianism "on the plan of Priestley and Belsham."[43] But even if religion is primarily regarded as feeling, this feeling must concentrate on some central ideas, which constitute the religion or at least the religiosity in question.

The religion advocated by Brownson was essentially the Unitarianism preached by William Ellery Channing. The latter, though the founder of the American Unitarian Association, was no strictly dogmatic Unitarian like Andrews Norton, but cherished views and sentiments which heralded Transcendentalism. Therefore, Channing was hailed by the younger generation of Unitarian ministers as their great spokesman and inspirer. Later, however, when he realized where his "disciples" were tending, even the liberal Channing seems to have had some misgivings.

Brownson praised highly Channing's earlier mentioned sermon on "Likeness to God."[44] In this sermon, "the most remarkable since the Sermon on the Mount," Channing emphasized the essential similarity of the divine and human natures. To Brownson, Channing's idea of "the likeness of a kindred nature" implied another and even more momentous idea, namely, that the God-Man, or Jesus, is not "a being alone of its kind."[45] Thus in principle incarnation loses its special character and instead becomes valid for every human being. The difference between Jesus and other men is not one in kind, but in degree. Channing himself, however, seemed to stop short of a similar conclusion. According to Brownson, Channing held Arian views on the person of Christ, or at least regarded him as a superangelic being.[46]

The idea of the general incarnation, which Brownson gave a fuller treatment in his article "Church of the Future," is no doubt representative of the Transcendentalist outlook.[47] Frederic Henry Hedge, for instance, believed "in the ever-proceeding incarnation of the Spirit of God in human life."[48] It is even possible that Brownson was the first among the Transcendentalists to state this doctrine. In any case, he was the one among them to emphasize it most strongly.

The doctrine of the general incarnation, which in principle raises all human beings to the same level, expresses respect for and faith in every individual man and woman, and represents the religious-democratic aspect of Transcendentalism. To Brownson, if to anyone, this idea was indeed no abstract formula only:

> The human mind, allied as it is to the divine, is too valuable to lie waste or to be left to breed only briars and thorns. Those children, ragged and incrusted with filth, which throng our streets, and for whom we must one day build prisons, forge bolts and bars, or erect gibbets, are not only our children, our brother's children, but they are children of God, they have in themselves the elements of the Divinity and powers which when put forth will raise them above what the tallest archangel now is. And when this is seen and felt, will those children be left to fester in ignorance or to grow up in vice and crime? The whole energy of man's being cries out against such folly, such gross injustice.[49]

In Brownson's view, it was just the common man who, 1800 years ago, went forth with glowing enthusiasm to conquer the world for Christianity. And the inspiration which in the first century dominated "the Christian movement of the people," is by no means extinct today. Manifesting itself in present-day associations of all kinds, the popular inspiration, helped by the Eclectic philosophy, will usher in the longed-for Christian renaissance, the synthesis of spirit and matter.[50]

In two important respects, however, Brownson's views differed from those held by most of the Transcendentalists.

First, he did not share their dislike of churches and institutions. He maintained that men "must and will embody their ideas of the true, the beautiful, and the good—the holy, in some institution."[51] Yet this idea, which he later was to develop further and which led him in the direction of the Catholic Church, in 1836 was still in its embryonic state.

Second, Brownson's skeptical attitude toward Protestantism as such was not typical of most Transcendentalists. Theirs was an opposition to Calvinist orthodoxy, not to the Protestant emphasis on individual reason and conscience. Nor did they generally share Brownson's positive appraisal of medieval Catholicism; in his own words: the Middle Ages "are deemed . . . to be 'dark ages' only because we have not light enough to read them."[52]

Such ideas were already pointing out the road of his own development. Though Brownson at that time did not dream of converting to Catholicism, which he thought to be hopelessly behind the times, Victor Cousin's Eclecticism and the writings of Benjamin Constant and the Saint-Simonians had made him understand and appreciate the historical mission of the Catholic Church. And eight years later the former herald of a new church came to the conclusion that to him the Church of the Past was after all the Church of the Future as well.

In the January, 1842, issue of the *Boston Quarterly Review* Brownson "reviewed" his book *New Views*. Yet his article "Church of the Future"[53] was no revision of his ideas, but rather a clarification and elaboration of some of his statements.

As in his *New Views*, Brownson stressed the need of "a broad and generous synthesis" of spirit and matter as an ideal of the Church of the Future.[54] He restated his view of Catholicism and Protestantism, favoring the former at the expense of the latter even more than he had done in his book. True, he was still very skeptical as to "the old church:" "She has ceased to aspire. She has no words of authority. Men laugh at her puerile duties and her idle threats."[55] But, paradoxically enough, he could also state in the same essay that the Church of the Future "will not be a destruction of the old church, but her fulfilment. She will be the church of the past, enlarged, modified, converted into the church of the future." The condition, however, was that "the old church" accepted the two ideals *Equality* and *Progress:* "She is already an organism for that purpose, did she but know it."[56] She certainly did not "know it," because "equality" to Brownson implied the doctrine of the general incarnation, and as far as his view of "progress" was concerned, it was limited to "the natural order" only.[57] But after all, he was beginning to look upon "the old church" as a still living "organism" and not only as an organization of the past.

While his attitude toward "the old church" was somewhat ambivalent, his view of Protestantism was little more than a total rejection. "In its excessive rationalism, in its rejection of sentiment, of inspiration," Protestantism had not only made "the temple-service" a barren affair, but had also made "the power of love" homeless among its adherents.[58] In short, Protestantism was a downright "denial."[59]

But even though Brownson still advocated his gospel of the unity of spirit and matter, he seemed to be more concerned with another principle, because he had not dealt with it so extensively in *New Views*. This principle was the generalization of the doctrine of incarnation. He pointed out that incarnation was not something exclusive, restricted only to Jesus, as the church had always held. On the contrary, divine incarnation included all human beings. Brownson applied Cousin's Eclectic method when declaring: "The church was right in what she asserted, wrong in what she denied. When she asserted the incarnation of the ideal in Jesus, she asserted the truth; when she asserted that it was and could be incarnated in him only, she erred."[60] So even if Brownson considered Jesus "the real Mediator between God and men, and the literal Saviour of our souls,"[61] his doctrine of the general incarnation after all meant that there is no *essential* difference between Jesus and the most "ordinary" human being. Thus, despite some traditional figures of speech, Brownson's conception of Jesus had not come nearer to that of traditional Christianity. Even his statement: "there is no God, but God 'manifest in the flesh' " only served as basis for his idea of the general incarnation: "Man is this visible manifestation."[62]

To all intents and purposes, Brownson's religion was still a "religion of humanity," and the new church he was dreaming of was still "the church of the ideal" to be realized sometime in the future.[63] But more distinctly than in 1836, when he wrote his *New Views*, he now regarded the Church of the Past as a possible foundation on which to build the Church of the Future. For "the old church" was still an "organism."

[1] *Works*, IV, 1–56. Hereafter referred to as *New Views*.
[2] *Works*, IV, 57–78.

[3] *The Convert*, p. 83.
[4] XXII, 3rd series, IV (March 1837), 127–130, esp. 128, 129.
[5] *New Views*, p. 5.
[6] *Ibid.*, p. 22.
[7] *Ibid.*, p. 27.
[8] *Ibid.*, p. 28.
[9] *Ibid.*, p. 34.
[10] *Ibid.*, p. 50.
[11] *The Convert*, p. 86.
[12] *Ibid.*, p. 85. Evidently, such a sweeping idea was liable to charge. Thus Emile Faguet, in his book *Politiques et moralistes du dix-neuvième siècle* (2e série, 5e éd.; Paris, 1903), wrote that an affirmation itself means a negation of that which it excludes, and suggested that Cousin's philosophy might be called exclusivism with no less justice than Eclecticism (p. 252).
[13] In his work *Victor Cousin et son Oeuvre* (3e éd.; Paris, 1893), Paul Janet calls attention to the fact that philosophical generalizations were typical of the age, citing as examples Auguste Comte's theory of the three stages and the Saint-Simonian doctrine of the "critic" and the "organic" epochs of history (p. 355). And after all, Janet finds Cousin's classification of philosophical systems "la plus plausible et la plus rationelle que l'on puisse essayer" (pp. 354–355).
[14] Janet, *op. cit.*, p. 453. In his dissertation on *Victor Cousin, Hegel und die französische Romantik. Einflüsse und Wirkungen* (Oberviechtach, 1932), Bernhard Knoop says that Cousin, although strongly influenced by Hegel, made at least one original contribution to philosophy, i.e. his theory of identity between philosophy itself and the philosophical method (p. 58).
[15] Brownson's use of "materialism" instead of "sensualism," which was used both by Cousin and Heine, was perhaps quite incidental. Yet in 1860, when making some comments on dictionaries, he said he preferred "sensism" to "sensualism," which to him signified a moral rather than an intellectual or strictly philosophical system (*BrQR*, 3rd New York series, I, 262). In any case, in *New Views* he called Locke's philosophy "sensism" (p. 21).
[16] Heinrich Heine, *Zur Geschichte der Religion und Philosophie in Deutschland, Gesammelte Werke*, hg. G. Karpeles, V (3. Ausg.; Berlin 1909), p. 42.
[17] *Ibid.*, p. 63.
[18] *New Views*, pp. 36, 39.
[19] Though a staunch and very often an aggressive opponent of Protestantism throughout his Catholic period, Brownson in the early 1860's took a more balanced position regarding the Reformation. He maintained that the Reformation was originally "a movement in the church, by Catholics, and it became Protestant only subsequently, after it had been expelled from the church." And he even wrote: "By an unwise resistance ecclesiastical authorities drove the reformers into heresy and schism" (*Works*, XII, 565).
[20] Heine, *op.cit.*, p. 53.
[21] *Unitarian*, I (June 1834), 286.
[22] *New Views*, p. 47.
[23] *Ibid.*, p. 50.
[24] *Ibid.*, pp. 49, 50.
[25] *Ibid.*, p. 45.
[26] *Ibid.*, p. 1.
[27] *Ibid.*, p. 10.
[28] *Ibid.*, p. 11.
[29] *Ibid.*, p. 9.

[30] *BrQR*, II (Oct. 1845), 544.

[32] "The Reunion of All Christians" (Jan. 1862), *Works*, XII, 475, 476.

[32] *Ibid*., p. 479.

[33] *Ibid*., p. 481.

[34] *Works*, VIII, 224–225.

[35] "Historic Notes of Life and Letters in New England," *The Complete Works, Concord Edition*, X (Boston and New York, 1904), pp. 341–342.

[36] Joseph L. Blau, *Men and Movements in American Philosophy* (New York, 1953), p. 110.

[37] Lindsay Swift, *Brook Farm, Its Members, Scholars, and Visitors* (New York, 1900), p. 7. Yet according to Emerson, Brownson attended at least three meetings of the Club *(The Journals and Miscellaneous Notebooks of Ralph Waldo Emerson* (ed. William H. Gilman et al., V: 1835–1838 [Cambridge, Mass., 1965], pp. 194, 218, 338).

[38] Emerson's quotation of a phrase made by a non-Transcendentalist about some members of the Transcendental Club *(The Complete Works*, X, 342).

[39] Odell Shepard, editor, *The Journals of Bronson Alcott* (Boston, 1938), p. 130. The occasion was a "conversation" between the two "polarities" Brownson and Jones Very in 1839. "It was comic to behold them," wrote Alcott. "They tried to speak, but Very was unintelligible to the proud Philistine."

[40] Clarence L. F. Gohdes, *The Periodicals of American Transcendentalism* (Durham, N. C., 1931), p. 40. The exact titles of the books of Bronson Alcott and William H. Furness were *Conversations with Children on the Gospels* and *Remarks on the Four Gospels*.

[41] Yet Clarence L. F. Gohdes calls *New Views* "a transcendental treatise" *(op. cit*., p. 40).

[42] *New Views*, p. 3.

[43] *Ibid*., p. 27.

[44] *The Works of William E. Channing, D. D., Eighth Complete Edition*, III (Boston and New York, 1848), pp. 227–255.

[45] *New Views*, p. 46. See also "Likeness to God," p. 233.

[46] *The Convert*, p. 79.

[47] *Works*, IV, 62–65.

[48] Blau, *op. cit*., p. 117.

[49] *New Views*, pp. 48–49.

[50] *Ibid*., pp. 40, 41–44.

[51] *Ibid*., pp. 28–29.

[52] *Ibid*., p. 27.

[53] *Works*, IV, pp. 57–78.

[54] *Ibid*., p. 78.

[55] *Ibid*., p. 76.

[56] *Ibid*., pp. 75, 77.

[57] In 1873 he wrote that he had believed in the idea of "progress" until the end of 1842 *(Works*, IX, 485), but from that time he came to realize that progress was possible only through supernatural intervention (see, for example, *Works*, IX, 328).

[58] *Works*, IV, 74.

[59] *Ibid*., p. 78.

[60] *Ibid*., p. 63.

[61] *Ibid*., p. 64.

[62] *Ibid*., p. 63.

[63] *Ibid*., p. 76.

IX
Approaching Politics

As Brownson himself declared, the views put forth in his little book were the principles on which his Society for Christian Union and Progress was founded.[1] But if someone wanted "inside" information about the society and its minister, he would have to pay some visits to Lyceum Hall and, already from the beginning of July 1836, to the Masonic Temple in Boston, where the meetings of the society were held.[2]

On entering the assembly room, our visitor would observe a congregation whose members for the most part were of the laboring class.[3] Then his eyes would turn to a tall, lean fellow just about to enter the pulpit. In a determined, perhaps a little too self-assured manner the minister would begin to speak. His voice was strong and distinct, but often lacked that undefinable warmth which puts the preacher into direct, personal contact with his audience. Isaac T. Hecker relates that Brownson once, when preaching to John Freeman Clarke's congregation, tried hard to be pathetic, but obviously with little success. And young Hecker himself, who got to know Brownson later,[4] "did not go to him for emotion, but for thoughts."[5] In fact, Brownson "was essentially a philosopher," Hecker wrote, "and that means that he never could be what is called popular." But to those who had philosophical interests, he was a fascinating speaker who often roused their enthusiasm. And to all listeners, whether philosophical or not, Brownson "was one of the few men whose power is great enough to advertise himself. Wherever he was he was felt. His tread was heavy and he could make way for himself."[6] First of all, the unfailing honesty and the simple earnestness with which he spoke could not fail to make impression both on members of the society and casual visitors.

Among the latter was the talented woman publicist Elizabeth P. Peabody. In marked contrast to several liberal Christians who gave to a certain one of Brownson's sermons the not flattering epithets "anti-

Christian" and "blasphemous," Miss Peabody declared in a letter of July 14, 1837, to Brownson that she had been "very much affected and stirred up by the glowing faith in Christ, which so strongly pervaded it." According to her, Brownson did not say that it was unnecessary to believe in God, nor that the clergy were infidels; but he said they lacked "faith in man's becoming equal to Christ," and Miss Peabody added convincedly: "Is it not so?" No less convincedly the lady concluded: "The whole of this exhortation was perfectly thrilling."[7]

Another and even more important casual visitor was the intelligent, energetic Englishwoman Harriet Martineau. She established her fame as a writer of religious stories, which were much read both in her home country and abroad. But this little woman, who was already handicapped by deafness, won an even greater reputation through her popularizing tales on the principles of Adam Smith and other economists. In 1834 she visited America and made a long tour of more than two years. Among the places she visited was Boston. As a sister of James Martineau, one of the leaders of English Unitarianism, she must have been particularly interested in visiting Boston, the center of American Unitarianism. She was in the city when Brownson was about to start his society. And in fact, she was very much impressed by this minister who seemed so earnest and straightforward when standing in the pulpit. She even had his discourse on the "Wants of the Times" printed in her own book *Society in America*, and Brownson, for his part, hardly complained of this unexpected publicity.[8]

This discourse which served as a kind of manifesto for his society founded some weeks later was delivered in Lyceum Hall, Hanover Street, on Sunday, May 29, 1836. Brownson emphasized that the two great principles of the age were free inquiry and democracy. In contrast to the "infidels" the church had neglected these principles, though they were closely connected with Christianity. The Christian message had to be adapted to the time and circumstances: "I accuse no preacher of not preaching the truth. The truth is, I believe, preached in all churches, of all denominations, to a certain extent at least; but not the right kind of truth, or not truth under the aspects demanded by the wants of the age, and country."[9]

In the preacher's view, people were no longer content with "Jewish threats" of hellfire, nor with "beautiful essays, and rounded periods on some petty duty, or some insignificant point in theology."[10] Evidently, Brownson's attack was not only directed against Calvinism and revivalistic movements, but also against the form and themes of current Unitarian preaching. Instead of Calvinist orthodoxy Brownson launched the idea of "free, unlimited inquiry," and instead of conventional, upper- and middle-class Unitarianism—"the aristocracy of our churches"—he praised "the democratic spirit" of Christianity: "I say again that Jesus was emphatically the teacher of the masses, the prophet of the workingmen if you will, of all those who 'labor and are heavy laden.' "[11]

Although Jesus did not directly appeal to any definite class, he might, nevertheless, be called a prophet of the people, because he lived and died for principles which, in the course of time, had improved the lot of the lower classes. His spirit had led to the abolition of slavery in almost all Christendom; besides, it had done away with the aristocracy of war and nearly also the aristocracy of birth.[12]

Yet Brownson was also careful to point out that he was by no means any "destructionist:" "I would improve, preserve whatever is good, and remedy whatever is defective, and thus reconcile the *Conservator* and the *Radical*." In fact, by now there was little left of radicalism proper in the former adherent of Frances Wright, if he had ever been a thoroughgoing radical. Above all, religion, which some years ago he regarded as a barrier to individual and social progress, had become to him the true principle of reform.[13] Also, just as in his theological and philosophical speculations he was trying to reconcile spiritualism and materialism, in his social and political views he was trying to reconcile conservatism and radicalism.

Nevertheless, he was charged with being a real radical or a "leveller," a charge which indicates that at least some Unitarians looked with suspicion upon this newcomer who so confidently addressed the workingmen. No doubt, Brownson's attack on the existing pew system could not but irritate some well-to-do churchgoers.[14] On the other hand, some leftists blamed him for not espousing the cause of the workingmen strongly enough.[15]

To Brownson, who wanted to "reconcile the *Conservator* and the *Radical*," the old question presented itself anew: How to achieve social progress? In an article in the *Christian Examiner* for May 1836, he restated his old thesis that education, of both grown-ups and children, was the only *efficient* means of all social progress.[16] Yet he had by now modified his view of individual "reform" as the only prerequisite to social progress. While one year before he had written that "all social reforms must be the effect of individual reform,"[17] he now contended that certain social improvements were necessary for a great many members of society: "Perfect every individual, and undoubtedly you would perfect society; but it is necessary that the perfection of both be carried along together."[18]

Not only his sermons to his association, but also his writings in the *Boston Reformer*—a weekly journal which he edited for some time—indicated his growing concern with social and political problems. But just as he did in his programmatic sermon, the new editor stressed that he was not "a revolutionist," but "much more of a conservative," one who believed in "orderly, legalized progress." His reasons were twofold. First, he looked upon religion—the "active principle" in man—as a lever of reform, and second, he had, increasingly, come to consider the American system of government established, at least in theory, "in the interests of the many" and not the few. These two points of view motivated Brownson's middle course between extreme conservatism and extreme radicalism.[19]

Since he left the Workingmen's Party after "a year's devotion to it,"[20] Brownson had not taken active part in politics. In the early 1830's he kept away from political work and political parties altogether. In his Fourth of July Speech at Dedham, 1834, he said bluntly that he regarded with "almost perfect indifference" the struggles between the politicians, because "the country, humanity, moral and social progress are not in those struggles."[21]

One might have expected that he would join a second time the small Workingmen's Party, which, although extinct in New York, still existed in Boston. This, however, Brownson was not willing to do. In fact, he even went as far as to encourage the workers themselves not to join the party. According to his—albeit by now somewhat modified—belief in education and "self-culture," he dissuaded the workers from trying to achieve their aims through legislation.[22] Thus he was against their attempts to introduce by political means a ten-hour day, and advised them instead to make advantageous agreements with their employers in advance concerning working hours.[23] His skepticism of political legislation was also due to his general idea of the role of government,[24] and his "organic" conception of society.[25]

Yet Brownson gave the workingmen his moral support, both as minister to his society and as a more or less convinced member of the Democratic Party. As a minister he emphasized the social side of religion, maintaining that the church ought to ally itself with liberalism, and that the clergy should be the advocates of the people or of the "Reform Party."[26] As a supporter of the Democratic Party,[27] he thought this party able to warrant and aid social progress. Yet he did not think it advisable to link the workingmen's cause too closely with one party.[28]

Even if Brownson in general was skeptical of party organizations[29] and professional politicians, he was not indifferent to political principles or great issues. From social background and general outlook he was early induced to sympathize with the Democratic Party. Yet, in the 1820's at least, he was no Jacksonian Democrat. It is noteworthy that neither in 1824 nor in 1828 did he want Andrew Jackson to be president, but preferred, in 1824, the more moderate candidates William Harris Crawford and John Caldwell Calhoun and, in 1828, John Quincy Adams.[30] Now, in the latter part of the 1830's, Brownson wanted to strengthen his oldtime affiliations with the Democratic Party.

Yet he did not seem willing to strengthen those affiliations too much. Instead of committing himself warmly to the party, its principles and causes, he made some cool reflections on what he considered its chief doctrine, the sovereignty of the people. Not satisfied with "sovereignty" as such, he went a step further, asking: "Is that will right? Is it just? ... Were we in office, however, we should feel ourselves bound to obey it or not to act at all, that is, where the will was clearly and formally expressed by the people themselves, in the same manner in which we were elected." But, he continued, "left to our own discretion, we should act in reference not to their will, but to our own convictions of right."

Then he gave his own definition of popular sovereignty: "We admit the sovereignty of the people when the question is of many or few; we deny it when we speak absolutely. The people are not sovereign. There is no sovereign, but the Infallible, that is, God, that is again, the Right, the Just. We dissent from the democratic party, therefore, and of course from the popular doctrine of the day, by denying the infallibility of the people, and the absolute sovereignty of their will."[31]

Throughout his life, Brownson was consistent in his disavowal of the doctrine of popular sovereignty, and his devotion to first principles carried him, at least in this field, too far. It is difficult to imagine that leaders and theorists of the Democratic Party interpreted the sovereignty of the people to be the infallibility of the people, though some might have stressed unduly—as, for example, John L. O'Sullivan, the editor of the *Democratic Review*, did in 1843—the "absolute and unchecked government" of the majority. But even O'Sullivan believed Providence to be above the popular will.[32] More important, the leading Democrat and the later well-known historian George Bancroft formed the aphoristic phrase: "Eternal justice ruling through the people." On the other hand, it is interesting to note what the acute French observer Alexis de Tocqueville at the same time wrote about "the Sovereignty of the People in America:" "The people reign in the American political world as the Deity does in the universe. They are the cause and the aim of all things; everything comes from them, and everything is absorbed in them."[33] Obviously, both Brownson and de Tocqueville pointed to a danger latent in all democratic societies, but in the light of later developments it is not wrong to say that they both, or at least Brownson, overemphasized this danger.

However, in a larger perspective Brownson's idea of the sovereignty of the Right and the Just was, in a way, a version of "the higher law," a concept which has played an important part in American intellectual history. His idea is even part of a still broader tradition: his wish as a possible political representative to act according to his "own convictions of right" re-echoes the words of Edmund Burke in his speech, in 1774, on the duties of the member of Parliament: "It is his duty to sacrifice his repose, his pleasures, his satisfactions, to theirs [those of his constituents]; and above all, ever, and in all cases, to prefer their interest to his own. But, his unbiassed opinion, his mature judgment, his enlightened conscience, he ought not to sacrifice to you, to any man, or to any set of men living. These he does not derive from your pleasure; no, nor from the law and the constitution. They are a trust from Providence, for the abuse of which he is deeply answerable."

However, to many readers of his journal Brownson's philosophical distinction between sovereignty and infallibility was, probably, of little interest. In any case, some subscribers complained that there was too much of religion in the paper.[34] One person, though, appreciated Brownson's mode of thinking: George Bancroft. Like Brownson who despite his theory of the popular sovereignty believed that "the people are the only rightful depositories of political power,"[35] Bancroft maintained that "the best government rests on the people and not on the few, on persons and not on property."[36] Yet, like Brownson, he did not believe that popular sovereignty *per se* was, of necessity, identical with the supreme good and the supreme right. In a letter to Brownson

(Sept. 21, 1836) he wrote: "The people need a higher conviction, a clearer consciousness of its democracy."[37] And finally, like Brownson, Bancroft was interested in principles rather than the work of everyday politics. Accordingly, he gave credit to Brownson who in his reasoning was guided by principles, "that deep philosophy which by the unerring standard of human consciousness, tries the merit of every measure."[38]

In the same letter, which was written after the election and instalment of the new Democratic President Martin Van Buren, Bancroft also said that Brownson was "rooted and grounded in the true doctrine." Yet in one important respect Brownson's view was no longer "rooted and grounded." Under the impact of the economic crisis of 1837, Brownson became acutely aware of the class problem in American society. This led him to a reappraisal of his optimistic belief in an "orderly, legalized progress." Simultaneously, he seemed to lose faith in his old doctrine of the coöperation of all classes to ameliorate the lot of the poor.

His sermon "Babylon Is Falling," preached on May 28, 1837, was representative of his changed outlook. To Brownson, two different kinds of principles were opposed to each other: Liberty, Equality, Peace against Privilege, Inequality, War. A terrible encounter between them was to be feared, if the battle had not already begun. In fact, one of these "parties" had to be extinguished before peace could be established.[39] In this struggle Brownson wanted to be a "soldier of equality," fighting, if not for equal wealth for all, at least for equal chances to all members of society, and to each one according to his ability."[40] In order to extinguish the "party" of inequality or, possibly, to avert a terrible final clash between the two "parties," such "soldiers" would be much needed. Brownson maintained that the gap between the main classes of contemporary society was steadily widening. Even in spite of labor-saving machinery, the workingmen as a class were not better off than before. On the contrary, they had to work harder for the same pittance of wages.[41]

No doubt, these were new tones. Brownson, who for several years had believed in an organic social progress, suddenly began to speak about a probable social revolution. This has led Helen S. Mims to maintain that the year 1837 opened a new period in Brownson's thinking, "marked by a trend toward materialistic monism" and an "emphasis on the class struggle as the basic fact in the social process."[42]

On the whole, Brownson never shrank from revising or modifying his views when circumstances obviously demanded it. Although devoted to first principles, Brownson was eminently a practical man who let his ideas serve—in the widest sense—practical purposes. This contrast was also one of the strange paradoxes in Brownson's character. His most notable change of outlook was caused by the Civil War, which forced him to revise, essentially, his former states' rights doctrine. But typical of his consistency as to the general theories of government, a large portion of his book *The American Republic* (1866), which, by the way, was dedicated to his old friend George Bancroft, consisted of articles written about twenty years before.

As far as the crisis of 1837 was concerned, it could not be ignored by any thinking person. Already before the presidential election of 1836 there had been strikes and labor conflicts, "things which"—according to William Graham Sumner—"were almost unprecedented in the United States."[43] And the next year saw the so-called "bread riots" in New York, when the excited populace destroyed five hundred barrels of flour and one thousand bushels of wheat, and the militia had to restore order.[44]

However, Brownson's views as presented in his sermon are somewhat ambiguous. First, it is noteworthy that he did not see the real enemy in one particular class of society. To him, the enemy, or the deep reason for the latent social struggle was "the *Spirit of Gain*, the Commercial Spirit, or System," which is universal and, therefore, not characteristic of one class.[45] Second, Brownson even now, under the pressure of the economic and social crisis, stressed self-improvement as the great objective. Equal chances to all or "physical" advantages like riches were in themselves of little importance, if they did not serve as means of individual progress.[46] So even now he was trying to steer a middle course, although the form in which he presented his views indicated a more extremist stand.

Although this sermon and similar ones, e.g. the sermon with the incendiary title "The Rich against the Poor,"[47] made Brownson even more suspect, in some circles, as a dangerous "leveller," George Bancroft realized that Brownson might be useful to the Democratic Party. As the recently appointed Collector of the Port of Boston, Bancroft offered him the post of Steward of the Marine Hospital at Chelsea.

This post would mean economically a good deal to Brownson and his family. Its duties were mostly nominal, and in addition to an annual salary of 1,600 dollars he would get a good, rent-free house to live in.

Yet he seems to have wavered a little before he accepted the offer. It was only on condition that he might write and speak just what he wanted about political matters without any express party orders that he accepted.[48] And thus he was well prepared to start his *Boston Quarterly Review* the next year.

1 *New Views*, p. 2.
2 *Early Life*, p. 140. Lyceum Hall seems to have been used before the society was officially organized.
3 *Ibid*., p. 141. Yet, according to Henry F. Brownson, some well-to-do people supported the society. He also says that the congregation averaged five hundred (*Ibid*., p. 140).
4 According to Hecker, he heard Brownson for the first time "somewhere about 1834" in New York (*Catholic World*, XLV [May 1887], 202). But this is disputed by Theodore Maynard, who maintains that "the first record we have of Brownson in New York . . . was in 1841" (*Orestes Brownson*, p. 57). Maynard bases his argument on Vincent V. Holden's book *Early Years of Isaac Thomas Hecker* (Washington, 1939).
5 *Catholic World*, XLV (July 1887), 472.
6 *Catholic World*, XLV (May 1887), 204.
7 *Early Life*, pp. 152, 157, 158.
8 Harriet Martineau wrote two books on America, each of three volumes: *A Retrospect of Western Travel* (London, 1838) and *Society in America* (London, 1839). Brownson's discourse was printed in Vol. III, pp. 342–359.
9 *A Discourse on the Wants of the Times* (Boston, 1836), pp. 8, 9 ff.
10 *Ibid*., p. 9.
11 *Ibid*, pp. 8, 19, 20, 21.
12 *Ibid*., p. 20.
13 *Ibid*., pp. 4, 12, 14, 18, 21.
14 *Ibid*., pp. 4, 7–8.
15 *Early Life*, pp. 146, 147.
16 XX, 3rd series, II (1836), 155.
17 "Progress of Society," *Christian Examiner*, XVIII, New series, XIII (July 1835), 357.
18 *Christian Examiner*, XX, 3rd series, II (1836), 160.
19 *Early Life*, pp. 162, 163.
20 *The Convert*, p. 63.
21 *Dedham Address*, pp. 17–18.
22 *Early Life*, p. 170.
23 *Ibid*., p. 171.
24 *Dedham Address*, p. 17.
25 *The Convert*, p. 64.
26 *A Discourse on the Wants of the Times*, pp. 18 ff.; *Early Life*, p. 172.
27 *Early Life*, p. 182.
28 *Ibid*., p. 179.
29 *The Convert*, p. 63.
30 *Early Life*, p. 178.
31 *Ibid*., p. 182.
32 New series, XII (May 1843), 537–544.

[33] *Democracy in America*, ed. Richard D. Heffner (A Mentor Book; New York, 1956), p. 58.
[34] *Early Life*, p. 171.
[35] *Ibid.*, p. 169.
[36] "The Office of the People in Art, Government, and Religion" (1835). Quoted in *Living Ideas in America*, ed. Henry Steele Commager (New York, 1951), p. 228.
[37] *Early Life*, p. 180.
[38] Letter of July 9, 1837 (*Early Life*, p. 184).
[39] *Babylon Is Falling* (2nd ed.; Boston, 1837), pp. 5–6, 20.
[40] *Ibid.*, pp. 9, 11.
[41] *Ibid.*, p. 16.
[42] "Early American Democratic Theory and Orestes Brownson," *Science and Society: A Marxian Quarterly*, II (Spring 1939), 184.
[43] *Andrew Jackson* (Boston and New York, 1899), p. 449.
[44] *Ibid.*, p. 450.
[45] *Babylon Is Falling*, pp. 3–4.
[46] *Ibid.*, p. 14.
[47] Delivered in June, 1837 (*Early Life*, p. 151).
[48] *Early Life*, pp. 211, 212.

X

An Eclectic Reasoner

When, in January, 1838, Brownson commenced his *Boston Quarterly Review,* he entered upon an important phase of his career. Up to that time he had edited several small papers or journals. But to be responsible for a periodical, each number of which containing about 130 pages, was something different.

The *Boston Quarterly Review* existed five years and, according to *The Convert* (page 89), was conducted almost singlehandedly. Its articles were meant to treat, and also did, a vast variety of topics under the headings of religion, philosophy, politics, and general literature. Obviously, the editor wanted to put his own stamp on the review and, perhaps, even intended to write most of the essays himself. On the other hand, wanting to make his *Quarterly* representative in tone and character, he probably hoped for more contributions from other writers than he really got.

However, since the articles were not always signed, it is sometimes difficult to state whether an article in question was really written by the editor himself. According to Henry F. Brownson, there were, among others, the following contributors to the *Boston Quarterly Review:* George Bancroft, George Ripley, Bronson Alcott, Margaret Fuller, Anne Charlotte Lynch, Sarah H. Whitman, Miss R. A. Tylor, Elizabeth Peabody, B. H. Brewster, H. S. Patterson, A. H. Everett, and Theodore Parker.[1] To these names may be added Albert Brisbane, John F. Tuckerman, J. S. Dwight, William Henry Channing, and S. D. Robbins.[2] The editor certainly hoped that Emerson would have been among the contributors, but in a letter of November 15, 1837, he declined to write an article for the first number of the review. Although he expressed the hope of being able to do something for the periodical later, there is no indication that he ever wrote anything for it.[3]

What concerns us here are Brownson's own contributions to his review. If the signature of the author or other clear indications are lacking, the style, the technique of composition and, to some extent, the substance of the article are the indirect means by which I try to decide Brownson's possible authorship. In dubious cases, the articles in question will not be accounted for.[4]

When Brownson later looked back on his *Boston Quarterly Review*, he stressed that his aim as an editor was not to dogmatize, but to inquire, not to state fixed doctrines on any subject, but to stimulate to free thought. From his Catholic position he characterized many of his views which he held at that earlier time as "crude, rash, and thrown out with a certain recklessness," but even if "none of his countrymen are less disposed to accept entire the speculations, theories, and utterances of that *Quarterly Review,* than I am," he yet believed "it deserves an honorable mention in the history of American literature." Though, on the one hand, admitting that among all the topics he dealt with in his review only certain political questions were given a clear and consistent treatment, he confidently stated, on the other hand, that "the opinions it enunciates, on a great variety of topics are substantially such as I still hold on the same topics." All in all, Brownson thought his review had accomplished what he intended: to provoke the readers to think for themselves. Yet, according to the editor, this purpose was not always appreciated by his readers, who regarded him as a bold and vigorous writer, but also as an eccentric, extravagant person who loved to change his opinions constantly.[5]

Although the circulation of the review was limited,[6] its importance should not be underrated. In some circles it seems to have been received and read with great enthusiasm. Said, for instance, Sarah H. Whitman in a letter of November 19, 1840, to Brownson: The *Boston Quarterly Review* is read to pieces long before other periodicals in the Athenaeum, Providence![7] In his above-mentioned letter of December 30, 1837, young Henry David Thoreau told his former benefactor that he had "perused with pleasure the first number of the 'Boston Review' [sic]. I like the spirit of independence which distinguishes it. It is high time that we knew where to look for the expression of *American* thought. But the doubt speedily vanishes when we can depend upon having the genuine conclusions of a single reflecting man."[8] The young Unitarian minister Theodore Parker, contrasting the *Dial*, the professed organ of the Transcendentalists, to the *Boston Quarterly Review*, compared the former with an "innocent" procession of children, but the latter with a "real" procession of men.[9] And in his autobiography Parker called attention to the fermenting 1830's, when Brownson and the *Boston Quarterly Review* made themselves manifest: "In this he diffused important philosophic ideas, displayed and disciplined his own extraordinary talents for philosophic thought and popular writings, and directed them towards Democracy, Transcendentalism, 'New Views,' and the 'Progress of the Species.' "[10]

The very best recommendation of the review was in all probability given by William Henry Channing, who, in 1843, wrote in his periodical *The Present:* "In an age like this, superficial and perplexed, and yet learning, as it is, its own ignorance at least . . . a man must be akin to a seraph or a stock not to change. The only consistency one would now desire to keep is the *consistency of progress,* and this Mr. Brownson may proudly proclaim . . . Take it all in all, it was the best journal this country has ever produced, at once the most American, practical and awakening; the more so because its editor was a learner and shared his studies with his readers."[11]

In his "Introductory Remarks" to the *Boston Quarterly Review* Brownson wrote: "Man is a seer and it is each man's duty to declare simply what he sees, without attempting to fix its precise value."[12] From a general point of view, such a statement indicates an "eclectic" attitude in the sense of a searching mind. Thus, already as a "Free Enquirer" Brownson had declared that his creed was truth wherever he could find it,[13] and as an independent preacher he believed that "all have some truth, all have some errors."[14] In this broad sense of the term Brownson was an "eclectic" also during the five years while he edited the *Boston Quarterly Review.*

Yet, above all during the first two years when the influence of Cousin was strong, Brownson might even be termed an *E*clectic. Not only did he share and apply Cousin's basic approach: "all systems are true in what they affirm, false only in what they deny, or only in that they are exclusive,"[15] but he was also strongly influenced by Cousin's philosophy in general. And whether an Eclectic or an "eclectic," Brownson was always trying to reconcile opposites.

In his introduction to the *Boston Quarterly Review* Brownson presented his basic views on religion, philosophy, and politics. In "the great Movement commenced by Jesus . . . and which is manifesting itself now in a manner that makes the timid quake, and the brave leap for joy," he found the necessary resources to carry on "a reform in the Church, giving us a purer and more rational theology;" further, this "Movement" would help to make philosophy "something profounder and more inspiring than the heartless Sensualism of the last century;" finally, this same "Movement" would elevate the workingman and free the slave.[16]

His thoughts of "a purer and more rational theology" were partly presented in an article with the suggestive title: "Christianity not an Original Revelation with Jesus, nor a System of theological Doctrines, properly so called." Premising the axiom "All truth is immutable and eternal," Brownson maintained that historical Christianity could not be an original revelation. Another argument was furnished by the Bible itself: according to St. Paul, God preached the gospel already to Abraham; and Jesus himself said: "Before Abraham was, I am." To Brownson this indicated a difference in meaning between the names of Jesus and the Christ. While the Christ is the principle of love, Jesus was only an individual who "possessed the Christ," though he did so much more than any other human being. In this distinction between "the individual Jesus" and the Christ, Brownson found the solution to the mystery of the two natures attributed to Jesus.[17]

Brownson, like other contemporary Christians of the liberal kind, often preserved the traditional dogmatical terms, but gave them an unorthodox interpretation. Indeed, his basic conception of Christianity was unorthodox: "Nothing is more certain than that one becomes a true Christian according to the New Testament, by living and only by living the life which Jesus lived,–not by believing what he may have taught, but by being what he was, righteous as he was righteous." In Brownson's view, Christianity was no specifically revealed religion, and whoever loved "the Divinity" with all his heart and his neighbor as himself–whether he be a Jew, a Moslem, a Pagan, or a professed Christian–was "a Christian in the highest and only worthy sense of the term."[18]

But although Christianity was no original revelation with Jesus, he and "the Christian Movement" might, in a certain sense, be called "original and peculiar."[19] Brownson stressed that the originality of Jesus did not consist in his nature; further, his originality did not consist in his doctrine of salvation, since "the conditions of salvation never change;" finally, his originality was not manifest through his martyrdom, because "humanity is rich in martyrs."[20] His originality consisted in his grand vision of love as something comprising all humanity, not only one's own family, caste, tribe, clan, or country: "In him the Christ attained to Universality." Abraham, Moses, and David—the representatives of the Jewish people and Judaism—did not embrace this conception of universal love, but restricted their sympathies to the members of their tribe or nation. In contrast to the Jews, the ancient Greeks had developed a cosmopolitan spirit, but even the great Socrates had "nothing of the completeness we perceive in Jesus."[21]

Just as Jesus loved mankind, the Christian movement must center on philanthropy, and not exclusively on piety, patriotism, art, or science. Indeed, Christianity was a definite advance on Judaism, which had only developed the religious element of human nature, or piety. The mission of the Son of Man was not to make us love God less, but man more. Also, Christianity was a definite advance on the Greek and Roman cultures. Neither the Greeks through all their achievements in art, science, and philosophy, nor the Romans with their contributions to jurisprudence and their strong patriotic feelings realized the love of man as MAN. Brownson stressed that this love made religion not exclusive, but all-comprehensive.[22]

Brownson developed his idea of Christianity as essentially a philanthropic movement in the article "Democracy of Christianity." Reviewing the book *Principles and Results of the Ministry at Large in Boston* (1838) by the Unitarian minister Joseph Tuckerman, and two books by the well-known Frenchman Félicité Robert de Lamennais: *Affaires de Rome* (1837) and *Paroles d'un Croyant* (1833), Brownson emphasized the double mission of Jesus. One of his objects, and "perhaps" the more important one, was to make atonement for sin and save the soul of man for the hereafter. Brownson, apparently in an offhand manner, declared that he had nothing to say about this "more exclusively theological object" in his journal. What really concerned him was the alleged other mission of Jesus, i.e. to establish a kingdom of righteousness and peace on earth "for men while yet in the flesh." Christianity, then, had a distinct social and political aspect, which, according to Brownson, had been much neglected. Assuming that the great aim of Christianity was to raise everyone up to the "stature of perfect man in Christ Jesus," Brownson maintained that no element of human nature, whether the religious or the social element, must be neglected in order to reach this aim. Therefore, Christianity could not be exclusively a theological affair, but must cover all the departments of life.[23]

To Brownson, as to Lamennais, Jesus was "the prophet of the democracy," of the people, a man sent from God to preach glad tidings to the poor.[24] Both of them stressed Christianity as a social gospel. Brownson, like Lamennais, criticized the church and the clergy, who, to them, ignored the truly democratic character of Christianity. The church, instead of being a social lever, seemed to act too much as a conservative, even constabulatory force in civil matters.

Yet the cause of democracy, which was linked with the cause of liberty, could not be defeated, and the only thing the church could do to save itself was to ally itself with that triumphant cause. Even papal bulls and anathemas as, for instance, in the case of Lamennais, had no effect.[25]

Since most people identified Christianity with the church, they were disposed to reject Christianity if they rejected the church. But–Brownson stated–a people deprived of the influence of religion would not at all be able to carry out real social improvements; and instead of order and liberty, anarchy and license would be the result. He emphasized the view of Lamennais that liberty is "true order," that family and property are the two foundations of society, and that social reforms, or reformism, are highly preferable to revolutions. But to both true order and social progress the influence of religion is indispensable.[26]

In *The Convert* (page 100) Brownson wrote that this "Christian democracy" was the core of his preaching for ten or eleven years. In fact, "Christian democracy" was only another name of his "religion of humanity," whose aim was man's earthly happiness. For this aim he labored–as he stated in *The Convert* (page 48)–"steadily and without wavering from 1828 till 1842," and, in trying to obtain the means by which to reach this aim, he was finally led to the Catholic Church.

True, some time after his conversion he advised possible reformers as follows: "Would you reform society? Go, then, and study at the foot of the cross, and learn to trample the world beneath your feet."[27] But in 1857, though regarding his pre-Catholic belief in "Christian democracy" as such as "the great heresy of the nineteenth century," he immediately added in his autobiography (page 101) that the doctrine had "its side of truth." And in 1858 Brownson let Herr Diefenbach, one of his fictitious persons in "Conversations of Our Club," say: "Lamennais had a glimpse of the truth. The democratic spirit must be turned to the advantage of religion."[28] More important, in 1862 Brownson stated—and manifestly in his own behalf—that the Christian popular movement in France of the 1830's, which was led by Lamennais and Père Lacordaire, had inspired him to believe in the possibility of a reconciliation between religion and modern society. This French movement directed even for the first time his attention toward "the old church," and gave him "a glimpse of her grandeur, as a social institution."[29] Yet he added that the excommunication of Lamennais made him conclude that the Catholic Church was dead and made him even waste twelve years of his life in futile attempts at founding a new church.[30]

From a historical point of view, just as the movements led by Lamennais and Lacordaire anticipated the "prêtres-ouvriers" of the twentieth century, Brownson's ideas of a "Christian democracy" and the "Church of the Future" anticipated the "Social-Gospel" Movement, initiated by Walter Rauschenbusch.[31] More particularly, Brownson's earlier views were in some measure reflected in his own attempts in the 1860's to reconcile Catholicism with modern society and civilization, especially in their American aspects.[32]

However, as he also stated in *The Convert,* Brownson was not the only American at the time who espoused "Christian democracy" or social Christianity. The Unitarian clergyman Joseph Tuckerman, whose book Brownson reviewed, dedicated much of his life to working in the slums of Boston. His colleague Edwin Chapin followed his example in New York. More distinctly than many others, Elias L. Magoon, a Baptist minister, pointed to the social character of Christianity in his book *Republican Christianity* (1849). In the spirit of Lamennais he demanded that the church "work for the millions rather than for the aristocratic cliques," and that she be the "patron of the aspiring, the fortifier of the weak, the deliverer of the oppressed."[33]

Although Brownson in his interpretation of Christian dogma was far from the orthodox position, he did not embrace such radical views as Emerson, who in his "Divinity School Address" of 1838 encouraged the students to reject outright all formal creeds and instead wait for a direct, new revelation from God. This address, which provoked strong reaction and eventually closed the pulpits to Emerson, was reviewed by Brownson in the October, 1838, issue of the *Boston Quarterly Review.*

He praised the address for "its life and freshness, its freedom and independence." And he paid homage to the speaker, too: "No one can know him or read his productions without feeling a profound respect for the singular purity and uprightness of his character and motives." But, on the other hand, he criticized the address for its vagueness, its inconclusive reasoning, and its incoherent, fragmentary ideas.[34]

Insofar as the address contained any specific doctrine, it was that of the supremacy of the individual soul, to which all things in the universe were supposed to be subordinate. According to Emerson, as Brownson understood him, Man is his own lawgiver. Brownson reacted strongly against this doctrine, which he called a doctrine of "transcendental selfishness" or "pure egotism:" everything out of me is nothing in itself; if it be anything, it is only because it is something to me. By contrast, Brownson maintained that man feels himself obliged to obey a law, not emanating from his own soul, but imposed upon him by "a supreme lawgiver," i.e. God. In principle, Emerson's advice "Act out thyself!" might even lead to sensual licentiousness. The Christian commandment "Deny thyself, and love thy neighbor as thyself!" signified, in Brownson's view, a definitely higher view of ethics. Above "the good of the individual" Brownson placed "the good of the universe" or "absolute good."[35]

But after all, morality was only the *cultus exterior*, the outward worship of God. While the moral sentiment only led to or disclosed the idea of "universal order," the religious sentiment led to the idea of God, "the Father of universal order." Brownson defined the religious sentiment as a craving of the soul to fasten itself on an object above itself, a being all-sufficient, omnipotent, immutable, and all-holy. This sentiment was derived both from a sense of dependence and from an intuition of an invisible power on whom man could depend. If, then, the soul were sufficient for itself, religion would be out of the question. Even if Brownson did not undervalue the divine capacities of the soul, he was not at all willing to identify it with God himself: "He is in us, but not us."[36]

It is interesting to note that when, in the early 1830's, Brownson was speaking and writing about the inner light and the religious sentiment, he was not so careful in drawing the line between the sentiment as such and its object, i.e. God. It is also noteworthy that Brownson, who in another context wrote about "the theological mission" of Jesus as a matter of no concern for his review, now admitted that he felt oppressed by his own weakness and even sinfulness.[37]

Brownson thought Emerson to be praiseworthy insofar as he urged men to reproduce Christianity in their own souls and not base their faith on historical documents as such. Yet Brownson could not accept Emerson's view that the Christianity of the past had ceased to have any interest for us at all. To Brownson, "Christianity results from the development of the laws of the human soul, but from a supernatural, not a natural, development." In different ages God had, by supernatural means, enabled men to see the truths necessary to our progress. Thus the individual experience of Christianity must be supplemented by that of the race, or "the psychological Christ" have his indispensable counterpart in "the historical Christ." While the church had overemphasized the historical Christ, Emerson seemed to go to the other extreme of preaching only a psychological Christ. Brownson, anticipating his later doctrine of life, said that the life of Jesus "is the life we now live, so far as we live any life at all."[38]

No doubt, Brownson, in his opposition to Emerson, was nearer to orthodoxy than he had ever been since he left the Presbyterians. From that time Christianity had hardly been anything more to him than what was meant by natural religion. Now he used the word "supernatural" in clear contrast to "natural," just as he stressed that God, though in us, is not us.

Moreover, the essay is symptomatical of the essential difference between Brownson and Emerson in their respective views of the role of tradition. While Emerson, as a "pure" Transcendentalist, was highly skeptical as to everything traditional, and wanted to clear the ground in order to create completely new things, Brownson became more and more convinced that the experience of the past was indispensable to the contemporary and future generations.

In an essay on Brownson and Emerson, A. Robert Caponigri states that Emerson stressed the identity between the individual soul and the absolute cause, whereas Brownson believed that "the mind apprehends its object not in virtue of a radical identity but of an ultimate polarity." And as for the role of tradition or history, Emerson saw in it only a representative value, something serving as symbol or analogy of spiritual facts, while Brownson, on the other hand, more and more came to consider it a real medium through which absolute or transcendental ideas manifest or actualize themselves.[39] Thus, by 1838, the differences in outlook between Brownson and Emerson were beginning to appear. And no less characteristically, Brownson also objected to Bronson Alcott's idea of the identity between God and man, and between

God and nature. To Brownson, God is in His works, but also separate from them.[40]

Apparently, Brownson who, in René Wellek's words, was standing "somewhat apart," though he had much in common with the Transcendentalists, saw more clearly than they the danger of subjectivism and expounded more and more "an extreme objectivist intuitionism."[41] Later, Brownson was to develop his views on intuition; but already as a Universalist he declared that "intuition is undoubtedly the strongest evidence we can have,"[42] and in his essay on Emerson's Address he contrasted the latter's "primitive intuition" based on subjective instincts with "an intuition of an invisible Power, Father, God, on whom we may depend," an intuition which does not derive from the religious sentiment, but which constitutes it.[43]

Victor Cousin, whom Brownson at that time regarded as *the* philosopher, most probably influenced, or at least justified, his view of tradition and its worth. Cousin's Eclecticism was to a large extent identical with the history of philosophy. Evidently, Brownson had Cousin's Eclecticism in mind when writing: "As in philosophy, we demand history as well as psychology, so in theology we ask the historical Christ as well as the psychological Christ."[44]

When writing his *New Views*, it was just the eclectic character of Cousin's philosophy which caught Brownson's attention, whereas the Frenchman's views of ontology and psychology were admittedly words of no or little sense to him.[45] However, he soon began to study those elements of Cousin's philosophy, and already on November 15, 1836 (the preface of *New Views* was dated November 8), he wrote a letter to Victor Cousin, where he indicated his grappling with psychological and ontological problems: "Your works, Sir, found me sunk in a vague sentimentalism, no longer a sceptic, but unable to find any scientific basis for my belief. I despaired of passing from the Subjective to the Objective. You have corrected and aided me; you have enabled me to find a scientific basis for my belief in Nature, in God and Immortality, and I thank you again and again for the service you have done me."[46]

Brownson did more than write letters. He wrote two articles for the *Christian Examiner*. Already in the first article, which appeared even before the publication of *New Views*, Brownson was concerned with Cousin's notions of psychology and ontology, or of the "passing from the Subjective to the Objective." Like Cousin, Brownson emphasized that "the spontaneous reason," which, in the last analysis, is

God himself, intuitively "reveals to us God and the world on precisely the same authority as our own existence, or the slightest modification of it." As it is the task of psychology to disclose the nature and workings of "reason," psychology, according to Cousin, "conducts of itself to ontology."[47] Cousin liked to present himself as a philosopher who, in contrast to German idealistic philosophers, constructed his system of thought on an inductive basis.

However, Cousin's favorite contention that he began modestly in psychology and finally reached ontology may be disputed. Since he presupposed *a priori* a "spontaneous reason" identical with God in us, but not of us, one may just as well maintain that he began in ontology and ended in psychology. Thus Brownson wrote that Cousin followed Schelling and Hegel "very nearly, in going from God to nature and humanity," but immediately after he told his readers that the French philosopher began with the study of human nature, while the two German philosophers at once soared to the Absolute.[48]

Therefore, the problem remains whether the connection between psychology and ontology, in Cousin's system, has been sufficiently established. Hippolyte Taine, a severe critic of Cousin's philosophy, though an admirer of his style, made short process of Cousin's philosophizing: "Il construit des édifices admirables, hardis, élégants, d'une architecture nouvelle et symétrique; et ce sont des châteaux de cartes."[49] Even Brownson doubted whether Cousin had really built "a bridge over the gulf which separates ontology from psychology," but confiding in Cousin's conception of "reason," he thought he could leap the gulf without any bridge at all.[50]

Undoubtedly, Cousin himself must have felt the difficulty of building that bridge. In Brownson's interpretation, Cousin stated that "no fact of consciousness is possible without the conception of our own existence, the existence of the world, and that of God . . . Ourselves, nature, and God are, then, necessarily asserted in every word, in every affirmation, in every thought." And, Brownson added, one could not conclude from the finite to the infinite, because the ideas of the finite, the infinite, and their relation exist in consciousness and "are developed simultaneously in the first act of the intellectual life."[51]

In the preface to the third edition of his *Fragments philosophiques* (1838), Cousin mentioned Brownson's articles in the *Christian Examiner*, making some laudatory comments on their author: "un rare talent de pensée et de style." Cousin also referred to a third article by Brownson: "Philosophy and Common Sense" in the first number of the *Boston Quarterly Review*.[52]

In this very article, which, in part, was an answer to an essay of Francis Bowen on Locke and the Transcendentalists in the *Christian Examiner*, Brownson presented some leading doctrines of Cousin's philosophy. Above all, he dealt with the doctrine of "the spontaneous" and "the reflective reason." To Cousin and Brownson, "common sense" was identical with the universal beliefs of mankind, beliefs which were given by the Spontaneous Reason. Philosophy, on the other hand, was the work of the Reflective Reason, whose task was to examine these universal principles. According to this distinction between common sense and philosophy, the greater part of mankind, even if they are not inclined to philosophical reflection, are not necessarily of a lower human standard than educated people: "We shall, if we seek, often find those to have the inward experience required, who have been to no school but Nature's, and had no instructors but the internal whisperings of God's Spirit."[53] Brownson, then, gave to Cousin's doctrine of the Spontaneous Reason an interpretation in favor of the masses, while at the same time maintaining that Locke's *tabula rasa* doctrine had an undemocratic character: "True and holy for us then are the instincts of the masses; true and holy for us then are the universal beliefs of mankind."[54]

However, Brownson's article was no defense of Transcendentalism, as far as this term was considered identical with the contemporary German idealistic philosophy. At least to some extent he was inclined to accept Bowen's criticism of "what is properly called the Transcendental Philosophy." Instead, Brownson stated, "the genius of our countrymen is for Eclecticism."[55] Yet, as Brownson was well aware of Cousin's indebtedness to Schelling and Hegel, his criticism of contemporary German philosophy primarily concerned the form, not the substance. Typically enough, Brownson wrote to Cousin at about the same time: "We like Germany all the better for being filtered through the brain of France."[56]

Clarence L. F. Gohdes thinks Brownson's choice of the word Eclecticism was—as "a matter of policy"—well justified, because many already considered "Transcendentalism" nothing but "rabid speculation."[57] For another reason, too, Brownson's choice of term might be called "a matter of policy." Thus, in the polemic against Bowen who stated categorically that "either one party or the other is entirely in the wrong,"[58] Brownson was not unwise in setting forth the more tolerant Eclectic maxim: truth may be found in every philosophical system.[59]

However, just this statement of Brownson shows that the term "Eclecticism" was more than a mere matter of policy to him. As stated before, the very eclectic character of Cousin's philosophy had a strong hold on him. While in his *New Views* he had applied the thesis to religion, he now also tried to give the thesis a social and political application. In an address Brownson interpreted the doctrine of the sovereignty of the people in the light of Cousin's Eclectic principle, i.e. all systems are true insofar as they are affirmative, false insofar as they are negative, i.e. exclusive.

From his starting point Brownson argued as follows: the affirmative part of the doctrine of popular sovereignty is its emphasis on the rights of the people, in contrast to the exclusive sovereignty of the clergy and nobility. Yet the doctrine is false–because it is exclusive–if the sovereignty of the people means the right of the majority to tyrannize the minority. This doctrine, therefore, should be replaced by another, which is not exclusive: "the sovereignty of justice."

Reflecting further on the character of a real democracy, Brownson maintained that it is a "chemical compound" of monarchy, theocracy, and aristocracy. The sovereignty of the king (exclusive principle) has been replaced by the sovereignty of justice; the idea of God is identical with "universal reason" and not with the clergy (exclusive principle); finally, a real democracy has adopted and acts on the affirmative principle of aristocracy, i.e. that some are more fit to govern the State than others, whereas the aristocratic privileges of birth, exclusive as they are, find no place in a real democracy.[60]

Obviously, to Brownson Cousin's philosophy might serve different purposes. Thus Cousin's doctrine of the Spontaneous Reason provided Brownson with a firm basis for his belief in the masses of mankind, but the Eclectic method also justified his rejection of the doctrine of popular sovereignty in the sense of absolute majority rule, which, in theory, excludes the rights of the minority.

Brownson, then, linked Cousin's philosophy with the cause of the democracy. But this connection might seem a bit arbitrary. In Cousin's own country Eclecticism was hardly looked upon as a system backing left-wing political movements. To Pierre Leroux, for instance, Cousin's Eclecticism was an exponent of what he considered the contemptible *juste-milieu*: "Prenez une dose de monarchie, une dose d'aristocratie et une dose de démocratie, vous aurez la restauration ou le juste-milieu, et ce sera l'éclectisme."[61] And in the United States Caleb Sprague Henry, the Episcopalian clergyman-philosopher, who translated Cousin into English, sought, according to Brownson, "to link it [i.e. Eclecticism] with the past both in theology and politics."[62]

Indeed, Cousin's philosophy seemed to be a flexible system—or a "brilliant mosaic" as Parker called it[63]—which might "legitimate" quite different views. Even Brownson himself made the conception of the Spontaneous Reason serve two different purposes. The Spontaneous Reason was not only supposed to represent the universal beliefs of mankind, but also stand for the inspired, creative power of a great prophet or a great poet. Thus Brownson described the character of Jesus as "a spontaneous production, as coming into the world already formed, perfected and finished by the Creator's hand at one stroke."[64] And reviewing some poems by John G. Whittier, Brownson contrasted Shelley with the American poet in these interesting, though not quite convincing terms: "Whittier is the true poet of the two; and freedom is more living in him than it was in Shelley ... In one it was the result of reflection ...; in the other it is the spontaneous expression of his very soul, the outpouring of his inner and higher life."[65]

So even if Brownson adopted the term and the cause of Eclecticism while avoiding the term "Transcendentalism" about his own basic views, his idea of the Spontaneous Reason clearly shows that from a general point of view he and the Transcendentalists stood on the same ground. Thus Emerson, in his essay on "Intellect," expressed the same thought as Brownson on spontaneity and reflection: "If we consider what persons have stimulated and profited us, we shall perceive the superiority of the spontaneous or intuitive principle over the arithmetical or logical."[66]

On the whole, Brownson might be classed with the Transcendentalists, insofar as they all rejected the sensist philosophy of Locke and believed in the capacity of the soul to perceive intuitively ideas transcending the world of the senses.

More important, in this general sense, Brownson throughout his life remained a "Transcendentalist." Even O. B. Frothingham, who accused him of intellectual instability, stressed that "the Romanist," when writing *The Convert*, was "essentially a Transcendentalist." To this effect Frothingham quoted Brownson's statements in *The Convert* (page 135) that truth is the mind's "object, and it seeks and accepts it intuitively," and that "the office of proof or even demonstration, is negative rather than affirmative."[67]

In fact, Brownson, logician though he was, would have no difficulty in accepting–in the critic Harold Clarke Goddard's definition–the general Transcendentalist view of intuition: "no truth worth the knowing is susceptible of logical demonstration."[68]

But, as indicated above, already from 1838 there was an increasing difference between Brownson and the Transcendentalists "proper," above all, Emerson and Bronson Alcott, regarding the character of intuition. Brownson, having "despaired of passing from the Subjective to the Objective," was increasingly concerned with the problem of establishing the objective basis of truth, and he seems to have found a temporary solution to his problem in Cousin's philosophy.

Generally speaking, the essential difference between Transcendentalist subjectivism and Brownson's "objectivist"[69] view might be illustrated through the words of Frederic H. Hedge: "For truth is not a form of words, but a vision of the mind."[70] By contrast, Brownson would have called truth a vision *to* the mind. The following words on intuition–written in 1862–reflect both his own general "Transcendentalist" position and his own particular emphasis on the objective basis of intuition: "All principles are intuitive, given intuitively, as the condition *a priori* of the existence and activity of the mind, and our knowledge never extends beyond what is embraced in our intuitions."[71] To Brownson, then, not only were "all principles" intuitive, but they were also "given" intuitively.

But for the time being Brownson felt himself attached to the Transcendentalists, and it was not without a certain pride that he wrote in 1845: "It cannot be denied, that, in a history of American transcendentalism, the Editor of the *Boston Quarterly Review* should not be forgotten, pronounced as he was by *Blackwood's Magazine* the Coryphaeus of the sect, and by Victor Cousin one who promised to be 'a philosophical writer of the first order.' "[72]

Indeed, whether "the Coryphaeus of the sect" or one standing "somewhat apart," Brownson had much in common with the Transcendentalists. Also, in contrast to "the Old School" of Andrews Norton and Francis Bowen, they were skeptical as to much of the English philosophical and literary tradition. Instead, they hailed with enthusiasm the new philosophical and literary trends of France and Germany. Brownson's friend George Ripley set about editing a series of volumes containing different writings of French and German authors and philosophers. The first volume, containing miscellaneous writings of Cousin, Constant, and Jouffroy, was heartily welcomed by Brownson. To him, modern French and German literature was much more democratic than the English, and dealt with the two elements which constituted a real democracy: order and freedom; moreover, this philosophical literature tried to give an answer to the most vital questions of life, and if it should not succeed in giving the right answer, it furnished at least "the true method of philosophizing, of legitimating scientifically the universal beliefs of mankind." And Brownson paid a special tribute to Cousin, "the chief of the New French Philosophy."[73]

In his *Boston Quarterly Review* Brownson was careful to point out that he was no Democrat in the strictly partisan sense of the word. Being an Eclectic also in political matters, he accepted truth wherever it could be found.[74] Even less he seemed inclined to take part in the daily strife and turmoil of partisan politics. Brownson, making some reflections on the former President John Quincy Adams, whom, by the way, he considered an exception to the general rule, characterized as follows "an old statesman:" "There is something in the strifes of party, through which he has passed, so destructive to the moral sensibilities.... You would not look for reformers among statesmen."[75] However, despite his general dislike of practical politics and his skepticism about the doctrine of popular sovereignty, Brownson was a *D*emocrat in the broad sense of the term. And, consonant with his left-wing sympathies, accentuated by the economic crisis of 1837, he maintained that "productive labor" needed help and protection from government,[76] though primarily from the state governments.[77] Moreover, he generally stressed the need of the active role of government in promoting social progress: "Moral progress and social progress should never be separated."[78]

But even if he was apt to modify the old Jeffersonian doctrine that the best government is that which governs least, he followed the Jeffersonian tradition when describing "the American democrat" as "one who is jealous of power," especially the power of the Federal Government: "His first duty is to watch that the Federal Government do not swallow up the State governments."[79]

Brownson, in keeping with this broad tradition, expressed fear of the alleged strong tendency toward centralization, manifesting itself in the Federal Government as well as in the many different associations of the day. To Brownson, this general tendency threatened to merge the individual in the State and in the mass. And, anticipating his later concern with the rights of the minorities, he declared that "we must throw around each individual a bulwark of sanctity, and not permit society to break through it, though it were to do the individual an unspeakable good."[80]

To Brownson, this bulwark already existed in his own country. The Bill of Rights, trying to define the natural rights of man, protects the individual from encroachments of the State.[81]

It is interesting to note that the Frenchman Alexis de Tocqueville, whose book *Democracy in America* appeared in 1835, put forth almost the same view of the centralization of power in the United States. De Tocqueville, although stressing the importance of local authority in the country (states and townships), was convinced that "democratic nations are most likely to fall beneath the yoke of a centralized administration." The chief cause of this was the tendency "to concentrate all the strength of the government in the hands of the only power which directly represents the people."[82] However, de Tocqueville differed from Brownson in his conception of political and other associations. While Brownson regarded the associations as dangerous to individual freedom, the Frenchman considered them necessary guarantees of minorities against the tyranny of the majority.[83]

Brownson's skeptical attitude toward the growing centralization of power in the Federal Government and in the various associations came to the fore in his view of slavery and Abolitionism. On the question of slavery itself there could be no doubt: "Slavery in any form is an evil, and should be removed as soon as it can be." But he doubted both the right and the expediency of forming associations in the Northern States for the removal of slavery in the South. The only argument of the Abolitionists as of every association was "the argument of numbers," which every thinking man would refuse to listen to. The only arguments to be recommended were, as Brownson saw it, those addressed to the reason and conscience of "our Southern brethren."[84]

Since, according to Brownson, slavery was no national or federal institution, and since the states were older than the Union, the Abolitionists opposed both international and federal law, which gave the Southern States the right to solve their own slave problems. Brownson even feared that the Abolitionists, through their unwise proceedings, might consolidate slavery in the South. Hardly less detrimental to the cause of the Negro was the increasing power of the central government. In Brownson's view, the plantation owners, when they no longer feared the tendencies toward centralization from the North, would improve the conditions of the Negroes.[85] Moreover, he believed the spirit of the American institutions together with "the secret but sure workings of Christian democracy" would gradually do away with slavery. For the time being, he thought his countrymen in the North should be concerned with more immediate problems, such as the Sub-Treasury Bill, which would mean the divorce of the banking system from the Federal Government, and social reforms, which he believed to be more needed in the North than in the South.[86]

It is possible that Brownson at that time, like many other Democrats, overlooked "the affirmative or positive" aspect of the Abolitionist cause, expressed as follows by Edward M. Shepard, Martin Van Buren's biographer: "With unquenched vision they [i.e. the Abolitionists] saw the horrid picture of the individual slave life, not the general features of slavery."[87]

But after all, Brownson emphasized the rights of the individual. In principle, therefore, Brownson and the Abolitionists stood on the same ground, and later, during the Civil War, he was, to a large extent, to make common cause with them. So it was perhaps more than an incident that Brownson praised the Abolitionist poet John G. Whittier as the prototype of the American poet, whose mission was to present to the world "the American Idea" or the "perfect law of liberty:" "The realization of justice and love in the case of each individual member of the human race" and "the liberty which ... secures to every man, whether white, red, or black, high or low, rich or poor, great or small, the free exercise of all the rights and faculties, which God has given."[88] And whether called Eclectic or not, this idea was–and is–not exclusive.

Generally, throughout the year 1838 Brownson applied the Eclectic method, trying to find affirmative principles and reconciling opposites or polarities, while avoiding "Ultraism."[89] In religion, he combined "the psychological Christ" and "the historical Christ;" in philosophy, he tried to reconcile the Subjective and the Objective as "developed simultaneously in ... intellectual life;" in politics, he stressed the need for order and liberty. Consistent with his earlier position, he called for the reconciliation between reason and faith,[90] and, referring to his *New Views*, he declared that "in love ... God and man meet, lose their antithesis, and become one."[91]

Brownson, considering the first year of his *Boston Quarterly Review*, stated that although his success had not been great, it was at least greater than he had expected.[92] So not without confidence he entered upon the second year as editor of his periodical.

In religion, Brownson took active part in the controversy between "the Old" and "the New School." In a polemical article against Professor Andrews Norton, Brownson blamed him for giving only "the probable truth of Christianity" and not "its certain truth." Since, according to Norton, the authority of Christ as a teacher from God rests on his alleged miracles only, it would be necessary to lay down a canon of criticism by which to distinguish real miracles from false "miracles," genuine texts from spurious texts. But Brownson did not discover this criterion in Norton's argument, and, not willing to base his religious belief on what he thought was debatable historical evidence, held that the truths of Christianity rest on the authority of "the infinite Reason, –'a portion of which is given unto every man to profit withal,' and which [St.] John assures us 'is the true light which enlighteneth every man who cometh into the world.' " Indeed, "that truth lights her torch in the inner temple of every man's soul, whether patrician or plebeian, a shepherd or a philosopher, a Croesus or a beggar. It is only on the reality of this inner light, and on the fact, that it is universal, in all men, and in every man, that you can found a democracy, which shall have a firm basis, and which shall be able to survive the storms of human passions."[93]

No doubt Brownson expressed the same general views as those of Cousin and the American Transcendentalists. Said Victor Cousin in his University lectures of 1817: "La raison aperçoit spontanément et sans regard au moi une vérité absolue, plus quelque chose d'existant réellement en soi à quoi elle rapporte la vérité absolue." And he also declared: "La raison révèle l'être infini."[94]

George Ripley, who during the years 1839–1840 was particularly engaged in the controversy with Andrews Norton, wrote in his farewell letter of October 1, 1840, to his congregation in Purchase Street: "They [i.e. the Transcendentalists] believe in an order of truths which transcends the sphere of external senses. Their leading idea is the supremacy of mind over matter. Hence they maintain that the truth of religion does not depend on tradition, on historical facts, but has an unerring witness in the soul. There is a light, they believe, which enlighteneth every man that cometh into the world; there is a faculty in all—the most degraded, the most ignorant, the most obscure—to perceive spiritual truth when distinctly presented;..."[95]

And Theodore Parker, who also made his contributions to the controversy between "the Old" and "the New School,"[96] later characterized the gist of Norton's thought as follows: "the mass of men must accept the doctrines of religion solely on the authority of the learned, as they do the doctrines of mathematical astronomy;..."[97]

Such statements indicated the broad democratic appeal of "the New School."

Obviously, Brownson reacted against "the Old School" for its alleged logical inconsistency and too narrow views of religion. He questioned the necessity of proving by supposed supernatural events that the *man* Jesus was an authorized teacher from God. Moreover, as Andrews Norton followed Locke's principle that there is nothing in the mind not derived from sense experience, the conclusion would be that nothing can be known and decided about God and the soul, since these conceptions undoubtedly transcend human observation.[98]

In order to give more strength to his own argument about the inner light, he called to his support the famous theologian Jonathan Edwards, whom he called "the father of New England theology" and some of whose writings he had read as a boy but without understanding them. But now, taking up the study of this great Puritan theologian and philosopher, Brownson was "astonished at the wealth of his intellect, and the depth of his philosophy, and delighted with the rational and spiritual character of his theology. He had grasped some profound and universal truths, which are now almost for the first time finding their true place in our systems of philosophy; and if he still retained many errors as to his theological or metaphysical formulas, his mind stood in the front rank of the master minds of his day."[99]

Edwards held that the power of seeing and understanding the truth of the Gospel revelation was superinduced upon the soul by regeneration, while Brownson considered this power "one of the original powers of the soul." But he thought this difference to be unessential, because Brownson, too, regarded this power "as an immediate gift from God," as the light which "is in us, but is not *us*," but without which "we could have no spiritual vision." So whether this power be original in all men, i.e. given to all men originally, or given only to some men by regeneration, in both cases the power was "an immediate gift from God."

In fact, Jonathan Edwards with more or less success was made to fit into the Eclectic as well as into the Transcendentalist pattern. Brownson declared that Cousin "contends for no more than Edwards did,"[100] and from an Eclectic point of view, Brownson's generalization of Edwards's doctrine was throughout "affirmative," because it did not exclude anyone.

More important, Perry Miller, stressing the mystical aspect of the Puritan tradition, indicates a line of thought from Edwards to the Transcendentalists, and points out that tendencies toward pantheism and mysticism in Edwards's philosophy, especially his doctrine of emanation, anticipated Transcendentalism.[101] Yet it should be added that Brownson, for one, tried to avoid pantheism by distinguishing between "the Light" itself and the human soul.

Although Brownson interpreted Jonathan Edwards's doctrine of the "Spiritual and Divine Light"[102] in a rather unorthodox manner, the fact remains that he appealed to an orthodox Calvinist theologian against a Unitarian professor.

On the whole, Brownson seemed to show a growing positive understanding of orthodoxy. He thought Unitarianism to be mainly a negative system, a protest against certain antiquated tenets of belief. Its great positive doctrine, the Unity of God, was, after all, nothing unique, because not only the Trinitarians, but even the Jews and the Mohammedans believe in this doctrine. However, although Trinitarianism itself, in its formalistic-orthodox shape, was, in Brownson's view, just as obsolete as Unitarianism, he thought the faith of the Orthodox, i.e. the Calvinists, to be richer than that of the Unitarians, and he would even prefer joining the former! But what he really believed in was "a wise Eclecticism," which would combine Unitarianism and Trinitarianism in a "harmonious whole." He felt sure that the Unitarians, once they had discovered the great truth hidden under the symbol of the Trinity—a truth which the Trinitarians themselves did not see—would understand that they did not need to give up their views, but enlarge them.[103]

Obviously, Brownson by now felt his attachment to Unitarianism and the Unitarians to be only nominal. On the other hand, he stressed the importance of the doctrine of the Trinity, and along "affirmative,"

Eclectic lines: "The denial of this doctrine has been almost universally felt to be a rejection of Christianity. This feeling has been just." But, he added, "the Church has never comprehended the deep significance of the symbol it has adopted and contended for." However, Brownson scarcely convinces the reader that he himself had comprehended its deep significance. To him, the Trinity was Jesus, Truth, and Love.[104]

Brownson's eclectic attitude was also manifest in his sympathetic treatment of Catholicism. Reviewing a book on Cardinal Cheverus, Archbishop of Bordeaux and formerly Bishop of Boston, Brownson defined Protestantism, as far as it was any religion, as only "a reminiscence of Catholicism." The great fault of both Catholics and Protestants, however, was their too strong belief in human authority and their denial of reason. The Catholics made their faith dependent on the alleged infallibility of the Pope, while the Protestants made their faith dependent on the written word and its interpretation. And he did not think the Protestants any better than the Catholics: "With the Episcopalians, you must bow to the Lords Bishops; with the Presbyterians, to the Lords Presbyters; with the Congregationalists, to the Lords Brethren." Re-echoing his *New Views*, he stated that Protestantism as such was "akin to infidelity, and the resemblance between Luther and Voltaire . . . is very great." As Luther denied the authority of the Pope, Voltaire later denied the authority of the Bible. Thus Brownson, making a tremendous jump from his premise to his conclusion, confidently stated that "Voltaire was the complement of Luther." And just as Brownson now preferred Calvinism to Unitarianism, he preferred Catholicism to Protestantism.

But first of all, he preferred the Quakers, who were neither Protestants nor Catholics, and asserted only "the infallibility of the Spirit of God, a portion of which is given unto every man, and whereof every man is his own interpreter. To this the Christian world must come at last, and then the Church really universal, the true Catholic Church, will be constituted."[105]

Obviously, Brownson, applying the Eclectic formula that "each sect has an element of truth,"[106] gradually got a more positive view of religious orthodoxy, whether Calvinist or Catholic. In the *Boston Quarterly Review* of 1839 this tendency was clear, while his opposition against the Unitarianism of the Norton type was no less manifest. Yet he did not accept orthodox beliefs as such. What he still stood for, was a spiritualized liberal religion. With his emphasis on terms like "the inner light" and "the infinite Reason," his dislike of Locke's sensism and, finally, his unorthodox interpretation of orthodox dogma, Brownson was a typical representative of "the New School." The aim of the Transcendentalists, as far as religion was concerned, was mainly the same as Brownson's, i.e. to make Unitarianism more spiritual, even by means of orthodox symbols. In fact, several Transcendentalists were seeking for the symbolic meaning of the orthodox doctrines. Thus Margaret Fuller held that, since Unitarianism could not satisfy any more, the old dogmas had to be given a new interpretation,[107] and Frederic Henry Hedge reasoned along the same lines as, for instance, on the doctrine of Incarnation.[108] In the eyes of both "the Old School" Unitarians and of the Orthodox, however, the Transcendentalists, and Brownson among them, represented "the latest form of infidelity."[109]

But, as shown above, it was first of all on the basis of "a wise Eclecticism" that Brownson tried to formulate his views on religion. In fact, he was not the only American intellectual at that time who regarded Cousin's philosophy as a system to explain or justify beliefs in religious doctrines. George Ripley, who deplored the "open dread of philosophy and a secret doubt of religion in the midst of us," and declared that "we are believers in a spiritual religion; but we are not masters of a spiritual philosophy," recommended Cousin's philosophy, which appealed to the philosophic mind and established "on a rock the truth of the everlasting sentiments of the human heart."[110] And the Episcopalian C. S. Henry believed Cousin's philosophy "calculated to establish the very foundations of morality and religion against the subversive principles of Locke and Paley."[111]

Cousin himself was also aware of this American attitude toward his philosophy. In 1838, after duly praising Brownson for his articles on the new French philosophy, he called attention to the fact that it was above all "son caractère moral et religieux" that appealed to Boston and New York.[112] In any case, this was true of Brownson.

Broadly speaking, Brownson, in harmony with the "pragmatic" mainstream of American intellectual tradition, considered philosophic thought not an end in itself, but an arsenal of fundamental principles, which were to serve as a basis of his views of religion and politics. This view of philosophy as a guide to and a vindicator of truth made him emphasize the real or supposed ideological, although not narrowly "practical," tendency of "first principles." For example, in his criticism of "the Old School" Unitarianism, he stressed the point that Locke's sensism or empiricism through the minds of the more logically consistent French philosophers was turned into sheer materialism and infidelity: "All the leading French Infidels, they who did the most to overturn the Church and prepare the Reign of Terror, were disciples of Locke and anglo-maniacs."[113]

Evidently, Brownson loved to push premises to their extremes, above all, as far as the views of his opponents were concerned. For this reason, he regarded Voltaire as "the complement of Luther" and the French revolutionaries as Locke's disciples. Augustine F. Hewit was right when maintaining that Brownson in argument was like Thor with the hammer, but, like the Norse god, he lacked "subtlety of thought, fineness of discrimination, completeness of induction, and minute, accurate analysis."[114]

At first sight, his love of pushing principles to extremes and, on the other hand, his love of "a wise Eclecticism" or of reconciling opposites might seem a contradiction. But as for his own basic views, his very starting point was most often of a synthetic nature. In the above-mentioned article of his on "Cousin's Philosophy" in the *Christian Examiner* (1836), he declared that the ideas of the finite, the infinite, and their relation "are developed simultaneously in the first act of the intellectual life;" and the same basic approach some years later motivated his synthetic philosophy and his doctrine of life and communion. On this background Hewit was also right in maintaining that "in the capacity of grasping a first principle and following it out on the synthetic method lay his great power."[115] But obviously, the method Brownson used in stating the alleged tendency of Locke's philosophy was purely "analytic" and not "synthetic."

In fact, Brownson was often "analytic" in the sense of strongly one-sided. Above all, this was the case during the first years after his conversion to Catholicism and during the last years of his life. But also in his more marked "eclectic" and "synthetic" periods, his strong feelings influenced his thinking and gave it a tinge of extremism. This characteristic tendency, however, mostly found expression in categoric statements about specific phenomena and, on the whole, colored the presentation of his views; much less it concerned his basic views themselves. Also, his inclination to extremism was strengthened by a self-assertiveness not altogether sympathetic. In 1839, in an article on education, he challenged his readers in the following brusque manner:

"What theological seminary would have selected Jesus, Paul, or John, in their lifetime, for a professor of theology? Nay, what Board of Education on earth, would make the editor of the *Boston Quarterly Review* a professor in a Normal School?"[116] But, it should be added, Brownson also bluntly confessed, as he did, for example, in 1862, that he had "no humility to boast of."[117]

He was, indeed, a bundle of or even a prey to contradictory feelings. Moments of anger were followed by moments of remorse, his craving for fellowship and contact, and his desire to be gentle were in constant conflict with the aggressive tendencies of his character. Symptomatically, in 1845, just after his conversion to Catholicism, he felt assured that "we as Catholics can afford to be even generous towards our opponents." But, pen in hand, he suddenly turned belligerent and burst out: "We are strong enough, we hope, to knock down their strongest men."[118]

True, Brownson, aggressive debater that he was, made vigorous attempts to "knock down" his opponents with his formidable logical powers. And if logic did not silence his adversaries, he even sometimes used the less convincing "logic" of his fists. This once happened to a certain Hoover, who in the office of Benjamin Greene, the publisher of Brownson's review, ventured to attack the Catholic Church. Brownson resolutely threw him over the stove, or "hooverized" him, as people called similar actions later.[119] Even Brownson's friend Isaac T. Hecker found his temper very vigorous in conversations, so vigorous, indeed, that one had better take courage when disagreeing with him![120] And in 1864, though under the impact of the Civil War and in a discussion about capital punishment and the prison system, Brownson stoutly declared that "the only good use you can make of some men is to hang them."[121]

Of course, such statements must be taken with a grain of salt, and the circumstances motivating them must be accounted for. Nevertheless, utterances of that kind reflected his truculence of mind and his gruff, even scaffold-like humor. But like most people of a similar nature, Brownson seldom, if at all, bore a grudge to anyone very long. His anger was sudden and explosive, and if it was destructive, it was mostly so to himself.

His enthusiastic support of certain authors and philosophers, and his no less temperamental dislike of others also indicated his tendency to "analytic" extremism. Two examples may be sufficient. In 1864 he praised in glowing terms Vincenzo Gioberti, who had "a science, an ability, and a genius for grappling with the profoundest and most abstruse philosophical and theological problems never surpassed, if equalled, since St. Augustine."[122] On the other hand, in 1876, in his very last article, he characterized men as Charles Darwin, Thomas Henry Huxley, and Herbert Spencer as "miserable charlatans."[123]

Much owing to his strong, emotional attachment to his principles as well as to his lack of "subtlety of thought," Brownson also sometimes seemed to think even the most complicated philosophical problems to be extremely easy. Generally speaking, he never, except for the time of his brief experience with the "Free Enquirers," had any serious metaphysical doubt of God's existence. His lifelong problem was to establish philosophically the basis of his belief in God and objective, absolute ideas; but he did not doubt that they existed. In 1840, at a time when he was highly skeptical as to priesthood and churches, he wrote: "We may know that God exists as positively, as certainly, as we may know that we feel hunger or thirst, joy or grief."[124] Therefore, he reacted strongly against Norton's thesis of "the probable truth of Christianity" and not "its certain truth," and his later criticism of John Henry Newman's *An Essay on the Development of Christian Doctrine* had, partly, the same motivation.[125] And in 1874, when commenting on Cousin and his method, Brownson confidently stated that if the theory of the bridge or transition between the Subjective and the Objective be removed, philosophy would be as easy as the multiplication table![126]

But this last example also shows that Brownson, despite his tendencies to extremism, had essentially the same *primum philosophicum* or the same basic philosophical views in 1874 as in 1839. And these views were "eclectic" or, better, "synthetic," and not "analytic."

However, not all American spokesmen for the new French philosophy passed a similar rash judgment on Locke's empiricism. C. S. Henry, for one, stressed the view that it was not at all identical with the French sensist philosophy. In Locke's system, empiricism covers both sensation and reflection, while the French reduced his term to signifying sensation only.[127] And H. G. Linberg underscored the "practical wisdom" of Locke, who, contrary to the French sensist philosophers, had sufficiently common sense not to draw the most extreme conclusions of his premises.[128]

Nonetheless, to most American interpreters Cousin's philosophy pointed clearly in another direction. To Brownson it was "the only one, that has come to my knowledge, which enables me to explain, on rational principles, the phenomenon of revelation, and to find firm ground for my faith as a Christian."[129]

Commenting on an article by a contributor who maintained the necessity of God's specific revelation contained in the Bible, and, therefore, rejected Cousin's idea of Reason imparting to all men the idea of the infinite, Brownson argued that there was no factual distinction between the biblical revelation and Cousin's theory of Reason, since the idea of the infinite, according to Cousin, comes spontaneously as a revelation from without and not as a result of the activity of the human mind.[130]

Brownson did not only apply Cousin's notion of the Spontaneous or Objective Reason to support his faith in the Christian revelation; more particularly, he accepted Cousin's philosophical argument for the doctrine of the Trinity: In the Oriental religions the idea of the infinite ended in pantheism, except for the Jewish religion; but in the religions of Greece and Rome the idea of the finite ended in polytheism. The combination of pantheism and polytheism led to triunity, a conception of God as no pure unity or pure totality, but simultaneously infinite and finite, one and many, identity and diversity. However valid the argument, it helped Brownson form a broader view of the role of religious tradition: "This is the sublime God of the Christian, of the true philosopher also, the God of whom Plato had some clear intimations, and in whom the whole Orthodox Church has believed, and still believes."[131] To Brownson, the Objective Reason might even legitimate philosophically the belief of the church in Christ as the second person of the Trinity, i.e. the Objective Reason might be synonymous with Logos as described by St. John. In this case, Brownson added, those attacking the doctrine of the Trinity would be just as unphilosophical as unorthodox.[132]

Cousin himself held that, although philosophy as such cannot be a religion, Christianity was *the* religion of his "philosophie spiritualiste," while the latter was the philosophy of Christianity, but on condition that Christianity "se place, ainsi qu'il le fait souvent, dans les limites de la raison naturelle."[133] After all, these last words also signify the limits of his own understanding and acceptance of Christianity. Cousin even seemed to hold religion, included Christianity, in lower esteem than philosophy. While religion appeals to the masses, philosophy only appeals to the intelligence of the small numbers of persons making up the *élite*, the *avant-garde* of mankind.[134]

Ernest Renan, himself no orthodox Christian, but an admirer of Cousin, wrote that Cousin's greatest difficulty was to establish the alliance between his own philosophy and Christianity, and he indicated the reason: "Il est bien permis de dire cependant que ce qui frappe dans le caractère général de l'œuvre de M. Cousin n'est pas ce qu'on entend d'ordinaire par le sentiment chrétien."[135] Another French critic put it in this way: "Ils [i.e. the Eclectic philosophers] ne sont pas moins étranges au sentiment religieux, et ils n'ont pas, surtout Cousin, cette intelligence des questions religieuses, qui est faite d'abord de sympathie."[136] Above all, Emile Faguet's pointed remarks should be mentioned. He declared that Cousin had never a "sentiment religieux," but an "esprit religieux." Both to him and to Renan, Cousin's philosophy was–in Renan's words–a "sorte de philosophie d'Etat,"[137] i.e. a spiritual philosophy satisfying the demands and interests of the liberal *bourgeoisie*. But, Faguet continued, Cousin's system, *half* religious that it was, could not in the long run satisfy either the religious people or the others. The former group, therefore, were to ("devaient") return to Christianity.[138]

This statement was at least true of Brownson, who was even to accept the most orthodox form of Christianity, Roman Catholicism. In 1867, twenty-three years after his conversion to Catholicism, he wrote, in his categoric manner, that Cousin's philosophy with is "subtile and refined rationalism" might be more dangerous to religion and society than the "sensism" of Condillac and the gross materialism of Cabanis, Garat, and Destutt de Tracy.[139] But in 1839 Cousin's spiritualistic philosophy was eminently suited to strengthen Brownson's belief in his "religion of humanity" or "Christian democracy."

Yet to liberal and orthodox Christians alike, the idea of a personal God was indispensable; and Cousin's spokesmen in the United States as elsewhere had to defend him against repeated charges of pantheism. Taine remarked that Cousin in 1828 and 1833 had put forth a statement which showed such unmistakable signs of pantheism that Cousin himself, who denied having ever been a pantheistic philosopher, simply left out the questionable statement in later editions of his work. The dubious thesis read: "Selon lui [i.e. Schelling] la philosophie doit s'élever d'abord à l'Etre absolu, substance commune et commun idéal du moi et du non-moi, qui ne se rapporte exclusivement ni à l'un ni à l'autre, mais qui les comprend tous deux, et en est l'identité. Cette identité absolue du moi et du non-moi, de l'homme et de la nature, c'est Dieu. Il suit de là que Dieu est dans la nature aussi bien que dans l'homme. Ce système est vrai."[140]

Taine also quoted another statement of Cousin, but this statement was not so indicative of pantheism as the former and was, therefore, not omitted by Cousin in later editions: "Le Dieu de la conscience n'est pas un Dieu abstrait, un roi solitaire, relégué par-delà la création sur le trône désert d'une éternité silencieuse et d'une existence absolue qui ressemble au néant même de l'existence; c'est un Dieu à la fois vrai et réel, un et plusieurs, éternité et temps, espace et nombre, essence et vie, indivisibilité et totalité, principe, fin et milieu, au sommet de l'Etre et à son plus humble degré, infini et fini tout ensemble, triple enfin, c'est-à-dire à la fois Dieu, nature et humanité."[141]

However, although Cousin seemed to give up his notion of one all-comprising substance, or the absolute identity of man and nature, his view of God as creator, indicating God's necessity of creating, made him suspect of pantheistic thought. The fact that there was a close connection in his mind between these two ideas is seen in the following quotation: "Dieu n'étant donné qu'en tant que cause absolue, à ce titre, selon moi, il ne peut pas ne pas produire, de sorte que la création cesse d'être inintelligible, et qu'il n'y a pas plus de Dieu sans le monde, que de monde sans Dieu."[142] The idea of God as absolute substance identical with God as absolute cause he developed as follows: "Il n'y a point de substance et d'être en soi; que l'être en soi, c'est le néant; que tout être, s'il est, est déterminé; que sa perfection est dans celle de ses déterminations . . ."[143]

George Ripley, recalling Jonathan Edwards's doctrine of emanation, of God's "disposition" to create, said that, according to Cousin, God's will, which is essentially free, does not lie in His intelligence, which is subjected to necessity, but in His act of creating after the decision has been made.[144] C. S. Henry, defending Cousin against a charge in the Calvinist *Princeton Review* that the French philosopher was a pantheist and fatalist, maintained that Cousin presented the world and the human mind as objective realities separate from God.[145] Reasoning along the same lines of thought, a writer in the *Boston Quarterly Review* also defended Cousin against charges of pantheism and fatalism. After stating that, in Cousin's system, the *me* and the *not-me* are finite substances, while God is the infinite substance, the writer argued that God as a force is "essentially a creator." God's spontaneity in the act of creation is essentially free although accompanied by no deliberation.[146]

However, these more or less spasmodic efforts to present Cousin's philosophy as weathertight against pantheism do not sound wholly convincing. Taine's references to some of Cousin's own statements have already been mentioned. Another, although not so famous critic, Jesse Cato Daniel, claimed that Cousin's own defense against charges of pantheism did not help him. Daniel, even enlisting the support of Sir William Hamilton, said that God is not forced to create, since in that case God as absolute cause would be dependent on something else. At most God's obligation to create can only be a moral one, by no means a natural or physical necessity as, according to Daniel, maintained by Cousin.[147]

As for Brownson himself, he defended for the time being Cousin against charges of pantheism. Since Cousin maintained that the ideas of the infinite and the finite are both fundamental elements of Reason, Brownson concluded that he was no pantheist, and as for Cousin's doctrine of God as "absolute and ultimate cause," Brownson stated that "we cannot conceive of an actual creator without conceiving of an actual creation."[148]

Yet later he came to the conclusion that Cousin was liable to charges of pantheism. In a friendly letter of December 22, 1858, Brownson, after expressing his gratitude to the French philosopher, suggested objections to Cousin's idea of "being as being only in so much as it is cause," which "would make creation a necessity of his own [God's] nature."[149] But in 1867 Brownson stated point blank that Cousin was wrong in maintaining that substance was essentially cause. Even though God is *vis activa*, this does not mean that he is forced to act *ad extra*, or to create, Brownson concluded, and labeled outright Cousin a "pantheistic philosopher." And since Cousin failed to vindicate the liberty of God, he failed to vindicate the liberty of man, too. Thus, according to Brownson, his pantheism, as all pantheism, ended in fatalism.[150]

Already in 1839 Brownson indicated the difficulty of distinguishing, according to Cousin's system, between the objective or spontaneous and the reflective or subjective aspects of Reason.[151] Brownson increasingly felt that Cousin had not solved his difficulty, and in *The Convert* (page 128) he wrote that "it was always an objection in my mind to his philosophy." And in 1855 he concluded that Cousin had not succeeded in distinguishing between the spontaneous and the reflective actions of Reason and, therefore, had fallen into pantheism or egoism, which both exclude causality.[152]

As far as Cousin's Eclectic method was concerned, Brownson, particularly in the late 1850's and the early 1860's, restated his belief in the formulas "each sect has an element of truth" and "all systems are true in what they affirm, false only in what they deny, or only in that they are exclusive." In 1855 he declared that "every erroneous theory has as its basis some truth, or truth under some aspect" and "that to ascertain and accept the truth of different schools is the best way to refute their errors."[153] And in 1861 he wrote that the whole truth ought to be presented in such a manner that those addressed would find it to be in harmony with the elements of truth they already held.[154]

On the other hand, Brownson soon thought to discover the supposed "syncretic" character of Cousin's method. Pierre Leroux contended that a conciliation of two systems was possible only on condition that there be a third system superior to them both, and in his eyes, Cousin's Eclecticism was nothing but a "misérable syncrétisme," politically as well as philosophically.[155] Even more scathing–and humorous, at that –was Emerson's indictment of Eclecticism in 1838:

> Take for example the French Eclecticism, which Cousin esteems so conclusive; there is an optical illusion in it. It avows great pretensions. It looks as if they had all truth, in taking all the systems, and had nothing to do but to sift and wash and strain, and the gold and diamonds would remain in the last colander. But Truth is such a fly-away, such a slyboots, so untransportable and unbarrelable a commodity, that it is as bad to catch as light. ... Translate, collate, distil all the systems, it steads you nothing; for truth will not be compelled in any mechanical manner.[156]

Brownson reasoned much along the same lines, though less poetically, when, in 1842, he wanted to replace "eclecticism" by "synthesis," or "a system composed of shreds" by "an entire new garment woven without seam from top to bottom."[157] In a letter of September 1, 1844, to Cousin, Brownson wrote that he had "departed in some respects from the views he had gathered from the study of your own writings." More distinctly than Cousin, he found the fact of consciousness to be "the *resultante* of the conjoint activities of both subject and object," and postulated "the indissoluble synthesis of subject and object" as "the point of departure of philosophy." "Hence," he concluded, "I am synthetic rather than eclectic."[158]

But even if, as stated both in this letter and in *The Convert* (pages 128 ff.), Pierre Leroux directed his attention to the analysis of thought, Cousin had, at least indirectly, led him on the track by stating that "thought, or the fact of consciousness, is a phenomenon with three elements, subject, object, and their relation" (page 128). For this reason, Brownson in his letter of December 22, 1858, to Cousin, wrote that there was, after all, little difference between their systems. He had even "been led to think that it [i.e. his own synthetic philosophy] simply completes and renders consistent your own doctrine of reason. It substitutes synthetism for eclecticism, indeed, but escapes syncretism, and avoids alike pantheism and what I call Deism." And he added that "without your labors, I should never have been able even with the aid of Gioberti to have obtained the formula I insist on as the primum philosophicum [i.e. *Ens creat existentias*]."[159]

In 1864 Brownson even maintained that Cousin, more clearly than any one else, had proved the impossibility of deducing all science only from one single principle, and he continued:

> The Eclectic, as Cousin himself maintains, cannot safely proceed at random in his selection, but must have a scientific rule by which to determine what he will take or what he will leave. This rule is possible only on condition that he has already in principle the truth in its unity and integrity; or, in other words, we must have the true system which embraces science in its unity and universality, before we can say what in the several systems is true, or what is false. The ideal formula must be, not eclectic, but synthetic. ... It is the *Ideal* formula, the ideal judgment, which enters into every judgment of experience.[160]

Therefore, both in a broad, general sense and in a more specific sense Brownson might be called "an eclectic reasoner," and it is apt to close this passage with Brownson's own words about Cousin and his influence upon him. These words were written in 1842, when he had become more skeptical than before as to the French Eclectic philosopher: "His writings contain nearly all the materials requisite for constructing a sound system of philosophy. There is scarcely a point involved in the whole subject, on which he has not shed more or less light. We have borrowed from him the very light by which we have been enabled to criticise him; and if we are able on some points to offer a more satisfactory explanation of our mental phenomena than he has done, it is to him that we are indebted for our ability."[161]

However important all these aspects of Cousin's philosophy became to him later, Brownson for the time being particularly stressed the spiritualistic, anti-Lockian character of the Frenchman's philosophical system. Brownson, trusting the power of abstract ideas more than the efficiency of practical politics, took his ideological weapons from Cousin's arsenal to defend the cause of the democracy: "Nothing but spiritualism has the requisite unity and universality to meet the wants of the masses."[162]

To Brownson, the struggle of the parties before the election of 1840 was fundamentally a controversy between two contrasting philosophies. The Whigs, representing the moneyed classes which did not want any change, were adherents of Locke and Hobbes, i.e. of external authority in all fields. The Democrats, on the other hand, representing all humanity and not any particular class, believed that there is "a spirit in man" and "recognize in man the criterion of truth, the universal reason, whereof each man is made a partaker, the ultimate authority in all matters pertaining to religion and politics."[163] Since the Democrats believed in the "spirit in man" and rejected all "belief on authority," this party of progress was sure to win, while the Whigs were sure to lose.[164]

Obviously, Brownson had an emphatic, almost naive confidence in the power of ideas and "first principles." Yet it is doubtful whether his philosophical vindication of the Democratic Party was really understood and appreciated by most of its adherents. Even Brownson himself was skeptical on that score, and rebuked the party for being too "intent on office, on maintaining itself as a party, and too indifferent to the progress and application of free principles." But although no "party man" in the narrow sense of the word,[165] he regarded the Democratic Party as the American branch of the great democratic movement of the time and, therefore, as a highly useful instrument for carrying through reforms of the American society. And these reforms, Brownson maintained, should come as the result partly of legislation, partly of education, which ought to be religious, social, and political.[166]

Brownson's political articles in the *Boston Quarterly Review* of 1839 were rather philosophical or ideological, and as far as particular causes were concerned, such as education, slavery, and the bank system, his views were far from incendiary. But though his attitude toward central political issues of the day was moderate, his strong, almost "romantic" optimism on behalf of the Democratic Party and its future cannot but strike the reader. It is curious to note that Brownson, who shunned every kind of fatalism in his conception of God as creator, had an almost fatalistic belief in the perfectibility of man, and, at least for the time being, in the right decisions of the masses. He was quite convinced of the victory of the Democratic Party in 1840, especially so if President Martin Van Buren identified himself with the cause of the people. For Brownson there was now little doubt, apparently, that the voice of the people was the voice of God,[167] and his formerly expressed fear of the sovereignty of the people and unchecked majority rule seems to have been temporarily suppressed. But the next year was to see not only the defeat of the Democratic Party, but also the shattering of Brownson's illusions.

Also, Brownson's views of literature were, in 1839, further developed on the basis of Cousin's philosophy, especially on his distinction between the Spontaneous and the Reflective Reason. Poetry is the expression of the spontaneous, of God in man, "the spirit of his [i.e. man's] spirit," while philosophy is man's own reflection. Since God speaks in poetry, but man in philosophy, poetry is in a higher sense more "true" than philosophy. Obviously, Brownson, like Cousin, adhered to the common Romantic theory of the poet as a divinely inspired seer. God speaks through the poet as his medium: "He does not seek his song; it comes to him. It is given him. He is, to a certain extent, a passive, though not an unmoved recipient of it."[168]

However, the Spontaneous Reason, or "Word of God," is universal, i.e. it reveals truth, beauty, and goodness not only to the poet, but to every man.[169] The difference is only in degree, not in kind. Perhaps more than Cousin's other followers, Brownson emphasized the democratic aspect of the idea of the Spontaneous Reason. Buoyantly confident in the judgment of the people, Brownson exclaimed: "The popular voice is the only authority to which we may appeal in matters of poetry, or any of the fine arts . . . To say of a poet that he is unpopular, is about the same as to say that he is no poet at all."[170]

More interesting than a general outline of his literary theory is to see how he applied it, especially to the English poet William Wordsworth. Though Brownson admitted that Wordsworth had poetic sensibility to a high degree, his poems were essentially "creations of reflection," not of spontaneity. Even his praised simplicity was artificial and, worse still, he did "not seem to us capable of being simple without approaching the silly."[171] The resentment of the elder Wordsworth to the great French Revolution was another reason why, in Brownson's opinion, he was not a "popular" poet. Evidently, it was the democratic aspect of this revolution Brownson had in mind, and not its religious character.

He admitted that Wordsworth often wrote about poor people, whom he regarded with sympathy. But, the reviewer asserted, this sympathy was scarcely anything more than condescension. Wordsworth would like to give alms to the poor, but not make any serious attempts to abolish poverty. True democracy, Brownson eloquently stated, does not idealize the beggar, but loves the man in the beggar.[172] Although Brownson stressed man's need for strong activity, he conceded that Wordsworth with his different emphasis somehow fitted into the quiet times that had to come after the stormy eighteenth century. Notwithstanding, he also complained that Wordsworth was not made of "sterner stuff," that he was not more "robust and manly," and instead praised the "passive virtues," like innocence. Brownson, for one, did not hold innocence in high esteem: after all, "it consists in the absence of sin, not in the presence of virtue."[173]

Finally, Brownson reacted against what he called Wordsworth's "babyworship:" "It is a fact well attested by experience, that the corruptions of parents descend to their children; and who dare say that the corruptions of Adam's nature, by his transgression, have not passed upon all his posterity?"[174] This statement indicated that Brownson, although he believed that every man was partaker of "the universal reason, or Word of God, uttering itself in us,"[175] did not accept Rousseau's doctrine of man's natural goodness.

In fact, Brownson's general impression of Wordsworth was far from flattering: "Wordsworth's mind is full of narrow and local prejudices, as is unfortunately the case with most Englishmen."[176] However, Emerson, who in general was more wary of expression than Brownson, was no less blunt in his appraisal of Wordsworth after visiting him in 1833: "He surprised by the hard limits of his thought. To judge from a single conversation, he made the impression of a narrow and very English mind; of one who paid for his rare elevation by general tameness and conformity."[177]

It has been said that Wordsworth's "appeal is to the mature mind."[178] However this may be, Wordsworth's poetry never appealed to Brownson. In an essay on the English poet written sixteen years later, Brownson expressed in general the same view as he did in 1839, and he even pointed out more strongly that Wordsworth lacked intellectual power and was too fond of "descriptive poetry." His popularity (with Brownson, this word had certainly been devaluated since 1839) rested on a "dreamy and misty German subjectivism, which tends to conceal the poverty of meaning and his want of manly vigor." Brownson made allowance only for his minor poems, such as "We are Seven," which he thought to be beautiful.[179]

In contrast to the alleged languid and dreamy poetry of Wordsworth, Brownson wanted a literature about "the really living, moving, toiling and sweating, joying and sorrowing people."[180] Moreover, literature should never be regarded as an end, only as a means. The principal task of American literature was to present and embody the ideas of democratic liberty and equal rights, political and social, of every human being. Since literature was the expression of the national life, and the great authors were themselves representative of the spirit of the age, no particular efforts to create an American literature were necessary. As Brownson saw it, literature was determined by invariable and necessary laws. Yet American writers, instead of drawing "their inspirations from books, from the past, from a clique or coterie," which they had been inclined to do, should accelerate the coming of the real American literature by appealing to and mingling with the common people.[181]

In an address on American literature, delivered before the United Brothers Society of Brown University, at Providence, R. I., on September 3, 1839, Brownson more particularly stressed the social character of the coming American literature. In the economic and social struggle between "the accumulator of wealth" and the workingman, to him the real producer of wealth, American literature would be born.[182]

But his very suggestion of a coming economic and social class struggle indicated that Brownson's "Christian democracy," which he thought to be "a wise Eclecticism" or a combination of Christianity and democracy, was beginning to assume a more "militant" or extreme character.

[1] *Early Life*, pp. 214, 215, 220, 230, 233.
[2] Clarence L. F. Gohdes, *The Periodicals of American Transcendentalism*, p. 48.
[3] *Early Life*, pp. 214–215.
[4] As for the first volume (1838), the Boston Public Library possesses the copy of Theodore Parker, who wrote in the margin the names of the authors (Gohdes, *op.cit.*, p. 48).

5 *The Convert*, pp. 89–90.
6 *Ibid.*, p. 90.
7 *Early Life*, p. 216.
8 *Ibid.*, p. 206.
9 Letter to Convers Francis, December 18, 1840 (Gohdes, *op.cit.*, pp. 81–82).
10 *Experience as a Minister*, p. 314.
11 Gohdes, *op.cit.*, p. 81.
12 *Boston Quarterly Review*, I (Jan. 1838), p. 4. Hereafter referred to as *BQR*.
13 *Free Enquirer*, II (Jan. 2, 1830).
14 *Philanthropist*, II (Jan. 14, 1832), 87.
15 *The Convert*, p. 85.
16 *BQR*, I (Jan. 1838), 6.
17 *Ibid.*, pp. 10, 11, 18.
18 *Ibid.*, pp. 15, 20.
19 *BQR*, I (April 1838), 129.
20 *Ibid.*, pp. 130–132.
21 *Ibid.*, pp. 133–137.
22 *Ibid.*, pp. 140–148.
23 *BQR*, I (Oct. 1838), 445–446.
24 *Ibid.*, p. 447.
25 *Ibid.*, pp. 460–464.
26 *Ibid.*, pp. 448, 451, 453, 465.
27 *Brownson's Quarterly Review*, III (July 1846), 408.
28 *Works*, XI, 348.
29 "Lacordaire and Catholic Progress," *Works*, XX, 258, 262.
30 *Ibid.*, p. 262.
31 See *American Christianity: An Historical Interpretation with Representative Documents*, ed. H. Shelton Smith et al., II (New York, 1963), pp. 361, 401–407.
32 See, for example, "The Church Not a Despotism" *(BrQR*, 1862), *Works*, XX, 235–236, and "Civil and Religious Freedom" *BrQR*, 1864), *Works*, XX, 322.
33 Merle Curti, *The Growth of American Thought* (2nd ed., New York, 1951), pp. 307–308.
34 *BQR*, I (Oct. 1838), 501, 513.
35 *Ibid.*, pp. 502, 504–505.
36 *Ibid.*, pp. 507–509.
37 *Ibid.*, p. 509.
38 *Ibid.*, pp. 510–512.
39 *New England Quarterly*, XVIII (Sept. 1945), 368–390, esp. 376–380.
40 *BQR*, I (Oct. 1838), 431.
41 "Emerson and German Philosophy," *New England Quarterly*, XVI (March 1943), 61.
42 *G. A.*, VII (Feb. 7, 1829), 37.
43 *BQR*, I (Oct. 1838), 506, 508.
44 *Ibid.*, pp. 511–512.
45 *The Convert*, p. 85.
46 *The Brownson Papers* at Notre Dame University.
47 "Cousin's Philosophy," *Christian Examiner*, XXI, 3rd series, III (Sept. 1836), 45, 54, 57.
48 *Ibid.*, 44, 62. Jesse Cato Daniel, among others, maintained that Cousin was always operating with *a priori* principles (Introduction to *The Philosophy of the Beautiful* [London, 1848], pp. xiii–xxx).
49 *Les philosophes classiques du XIXe siècle en France* (5e éd.; Paris, 1882), p. 83.

[50] "Cousin's Philosophy," p. 63. George Ripley, too, thought the only justification of concluding from the finite to the infinite lay in "the necessity of our reason" *(Specimens of Foreign Standard Literature*, ed. George Ripley, I [Boston, 1838], pp. 203–206). And the clergyman-philosopher Caleb Sprague Henry contended that faith alone could leap the gulf between the finite and the infinite (Preface to 3rd ed. of his translation of Cousin's *Elements of Psychology* [Ney York, 1842], p. xvi).

[51] "Cousin's Philosophy," pp. 49, 50.

[52] Quoted in Victor Cousin, *Fragments philosophiques*, V (5e éd.; Paris, 1866), p. lxxxiii. The second article in question was "Recent Contributions to Philosophy," *Christian Examiner*, XII, 3rd series, IV (May 1837), an article which primarily dealt with the ethical aspect of Cousin's philosophy.

[53] *Works*, I, 14.

[54] *Ibid.*, pp. 15, 17. Yet he added that truth, philosophically exposed, was for the few (p. 18).

[55] *Ibid.*, p. 3. See also "Recent Contributions to Philosophy," p. 186.

[56] Letter of Nov. 15, 1836 to Cousin: *The Brownson Papers* at the University of Notre Dame.

[57] *The Periodicals of American Transcendentalism*, p. 52.

[58] "Locke and the Transcendentalists," *Christian Examiner*, XXIII, 3rd series, V (Nov. 1837), p. 183.

[59] "Philosophy and Common Sense" *(BQR*, I), *Works*, I, 2. See also "Recent Contributions to Philosophy," pp. 195–196.

[60] "Democracy" (Address of the Democratic State Convention of Massachusetts, held at Worcester, Sept. 20, 1837), *Works*, XV, 3, 17–19.

[61] *Réfutation de l'Eclectisme* (Paris, 1839), p. 69.

[62] Letter of June 23, 1838 to Cousin: *The Brownson Papers* at Notre Dame University.

[63] *Experience as a Minister*, p. 301.

[64] *BQR*, I (April 1838), 138.

[65] *BQR*, I (Jan. 1838), 25.

[66] Quoted in *Essays, First and Second Series* (Everyman's Library; London and New York, 1947), p. 182.

[67] *Transcendentalism in New England* (New York, 1876), p. 132.

[68] *Studies in New England Transcendentalism* (New York, 1960), p. 5.

[69] See n. 41.

[70] *Theological Progress during the Last Half Century: A Sermon* (Providence, 1878), p. 10.

[71] *Works*, I, 515.

[72] *Works*, IV, 25.

[73] "Specimens of Foreign Literature," *BQR*, I (Oct. 1838), 443, 444.

[74] "Democracy" *(BQR*, I), *Works*, XV, 106.

[75] *BQR*, I (April 1838), 152, 153.

[76] "Sub-Treasury Bill" *(BQR*, I), *Works*, XV, 106.

[77] See *BQR*, III (April 1840), 215.

[78] BQR, I (Jan. 1838), 127.

[79] "The American Democrat" (Review of J. F. Cooper's book of 1838 with the same title), *BQR*, I (July 1838), 375.

[80] *BQR*, I (July 1838), 377.

[81] "Democracy," *Works*, XV, 27.

[82] *Democracy in America*, ed. R. H. Heffner (New York, 1956), p. 71.

[83] *Ibid.*, p. 97.

84 *BQR*, I (April 1838), 191.
85 "Slavery – Abolitionism" *(BQR,* I), *Works,* XV, 48, 54–55, 60–61, and "Abolition Proceedings" *(BQR,* I), *Works,* XV, 69, 78.
86 *Works,* XV, 77, 84, 45, 85 (from the same articles mentioned in n. 85).
87 *Martin Van Buren* (Boston and New York, 1899), p. 270.
88 *BQR*, I (Jan. 1838), 23–24.
89 Title of article in *BQR*, I (July 1838), 377–384.
90 *BQR*, I (April 1838), 178.
91 *Ibid.*, 148.
92 *BQR*, I (Oct. 1838), 516.
93 "Norton on the Evidences of Christianity," *BQR,* II (Jan. 1839), 89, 96, 97, 111.
94 Quoted in Victor Cousin, *Premiers essais de philosophie* (6e éd.; Paris, 1873), pp. 264, 313.
95 Octavius Brooks Frothingham, *George Ripley*, pp. 84–85.
96 O. B. Frothingham, *Transcendentalism in New England*, p. 132.
97 *Experience as a Minister,* p. 312.
98 *BQR*, I (Jan. 1839), 97, 105.
99 *Ibid.*, pp. 99–100.
100 *BQR*, III (July 1840), 306.
101 "From Jonathan Edwards to Emerson," *New England Quarterly,* XIII (Dec. 1940), 589–617.
102 Quoted in Walter Fuller Taylor, *A History of American Letters* (New York, 1947), p. 31.
103 *BQR*, II (July 1839), 379–384.
104 *Ibid.*, p. 335.
105 *Ibid.*, pp. 387–389.
106 *Ibid.*, p. 385.
107 *Memoirs,* II (Boston, 1884), 84–85 (Quoted in Perry Miller, "From Jonathan Edwards to Emerson," *New England Quarterly,* XIII [Dec. 1940], 612).
108 Joseph L. Blau, *Men and Movements in American Philosophy* (New York, 1953), p. 117.
109 Andrews Norton's well-known characterization of Transcendentalism in the very title of his *A Discourse on the Latest Form of Infidelity; Delivered at the Request of the "Association of the Alumni of the Cambridge Theological School," on the 19th of July, 1839* (Cambridge, Mass., 1839).
110 "Victor Cousin. Introductory Notice," *Specimens of Foreign Standard Literature,* ed. George Ripley, I (Boston, 1838), pp. 37, 38, 41–42.
111 "Preface" to his translation of Cousin's *Elements of Psychology* (3rd ed.; New York, 1842), p. xviii.
112 "Avertissement – de la troisième édition" (1838), *Fragments philosophiques,* V (5e éd.; Paris, 1866), p. lxxxiii.
113 *BQR*, II (Jan. 1839), 106.
114 Obituary in *Catholic World,* XXIII (June 1876), 371.
115 *Ibid.*, p. 371.
116 *BQR*, II (Oct. 1839), 410.
117 "The Church Not a Despotism" *(BrQR), Works,* XX, 223.
118 *BrQR*, II (Oct. 1845), 548.
119 *Middle Life*, p. 635.
102 "Dr. Brownson in Boston," *Catholic World,* XLV (July 1887), 469. Yet Hecker added that Brownson did not want any submissive consent to his views.
121 *BrQR*, National series, I (April 1864), 255.

[122] "The Giobertian Philosophy" *(BrQR), Works*, II, 212.

[123] "Philosophy of the Supernatural" *(American Catholic Church Review), Works*, II, 277.

[124] *BQR*, III (July 1840), 275.

[125] Newman's support of the Anglican Bishop Butler's thesis: "a collection of weak evidences makes up a strong evidence" *(An Essay on the Development of Christian Doctrine*, p. 107) could hardly expect any sympathy from Brownson. (I take the reference from Maynard's biography on Brownson, p. 199.) See also *Apologia pro vita sua* (London and New York, 1955), pp. 44, 186–187.

[126] *BrQR*, Last series, II (Oct. 1874), 561–562.

[127] "Introduction" to his translation of Cousin's *Elements of Psychology* (2nd ed.; New York, 1838), pp. xiii–xiv n.

[128] "Notes by the Translator" in his translation of Cousin's *Introduction to the History of Philosophy* (Boston, 1832), p. 454. Linberg added that the Scottish philosophers, "the American revolution and the constitution of the United States were the effects of British spirit as well as of British wisdom."

[129] *BQR*, II (Oct. 1839), 454–455n.

[130] *Ibid.*, pp. 449–477.

[131] *Ibid.*, p. 456.

[132] *BQR*, II (April 1839), 179.

[133] "Avertissement de la seconde édition" (1845) of *Premiers essais de philosophie* (6e éd.; Paris, 1873), pp. 13–14.

[134] "Préface de la deuxième édition" (1833) of *Fragments philosophiques*, V (5e éd.; Paris, 1866), lxxi–lxxii.

[135] *Œuvres completes de Ernest Renan, Edition définitive établie par Henriette Psichari*, II (Paris, 1948), pp. 75, 78.

[136] Ch. Adam, *Cousin, Jouffroy et la métaphysique individualiste* (Dijon, 1893), p. 60.

[137] Renan, *op.cit.*, p. 70.

[138] *Politiques et moralistes du dix-neuvième siècle* (2e série, 5e éd.; Paris, 1903), pp. 229, 277.

[139] "Victor Cousin and his Philosophy" *(Catholic World), Works*, II, 326.

[140] *Les philosophes classiques du XIXe siècle en France* (5e éd., Paris, 1882), pp. 134–135.

[141] Cousin, "Préface de la première édition de 1826," *Fragments philosophiques*, V (5e éd.; Paris, 1866), xxvii, and Taine, *op.cit.*, 139.

[142] Taine, *op.cit.*, p. 139 (Quoted in the 2nd preface of 1833 of Cousin's *Fragments philosophiques)*.

[143] Cousin, "Avertissement de la seconde édition de 1845," *Premiers essais de philosophie* (6e éd.; Paris, 1873), p. 18.

[144] "Notes," *Specimens of Foreign Standard Literature*, I (Boston, 1838), pp. 255 274.

[145] "Preface" to the 3rd ed. of his translation of Cousin's *Elements of Psychology* (New York, 1842), pp. vi–xii, and "Preface" to the 4th ed. (New York, 1856), p. xliii.

[146] *BQR*, II (Oct. 1839), 435–448.

[147] "Appendix" to his translation of Cousin's *The Philosophy of the Beautiful* (London, 1848), pp. 183–186.

[148] *BQR*, III (July 1840), 291, 301–302.

[149] *The Brownson Papers* at Notre Dame University.

[150] *Works*, II, 316, 317, 318.

[151] *BQR*, II (April 1839), 178.

152 "The Problem of Causality" *(BrQR), Works,* I, 399.
153 "What Human Reason Can Do" *(BrQR), Works,* I, 310, 323.
154 *Works,* XX, 143.
155 *Réfutation de l'Eclectisme* (Paris, 1839), pp. 69, 70, 95.
156 "Literary Ethics – an Oration Delivered before the Literary Societies of Dartmouth College, July 24, 1838," *The Complete Works, Concord Edition,* I (Boston and New York, 1903), 171.
157 "Reform and Conservatism" *(BQR),* V), *Works,* IV, 87.
158 *The Brownson Papers* at Notre Dame University.
159 *Ibid.*
160 *Works,* II, 268, 269, 270.
161 *Works,* IV, 359.
162 *BQR,* II (Oct. 1839), 405–406.
163 *Ibid.,* p. 405.
164 "Democracy and Reform," *BQR,* II (Oct. 1839), 504, 505, 512.
165 *Ibid.,* pp. 513, 516.
166 *Ibid.,* pp. 402, 416.
167 "Prospects of the Democracy" *(BQR),* II), Works, XV, 44. See also "Sub-Treasury Bill" *(BQR,* I), *Works,* XV, 107.
168 *BQR,* II (April 1839), 143.
169 *Ibid.,* p. 141.
170 *Ibid.,* p. 150.
171 *Ibid.,* pp. 155, 159.
172 *Ibid.,* pp. 165 ff.
173 *Ibid.,* pp. 161–162, 168.
174 *Ibid.,* p. 162.
175 *Ibid.,* p. 141.
176 *Ibid.,* p. 168.
177 *The Complete Works, Concord Edition,* V (Boston and New York, 1903–1904), p. 24.
178 B. Ifor Evans, *A Short History of English Literature* (Penguin Books, Middlesex, England; New York, 1944), p. 37.
179 "Wordsworth's Poetical Works" *(BrQR,* II), *Works,* XIX, 425–428.
180 "American Literature" *(BQR,* II), *Works,* XIX, 18.
181 *Ibid.,* pp. 15–20.
182 "American Literature: An Oration, Delivered before the United Brothers Society of Brown University, at Providence, R. I., Sept. 3, 1839" *(BQR,* III), *Works,* XIX, 35, 37.

XI
"Charles Elwood"

Already in 1832 Brownson planned to write a book about his "conversion" from skepticism to "an unwavering and joyful belief in our God —my Father,"[1] and at about the same time he even foreshadowed his coming book by writing in his journal a kind of "short story," which reflected his own development from strict Calvinism to downright infidelity. In connection with this story, which bore the characteristic title "Priest and Infidel," Brownson, in harmony with his general inclination to steer a middle course, wrote about himself as follows: "The writer knows full well the evil effects of both extremes. He has grown dark and desperate under the influence of Calvanism [sic], and felt his affections wither and his sympathy die, under the dread dominion of scepticism." Instead, he had found comfort and strength in a "rational religion," which corresponded to and met the demands of the "religious sentiment natural to man."[2]

These words, sketchy though they were, really signalized both the contents of his forthcoming book and his purpose for writing it. In the preface to *Charles Elwood; or, The Infidel Converted*, which was published in 1840, but written for the most part as early as in 1834,[3] Brownson wrote: "I am willing the public should take the book as an account which I have thought proper to give of my own former unbelief and present belief. So far as it can be of any use, I am willing that what is here recorded should have the authority of my own experience."[4]

In order to make his book more attractive to the common reader and, as he himself pointed out later, to strengthen and throw into relief its arguments, Brownson chose the novelistic form. But he emphasized that the novelistic elements of his book were purely fictitious, and that the author was identical with Charles Elwood, "the hero of his story," only "so far as the purely spiritual experience detailed is concerned." And "beyond this," he added, having particularly the love story in mind, "he has nothing in common with him."[5]

But this mixture of novelistic ingredients and long conversations on theological and philosophical subjects hardly made the book more attractive, either to those who wanted a real novel and not lengthy discussions on abstruse topics, or to those who wanted such discussions and were distracted by literary features.

True, this blend of novel and treatise seems inorganic or, in Brownson's own terminology, "syncretic" and not "synthetic" or clearly indicative of "a wise Eclecticism." In any case, even if Brownson defended his own use of a love story in his book, and this because it presented the theme of the eternal struggle between human love and religion,[6] he later repeatedly criticized other writers for mixing theology and romance. Thus in 1847 he maintained that a combination of novel and theological treatise was nothing but a "literary hybrid."[7] In the following year he was more definite, declaring that a novel has a story, a plot, and demands action, whereas a logical discussion presupposes calm and interests the intellect. Consequently, no "unity of effect" can be obtained, so much the less because "profane love" and religion are virtual contrasts to each other like oil and water.[8] Obviously, it is the comparatively recent convert to Catholicism who speaks so categorically.

However, in 1871 Brownson gave a more complete and balanced view of the whole question. After stating that "this style of novel, half theology and half romance, is not to our minds the highest one," he emphasized the synthesis of nature and grace as the real purpose of Catholic novel writing. Novels, he declared, should be filled with Catholic spirit, but not with specific doctrines, not even special moral doctrines.[9]

The "slight thread of fiction"[10] or the plot of Brownson's novel is as follows: Charles Elwood is regarded as an infidel by the orthodox people in the village where he lives. When his *fiancée*, Elizabeth Wyman, turns Christian, the pastor of the orthodox church at the place exerts all his influence in making Elwood, too, a convert to the orthodox faith. But realizing that his efforts are of no avail, the minister, with the aid of Elizabeth's recently converted and fanatical brother George, forces her to break off her engagement with "the atheist." Yet she does so only after the severest struggles of conscience and a most moving, but vain appeal to her *fiancé* to become a Christian.

Charles Elwood, utterly despairing of anything religious, becomes a social reformer; but feeling lonely and growing disappointed with mankind, he finally gives up his work of world reform based on "enlightened self-interest." He comes under the influence of a Mr. Howard and a preacher, Mr. Morton, who advocate–as Brownson had written in the *Philanthropist*–a "rational religion" corresponding to the "religious sentiment natural to man." Stressing the point that free investigation and the support of the democratic cause are in harmony with Christianity, and justifying on an alleged rational basis the belief in God and the immortality of the soul, they finally manage to "convert" young Elwood to their, i.e. to Brownson's own, rational or natural religion.

During the long, didactic conversations on theology and philosophy, the reader almost forgets Elizabeth and her fate. Yet the author, recapturing his "slight thread of fiction," rounds out his novel with these words: " 'And Elizabeth, will you tell us nothing of her?' Pardon me. I have planted wild flowers on her grave, and watered them with my tears."[11]

True, the plot is meager, and the novelistic theme: the struggle between human love and religion, is only given a fragmentary treatment. But although Elizabeth's gentle character and her tragic fate may touch even a modern reader, the "story" is dangerously close to sentimentality. Yet from the point of view of fiction, the most serious objection to be raised against Brownson's book concerns his character drawing. Most of the characters, particularly the Calvinist ministers, are stereotypes rather than individuals. Elwood's contempt for them even makes him accuse them of downright hypocrisy, and he seems at a loss to find any conciliating feature at all in their behavior.[12] Brownson even called the bigot minister of the orthodox church in the village *Mr. Smith*, the very same name borne by the minister who had been pastor of the Presbyterian Church of which Brownson had once been a member. As might be expected, the Rev. Reuben Smith felt very much offended, but in the ensuing correspondence between him and Brownson, the latter wrote that the name used was wholly incidental, so much the more because it was very common. And this seemed to satisfy the real Mr. Smith.[13] In all events, Brownson's categoric condemnation of the orthodox ministers sounds little convincing. When satire and caricature are exaggerated and not even mellowed by humor as, for instance, in Sinclair Lewis's *Elmer Gantry*, they cannot but miss their aim.

No doubt, when writing this book, Brownson had his unhappy Presbyterian experience in mind. But even if he generally distrusted or even despised Presbyterianism and Calvinism, in this connection it might be just to mention one of the very few exceptions to this general rule. In

1869, when reviewing Henry Ward Beecher's novel *Norwood*, he declared that, though far from relishing Calvinism, he preferred Presbyterianism and "even" Methodism to rationalism or mere naturalism. And more particularly, he definitely preferred oldtime Puritans to modern liberals, who, like Emerson, "despise Christianity too much to offer any direct opposition to it."[14] Yet as far as "the Beecher genius" was concerned, Brownson, though admitting "passages of rare force and vigor" in Harriet Beecher Stowe's books *Uncle Tom's Cabin* and *The Minister's Wooing*, found that it was "not lyrical or dramatic, but essentially militant and prosaic."[15] However this might be, at least Brownson's own description of Calvinist ministers in his novel *Charles Elwood* was "essentially militant and prosaic."

The only minister who is something more than a cliché is the clergyman-philosopher Morton, but he is no Calvinist either. Instead, he seems more like Brownson himself, judging from this "portrait" of him given by the author:

> The preacher, a Mr. Morton, was a tall, well-proportioned man, with something a little rustic in his appearance, indicating that his life had not been spent in the circles of the gay and the fashionable. Though far from being handsome, his features were striking and impressed themselves indelibly upon the memory. His dark complexion, and small, restless black eyes bespoke an active and also an irritable disposition, and assured you that he might say some bitter things. His head was large, and his brow elevated and expanded. His face bore the marks of past struggle, whether with passion, the world, or sorrow, it was not easy to say. He was apparently under forty years of age, but you felt that he was a man who could speak from experience, that he was in fact no ordinary man, but one who had a biography, if you could only get at it. There was something almost repulsive about him, and yet you were drawn insensibly towards him.[16]

I have quoted this description at length, because it seems such an excellent "self-portrait" of the author. Comparing it with the daguerreotype of Brownson from about the same time (*Works*, IV), one cannot help being struck by the similarity. And as for the "interior portrait" of Mr. Morton, the similarity with the author himself is no less striking. Undoubtedly, Brownson had "an irritable disposition" and "might say some"—or even many—"bitter things." But although he might be "almost repulsive," at least some people "were drawn insensibly towards him."

At any rate, Morton is Brownson's own spokesman on religion and philosophy. As the author indicated in the preface to his book, Morton is "a kindred spirit with M. Victor Cousin, though perhaps more of a theologian."[17] Thus, Morton's eclectic approach to Christian doctrines is a theological application of Cousin's method; further, his idea of Reason in its spontaneous and its reflective modes and, also, his demonstration of God's existence clearly reflect Cousin's philosophy.

In a larger perspective, Morton voices views and sentiments representative of Transcendentalism. His emphasis on the inner light, the universal character of divine inspiration and the spiritual independence of the individual show his Transcendentalist leanings. Also, Morton's view of the biblical miracles and his symbolical interpretation of Christian dogma represent the Transcendentalist attitude. More important, his idea of spirit as "the only reality" makes him strike almost Emersonian tones: "That which is seen, which we examine with our senses, is never to us, did we but know it, the thing itself. It is mere appearance, shadow, pointing to a reality back of it, a substance which sends it forth, but which it is not. We always call that which is permanent, immutable, in the thing,–not its apparition,–the thing itself, and this always transcends the senses,–is transcendental. Spirit is, in fact, the only reality of which we ever do or ever can form any conception. Men are materialists only because they misinterpret or misname their own beliefs."[18]

And if Lindsay Swift is right in maintaining that the primary aim of Transcendentalism was to assure "the supremacy of man himself and of each and every man as well,"[19] Morton was, indeed, an eloquent representative of Transcendentalism:

They [i.e. some men] are afraid of crowds and look with a sort of contempt on the movements of multitudes. They have great confidence in the capacity of the people to be instructed, in their capacity of progress; but none in their spontaneous power of perceiving truth and obeying its impulses.... [They say] the people have no light in themselves. Here and there you shall find a man who may be called a sun shining with its own light, but all the rest are mere planets and satellites, shining only as they are shined upon. Now I protest against this doctrine. The true light enlighteneth every man who cometh into the world. Every man has the true light in himself, and is a sun, and not a planet. If the masses are not aware of this, the reason perhaps may be found in the fact that they are in the habit of looking outward, not inward. Each man, instead of looking into himself for light, looks abroad, and up to some great man, learned man, or, what is worse still, to some rich man.[20]

The fact that Brownson's book was published in 1840, although most of it was written six years earlier, indicates that his views did not undergo any considerable change during those years. But in *Charles Elwood* his Transcendentalist tendencies were more manifest than in his previous productions. Above all, in his *New Views* of 1836, despite his belief in the holiness of all things, he wanted to reconcile two real extremes: spirit and matter, whereas in *Charles Elwood* matter seemed to be "mere appearance" or a "shadow." True, as in *New Views*, the author of *Charles Elwood* showed a deep respect for the agelong "convictions" of "the church."[21] Yet in the latter book Brownson was not very much concerned with the historical development of the church; nor did he seem so skeptical about Protestantism as he was in his *New Views*. Even if Mr. Howard, Elwood's gentle host, praises Catholicism at the expense of Protestantism, he also seems to think that Protestantism contains germs of something better to come: "If Protestantism did not mark a transition to something better, I should arrange myself with the Catholics rather than with the Protestants."[22] Moreover, in *New Views* Brownson considered the new church not only an invisible power, but also an outward organization, while Morton in *Charles Elwood* declared: "The true church of Christ, the true catholic church, I hold therefore to be not an outward, visible church, but an inward and invisible church." In other words, "the church" should be a spiritual kingdom permeated by "righteousness and peace and joy in the Holy Ghost."[23]

Therefore, it is hardly beyond the mark to conclude that Morton's —and Brownson's—emphasis on spirit as "the only reality" and his idea of "the church" as something purely "inward and invisible" make *Charles Elwood*, as far as the main argument is concerned, a Transcendentalist treatise. And one may also conclude that Brownson's *New Views* with its highly critical attitude toward Protestantism and its positive appraisal of historical Catholicism was more indicative of his Romeward drift than *Charles Elwood*, published four years later.

However, as a result of Howard's and Morton's arguments young Elwood feels convinced that he has passed "from infidelity to an unwavering belief in God and the supernatural origin of Christianity."[24] Notwithstanding, he is still disowned by "the Christan world," which as before regards him as an infidel. This cannot but surprise him, because he thinks his views coincide with those of "the universal church, though presented perhaps in an uncommon light."[25]

From a traditional Christian point of view, not only his presentation of his ideas, but also these ideas themselves were rather "uncommon." Indeed, Elwood's spiritual guide Howard does not recognize Christianity as a distinctly "revealed" or "supernatural" religion. Premising that "Christianity is not a creed, but a life," he concludes that belief in Christ simply means love of "truth and goodness" and the realization of the natural qualities of man. The doctrine of an original Fall is not taken into account, nor does he think there is any difference at all between "the teachings of the universal reason" and "the revelations of God."[26]

In a later "review" article on his own book Brownson restated Howard's basic thesis: "there is no radical difference between the inward life of an honest, intelligent unbeliever and that of an honest, intelligent believer." Accordingly, the "conversion" of an infidel did not mean to give him or lead him to a new and different faith, but to enable him to understand the faith he already had, or to give him faith in his own faith. What "faith," then, did Charles Elwood have even in his "infidel" state? He had faith in social reforms and philosophical inquiry, and Howard showed him that this "faith" was in complete harmony with Christianity and not opposed to it, as he had been led to believe. What it all boiled down to was that Howard—and Brownson—presented Christianity as identical with "life" and not with any "speculative belief," and a Christian as one who is willing to die for truth and "the redemption of man, as Jesus did."[27]

Undoubtedly, this reasoning made Christianity lose almost every trace of its distinct character, and—at least in theory—reduced it to natural religion. Brownson's "religion of humanity," which he had advocated with more or less strength since the beginning of the 1830's, was again stated in its nakedness. No wonder, therefore, that Dr. Francis Wayland of Brown University in the orthodox *Christian Review* suggested another title of Brownson's book: *Charles Elwood; or, Christianity Converted.*[28]

However, Elwood's desire to be in harmony with the doctrines of "the universal church" at least indicated his respect for Christian tradition, and according to Henry F. Brownson, his father at that time really believed more of Christianity in its traditional sense than his book gave him credit for, and whittled down Christianity to its barest minimum in order to "convert" infidels. At any rate, Henry F. Brownson has an interesting point when maintaining that his father's later argument for the existence of God, as elaborated in his series of articles in "Refutation of Atheism" (1873–1874), was contained in germ already in *Charles Elwood*.[29]

In any case, despite Brownson's generally unorthodox conception of Christianity in this book, Morton's argument for the existence and attributes of God is primarily a philosophical question, which does not necessarily concern the theological differences between orthodox and liberal Christians. It was perhaps first of all Morton's reasoning on this subject that caused a reviewer in the liberal *Christian Examiner* to write: "the argument, by which Elwood was converted, together with its terminology, are from a philosophy, with which many of our readers have but little, if any acquaintance."[30]

Morton's argument is briefly as follows: The Spontaneous Reason is the direct revelation from God to the human mind and virtually constitutes the human belief in the existence of man, nature, and God. Therefore, "no man does ever really deny the existence of God. Men may reject the term, but never the reality." Even the atheist, then, will find God "at the bottom."[31] It was also for this reason that the gentle Elizabeth, though dominated by her stern "advisers," felt intuitively the religious core of Elwood's character when asking him: "Is not Christ in you, though you know it not?"[32] And many years after this conversation with Elizabeth, Charles Elwood concluded that "there must be a God within to recognize and vouch for the God who speaks to us from without."[33]

However, the Reflective Reason is needed to clarify man's intuition of the existence and attributes of God or the Supreme Being. Morton, basing his argument on the alleged intuitive conceptions of the true, the beautiful, and the good, maintains that these ideas, in order to be real, must be identified with substance. Hence he concludes the existence not only of substance, but of absolute substance. And since two or more absolutes would be an absurdity, there can be only one absolute substance. Concluding from man and nature that are both relative existences, he states that absolute substance must also be a cause, i.e. absolute cause. This absolute cause is identical with God, who in "our radical idea" of him is a cause, or, more specifically, creator.[34]

But this absolute cause, or God, must also be intelligent and "personal," or the argument would not go beyond pantheism. To demonstrate the intelligence of the absolute cause, Morton starts with the conceptions that are inherent in Reason and have authority beyond the individual consciousness. Since all its conceptions have a character of necessity, universality, and absoluteness, Reason itself is absolute. But as there cannot be two absolutes, Morton concludes that absolute substance is also absolute Reason. Further, since Reason is intelligence, God is not a blind cause, but an intelligent cause. To Elwood's question of if, according to this argument, his own reason would be identical with God himself, Morton answers that this is true only of Reason "in its fulness, in its Godhead," i.e. when it is above and independent of human conditions and frailties.[35] From God's intelligence Morton concludes God's personality. And since God is an infinitely free intentional causality, He must be infinitely more than a human being. Finally, he demonstrates God's moral attributes by concluding from the absolute ideas of justice and goodness inherent in Reason.[36]

God as absolute cause must create: "Creation then is necessary." But to avoid the charge of fatalism, Morton maintains that God creates not out of "a foreign necessity, but a necessity of His own nature." Yet Morton is more convincing when trying to refute the charge of pantheism. Although God is the life and substance of His works, He is not identical with them, but independent of them. God as the "permanent and indwelling cause" of the universe gives a sacred character to His works, above all to man, the highest manifestation of the Deity. Thus God and His creation are the very source and justification of human rights.[37]

In the foregoing chapter was pointed out Brownson's later critical attitude to some parts of Cousin's philosophy, even his conception of Reason; but in this context it is apt to emphasize that Cousin's very idea of the spontaneity and objectivity of Reason appealed to him and throughout his life motivated his philosophic thought.

Thus in his representative essays in "Refutation of Atheism" Brownson's conception of "the ideal" or "the *a priori* and apodictic element" of thought corresponded to Cousin's idea of the Objective and Spontaneous Reason.[38] And Brownson declared that "if we had not ideal intuition of real and necessary being, there is no possible demonstration of the existence of God."[39] Therefore, despite certain shifts of emphasis, a main line of thought can be traced from *Charles Elwood* to Brownson's essays on atheism in the 1870's, a fact which was accentuated by Brownson's homage to Cousin in these very essays: "our old master, to whom we owe the best part of our philosophical discipline."[40]

Perhaps no less important, Brownson's lifelong belief in intuition, which already in the 1820's he regarded as "undoubtedly the strongest evidence" of all, explains his skeptical attitude toward the "inductive" character of Scholastic philosophy. Thus, in 1875, the aging and thoroughgoing Catholic Brownson declared that St. Thomas's "five proofs" of God's existence might be accepted only on condition that the Creative Act of Being–i.e. implicitly God–is intuitively imparted and perceived.[41]

No doubt, Morton's argument for the existence of God is based on *a priori* principles subject to belief rather than to any accurate philosophical verification. Thus Emile Faguet, in contrast to Cousin and not unlikely with some right, maintains that the Reflective and not the Spontaneous Reason is universal;[42] and as for Morton's elaboration of his "proof," he constantly applies unproven data.

However, Morton's mode of reasoning is in keeping with Brownson's general philosophical attitude. He repeatedly stated that principles should precede method,[43] and his strong belief in the power and the objective reality of ideas made him–as indicated in his article on "An Old Quarrel" of 1867–unwilling to distinguish between "mundus logicus" and "mundus physicus." Or one might add 'mundus realis,' because he wrote in the very same article that ideas are "objective and real, and either the intelligible object itself or the objective light by which it is rendered intelligible or knowable."[44] And in 1873 he was even more distinct, when declaring "logic to be a real, not a merely formal science, and that it responds to the truth of things."[45]

On the other hand, he was little concerned with the examination of the cognitive faculty as such. Thus in the just mentioned article of 1867 he exclaimed: "How we do and can know seems to us an inexplicable mystery, as is our existence itself."[46] But he felt assured that we *do* know. In 1873 he even stated, in his categoric manner, that nothing is more certain than the basis of knowledge, because to him "ideas are the intelligible or non-sensible objects of thought, and without which the mind would have nothing to note," and that, accordingly, "every thought, whether intuitive or reflective, is a judgment affirming its object."[47] But what about the influence of human frailties? In *The Convert* (page 135) Brownson stated his answer: "The will may be perverse, and withdraw the intellect from the contemplation of truth; prejudice or passion may darken the understanding, so that it does not for the moment see or recognize the object; but, whenever the truth is immediately present, and reason looks it full in the face, it knows that it is truth without further evidence, without anything extrinsic to prove that it is truth. To deny this would be to deny to the soul the faculty of intelligence, the faculty of knowing at all."

In 1869 he stated more generally his view of the nature and mission of philosophy: "True philosophy joined with theology is the response to the questions, What is, or exists? What are the principles and causes of things? What are our relations to those principles and causes? What is the law under which we are placed? And what are the means and conditions within our reach, natural or gracious, of fulfilling our destiny, or of attaining to our supreme good? Not a response to the question, for the most part an idle question, How do we know, or how do we know that we know?"[48] In the light of this basic approach to philosophy may be seen his lifelong belief in God "at the bottom," as expressed in *Charles Elwood*, or, though in more philosophical terms, in his essays in "Refutation of Atheism:" "The objective validity of our knowledge rests on the non-psychical element of thought, not on the psychical."[49]

However, *Charles Elwood* is something more than a novel and even more than "a philosophico-religious work" or treatise.[50] Regarded as a spiritual biography of the author, the book has its undisputed value. More or less intentionally, Brownson, through his "hero" Charles Elwood, gives us the impression of his own keen sense of loneliness and isolation in different milieus. Like Elwood, Brownson also felt himself a kind of "outsider." With his unfailing interest in philosophical investigation and his social-radical sympathies he might easily be considered an intellectual troublemaker by conservative people. Yet what makes Elwood's and Brownson's sense of estrangement more keen and even gives it a tinge of tragedy, is that their deep and genuine need of religion is in part misunderstood by their surroundings. Of particular autobiographical interest are Elwood's–i.e. Brownson's–memories from childhood, when, despite the influence of a stern religion, he felt around him the mild presence and Providence of a charitable God father.

Consequently, although the book abounds in philosophical speculations, Brownson succeeds in convincing even readers of today that Elwood's religious feelings and aspirations are the really motivating force in his quest for truth. And the author no more than his "hero" was a dry theorist, but a seeker after living truth. But just for this reason he is interested in arguments and even admits, as George Ripley pointed out, "the full force of skeptical arguments, whenever they are founded in truth."[51]

Yet it was Brownson's all-absorbing interest in arguments, "skeptical" or not, that, strengthened by his highly individualistic disposition and his marked tendencies to "analytic" and emotional extremism, made him to some extent a lonely, isolated figure.

Already in his childhood and youth he seems to have had contact problems,[52] so that he had ample time left for his solitary contemplations on religious subjects. His Presbyterian experience soon exasperated him, and his six years' Universalist period had an even less glorious ending.[53] As a "Free Enquirer" he was soon disgusted with Frances Wright's educational schemes, and to the individualist Brownson, the task of organizing the Workingmen's Party, or any party whatsoever, could not have any lasting appeal. If in his Unitarian phase things seemed to go more smoothly, he did not escape charges of being a social "leveller" or "agrarian." And, despite his general Transcendentalist position, Brownson stood "somewhat apart," and in more than one sense of the term.

In fact, Brownson was no genial, pleasant fellow easy to come in contact with. Even his lifelong friend Isaac T. Hecker found him "sociable, but grave,"[54] and felt he had to brace himself up when daring to disagree with him. And George Ripley was said once to have had a terrible nightmare, finding himself to be in a hot stove almost like hell and, worse still, face to face with Brownson, who was eagerly shoveling coal in the direction of his agonized friend. Georgiana Bruce Kirby in her book about Brook Farm tells this story to illustrate her statement that "Brownson was not the prince of gentlemen in a debate."[55]

Of course, Brownson well knew that people regarded him as a logical hairsplitter, and in 1855 he blurted out: "We are supposed to have no heart, and are regarded as a mere logic-grinder, logic-chopper, or dialectic gladiator."[56] He reacted strongly against this charge, which, however, was not quite unfounded. Yet the charge was also to no small extent caused by the fact that Brownson was a very able logician, whom it was not easy to refute, once his premises had been admitted. But as Parke Godwin maintained about Brownson: "The absolute is his forte,"[57] one might with no less right maintain that "the absolute," i.e. his categoric, even aggressive manner of presenting his arguments, was also his weakness. True, his mode of arguing was not coolly intellectual; on the contrary, it was both caused and highly colored by his emotions. It was indeed not devoid of feeling as such, but often devoid of the right kind of feeling, the one that appeals to and convinces, and not repels the opponent. Or as a writer in the *American Catholic Quarterly Review* put it: "It was merely the storm-wind proclaiming in clear, loud, defiant blast what might have been conveyed as well and with undimmed, undiminished truth, in gentler tones." But, the writer continued, "some may question his prudence; none can doubt that he was prompted solely by his strong convictions and zeal for the truth."[58]

In fact, not even as a Catholic did he live any peaceful life. Brownson, who later said that he had lived "very much apart" before his conversion to Catholicism and had not, therefore, any very "tender ties" to break,[59] came to realize that "his Catholic brethren are wedded to many things to which he is a stranger, and must remain a stranger."[60] Obviously, similar utterances reflected his somewhat isolated position also in the Catholic milieu, and although they were not common, they were hardly apt to improve his position in this milieu.

Anyhow, even if this point should not be unduly stressed, the above-mentioned instances suggest Brownson's sense of a certain loneliness and isolation. Sometimes, though, he was inclined to exaggerate or dramatize this more or less marked psychological problem, as he did just after leaving the Universalists. "I was attacked on every hand," he wrote melodramatically about his recent Universalist past, "and every man's hand seemed against me."[61] And the same Ishmael-like outlook is reflected by his "hero" Charles Elwood: "My life has been a continual warfare with principles and doctrines which I have found in power, but which have appeared to me false and mischievous. I have almost always stood alone, battling single-handed for the unpopular cause, the unfashionable party, the heretical truth. My hand has been against every man, and every man's hand has been against me." Yet the gloomy picture of Ishmael at once vanishes, because Elwood—and the author—continues: "Yet have I ever yearned toward my race, and separated from them only with the keenest regret."[62]

But how much was Brownson's own fault and how much the fault of his surroundings concerning his position as an "outsider?" Perhaps the writer in the *Nation* was not wholly in the wrong when suggesting that "apparently there was too little character in proportion to the talent for the making of a profoundly influential man."[63] But apart from the extremely difficult task of appreciating "the character" of a person, another explanation seems no less reasonable: Brownson's undisputed talent, though marred by his truculent temper and his too logistic cast of mind, was too great to make him a so-called "popular" man. But this does not exclude influence, not even profound influence.

However, despite his aggressiveness in debate, Brownson convinced some people, if not always of the alleged correctness if his ideas, at least of his own basic qualities, such as tenderness and, surprisingly enough, even humility. One recalls Joseph Henry Allen's pointed remark about Brownson as the "rude, yet tender-hearted man."[64] And to Isaac T. Hecker, Brownson was "the friend and guide of my youthful struggles," a man whose piety was "simple, practical, and not without a flavor of devotional sentiment," a man with "so true a heart and so great a soul."[65] One might only regret that these qualities were "basic" also in the sense that they had obvious difficulty in coming into the open.

In any case, as early as in 1828 Brownson had come to realize that "the logick of the heart has peculiar force," that it has, indeed, "more power than the mere logick of the head, to silence those angry disputants which a man sometimes feels within himself."[66] Perhaps the reason was that he found God in the heart, or "at the bottom."

Two years after its publication, the author himself "reviewed" his book in the April, 1842, issue of the *Boston Quarterly Review.* His primary reason for commenting on *Charles Elwood* was to modify the views of Howard and particularly those of Morton; and the general tendency of his comments was to show the more specific character of Christianity and the value of its tradition, and to establish on a firmer basis the objective reality of absolute ideas.

Brownson the "reviewer" wanted to make clear, what Howard had neglected to do, that a person brought up in Christian civilization "lives necessarily the life of Christ"[67] to a greater extent than those living in less advanced civilizations. To him Christianity has, as it were, become "a second nature."

As for his revision of Morton's views, Brownson wanted to give the impression that it concerned the form rather than the content of these views. But one is apt to believe that it really reflected the author's own increasingly critical attitude toward Cousin's philosophy. He had also grown skeptical about Benjamin Constant's doctrine of the religious sentiment.

True, in *Charles Elwood* Morton had defined religion both as sentiment, i.e. the craving for the infinite, and certain ideas: the true, the beautiful, and the good. But Morton, according to Brownson in 1842, had not stated clearly enough the character of the religious sentiment proper and the religious ideas as objective realities. Now Brownson had come to consider these ideas not constitutive elements of reason, i.e. reason regarded as man's faculty of knowing; only the power or faculty by which we "think" them is innate.

Brownson, by stressing the distinction between "the seer" and "the seen," the human capacity to "think" these ideas and these ideas themselves, tried to distinguish more clearly than before between the Subjective and the Objective, the *me* and the *not-me*. This clarification or amplification of his views made him define his attitude toward the Transcendentalists as follows: "All ideas,–and we use the term in the original Platonic sense,–are transcendental. In asserting man's power to perceive them, we coincide with the transcendentalists; but in asserting, as we also do, that it is out of the soul, out of the *me*, and not in it, that they exist, and that we perceive them, we depart from what we suppose is a characteristic feature of American transcendentalism."[68]

But what about this innate power to aspire to the infinite and perceive the transcendental ideas of the true, the beautiful, and the good? Does man in his mere natural capacity aspire and does he perceive these ideas only out of his own energy, or is a "foreign or special agency" needed to quicken his innate power to aspire and perceive?

Evidently, also on this point there had been a shift of emphasis in the author's view since he wrote his book. Particularly under the influence of the writings of a new "light," the French philosopher Pierre Leroux, Brownson felt inclined to appreciate more highly than before the value of tradition, constantly nourished and increased by "a providential man, or some divine interposition."[69] To Brownson, this tradition was the tradition of Christianity; it was the Christian influence that quickened man's aspiration to the infinite and his capacity to perceive transcendental ideas.

This indicated that Brownson had modified and enlarged Constant's doctrine of the religious sentiment. Yet more important was his strong criticism of Cousin's doctrine of Reason. What he especially objected to, was Cousin's thesis that one and the same Reason was both divine and objective and a faculty of human nature. Now Brownson had come to the conclusion that if Reason was divine or objective, it could not also be part of a human being or a subject. Either it had to be only impersonal in the sense of non-human, which would mean the denial of the fact that we are persons with moral responsibility. Indeed, the doctrine of the Impersonal or Objective Reason might blot out all theoretical distinction between God's acts and ours, and pave the way for pantheism. Or Reason had to be a faculty of human nature, but then it would only be part of the subject and, therefore, purely subjective.

This alleged confusion in Cousin's doctrine of the Spontaneous and the Reflective Reason together with his psychological method no longer convinced Brownson that the French philosopher had proved the objectivity of the absolute ideas. As Brownson now understood him, Cousin after all considered these ideas only elements of human intelligence and, therefore, only subjective. Also the American Transcendentalists regarded them "as laws of the soul, sometimes as the soul itself," i.e. as something purely subjective.[70]

Brownson concluded that Cousin, owing to his doctrine of Reason, had not been able to refute Kant's idealism and Fichte's egoism, because "with all his eclecticism, he really establishes no distinction between subject and object." In opposition not only to Cousin and Fichte, but to Immanuel Kant as well, Brownson set forth the following theses, which he thought would solve "the whole mystery" and place philosophy and the universal beliefs of mankind on the same basis: "*The objective element of thought is always not-me*" and "*there is no purely subjective, or purely objective knowledge.*"[71] He admitted that Cousin had suggested the very same solution, i.e. the principle that the thinker, or the subject, and the ideas, or the object, are "given" simultaneously in the act of thinking, or in thought. The absolute ideas, too, are objects of thought and independent of the thinker, or the subject. Yet Brownson did not find Cousin's proofs sufficient, since the latter regarded these ideas in relation to the human intelligence instead of regarding them as objective to the "*whole me.*" This distinction, however, seems rather technical, and Brownson, at least indirectly, was indebted to Cousin for this doctrine as for other doctrines as well. Or as he expressed what he thought was the fertility of Cousin's mind: "Cousin has suffered few facts in metaphysics to escape him."[72]

Nonetheless, he had a growing feeling that Cousin's philosophy did not constitute a coherent whole, chiefly because it identified philosophy too much with the history of philosophy. More important, he felt a stronger need than before to establish firmly the objective foundation of truth. A searching question runs, as it were, throughout his whole essay: how to know that religion is objectively true and something infinitely more than the feelings of one's own subjective religious sentiment; how to know that the ideas of the true, the beautiful, and the good are something infinitely more than fancies of one's own fallible imagination? No wonder, therefore, that "the problem of God" concerned him much more than earlier.

In *Charles Elwood* Brownson—or Morton—maintained that the absolute, objective ideas in the last analysis were identical with God. Brownson now clearly stated that these ideas are not God, but only contain a revelation of him, as a man may enter into his own thoughts. Moreover, the "hero" of the novel seemed to be content with "the discovery of the logical necessity of God," while Brownson in 1842 was more concerned with the knowledge of God than with the theoretical "proof" of his existence. In addition, he also realized much more than in 1840 that God had to be studied in His works and in His Providence, not in logical abstractions. To Brownson, this was also "the sublime doctrine" of Christianity," which tells us to see the glory of the Father in the face of His Son.[73]

Undoubtedly, Brownson's growing interest in "the problem of God" and his emphasis on the concrete and the actual as manifestations of absolute ideas and even of God were new tones in his writings. Even if he did not expressly mention it, Brownson in his new approach to the idea of God seemed to differ more from Cousin than he did in his criticism of Cousin's system of philosophy. Yet in *The Convert* (page 128), although paying his tribute to Cousin, he stated bluntly that Cousin could only give him "an abstract God, and no living God, no real God at all."

By way of conclusion, which changes or shifts of emphasis had taken place in Brownson's attitude from 1840 to 1842? First, he had come to appreciate more the role of Christian tradition and civilization, although Christianity only as life, not as dogma. His was still a "religion of humanity," but Christianity had been given definite preëminence among the religions. Second, his quest of absolute, objective truths independent of the thinking and feeling subject had become more predominant and removed him from European idealistic philosophy and, partly, from American Transcendentalism. And third, he had begun to realize, although dimly as yet, that God was something more than a philosophical abstraction; instead, He was a living reality, manifesting Himself in concrete things and events.

1 *Ph.*, II (Feb. 14, 1832), 115.
2 *Ph.*, II (May 29, 1832), 209–222, esp. 221, 222.
3 "Charles Elwood Reviewed" *(BQR*, V), *Works*, IV, 316. According to Henry F. Brownson, most of the book was written at Walpole in 1834 and at Canton in 1835 *(Early Life*, p. 421).
4 *Charles Elwood; or, The Infidel Converted (Works*, IV), p. 173.
5 *Works*, IV, 317.
6 *Ibid.*, p. 320.
7 *Works*, XIX, 157.
8 *Ibid.*, p. 226.
9 *Ibid.*, p. 559.
10 *The Convert*, p. 89.
11 *Works*, IV, 316.
12 *Ibid.*, p. 220.
13 *Early Life*, pp. 416–420.
14 *Works*, XIX, 542, 543.
15 *Ibid.*, p. 533.
16 *Works*, IV, 252.
17 *Ibid.*, p. 174.
18 *Ibid.*, pp. 271–272.
19 *Brook Farm: Its Members, Scholars, and Visitors* (New York, 1900), p. 6.
20 *Works*, IV, 293.
21 *Ibid.*, p. 307.
22 *Ibid.*, p. 232.
23 *Ibid.*, p. 304.
24 *Ibid.*, p. 313.
25 *Ibid.*, pp. 314, 315.
26 *Ibid.*, pp. 241, 242, 251.
27 *Works*, IV, 322, 323.
28 *Christian Review*, V (Sept. 1840), 423.
29 *Early Life*, pp. 427 ff.
30 William Dexter Wilson, "Charles Elwood; or, The Infidel Converted," *Christian Examiner*, XXVIII, 3rd series, X, 194.
31 *Works*, VI, 206, 288–290.
32 *Ibid.*, p. 214.
33 *Ibid.*, p. 187.
34 *Ibid.*, pp. 273–276.
35 *Ibid.*, pp. 276–279.
36 *Ibid.*, pp. 279–280.
37 *Ibid.*, pp. 280–284.
38 *Works*, II, 47. See also *Early Life*, p. 391.
39 *Works*, II, 72.
40 *Ibid.*, p. 35.
41 "Father Hill's Philosophy" *(BrQR*, 1875), *Works*, II, 528.
42 *Politiques et moralistes du dix-neuvième siècle* (2e série, 5e éd.; Paris, 1903), p. 255.
43 See, for example, "Primitive Elements of Thought" *(BrQR*, 1859), *Works*, I, 409, and "The Giobertian Philosophy" *(BrQR*, 1864), *Works*, II, 248.
44 *Works*, II, 290, 301.
45 *BrQR*, Last series, I (April 1873), 281.
46 *Works*, II, 303.
47 *BrQR*, Last series, I (April 1873), 283.

[48] "Spiritualism and Materialism" *(Catholic World)*, *Works*, IX, 386.
[49] *Works*, II, 45.
[50] *The Convert*, p. 89.
[51] *Dial*, I (July 1840) 46.
[52] *Early Life*, p. 8.
[53] *Ph.*, II (Jan. 14, 1832), 88.
[54] *Catholic World*, XLV (May 1887), 206.
[55] *Years of Experience* (New York and London, 1887), pp. 147–148.
[56] *Works*, I, 339.
[57] *The Harbinger*, VI (Jan. 15, 1848), 84 (Quoted in Gohdes, *The Periodicals of American Transcendentalism*, p. 43).
[58] "In Memoriam: Orestes A. Brownson," *American Catholic Quarterly Review*, (July 1876), 564.
[59] *Works*, XIX, 581–582.
[60] "Present Catholic Dangers" *(BrQR*, 1857), *Works*, XII, 140.
[61] *Free Enquirer*, II (Jan. 23, 1830).
[62] *Works*, IV, 196.
[63] "Orestes A. Brownson's Latter Life, from 1856 to 1876," *Nation*, LXXIII (July 4, 1901), 17.
[64] *Our Liberal Movement in Theology* (Boston 1882), pp. 87–88.
[65] *Catholic World*, XLVI (Nov. 1887), 234, 235.
[66] *G. A.*, VI (Sept. 13, 1828), 289–294.
[67] *Works*, IV, 325.
[68] *Ibid.*, p. 336.
[69] *Ibid.*, pp. 336, 337.
[70] *Ibid.*, p. 345.
[71] *Ibid.*, pp. 346, 355, 356.
[72] *Ibid.*, p. 346.
[73] *Ibid.*, p. 349.

XII
A Social-Radical Transcendentalist

In the January, 1840, issue of the *Boston Quarterly Review* Brownson stated that his periodical would still be devoted to religion, philosophy, politics, and general literature. Declaring himself to be an "eclectic," he invited "the Transcendentalists, the Mystics, the Theosophists, the Idealists" to make this journal a forum for their own ideas, and thus give the *Boston Quarterly Review* as broad a scope as possible.[1]

True, Brownson was still an "eclectic reasoner" in the double sense of the term. He defended Cousin's general view of philosophy and, as a faithful guardian, tried to ward off repeated charges of atheism, pantheism, and fatalism leveled against his master.[2] And in the broader sense of the term, Brownson, in keeping with a basic tendency of his, reasoned in an "eclectic" manner when maintaining that "the true man, the *whole* man, neglects no interest, overlooks neither body nor soul, but seeks to bring about a reconciliation between spirit and flesh, mind and matter, God and man."[3]

To Brownson, this essential quality of "the true man" corresponded to similar laws both of the natural and the moral universe: just as external nature is determined by the two polar forces of "contraction" and "expansion," the moral world is characterized by two opposite forces, an active force and a passive one, and "without the conjunction of the two, nothing is generated." He continued: "Man is both active and passive; he acts, and is acted upon. . . . This fact is variously represented by the terms, liberty and necessity, fate and free will, human ability and divine grace, or the strength of the will and the force of circumstances." Brownson emphasized that this idea of conjunction of two forces, an idea which he also applied to the relations between the individual and society, was no abstract "systematic unity," but a fact of experience.[4] Yet some years later he tried to make a "systematic unity" out of this fact of experience through his synthetic philosophy and his doctrine of life and communion.

His "eclectic" approach to basic questions was also reflected in a discourse delivered to his society in 1838, but printed in the October, 1840, issue of the *Boston Quarterly Review*. In this speech, whose characteristic title was "Progress Our Law," he stressed the close relation between the past, present, and future generations. To Brownson, real progress had to be based on tradition, on the experience of mankind, which reflected the universal reason.[5]

Moreover, his "eclectic" attitude might be seen in his idea of Church and State. In his *New Views* of 1836 and in his review article of his book in 1842, Brownson was concerned with his "Church of the Future." Although this intended future organization was meant to comprise Church and State, at least its very name suggested a kind of church organization and a recognition of church principles. But already in 1838 he intimated that the name of this future unity of Church and State ought to be *the State*, and that the church as a visible corporation should cease to exist. The contribution of "the church" would be her "moral ideas," which were to sanction the "social theories" of the State.[6] Similarly, Morton in *Charles Elwood*, believing in "an inward and invisible church," also believed that "the state should be a church," and even that State and Church should not only become a unity, but an identity.[7]

Yet in the *Boston Quarterly Review* of 1840 this idea was brought more sharply into focus–an idea which Brownson both in 1838 and in 1840 compared with the old Puritan conception of a "Christian Commonwealth" minus the "theological phraseology" of the Pilgrim Fathers.[8] So after all, despite this shift of emphasis from "church" to "state" –a change, however, which was mostly formal and caused by tactical deliberations[9]–Brownson's purpose set forth in his *New Views* of combining the spiritual and the material reappeared in 1838 and in 1840. The only difference from 1836 was that his thesis of "spiritualism" and "materialism" as synonymous with Catholicism and Protestantism was not restated, though, according to *The Convert* (page 110), this thesis presupposed his idea of unity between Church and State.

Perhaps not wholly beyond the mark, J. Fairfax McLoughlin calls Brownson's scheme "a church of his own, a sort of miscegenated Catholic-Protestant Brownsonian cult, the chief business of which was to get rid of priests and parsons, and open a new road to heaven."[10]

Yet from a more positive point of view, Brownson wanted to build society on what he regarded as Christian principles,[11] an idea which, although under different circumstances, he restated in the 1860's,[12] and which already in 1838 he motivated on "eclectic" grounds: "Before modern civilization could achieve its destiny, all these elements were to be brought together and moulded into an harmonious whole."[13]

Yet Brownson's stronger emphasis than ever on the spirit of Christianity or "the Christianity of Christ" and his utter contempt for any institutional religion—"the Christianity of the Church"—together with his ("uneclectic") disregard of the historical importance of the church made him approach more closely to Transcendentalism than ever before. In self-reliant, almost Emersonian tones he exclaimed: "But why am I a man, why have I eyes, why have I a soul, if I may only reproduce Luther or Calvin?"[14] In his "Divinity School Address" of 1838 Emerson declared: "Wherever a man comes, there comes revolution. The old is for slaves. When a man comes, all books are legible, all things transparent, all religions are forms. He is religious. Man is the wonderworker. He is seen amid miracles." Therefore, Emerson concluded, "thank God for these good men [i.e. Wesleys and Oberlins, Saints and Prophets], but say, 'I also am a man.' "[15]

More particularly, Brownson's article in the July, 1840, number of his review with an almost unreserved defense of "the New School" clearly showed where his sympathies lay. Formally, this essay was a kind of review of two articles originally printed in the *Princeton Review* "Concerning the Transcendental Philosophy of the Germans, and of Cousin, and Its Influence on Opinion in This Country." But most probably, Brownson wrote his essay to support his friend George Ripley in the latter's controversy with Andrews Norton.[16]

First, Brownson stated that Transcendentalism rejected the sensist philosophy of Locke and, more particularly, Unitarianism of the Norton type. In fact, his criticism of Norton was far from sober: "It is said he usually sits in a room with the shutters closed, which has the double effect of keeping the light out and the darkness in. This may be slander, but his productions, it must be confessed, afford no satisfactory refutation of it."[17] By the way, it was also slandered, though much more good-humoredly, that to the young students of Harvard Professor Norton's most genuine and convincing "evidences of Christianity" were his three lovely daughters, who were often strolling in the garden and obviously not intent on keeping any light out.[18] Rather strange, however, was Brownson's appraisal of Norton's book *Statement of Reasons for Not Believing the Doctrines of Trinitarians* (1819): "He pared the Christian faith down to the smallest conceivable point, and in the opinion of most Christians, divested the Gospel of all its richness."[19] After all, had Brownson done anything else himself in his *Charles Elwood*, published in 1840? However, he paid his compliments to Norton, who–to Brownson–was almost the only "oldtimer" willing to wage a real campaign against "the New School."[20]

Yet, more difficult to state what Transcendentalism was against, was to state what it positively stood for, or to recognize any common platform of those who were called or called themselves Transcendentalists: "Some of them embrace the Transcendental philosophy, some of them reject it, some of them *ignore* all philosophy, plant themselves on their instincts, and wait for the huge world to come round to them. Some of them read Cousin, some Goethe and Carlyle, others none at all. Some of them reason, others merely dream."[21]

But although American Transcendentalists studied foreign authors, especially French and German, Brownson discarded the notion of many critics that Transcendentalism was an imported article. Even if "truth transcends both time and space," and "it matters little whether its first discoverer be a Frenchman, a Dutchman, or a Yankee," Brownson wanted to stress that American Transcendentalism was "really of American origin."[22]

The alleged European, especially German, origin of American Transcendentalism was used by many opponents as their conclusive argument against it. Thus, to Francis Bowen, for one, there could be no doubt as to the new philosophy: "There is *primâ facie* evidence against it. It is abstruse in its dogmas, fantastic in its dress, and foreign in its origin. It comes from Germany, and is one of the first fruits of a diseased admiration of every thing from that source, which has been rapidly gaining ground of late, till in many individuals it amounts to sheer midsummer madness."[23] And two years later, in 1839, Norton complained: "We have indeed but little to guard us against the influence of the depraving literature and noxious speculations which flow in among us from Europe."[24]

Obviously, the problem of influences, let alone the question of their moral character, is often complicated. But recent scholarship seems to support Brownson's thesis of American Transcendentalism as "really" a result of the American cultural heritage. As mentioned before, Perry

Miller has indicated a line of thought from Jonathan Edwards to the Transcendentalists, and it is hardly quite incidental that both Brownson and Ripley, as pointed out earlier, referred to Edwards with the view of supporting their arguments.[25] Anyhow, it is interesting to note the similarity between the views of Brownson and those of the twentieth-century scholar René Wellek regarding the origin of American Transcendentalism. In 1840 Brownson wrote that the "attachment" of the Transcendentalists "to the literatures of France and Germany is the effect of their connection with the movement, not the cause.... These distinguished foreigners are not our masters, but our fellow disciples."[26] In 1943 René Wellek, in an article on "Emerson and German Philosophy," said pretty much the same: "The Transcendentalists were merely looking for corroboration of their faith. They found it in Germany, but ultimately they did not need this confirmation. Their faith was deeply rooted in their minds and their own spiritual ancestry."[27]

To Brownson, American Transcendentalists were mostly concerned with the source of human knowledge. Some of them considered this problem as an end in itself; others considered it so as to legitimate their religious faith; and others, finally, studied the grounds of knowledge to "obtain a firm foundation for political freedom."[28] Brownson himself undoubtedly felt most akin to the last two groups. But more important, he declared himself a Transcendentalist, not only because he believed in the existence of a transcendental order, but also because he believed in the possibility of knowing truth intuitively "or of attaining to a scientific knowledge of an order of existence transcending the reach of the senses."[29]

Brownson directed his polemics against Andrews Norton, who allegedly denied the capacity of the human mind for absolutely certain knowledge beyond "the limit of momentary consciousness, a certainty that vanishes the instant it exists, and is lost in the region of metaphysical doubt."[30] Against Norton's belief "on testimony" the Transcendentalists claimed for man "the power, not of discovering, but of knowing by intuition the spiritual world."[31] Or as Emerson wrote in his essay on "Self-Reliance," published in 1841: "We denote this primary wisdom as Intuition, whilst all later teachings are tuitions. In that deep force, the last fact, behind which analysis cannot go, all things find their common origin."[32]

As Brownson understood them, the Transcendentalists did not deny the divine or specific mission of Jesus or even his miracles, but they maintained that the truths exposed by Jesus could be perceived directly by the human mind "without reference to the authority or endowments of him who first revealed them." Even Holy Writ itself bore witness to this human capacity of grasping the highest truths intuitively. Jesus said that to *know* God means everlasting life, and that if anyone will do God's will, he shall *know* that the teachings of Jesus are from God. From such biblical statements Brownson concluded that the truth of Christianity, "though it might need to be supernaturally revealed, is nevertheless, when revealed, an object of knowledge."[33]

However, neither Brownson nor other Transcendentalists clearly explained the nature and significance of Christ's "mission." Brownson seemed to hold that our "direct perception" of truth "in the actual state of humanity" stems from the fact that Christ revealed the truth 1900 years ago. But how is it possible to reconcile this idea with the view that the truths set forth by Jesus could be perceived without reference to him?[34]

The question remains how the Transcendentalists could justify their view of the specific "mission" of Jesus. Like the Unitarians of "the Old School" they rejected Trinitarianism and consequently the dogma of Jesus as the Son of God. But unlike these Unitarians they rejected the argument of historical evidence or belief "on testimony," which was at least an attempt to state the uniqueness of Christianity and its founder. In his criticism of "the modern German school of infidelity" Norton, after all, seemed to have a point; and as an irony of fate, Brownson was later to raise similar objections to Transcendentalism as Andrews Norton, who wrote: "The most generally received notion seems to be, that religion arises out of the nature of man; that it is a feeling, a sentiment, an apprehension of something, it is hard to say what, that is intuitive or spontaneous, though admitting of cultivation." And he continued: "Feelings and sentiments cannot be excited, unless their proper objects are believed or imagined to exist."[35]

The Transcendentalists said many eloquent and poetical things about the founder of Christianity, but they all amounted to praises of the Son of Man, preëminent among all sons of men, but not essentially different from them.[36] To Norton, too, Jesus was only a man, but endowed by God with supernatural attributes, which made him essentially unique among men, and whose teachings, in consequence, were "proper objects" of belief.

On the other hand, there was at least much soundness in the reaction of the Transcendentalists against a religion that regarded miracles as the only proofs of the truth of religious doctrines. However good the motive, it is a question if such a half-dogmatic system will, in the long run, be able to hold its own against the increasing inroads of rationalism. In any case, later generations of American Unitarians seem to regard the essentially unorthodox Channing, Emerson, and Parker rather than Norton as their spiritual forefathers.[37] Without drawing too sweeping conclusions, perhaps it is not utterly wrong to suggest that the traditional dogma of the Trinity is indispensable in order to secure a minimum of dogmatic stability to a Christian denomination. Brownson, at least, even in his Unitarian period repeatedly mentioned the doctrine of the Trinity as a very important doctrine, although he gave it a symbolic, unorthodox interpretation.

In any case, this debate between "the Old" and "the New School" shows how much the Transcendentalists—and Brownson among them—were preoccupied with religious questions, even when philosophical questions were being discussed. To many adherents of "the New School," Transcendentalism served as a basis of religious faith.

Yet more than most Transcendentalists Brownson stressed the allegedly broad, popular appeal of the Transcendentalist doctrine. While the argument of historical testimony as the only proof of the truth of Christianity was, according to the Transcendentalists, only for the erudite and not for the people at large, the "witness within the soul" or "the transcendental element of human nature" made everyone perceive directly the essential religious truths. And not quite unexpectedly, Brownson stated that this doctrine, establishing the real worth and dignity of every individual, would in due time lead to the destruction of every "sacerdotal caste" and save "Humanity from ecclesiastical dominion."[38]

Thus Brownson's Transcendentalist beliefs motivated or justified his scathing attacks which he made during the same year on priestcraft and the church system, and also partly motivated his social-radical views which reached their climax in 1840.

In the July and October, 1840, issues of his *Boston Quarterly Review*, Brownson wrote his incendiary articles on "The Laboring Classes," in which he presented his views of the church, Christianity, and society in a more radical manner than he had done before. True, his general conceptions of Christianity and the church were the same as they had been from 1830, when—in his own words—he "publicly announced his conversion to the Christian Faith,"[39] or, in the more appropriate term which he adopted later about this form of faith, the "religion of humanity." And already in his *New Views* of 1836 he had contrasted "the Christianity of Christ" to "the Christianity of the church." But much more strongly than before he now stressed the social side of Christianity, and much more strongly than before he blamed the church, which in his eyes was too much allied with the moneyed interests: "Not a few of our churches rest on Mammon for their foundation. The basement is a trader's shop."[40] In her all-absorbing concern for the salvation of the soul, the church completely neglected her duty to improve the conditions of mankind on earth.

Brownson really despaired of "the Christianity of the Church." He was convinced that "one might as well undertake to dip the ocean dry with a clam-shell, as to undertake to cure the evils of the social state by converting men to the Christianity of the Church."[41]

And the core of the church was the priesthood. Although the priests were needed in the original, savage state of mankind to alleviate or destroy the extreme, barbarous individualism, the "iron despotism of the theocrat" in the long run had a devastating effect on the masses of people. Indeed, so devasting had this alleged effect become that the indignant writer blurted out: "The remedy is first to be sought in the destruction of the priest."

And priestcraft should be abolished by Christianity itself: "the sublimest protest against the priesthood ever uttered, and a protest uttered by both God and man; for he who uttered it was God-Man." The mission of Jesus was to call priestcraft to judgment and mankind to freedom. Instead of exposing any doctrinary religion, "he preached fraternal love, peace on earth, and good will to men."[42]

According to the religion of Jesus, or "the Christianity of Christ," every individual was considered a priest; moreover, this religion abolished all formal worship. To Brownson, there was no real difference between a Catholic priest and a Protestant minister, or between the Catholic Church and Protestant churches. All of them being authoritarian, all of them presenting "a vain show for the reality of piety," they "ought to go by the board."[43]

"The Christianity of the Church," then, was presented as socially conservative and authoritarian, dominated by an antiquated priestly hierarchy, whose "pseudo-gospel" was a formal religion of unintelligible dogmas, supposed to save men from imaginary sins and an imaginary hell. On the other hand, "the Christianity of Christ" was an undogmatic religion, focusing on Jesus as the great moral inspirer of men and of governments to carry out social reforms and elevate the poor classes of society. What Brownson really wanted was "to bring out Christianity as a means of social reform, and to enlist the Church on the side of the downtrodden masses." His aim was "to Christianize the democracy, and to *democratize* . . . the Church."[44]

After the destruction of the priesthood and the prevailing church system, the next step, according to Brownson, should be the revival of "the Christianity of Christ," this "prophetic," churchless religion with its heavy emphasis on intuitive social-moral principles.

No doubt, Brownson's attitude clearly reflected Transcendentalist thought: as intuition preceded tuition, as life preceded forms, the prophet preceded the priest. Or as Brownson put it: only *after* the prophet has stated a truth through persecution and death does the priest make his appearance on the scene.[45] By way of comparison, a reviewer in the Transcendentalist organ the *Dial* declared that "the prophetic administration of religion—free, bold, reaching forth and pressing forward to the future—will ever be too strong for the priestly—mechanical, servile, leaning largely upon the past," and another writer in the same periodical even seemed to consider himself a potential or real prophet, feeling assured that "Priestly Dignities . . . pass into brief accidents, and the self-conscious *I* is greater than they all."[46] Emerson was certainly right when in a letter to Carlyle (Oct. 15, 1842) he described the contributors to the *Dial* as follows: "They are all religious, but hate the churches."[47] And in Emerson's eyes, "the wise man" needed "no church, for he is a prophet."[48]

As Cameron Thompson points out, Emerson's belief that "revelation is the disclosure of the Soul," and Bronson Alcott's similar conviction that "experience of the soul is a revelation of God" made any priesthood and church system superfluous as mediators between God and man.[49] Even if Brownson did not accept a similar religious subjectivism and instead stressed the (formal) role of Jesus, the God-Man, as mediator, his sweeping denunciation of all organized religion past and present made him approach as closely as possible the Emersonian platform, and his earlier criticism of Emerson for preaching only a "psychological Christ" and ignoring "the historical Christ" or Christian history and tradition might now even be directed against himself.[50] In any case, Emerson must have felt a kindred spirit in the author of "The Laboring

Classes" and seemed particularly impressed by Brownson's style. To Margaret Fuller Emerson wrote that he had "read a part of Brownson's Laboring Classes. The last hero wields a sturdy pen which I am very glad to see. I had judged him from some old things & did not know he was such a Cobbett of a scribe. Let him wash himself & he shall write for the immortal Dial."[51]

After his more "eclectic" aproach to Christian and churchly tradition through his *New Views* and partly in his *Boston Quarterly Review* of 1839, it may seem surprising that Brownson in 1840 so vigorously attacked all churchly religion. In *The Convert* (page 104) he stated that he only drew the supposedly legitimate conclusions from Protestantism as such, but whether this argument was legitimate or not, it is strange that Brownson should take Protestantism as his premise, because already in his *New Views* he had found Protestantism insufficient as a religion and wanted instead a reconciliation between the affirmative parts of Protestantism and Catholicism, or the material and the spiritual. Interestingly enough, this is an example of the Catholic Brownson's polemic method, which was to deduce all his own "heresies" and extravagant views in his pre-Catholic phase to Protestantism.

Most probably, the virtual reason of his marked Transcendentalist attitude in 1840 was the increasingly heated controversy between "the Old" and "the New School." This controversy with its increasing moral demands of clear-cut positions was by now rapidly verging toward its climax. Ripley, when in October, 1840, taking leave of his Unitarian congregation in Purchase Street, unequivocally stated his Transcendentalist position;[52] and the young Theodore Parker, in a pamphlet under the pen-name of "Levi Blodgett," made short process–or "bloodshed"–not only of all churches, but of the Bible as well.[53] Even if Brownson, too, in his own words made "a clean breast of it,"[54] he did not push matters to that extreme, but instead used the Bible as his arsenal against the priesthood.[55] Yet to all intents and purposes Brownson felt it both a moral duty and a personal relief to come out strongly on the side of "the newness."

Interestingly enough, Brownson's outright rejection of the priesthood and the churches was in harmony with the views he held in his Universalist phase. As Arnold Smithline points out, a main line of thought can be traced from deism to Transcendentalism. Both the deists and the Transcendentalists believed in "innate ideas," and even though the former "followed the path of reason" and the latter "the path of intuition," they both believed that "the religious state is achieved without the 'crutch' of codes of morality or articles of faith artificially imposed." In fact, Thomas Jefferson's distinction between "the religion of the priests and that of the Gospels"[56] was restated in Brownson's similar distinction between "the Christianity of the Church" and "the Christianity of Christ."

Obviously, Brownson's general views in 1840 did not mean a complete return to his earlier deistic, rationalistic position. In 1840 he considered the Christian religion a mighty lever of moral and social reform, and he even confessed belief in the traditional Christian dogmas, though in a rather unorthodox interpretation of them.[57] On the whole, Transcendentalism in its religious aspect may be described as a spiritualized rationalistic religion, which had stripped deism of its mechanical and utilitarian features. But after all, Brownson's religion, both in its deistic-Universalist period and in its Unitarian-Transcendentalist phase, was essentially a "religion of humanity," and not Christianity as a specific, supernaturally revealed religion. His articles on "The Laboring Classes," then, serve to show a certain similarity between deism, radical Universalism, and Transcendentalism, as well as his own consistency within the sphere of natural religion from 1825 to 1840.

When this spirited, unchurchly "Christianity of Christ" had operated on men's minds for some time, Brownson believed that the whole atmosphere of society would be ripe for the necessary social-political reforms. And he added: "We have no faith in those systems of elevating the working classes, which propose to elevate them without calling in the aid of the government."[58]

In 1838, under the impact of the economic crisis, he declared that it was "a *Christian* duty to seek to perfect society no less than it is to perfect the individual." He even thought to find an element of egotism in the idea of "self-culture," and stated that "man can never perfect himself, so long as he makes his own perfection the end of his exertions."[59] And in 1839 he wrote that the State had certain duties concerning the material interests of the people.[60]

Yet it should be borne in mind that Brownson already in 1828 expressed the view that "suffering or misery proceeds . . . from the imperfect state of society," and that "man is to be considered in the aggregate or in his collective capacity, as well as individually."[61] In 1830 he sympathized with the views of Frances Wright, who had combined the environmentalism of Robert Owen and the individualism of

William Godwin.[62] Also in the early and mid-1830's, although strenuously advocating inner reform, he repeatedly attacked the laws which favored the rich and unduly punished the poor. And—as a writer in the *Christian Register* also suggested—how could the penal code be changed except through legislation?[63]

However, in 1840 Brownson stressed much more strongly than before—or after—the necessity of founding through political means a better society. On the whole, he seems to have believed in political action during the same periods—i.e. about 1830 and during the years after the great Panic in 1837—when the workers thought to reach their aims primarily through political means.[64] And there could be no doubt about his general position. Thus, in the introduction to his *Boston Quarterly Review* (1838) Brownson, as a spokesman of the Democratic Party or even of its left wing, demanded reforms for "the elevation of labor with the Locofoco."[65]

So, in his essays on "The Laboring Classes" Brownson postulated that after the destruction of organized religion and the revival of "the Christianity of Christ," resort must be to the government, which, as the agent of society, must carry out the alleged necessary reforms. Some of the reforms he proposed were on the Democratic ticket, such as the divorce of the government from banking interests, and control, if not the breaking up, of the great business corporations; but his attacks on the beginning factory system, which he wanted to split up into small independent units, and particularly his proposal of abolishing the hereditary right of property, were definitely beside the platform of the party.[66]

Characteristically, Brownson now bluntly declared that the social evils stemmed from the system, not from any individual. On the other hand, he stressed that Christianity, rightly understood and followed, was indispensable to the elevation of the working classes. In fact, he even presupposed a certain level of individual morality before his proposed social-political reforms might be carried through.[67]

In his second article on "The Laboring Classes" he clarified his view on the relation between inner and outward reform, and the role of government:

> We would indeed restrict as much as possible the sphere of government, and enlarge that of the individual; but government, as the organ and agent of society, is a positive good, and can never be dispensed with. We have, moreover, no faith in bringing about the social order we desire, by the

agency of selfishness and strife. True democracy can never rest permanently on the maxim, 'I am as good as you;' but it must resort to this other maxim, 'You are as good as I.' The spirit, by which it must ultimately be sustained, is not the spirit that will not submit to tyranny, but the spirit that will not tyrannize.

Mind is undoubtedly superior to matter, and all reforms must come from within; but the mental and moral reform, effected in the interior of man, will prove insufficient, unless it come out of the interior, and remodel the exterior.[68]

Obviously, not even in 1840, at the height of his social radicalism, did Brownson leave out of account individual reform as a prerequisite to social reform. Instead, in harmony with his general mode of thinking, he tried to hit upon the "just medium" between or a combination of both, although by now he considered social reform preëminent.

By contrast, Channing and most of the Transcendentalists were still moving within the safe circle of "self-culture." Thus Channing in some lectures given shortly before the publication of Brownson's first essay on "The Laboring Classes" declared that "the elevation of the laboring classes" did not mean "an outward change of condition," nor did it mean "release from labor, . . . struggling for another rank" or "political power." Restating his firm belief in "Elevation of Soul," Channing seemed confident that, despite certain fears and misgivings, "the Inward moulds the Outward."[69]

The difference between Brownson's approach to the problem of reform and the purely individualistic attitude more typical of the Transcendentalists was indicated in an article written at the same time by Frederic Henry Hedge. "Secluded from without, and nourished from within, self-sustained and self-sufficing," the Transcendentalist—or "the scholar," as Hedge called him—had only little or nothing to expect from society. The implicit conclusion was: why care to improve society?[70]

In the same year a reviewer in the *Dial*, commenting on a pamphlet by Edward Palmer, a former minister, who, like Brownson, wanted to abolish "the present property system," was convinced that the cure of the social evils "must not be looked for in a change of system. The heart must be set right: the true purposes of life comprehended; the divine relations of man with man understood and acted on, before the most perfect outward organization could be carried into effect, even if it were discovered. . . . Society must be inspired with correct social ideas; the divine law of love must be proclaimed, until it commands the universal heart; and the true idea will not fail, in due time, to organize itself in a true institution."[71]

Compared with ideas like these, which verged strongly toward quietism, egotism, and indifference to social and political problems, Brownson's view of the general relation between man and society seems rather realistic.

Like his fellow Transcendentalists, Emerson, too, believed in inner reform and was perhaps even more reluctant than anyone to take any political action. But he expressed his ideas with such gusto, drive, and originality that they could not help breaking through the narrow circle of "self-culture" and even having a ringing social appeal. In his lecture on "Man the Reformer" (Jan. 25, 1841) he told the audience that it was "better to work on institutions by the sun than by the wind;" in his lecture on "The Conservative" (Dec. 9, 1841) he declared that "the order of things is as good as the character of the population permits," and in "The Transcendentalist" (Jan. 1842) he formulated the following credo: "You think me the child of my circumstances: I make my circumstance." Most vigorously Emerson stated his extreme position in his "Lecture on the Times" (Dec. 2, 1841), although it should be added that this statement did not exhaust his views of slavery: "Then again, how trivial seem the contests of the abolitionist, whilst he aims merely at the circumstance of the slave. Give the slave the least elevation of religious sentiment, and he is no slave,—you are the slave; he not only in his humility feels his superiority, feels that much deplored condition of his to be a fading trifle, but he makes you feel it too."[72]

Obviously, compared with Channing, whose "real mission"—in Ernest Renan's words—"was wholly moral,"[73] and Emerson, who said he made his own circumstance, Brownson had a more "eclectic" or double approach to the problem of reform. As Arthur I. Ladu points out, Brownson, in contrast to other Transcendentalists, called for the interference of the State to improve the lot of the individual. But Ladu also emphasizes that their common aim was "spiritual culture,"[74] a term with a more comprehensive meaning than "self-culture," which generally seemed to imply certain private or personal virtues like temperance, frugality, and benevolence, and a certain level of knowledge.

Brownson must have had this more farreaching aim in mind when, in 1838, he wrote that "in laboring to perfect the individual, we are laboring for but an insignificant unit of an innumerable multitude," but, he added, "still the perfection of the social state is a means to attain it."[75]

And in 1840 it was undoubtedly "spiritual culture" he envisioned when declaring in "The Laboring Classes" that "though man's first step in civilization was slavery, his last step shall be freedom."[76]

After all, there may be some truth in Lawrence C. Porter's a bit too sweeping statement: "As is common with reformers, the Transcendentalists saw themselves as dwelling above the crowd."[77] And at least to the modern eye, the almost exclusive insistence of the Transcendentalists on inner reform might easily lead to a tacit approval of any prevailing political, social, and economic systems. In contrast, one feels that Brownson had a point when contending that tyrants would gladly accept the idea of inner reform, which might enable them to maintain their power.[78] But on the background of his own time and society, Brownson's emphasis on political action or direct outward reform struck a rather peculiar note.

In fact, not only the loosely knit group called the Transcendentalists, but most contemporary reformers had little belief in the efficiency of direct political action. Carl Russell Fish, dealing with the period 1830–1850 of American history, writes that political reforms "were regarded as a mere extension and application of principles already accepted and proved."[79] At least to some extent this seems to have been true of President Van Buren's order of March 31, 1840, establishing the ten-hour day on all government works.[80] Even the Abolitionists, at least before 1850, were mostly no-government men.[81] The French Revolution of 1789 perhaps still cast its "long shadow," making Americans of the 1830's and 1840's distrust abrupt changes of social and political institutions.[82] And, as a more immediate reason, the "spoils"-system, introduced or at least strongly accentuated by the Jacksonian administration, hardly increased the general respect for politics and politicians. But first of all, this widespread skepticism of politics among Americans during that period was caused by the vast possibilities of individual enterprise, reinforced by the Jeffersonian doctrine of a weak central government. Even as late as in 1847 Walt Whitman declared that "although government can do little *positive* good to the people, it may do an *immense deal of harm,*" and that "indeed sensible men have long seen that 'the best government is that which governs least.' "[83]

But no less interesting than Brownson's general emphasis on the need of outward reform and on the positive role of the government is his critical, almost Marxian analysis—before Marx—of contemporary American society. In his essays on "The Laboring Classes" he wanted to put in focus the increasing social and economic differences between the workers and the employers, resulting from the steadily growing factory industry.

Reviewing Thomas Carlyle's recently published pamphlet *Chartism* (1840), Brownson stated his own views on the burning social problem in Great Britain and the United States. He put no trust in the so-called middle classes, which, to him, did not care anything at all for "the real *proletarii.*" He even felt sure that England in her wars against revolutionary France did not fight primarily for monarchy, aristocracy, and religion. What she really fought for were the interests of the middle classes, of business and industry, against the interests of the workers, represented by the French Revolution of 1789. Now, even fifty years after this revolution, whose *bourgeois* origin and nature Brownson seemed to overlook, the social gulf between the classes, between the employers and the workers, was far from being bridged. In fact, he felt certain that sooner or later a terrible social war between the rich and the poor would break out. Yet this final struggle between the classes, however brutal and merciless it would be, was in the last resort not subjected to blind, materialistic forces: "The day of vengeance is sure; for the world after all is under the dominion of a Just Providence."[84]

So far, however, Providence had not intervened. Instead, injustice held the ground in the reigning social and economic system: "It may be laid down as a general rule, with but few exceptions, that men are rewarded in an inverse ratio to the amount of actual service they perform." Even in so-called "good" times many workers were unemployed. Worse still, it was not uncommon that people even died of hunger in the United States. Brownson especially emphasized the extremely bad plight of the seamstresses. With caustic irony he described their situation: "The bills of mortality in these factory villages are not striking, we admit, for the poor girls when they can toil no longer go home to die." In Brownson's eyes, the wage system was even worse than the slave system. Though warring against both systems, he regarded slavery as the lesser evil, because the slave owner, in contrast to the employer, had at least some responsibility for *his* slaves.[85]

To Brownson, a gradual improvement of the lot of the factory workers within the system was hardly possible. In any case, there was no "reasonable chance" that a large group of the workers would become independent of their employers within the pattern of the wage system.

Deep in his heart Brownson loathed industrialism, and he never overcame this hearty dislike. Fearing that the tendency inherent in the factory system toward increasingly larger units would make the workers more and more dependent on the factory owners, he dreamed of establishing the pre-industrial pattern of small workshops owned and run by single individuals. The wage system should be tolerated only as a means to enable the worker to settle down later as an independent owner of a workshop or a store.

Yet the possibilities of the workers to gain economic and social independence were constantly shrinking. Although the social and economic differences between the classes were less marked in the United States than elsewhere, the causes were purely "accidental:" the original equality of the first settlers and the low price of land. But these causes were constantly losing their significance. There was no trace left of the equality of the first settlers, and the price of land was too high in the old states and was steadily rising in the West. Immigration would only accelerate this development. Fifty years earlier almost every inhabitant could with good reason aspire toward social and economic independence. But now, as "the wilderness has receded, and already the new lands are beyond the reach of the mere laborer," the latter, Brownson concluded, was at the mercy of his employer.[86]

Brownson's analysis of the contemporary social and economic conditions in his country and his conviction of a coming war between the classes must be seen in the light of the great Panic of 1837 and its long aftermath. Only in 1842 could the country "lift its head from under the wreck" and recover temporarily for a couple of years, but not until well into the 1850's did the "hard times" come to an end.[87] Although in 1840 Chief Justice Shaw of Massachusetts ruled that strikes were not illegal, the depression period and the competition for jobs made strikes almost impossible.[88] In particular, the steadily growing stream of immigrants–2½ million from 1839 to 1850[89]–glutted the labor market and tended to reduce wages to a minimum.

As Helen S. Mims points out, Brownson seemed to hold that in the United States, which had no feudal caste, the class struggle would accelerate faster than in Britain and France,[90] and already in 1844 Friedrich Engels observed that American industry during the last ten years had made a tremendous leap and was already coping with the British industry.[91] One might expect that the right to vote, which had been granted to American workers, but not to their British comrades, would efficiently counteract the evils of industrialism. But according to H. E. Hoagland, the right to vote, "instead of lifting the wage-earners, had strengthened middle-class politics."[92] Although Carlyle in a letter of January 6, 1840, to Emerson wrote that the topics discussed in *Chartism* were "altogether English," and, therefore, not "likely to concern *New-*Englishmen very much,"[93] at least Bronterre O'Brien, the so-called "Chartist schoolmaster," was very much concerned with the labor problem in the United States. Believing that universal suffrage was only a beginning, he was convinced—like Brownson—that the root of the evil was the property system, and he pointed to the United States, where universal suffrage had not abolished the evils of capitalism.[94] Consequently, Brownson seemed to be more of a "Chartist" than Carlyle, who primarily suggested education and emigration as remedies,[95] and who, despite all his sympathy with the British workers, was not—as he wrote in a letter of January 17, 1840, to Emerson—accused by them "of being an incendiary and speculative sansculotte threatening to become practical, but of being a Tory,—thank Heaven."[96]

Schlesinger finds Brownson's analysis to be "perhaps the best study of the workings of society written by an American before the Civil War."[97] Yet Brownson seemed to underrate the future positive roles of the frontier and industrialization in American society[98] as well as the modifying, albeit often slow, workings of the check-and-balance system of a capitalist democracy.

Even if the author of "The Laboring Classes" felt sure of a coming class war, he tried to ward off the impending conflict by proposing the adoption of measures already mentioned. Of course, his proposal regarding property with the view of stemming the tide of industrialism and recreating a basically agrarian society was both unrealistic and impracticable, and contrasted strangely with his critical appraisal of contemporary society.

But Brownson the logician should at least be given credit for consistent reasoning. He held that the abolition of the hereditary monarchy and the hereditary nobility must be followed by the abolition of the hereditary right of property, this "anomaly in our American system." And he saw "no means of elevating the laboring classes which can be effectual without this."[99]

To Brownson, the Democratic Party, which even in an official document was called "The party of equality against privilege," was morally obliged to advocate the abolition of all privileges, including the hereditary descent of property. As a more general argument Brownson referred to the maxim of equal chances for all, a maxim held in esteem by all Americans. In his opinion, this motto would certainly justify the abolition of the hereditary right of property. The mission of the American people was to state the principle of equality and carry it into practice, not only in the political, but also in the social and economic fields. More particularly, the mission of his country was to make every worker a proprietor, and to Brownson the abolition of the hereditary descent of property would mean a big step toward the realization of the American idea, i.e. to "combine labor and capital in the same individual."[100]

To support his radical proposal Brownson also referred to writers like the American jurist James Kent (1763–1847), the English jurist William Blackstone (1723–1780), Jefferson, Bentham, and Montesquieu, who all maintained that a man's *natural* right to his property expires at his death. Brownson pointed out that these writers did not regard the hereditary descent of property as a natural right, but as the expression of a social or political law. But in contrast to these jurists and philosophers, who defended the system as "a wise and effectual . . . establishment," based on the principle of "convenience" and "the parental instinct," Brownson held that society, in order to be consistent, must follow the natural law or, in other words, abolish the hereditary descent of property.[101]

Brownson emphasized that, so far, he was concerned only with the idea itself and had as yet "little time to spend in proving it practicable." Anyway, he did not believe that his cherished idea would be carried into practice until the next generation. But in the meantime he gave the general recipe for the division of property: "The general valuation of all the property in the commonwealth once fixed, the simple rule of division will determine how much is the portion of the new occupant. Then a valuation of that vacated will determine how much of it must be allotted to one individual." Thus the point of departure would be the same for all. But though the government was needed to carry out the division of property, it should not be entitled to interfere with the economic competition between the members of society. Given a just division of property, Brownson had no serious objection to the principle of *laissez-faire*.[102]

In *The Convert* (page 112) Brownson admitted that he had got his idea with regard to property from the Saint-Simonians. In the United States Thomas Skidmore, the late leader of the leftist faction of the

Workingmen's Party in New York, already ten years before had proposed an even more radical plan than Brownson's regarding property. In order to make property "equal among the adults of the present generation," he proposed to arrange common auctions of all property and equally divide the proceeds between the people. In addition, he advocated common ownership of the land. His audacious scheme led to the division, if not of property, at least of the Workingmen's Party in New York, but there is no evidence that Brownson at that time supported Skidmore's or similar ideas.[103]

Brownson's skepticism of the factory industry and his dream of a pre-industrial society consisting of small farms, stores, and workshops run by independent owners clearly reflected Jefferson's thought.[104] Paradoxically, then, there was an element of conservatism in Brownson's agrarian-radical ideas of property and industry,[105] and even in 1857 he would have carried out his schemes of 1840, if it had been practically possible.[106] But despite his lifelong distrust of the industrial or capitalist system, after 1840 he did not propose any outward measures, imaginary or not, in order to change or modify the system.

A closer analysis also reveals a marked element of Transcendentalism in Brownson's ideas of industry and property. Thus H. E. Hoagland points out that during the period in question the solution to the social problem "was sought in a return to an idealised colonial system of economics dominated by agriculture and domestic industry," and that this "system of small independent industry found its expression on the philosophic side of transcendentalism."[107] One might venture to suggest that the same basic thought that found its expression in Brownson's agrarian schemes, motivated George Ripley's project of Brook Farm. Both wanted to realize their idea of small independent units of farming and home industry, whether on an individual or a coöperative basis. It is, therefore, perhaps not quite incidental that not only to Brownson, but also to Albert Brisbane, the leading American Fourierist, "the great question . . . concerns the union of labor and capital in the same individuals," although Fourierism required the addition: "by a system of combined and organized industry."[108]

Generally speaking, Brownson's "agrarianism" accentuated the hearty dislike of the Transcendentalists for machine culture and "things."[109] Out of this very dislike, Emerson, in 1841, expressed his "preference of the agricultural life out of the belief, that our primary duties as men could be better discharged in that calling."[110] As for the question of property, the Transcendentalists, with the exception of Brownson, did not propose to abolish the right of its hereditary descent, but their strong belief in the supremacy of mind above matter made them inclined to minimize the importance of property. Emerson, for one, was convinced that "the advantage of riches remains with him who procured them, not with the heir," to whom they become master, and not means, as they should be.[111] And more militantly, Theodore Parker attacked "the great property establishment of the times."[112]

After all, then, Brownson, not only in his views of the priesthood and the common church system, but also in his views of property and industry, was within the broad Transcendentalist pattern. Like Emerson, he wanted "a new order" which should "replace all property within the dominion of reason and equity."[113]

Yet the real significance of Brownson's essays on "The Laboring Classes" reaches far beyond both Transcendentalism and the time when they were written. Like Schlesinger, the British socialist Harold J. Laski stresses Brownson's social analysis and even calls him an "intellectual giant" in this field.[114] Hardly less important, however, was Brownson's strong insistence on the social aspect of Christianity. Theodore Maynard maintains that Brownson's ideas anticipated the later Papal encyclicals on labor,[115] and on the Protestant side, Brownson's social Christianity suggested not only the later American "Social-Gospel" Movement, but even the ecumenical emphasis in the distant 1970's on the social responsibility of the churches.

Finally, Brownson's view of property may be said to reflect, though in a very accentuated form, certain tendencies in the broad American idealistic tradition: the half religious "stewardship" conception of property, the ideal of the self-made man, and the dynamic attitude toward material goods, whose worth supposedly lies in their acquisition rather than in their retention. Perhaps it was not quite incidental that the author of the Declaration of Independence listed among the "unalien able rights" the dynamic conception "pursuit of happiness" instead of the static one about right of property.

1 *BQR*, III (Jan. 1840), 19.
2 *BQR*, III (July 1840), 287 ff.
3 *BQR*, III (Jan. 1840), 13.
4 *BQR*, III (April 1840), 261–262.
5 *BQR*, III (Oct. 1840), 405.
6 "Tendency of Modern Civilization," *BQR*, I (April 1838), 216–217. In the *BQR* for July, 1840 (p. 448) Brownson particularly referred to this article.

[7] *Works*, IV, 304, 305.

[8] *BQR*, III (July 1840), 437–438, and *BQR*, I (April 1838), 217.

[9] *The Convert*, p. 110.

[10] *Catholic World*, LXXVII (June 1903), 312.

[11] *The Convert*, p. 110.

[12] See, for example, *The American Republic*, published 1866 (*Works*, XVIII), in which Brownson maintained that the religious mission of the United States was to bring about "the union, identity between church and state, that is between religious and political principles." Yet "their union of interior principles" did not concern the "external separation of church and state" (pp. 211, 217).

[13] *BQR*, I (April 1838), 216.

[14] *BQR*, III (Oct. 1840), 407.

[15] *The Complete Works, Concord Edition*, I (Boston and New York, 1903), 144, 145.

[16] *BQR*, III (July 1840), 265–323. The articles in the *Princeton Review* were "Transcendentalism" (Jan. 1839) by James W. Alexander and Albert B. Dod, and "The School of Hegel" (Jan. 1840) by Charles Hodge. The fact that Norton republished these articles written by scholars at Princeton Theological Seminary shows that he felt more akin to his old "foes" the Trinitarians than to his new "enemies" the Transcendentalists (See Cameron Thompson, "John Locke and New England Transcendentalism," *New England Quarterly Review*, XXXV [Dec. 1962], 454). For an instructive treatment of the Norton-Ripley controversy, see William R. Hutchison, *The Transcendentalist Ministers* (New Haven, 1959), pp. 52–97.

[17] *BQR*, III, 268–269.

[18] Henry Steele Commager, *Theodore Parker* (Boston, 1947), p. 29.

[19] *BQR*, III (July 1840), 268.

[20] *Ibid.*, p. 269.

[21] *Ibid.*, p. 270.

[22] *BQR*, III (July 1840), 271.

[23] "Locke and the Transcendentalists," *Christian Examiner*, XXIII, 3rd series, V (Nov. 1837), 175.

[24] *A Discourse on the Latest Form of Infidelity* (Cambridge, Mass., 1839), p. 8.

[25] See Chapter X, notes 99, 100, 101, 144.

[26] *BQR*, III (July 1840), 271.

[27] *New England Quarterly*, XVI (March 1943), 62.

[28] *BQR*, III (July 1840), 271–272.

[29] *Ibid.*, pp. 322–323.

[30] Quoted in Norton's *A Discourse on the Latest Form of Infidelity* (*BQR*, III, 272).

[31] *BQR*, III (July 1840), 275.

[32] Quoted in *Essays, First and Second Series* (London and New York, 1947), p. 41.

[33] *BQR*, III (July 1840), 278, 276.

[34] *Ibid.*, pp. 277–278.

[35] Norton, *op.cit.*, p. 49.

[36] *The Complete Works, Concord Edition*, I (Boston and New York, 1903), 125.

[37] See, for example, William C. Gannett, *A Hundred Years of the Unitarian Movement in America, 1815–1915* (Germantown, Pa., 1915), where Channing, Emerson, and Parker are considered "the truer 'Unitarians'" and "our three Great Masters until now" (pp. 30, 32); and Frederick May Eliot, *Unitarians Believe* (Boston, 1939): "Many times . . . I have quoted Emerson, and even

when there hasn't been direct quotation, there has very often been a strong reliance upon his thought" (p. 55).

38 *BQR*, III (July 1840), 280.

39 *BQR*, III (Oct. 1840), 428.

40 *Ibid.*, p. 369.

41 *Ibid.*, p. 376.

42 *Ibid.*, pp. 383—384.

43 *Ibid.*, p. 385.

44 *Ibid.*, pp. 390, 430.

45 *Ibid.*, pp. 386—388.

46 *Dial*, I (Oct. 1840), 268; I (Jan. 1841), 281—282.

47 *The Correspondence of Emerson and Carlyle*, ed. Joseph Slater (New York and London, 1965), p. 332.

48 Quoted in *Essays, First and Second Series* (London and New York, 1947), p. 320.

49 "John Locke and New England Transcendentalism," *New England Quarterly*, XXXV (Dec. 1962), 450.

50 *BQR*, I (Oct. 1838), 511—512.

51 *The Letters of Ralph Waldo Emerson*, II (New York, 1939), p. 373.

52 Octavius B. Frothingham, *George Ripley* (Boston, 1883), p. 85.

53 The title of the pamphlet, too, was rather funny: *The Previous Question between Mr. Andrews Norton and His Alumni Moved and Handled in a Letter to All Those Gentlemen* (Boston, 1840).

54 *The Convert*, p. 104.

55 *BQR*, III (Oct. 1840), 439—442.

56 *Natural Religion in American Literature* (New Haven, 1966), pp. 52, 56.

57 *BQR*, III (Oct. 1840), 429.

58 *BQR*, III (July 1840), 391.

59 *BQR*, I (Oct. 1838), 471.

60 *BQR*, II (Oct. 1839), 416.

61 *G. A.*, VI (Nov. 8, 1828), 359.

62 *The Convert*, p. 56.

63 *Chr. Reg.*, No. 2, XIV (Aug. 23, 1834), 6; No. 3, XIV (Aug. 30, 1834), 10.

64 See Mary Ritter Beard, *The American Labor Movement* (New York, 1928), pp. 45—57.

65 *BQR*, I (Jan. 1838), 5.

66 *BQR*, III (July 1840), 391—394.

67 *Ibid.*, pp. 390—391. See also *The Convert*, p. 108.

68 *BQR*, III (Oct. 1840), 476.

69 "Lectures on the Elevation of the Laboring Portion of the Community" (Feb. 11, 1840), *The Works of William E. Channing, Eighth Complete Edition*, V (Boston and New York, 1848), pp. 166, 207.

70 "The Art of Life – the Scholar's Calling," *Dial*, I (Oct. 1840), 178, 182. See also Perry Miller's anthology *The Transcendentalists* (Cambridge, Mass., 1950), pp. 473—475.

71 *Dial*, I (Oct. 1840), 254.

72 *Dial*, I (Jan. 1841), 537; *Emerson's Works*, I (Boston and New York, 1903), pp. 280, 313, 334.

73 See Warner Berthoff, "Renan on W. E. Channing and American Unitarianism," *New England Quarterly*, XXXV (March 1962), 86 (quoted in Berthoff's translation of Renan's article in *Revue des deux Mondes* of 1854).

74 "The Political Ideas of Orestes A. Brownson, Transcendentalist," *Philological Quarterly*, XII (Jan. 1933), 280—289.

[75] *BQR*, I (Oct. 1838), 471.
[76] *BQR*, III (July 1840), 383.
[77] "Transcendentalism: A Self-Portrait," *New England Quarterly*, XXXV (March 1962), 43.
[78] *BQR*, III (July 1840), 373.
[79] *The Rise of the Common Man, 1830–1850* in *A History of American Life*, ed. Arthur M. Schlesinger and Dixon Ryan Fox, Vol. VI of 12 vols. (New York, 1927), p. 256.
[80] Thus the Workingmen's Party, which sprang into existence in the late 1820's, mainly originated in the workers' demand for a ten-hour day (See John R. Commons et al., *History of Labour in the United States*, [New York, 1926], 169, 231), and in the 1830's the ten-hour demand was a recurrent theme in industrial bargaining and motivated strikes and formations of unions (See Fish, *op.cit.*, p. 272).
[81] See John Demos, "The Antislavery Movement and the Problem of Violent 'Means,'" *New England Quarterly*, XXXVII (Dec. 1964), 501–524.
[82] Helen S. Mims, "Early American Democratic Theory and Orestes Brownson," *Science and Society* (Spring, 1939), III, 190.
[83] Herbert W. Schneider, *A History of American Philosophy* (New York, 1947), pp. 131–132.
[84] *BQR*, III (July 1840), 363–366.
[85] *Ibid.*, pp. 367–371.
[86] *Ibid.*, pp. 371–373, 472–473.
[87] Commons et al., *op.cit.*, I, 455, 487.
[88] Fish, *op.cit.*, p. 273.
[89] *Ibid.*, p. 110.
[90] "Early American Democratic Theory and Orestes Brownson," pp. 186–187.
[91] Herbert M. Morais, "Marx and Engels on America," *Science and Society*, XII (Winter, 1948), 7.
[92] Commons et al., *op.cit.*, "Humanitarianism (1840–1860)," I, 493. 493.
[93] *The Correspondence of Emerson and Carlyle*, p. 256.
[94] Max Morris, "Chartism and the British Working-Class Movement," *Science and Society*, XII (1948), 405–406.
[95] *BQR*, III (July 1840), 364–365.
[96] *The Correspondence of Emerson and Carlyle*, p. 289.
[97] *Orestes A. Brownson*, p. 96.
[98] "Orestes A. Brownson and American History," *Catholic Historical Review*, XL (Oct. 1954), 259.
[99] *BQR*, III (July 1840), 392–394.
[100] *BQR*, III (Oct. 1840), 477–481, 467.
[101] BQR, III (Oct. 1840), 486–491.
[102] *Ibid.*, pp. 494–496, 475–476.
[103] Helen L. Summer, "Citizenship (1827–1833), " *History of Labour in the United States*, I, pp. 236–237, 244; and M. R. Beard, *op.cit.*, p. 43.
[104] Arthur M. Schlesinger, Jr., *The Age of Jackson* (Boston, 1950), p. 310.
[105] M. R. Beard, *op.cit.*, p. 115.
[106] *The Convert*, p. 118.
[107] Commons et al., *op.cit.*, I, pp. 493–494.
[108] Review of Albert Brisbane's book *Social Destiny of Man: or Association and Reorganization of Industry* (Phil., 1840), *Dial*, I (Oct. 1840), 266.
[109] *Dial*, II (July 1841), 117.

110 "Man the Reformer," *Dial*, I (April 1841), 527.
111 *Ibid.*, pp. 528–529.
112 *Dial*, I (Oct. 1840), 212.
113 *Dial*, III (July 1842), 16.
114 *The American Democracy* (New York, 1948), p. 310.
115 "Orestes Brownson, Journalist: A Fighter for Truth," *Commonweal*, XXXVII (1943), 392.

XIII

Toward Political and Religious Conservatism

In *The Convert* (pages 103, 112, 113) Brownson wrote that his first essay on "The Laboring Classes" was received by his countrymen "with one universal scream of horror" and that above all his radical views of property and the factory system caused anger and embarrassment among the Democrats and malicious pleasure among the Whigs. The latter party reprinted his article by thousands, if not by hundreds of thousands, in order to damage the cause of their political antagonists.

As for his views on the priesthood and the churches, prominent Democrats like George Bancroft and John C. Calhoun agreed with him, and on the whole, his rejection of organized religion did not give the most offense,[1] so much the less because the Democratic Party was not by any means devoid of anticlerical elements.[2] But religious periodicals, particularly those of an orthodox stamp, took clear issue against him, and not only on specifically religious topics. Thus in the *Christian Review* President Francis Wayland of Brown University warned against the idea of State interference to improve the lot of the poor, on the somewhat strange ground that a similar interference would lead to State despotism. No less interesting was his point-blank assurance that Brownson's desire of abolishing priestcraft and the hereditary right of property stemmed from his reading of French literature, because "it would at once occur to every reader, that these notions could never have *originated* in the bosom of a native-born American."[3] A Methodist organ, obviously in defiance of Brownson's social-radical thought, expressed its preference of a dictator like "Bonarte" [sic] to any mobocracy.[4]

True, Brownson's essay, being published during the hectic election campaign of the same year, was signalized and unfavorably commented upon by political foes and friends alike. At Bunker Hill Daniel Webster thundered against him, and a Whig paper wanted him to be handled by the treadmill, the penitentiary, the pillory, and the whippingpost. Though the Democrats hardly expressed similar wishes with regard to their troublemaker, at least one of them—Levi Woodbury—wrote indignantly to George Bancroft and wanted to know why he had not fired Brownson from his government job;[5] and Bancroft, in turn, wrote to McAllister, Savannah, Georgia (Aug. 15, 1840), that "the Democracy of Massachusetts is no more responsible for Brownson's notions, than the Whigs are for Mormonism."[6]

Yet current Democratic opinion about Brownson's essay seems to have been pretty much divided; he was hardly met by wholesale denunciation as indicated in *The Convert*. Schlesinger even maintains that "the essay did not seriously affect either Brownson's usefulness or his popularity in the Massachusetts Democratic party," so that to the very close of the campaign he was touring the state, being in constant demand as a speaker.[7] And even if he felt the opprobrium from many quarters, being denounced in the press and from the pulpit and the rostrum, he also seemed to relish the situation and felt that his action was "bordering on moral heroism." Moreover, logician that he was, he felt a kind of intellectual relief when he had carried his premise to its last logical, if not realistic conclusion.[8]

But neither the election campaign of 1840 nor the defeat of the Democratic Party in November of the same year were any intellectual relief to him. The Whig Party, "that strange amorphous group," consisting of old Federalists, adherents of a U.S. Bank and protective tariffs, Anti-Masons, and advocates of states' rights, had nothing more in common than their opposition to the Democratic administration, and according to Claude Moore Fuess, one of Webster's biographers, the energies of the party "were largely devoted to destruction, and it had little to propose in compensation except remedies which the people did not relish."[9] Yet political "remedies," let alone political principles, got little or no hearing in this campaign, whose big popular hits seem to have been the Whig candidate William Henry Harrison's log cabin and President Van Buren's public expenses for the White House furniture. In this campaign, which sometimes degenerated into a veritable circus, the Whigs tried to outdo the Democrats in folksiness, and their choice of a former general as their candidate obviously had a recent Democratic model.[10]

Yet to Brownson politics should be something more than cheap popular appeals, and he who believed in the just and holy instincts of the masses, could not understand that "the people" might be cheated by demagogues. At that time Brownson's general skepticism as to the doctrine of popular sovereignty seems to have been much weakened. In this connection an entry in Bronson Alcott's diary for April 13, 1839, is interesting: "*Vox populi* is not *Vox Dei,* save where interest or passion are [sic] silent. It is the still small voice of the private soul that is authentic. Multitudes always lie. The single man's oracle is alone authentic. My neighbour Brownson will christen me 'Political atheist' for writing this sentiment. But his name is 'Legion.' I know not how many devils he hath."[11]

In any case, about that time Brownson really seemed to believe that "multitudes" or the masses never lied, but were guided by "first principles." And as Brownson saw it, the Democratic Party stood for great social and political principles, whereas their opponents, the Whigs, had no real ideology. Yet, however sanguine his belief in the Democratic Party, Brownson was right about the Whigs. They did not adopt any ideological platform at all, and their genial, but hardly strong-willed candidate for the presidency came "like another Cincinnatus from his plough," presenting as his vague aim to diffuse prosperity and to end hard times.[12]

But ideology or not, the "hard times" was at least a point, and, rightly or wrongly, the Whigs blamed the administration for the economic depression. More important, prominent Whig leaders like Daniel Webster and Henry Clay, who both tried to keep the discussion within the sphere of common sense, stressed the danger of a too strong executive power and pointed at examples of corruption in the Federal Government.[13] And, according to Henry Cabot Lodge, another of Webster's biographers, "the people, smarting under bankruptcy, poverty, and business depression, were wild for a change; but nothing," Lodge continues, "did so much to swell the volume of public sentiment against the policy of the ruling party as these speeches of Mr. Webster, which gave character and form to the whole movement."[14]

As for "the ruling party," it stated certain principles such as a limited Federal power and the separation of public money from the state banks. Moreover, the party declared its opposition to a national bank and rejected the idea of giving Federal grants to certain industries at the expense of others. Finally, the party convention stated that Congress had no constitutional right to interfere with slavery in the states. Obviously, the Jeffersonian tradition with its anti-Federal tendencies and its emphasis on states' rights was still strong in the party.[15]

In his biography of Henry Clay, Carl Schurz says that there was never "more enthusiasm and less thought" in any presidential campaign than in the Whig canvass in 1840.[16] But if the Whigs conducted their campaign with little thought, the Democrats, too, were often dangerously close to thoughtlessness. Thus, in a convention address to the people, they tried to cast doubts on Harrison's military prowess and achievements and accused the Whigs of wanting to reintroduce the "iron rod of Federal rule."[17]

Beyond any doubt, the elections aroused an overwhelming interest. No less than 2,400,000 voters went to the polls, an increase of 900,000 from the 1836 elections. By comparison, the increase of votes from 1840 to 1844 was only 300,000. Although Van Buren's defeat was not great numerically—he got only 145,000 less votes than Harrison—these votes were after all pivotal, since Harrison's total number of electoral votes were no less than 234, while Van Buren got only 60.[18]

But to Brownson, both the election campaign and the Whig victory were even more pivotal. Indeed, as he declared in 1843, "the famous election of that year [i.e. 1840] wrought a much greater revolution in us than in the Government; and we confess ... that since then we ... have pretty much ceased to speak of, or to confide in, the 'Intelligence of the people.' ... They who had devoted their lives to the cause of their country, of truth, justice, liberty, humanity, were looked upon as enemies of the people, and were unable to make themselves heard amid the maddened and maddening hurrahs of the drunken mob that went for 'Tippecanoe, and Tyler Too.' "[19] In *The Convert* (page 120) he wrote that the election campaign of 1840 with its "means utterly corrupt and corrupting," disgusted him with democracy as a form of government and made him "distrust both the intelligence and the instincts of 'the masses'." And even as late as in 1873 Brownson had not forgotten the "lesson" that the 1840 election gave him: " 'Tippecanoe and Tyler too' upset my democracy, by showing how easily the people can be humbugged and carried away by a song. Till then I had believed in democracy, though I believed in little else." And he continued: "The people held with me then, in some respects, the place the church now holds with me."[20]

It is difficult to grasp fully why Brownson, who was proud of having never believed in the doctrine of popular sovereignty and in the supposed wisdom of majorities, should have been so extremely disappointed with "the people" in 1840. However, he believed that "the people" were a kind of depository of divine power, and he fully shared Bancroft's faith in "eternal justice ruling through the people." To the question of whether there was any essential difference between the doctrine of popular sovereignty and his own (and Bancroft's) belief, he would have answered that the former "puts the people in the place of God, and asserts not only people-king, but people-god," while the latter derived wisdom and justice from God *through* the people. Yet, strangely enough, Brownson's exaggerated confidence in the intelligence and the instincts of the masses in 1840 and his later utter disappointment indicate more a belief, albeit unconscious, in the "people-god" than a belief in the people as only a more or less trustworthy medium of divine wisdom and influence. After all, one can hardly escape the conclusion that Brownson in 1840, under the strong impact of his social-radical ideas and the Transcendentalist doctrine of the universal inner light, believed so intensely in the divine instincts of the masses that he almost completely forgot his previous skepticism of majority rule and the doctrine of the sovereignty of the people.[21]

In any case, after 1840 Brownson felt the need of retracing his steps. Through studies of Aristotle and other ancient authors he gradually came to the conclusion that government was not an agent of society, but an authority with the right and duty to govern society. As he wrote in *The Convert* (pages 120–121): "I became henceforth a conservative in politics, instead of an impracticable radical, and through political conservatism I advanced rapidly towards religious conservatism."

However, he did not arrive at these conclusions as fast as this statement might indicate; nor should one forget that Brownson with his repeated insistence on the value of tradition and the experience of the human race had already for a long time expressed certain conservative sentiments.

Anyhow, his political articles during the first half of 1841 had a clear radical tendency, and the change in his attitude to government began to be seen only in the July number of his review. In the first article of the January, 1841, issue of the *Boston Quarterly Review* Brownson stated bluntly that he was still a radical and repeated his thesis from the last year that each worker should be both "producer" and "accumulator."[22] As for government, it should still be the agent of society, i.e. an active, progressive government carrying through social reforms, and not yet "an authority having the right and the power to govern society."[23]

It should be borne in mind, however, that Brownson by the term "government" in this connection meant state governments, and not the Federal Government. On the question of states' rights he was still a stubborn Jeffersonian democrat, maintaining that the Federal Government had to do only with "communities," i.e. states, and not individuals. On the whole, Brownson shared for some time the general attitude and beliefs of the Democratic Party, and even for his particular theory of inheritance set forth in his articles on "The Laboring Classes" he still seemed to retain his predilection, but had lost all hope of seeing it come true until a very distant future.[24]

True, he expressed his disappointment with the people, who allegedly had voted against their best interests, but he attributed the defeat of his party mainly to its politicians, who in his opinion were vague, timid and compromising. Instead, they should have put forward such proposals that would destroy "the social fabric entirely, or reconstruct it as it should be." In fact, Brownson still considered himself a left-wing Democrat, or a Locofoco, i.e. in Brownson's definition, a Jeffersonian Democrat who endorsed social equality.[25]

It was the duty of the government to carry out reforms so as to approach the ideal: social equality. Brownson was still pessimistic about the influence of morality and religion if the social inequality was too great: "This inequality throws men into a state in which you cannot bring religious principle or moral force to bear upon them."[26]

Yet in order to be efficient, the action of the government must at least get some response from the people; or better, through "right" voting the people should enable the government to take the most suitable action. But the election of 1840 convinced Brownson that the people were not mature enough to understand their vital interests. What must have grieved him particularly was the attitude of some of the workers who seemed to misinterpret his very intentions. Thus his mention of the overheard remark: "She is only a *factory* girl, and you know what that means"[27]—was regarded as his own negative appraisal of the women working in the factories. In an open letter to his accusers he stated in dignified terms, but with a melancholy undertone, that he worked for social reform and wanted the workers to be independent of their employers, or—in other words—he wanted to "put the 'plough into the hand of the owner,'—and also the spindle and the loom."[28] Although his quoted remark about factory girls might easily be misunderstood if considered in itself and not in its context, such misinterpretations hardly strengthened his belief in "the people."

But if his belief in the masses was constantly dwindling, he became more and more concerned with the rights of the minorities and the individual citizen. The primary task of the State was to protect the individuals against each other, but also to protect the individual against the State. Under the impact of the recent elections, Brownson felt and feared that the conception of absolute democracy was gaining ground: "We are aware that there is growing up among us a feeling, that majorities can do no wrong, but we have not yet satisfied ourselves that this feeling has any warrant in theory or experience." However, insofar as democracy meant a system of government with the aim of securing to the individual his natural rights, Brownson declared himself to be a democrat.[29]

Instead of absolute democracy or arbitrary majority rule he recommended "constitutional government" which alone could secure "real liberty" and the rights of the citizen: "The constitution is then a real check on ordinary government and legislation, the real sovereign of the country, of which government in its restricted sense is merely the agent or minister." Influenced by the "distinguished American statesman" John C. Calhoun, Brownson contrasted the term "concurring majorities of the parts" with the term "numerical majority." He stressed the point that the Constitution was not an expression of the numerical majority, and as regards amendments, Rhode Island and New York were on the same footing. Without going into detail, Brownson recommended that the same system be more prevalent in the states themselves.[30] In any case, he had the feeling that a good government must be founded in compromise between the "concurring" parts, and that it was a rather complicated affair, indeed much more so than he had so far seemed to imagine.[31]

Evidently, Brownson had recourse to the American Constitution, which with its system of checks and balances he considered a conservative guarantee against encroachments of "the numerical majority." With the help of the Constitution, which he found to be "a miracle of wisdom," and for which he had a "sort of religious veneration," it would be possible to fight efficiently for the freedom and the rights of the individual.[32]

Thus after 1840 Brownson gave to the Constitution another main emphasis than the one he had given earlier. In the 1830's he considered it mainly an instrument or at least an inspirer of the masses to carry through social reforms, but now, stressing its conservative aspects, he came to regard it mostly as a protector of the rights of the individual against the masses.[33] However, Calhoun himself did not apply his doctrine of concurring and numerical majorities primarily along these lines, but chiefly in support of his extreme states'-rightism and, increasingly, in his defense of the whole Southern section with its "peculiar labor" system, or slavery.[34] But in any case, Brownson seized upon Calhoun's principle, and symptomatically, in the very same year he decided to work for Calhoun's presidential candidacy in 1844.[35]

Psychologically, Brownson's disappointment with the masses resulting in his firm trust in the Constitution clearly shows his need for "believing" in something. In 1838 he declared that the instincts of the masses were true and holy to him,[36] and in 1841 he looked upon the Constitution with "religious veneration." No doubt, his intense craving for a solid foundation of belief often made his analysis of the premises a too hasty affair, and it is a strange paradox that Brownson, the "eclectic" reasoner, was such an "extremist" in his feelings.

For the latter reason Brownson exaggerated the dangers of majority rule, thus running the risk of stressing too much stability and order at the expense of social progress. For the same reason he exaggerated the importance of the 1840 election and the ideological role of the Democratic Party. And finally, for the same reason he had thought too highly of "the people" to take a moderate, balanced view of them when they chose another party than he had expected. After all, perhaps a flexible system of "checks and balances" or "a wise Eclecticism" might have been useful even in his own evaluation of "the people."

As Brownson began to doubt the truth and the expediency of political radicalism, he also began to doubt if true religion were identical with a no-church system. Instead he had a growing feeling that "the Christianity of Christ" could not be regarded as absolutely independent of "the Christianity of the Church." He even admitted the great importance of the church in that it had always emphasized incarnation, i.e. God manifest in the flesh. After all, God was no bleak abstraction, but a concrete, living reality: "We worship the invisible in the visible, the Creator in the creature, the Father in the Son." Brownson now began feeling that through the doctrine of incarnation the church met the deepest needs of man: "The abstract exists not for the heart. It is not goodness that we reverence, but him who is good; it is not beauty that we love, but the being who is beautiful."[37]

But Brownson was still far from the traditional, orthodox interpretation of the dogma of the Incarnation. He pointed out that the church had erred in not giving the truth of incarnation a general validity: "The Church has contended for a general truth, a truth of all times, and of all worlds; but she has regarded it as a special truth, a truth in relation to one individual only." Consequently, Brownson still considered Jesus not a being essentially different from other men, but after all a star that differed from other stars only in brilliance.[38]

At least so far, Brownson only seemed to have resumed his earlier, "eclectic" position regarding the church and Christian dogma. No doubt, his view of incarnation was influenced by Cousin's thesis that all ideas are defective, if exclusive or strongly one-sided, and Brownson's view also reflected the general Transcendentalist attitude toward Christian dogma, which was supposed to cover more farreaching truths than their orthodox interpretation seemed to warrant. Yet his increasing concern with the Incarnation as something more than an abstraction, but the idea of God manifest in the flesh, seemed to signalize a new emphasis, at least compared with his spirited, unchurchly Christianity in his articles of 1840.

This new emphasis on the doctrine of incarnation made him more open to certain aspects of Catholic doctrine and practice. He stressed the point that the Catholic Church, "in permitting the invocation of Saints, and the worship of the Virgin, blest mother of God," at least modified the exclusive character of the dogma of incarnation. By contrast, the Protestant churches, by "dethroning the saints" and "denying the divinity of the Virgin," had "robbed the Godhead of all its sweetness, the universe of its living, loving heart, and given as an object of worship, only a stern, frowning, forbidding Majesty."[39]

In Brownson's view, the advance of Protestantism "on Catholicism has, in too many respects, been a retrograde movement towards Judaism" with the latter's conception of a stern and awful Jehovah instead of "the mild and beneficent Creator revealed by Jesus." If Protestantism had made any advance, this progress had only been in nonreligious fields. While the latter point recalled his *New Views*, his words about the Virgin and the Saints indicated a more positive appraisal of Catholicism than he had admitted so far. The real and not only formal role of mediators, which increasingly occupied Brownson's mind and finally led him toward Catholicism, had already begun to attract his attention.[40]

True, from the time of his *New Views* he had considered Jesus as mediator or God-Man, but this primarily because of his representative character. Now he seemed to approach a more orthodox conception of Jesus: "The conclusion to which our inquiries have led us is, that the Saviour was very God and very man, and in him we see the union of perfect God and perfect man. The Christ was one with God, was God, and the Christ, the true God, was incarnated in the man Jesus, a true man, and type of the perfect man." Correspondingly, his view of the atonement was also becoming more orthodox: Jesus was "the Son of God, one with the Father, through whom alone we can be cleansed from all sin, and presented blameless at the last day."[41]

While approaching traditional Christian beliefs, Brownson became increasingly skeptical about the half-dogmatic Unitarianism of "the Old School" and did not even regard it any longer as a living religion: "We would speak respectfully of unitarianism, as we would always speak of the dead." Admitting its great importance in the intellectual and the social fields, Brownson stated bluntly that "men never embraced unitarianism because they were pious, but because they would dispense with being pious. Unitarianism never spoke to the heart, to the soul; never waked any real enthusiasm, or called forth any religious energy of character. It is in its nature *un*spiritual, merely intellectual and material, a sort of baptized atheism."[42]

But although Brownson would not mourn the supposed death of Unitarianism, he did not overlook its historical importance. Interestingly enough, he stressed the sociological and not, primarily, the religious causes of Unitarianism. With the social and economic progress of American society, Puritan asceticism, combined with or resulting from the stern Calvinistic doctrines, had gradually lost ground. He believed that the old Puritans tried to do more than they actually could do in thinking themselves able to live on earth as one is supposed to live in heaven. For this reason, "Unitarianism was with us a protest against asceticism, even more than against the absurdity of Calvinism.... It was an effort of those who could not live in a perpetual lie, to reconcile their theology and their religion to their philosophy and their mode of living."[43]

However, when the Unitarians began to examine their beliefs, they found that from the point of view of religion Unitarianism stood for "materialism, dryness, coldness, deadness." Falling back on the religious element of their natures and seeking refuge in a more spiritual philosophy, they found themselves in a state of transition from materialism to spiritualism, from Unitarianism proper to a "modified orthodoxy." Brownson undoubtedly regarded William E. Channing as a spokesman for this general tendency. Even more important in this respect was Brownson's praise of Emerson's *Essays* (1841), a book which "marks a movement of the unitarian mind towards a higher, a broader, a more truly religious faith and life."[44]

It is noteworthy that Brownson called this tendency toward a more spiritual religion a "modified orthodoxy" and even recommended his "orthodox friends" to read Emerson's essays.[45] Yet it is more than doubtful if these "friends" found Emerson's essays to be a sample of "modified orthodoxy." Despite their general disagreement with the Unitarians of "the Old School," they had scarcely any objection to Norton's label on Emerson's ideas: "the latest form of infidelity." But in contrast to Norton, the Calvinists believed that this infidelity was the logical conclusion of dogmatic Unitarianism itself.[46]

On the whole, Brownson seemed to voice thoughts and sentiments not uncommon among Unitarians of "the New School." In the Transcendentalist organ the *Dial*, William Dexter Wilson, obviously dissatisfied with oldtime Unitarianism, maintained that Trinitarianism originated in Platonic philosophy and "possibly, also" in the Bible.[47] Consequently, he declared his belief in the doctrines of the Trinity and of Christ as "very God." But first of all, he wanted a revival of Platonism, "a spiritual philosophy" which was "transcendental" and "dynamical."[48]

Another writer in the *Dial* viewed Catholicism in a favorable light, praising the "Holy Mother" and the "countless saints" of the Catholic Church, and contrasting the Catholic "*Unity of the Faith*" to the "chaos" made by "the so-called Reformation."[49]

Finally, Brownson's idea of incarnation as God manifest in the flesh had also certain parallels. Thus a third writer in the same organ asked if God was not "revealed through the senses," and declared that "everything beautiful is emblematic of something spiritual."[50] Despite Emerson's "noble doubt" as to the reality of matter, one might even suggest a remote parallel between Brownson's idea and Emerson's belief that "every natural fact is a symbol of some spiritual fact."[51]

Brownson's approach to Christian tradition was more clearly manifested in his review of Theodore Parker's famous sermon "On the Transient and Permanent in Christianity" (1841). Parker maintained that the moral precepts preached by Jesus and sanctioned by men as God's voice in their hearts were the permanent elements of Christianity. On the other hand, the different theological systems were its transient elements. Thus, to Parker, the doctrine of the Trinity was of downright heathen origin and, consequently, of no intrinsic, lasting value. Brownson, who by now had come to see the Christian dogmas, including the doctrine of the Trinity, in a more positive light, contended that Parker emphasized too much the humanity of Jesus at the expense of his "divinity."[52]

However, what Brownson really meant by the "divinity" of Jesus is more difficult to understand. On the one hand, he expressed the traditional view that Jesus, or Christ, was and could be Saviour only because he was God. On the other hand, he was of the opinion that God's incarnation in Jesus was not essentially unique, nor was this incarnation a prerequisite for the redemption of mankind. After all, Jesus represented only "the type of the union" of the divine and human natures: "All Scripture . . . plainly teaches, and all Christians really believe, that we may become united with God as Jesus in his Humanity was, be sons of God in the sense in which he was a son of God, and joint heirs with him of the heavenly inheritance."[53]

In fact, Brownson's reasoning offered a curious mixture of orthodox and unorthodox elements, which could not easily be harmonized. Yet Brownson, who only one year before had raged against all churchly religion, now seemed to be more skeptical about similar views expressed by another. Even though he gave Parker credit for having "spoken out in the tones of a brave man on a great subject, as few men among us have dared to speak," he took pains to warn against too much radicalism. Interestingly enough, Brownson appealed to "universal usage" and the tradition of "the Church" when blaming Parker for applying the terms "a Hebrew youth" or "Galilean peasant" to Jesus. This appeal to the tradition of "the Church" was the more remarkable since it was made by one who only one year before had branded what he called "the Christianity of the Church."

The reason might be that Brownson had a deep, underlying sense of religious tradition. Although he had little respect for existing churches, he seemed to have a more or less conscious respect for "the Church," which, apparently, represented to him not an institution, but the general beliefs of Christians throughout the centuries. Parker's views, which coincided with Brownson's "religion of humanity," made him realize the barrenness of a sheer natural religion. Thus, strangely enough, Parker's presentation of naked naturalism which Brownson himself, in principle, had advocated, served as an eye opener to him about the value of "traditional faith."[54]

Judging from the *Boston Quarterly Review* for the year 1841, philosophical questions as such occupied Brownson's mind far less than political and religious problems. After the general election of 1840, Brownson entered a new phase of his intellectual development. Feeling the need of grappling directly with the burning political and religious questions themselves, he was probably inclined to think that a cool philosophical corroboration of his views might be postponed.

Another reason for the lack of essays on philosophy in the 1841 review might be the fact that Brownson had begun to lose his immense respect for Victor Cousin. Instead, a new "light" in contemporary philosophy, Pierre Leroux, was about to attract his attention. Thus, the year 1841 signified in Brownson's life a comparatively great degree of intellectual unrest and uncertainty, which affected all fields of his mental activity, but philosophy in particular. Predictably, Brownson preferred to wait some time before formulating his changed or modified philosophical views.

In the broad sense of the term he still regarded himself as a Transcendentalist: "All persons, who believe in God, in a reality of a spiritual world, and contend that their belief has any legitimate basis, are transcendentalists." According to this rather sweeping definition, Brownson placed the Puritan philosopher-theologian Jonathan Edwards and the philosophers of the Scottish School under the general heading "transcendentalists." More important, however, was his attempt at a more philosophical definition of Transcendentalism. He now defined it as a system of thought maintaining that God does not exist in space and time, but out of space and time. The categories of space and time belong to the senses. How to establish contact between the world of the senses and the transcendental world? Brownson postulated that Reason, the alleged God-given capacity to perceive transcendental truths, "rises immediately into a region where there is no time, no space," and perceives the eternal, absolute ideas of the true, the just, the good, and the fair. No less important to show his Transcendentalist position was his statement that he considered Reason "partly analogous to" Emerson's "Over-Soul."[55]

Thus, Brownson to a great extent still shared the views of the Transcendentalists. No less significant in this respect was his positive appraisal of Emerson's *Essays* (1841). But he had also some objections to make, and these objections taken together with his positive evaluation of the essays undoubtedly reflected his general attitude at the time toward Transcendentalism as such.

Viewing Emerson's *Essays* much in the same light as he had previously considered his "Divinity School Address," Brownson criticized Emerson for his too strong insistence on the transcendental world and the idea of unity at the expense of the world of the senses and the idea of multiplicity. To Brownson Emerson was apt to fall into pure philosophical idealism. Even more important, as Emerson seemed to think that the diversity and multiplicity of the sensory world were nothing but illusions, he was liable to fall into pantheism, or as Brownson called it: "ideal Pantheism." In Emerson's view, at least as Brownson understood it, God and the universe seemed to form an absolute unity. Brownson, on the other hand, wanted to stress both the reality and the multiplicity of the senses: "The idealist is as exclusive and as erroneous as the materialist."[56]

Such a statement both reflected Cousin's influence and represented Brownson's general mode of reasoning. Typically, his philosophical key word about God and the universe was "relation" in contrast to Emerson's key word "identity." According to Brownson, God and the universe are in the most intimate relation, but that relation is one of cause and effect, not of identity."[57]

Obviously, the term "relation," which he used in different connections, did not imply "antithesis." Restating his doctrine of his *New Views*, he declared that "according to Christianity the antithesis between body and soul insisted upon by the old religions, is done away, and now we should write 'Holiness to the Lord' on everything. Man's whole nature rightly exercised, is alike holy."[58] Rather, "relation" meant "harmony," which, in Brownson's view, ought to be brought about between "the will" of the individual and "the primordial laws of the universe."[59] Or as he expressed the similar ideas elsewhere: "Whoso has penetrated into the mysteries of the universe has done it only on the condition of placing himself in harmony with its laws, or, in other words, with the will of its Creator."[60]

Although not indicating "identity," similar statements at least remind one of Emerson's idea of coincidences and symmetry.[61] Obviously,

Brownson was trying to find "harmony" in religion and philosophy in order to counteract his impression of the disharmonies of contemporary society. And in the following year he made decisive steps in his search for his own religious and philosophical "harmony."

1842 was the last and, in the light of Brownson's intellectual development, the most important year of the *Boston Quarterly Review.* On the whole, his writings in this year signaled a marked trend toward political and religious conservatism and an increasing emphasis on traditional beliefs. But his interpretation of these beliefs was not altogether traditional.

In politics, Brownson's increasing contempt for the rule of majorities motivated his demand for "order" and a strong, although not authoritarian, government. Feeling convinced that "the voice of the multitude is rarely the voice of God," he was skeptical about an extension of suffrage.[62]

On the other hand, he regarded the geographical extension of the Union as a definite advantage, because the sectional differences would weaken the tendency toward the "horizontal division," i.e. the social and economic differences between rich and poor. He seemed to think that many, almost independent states within the Union might counteract the monopolizing tendencies of an increasingly centralized Federal Government.[63]

In fact, when Brownson was now professing his belief in government, he thought almost exclusively of state governments. Rejecting Thomas Paine's idea that government was "at best a necessary evil," he formulated two positive aims of government: to secure the rights of the individual and further the coöperation between all members of society. Yet Brownson had lost his confidence in radical social reforms that met with strong resistance. Thus his own attempt to weaken "the horizontal division" between the social classes in each state by proposing the abolition of the inheritance laws had not been successful. He had come to believe that changes would come through the influence of religion and morality rather than by the direct initiative of the government.[64]

The Whigs even contended that Brownson's "agrarian" notions were the main cause of Van Buren's defeat, but he defended himself against the charge.[65] Even Van Buren himself seems to have suggested the same, but in all likelihood Brownson's essays on "The Laboring Classes" did not have such an impact on the election.[66] And despite his misgivings, Brownson still considered himself an adherent of the Democratic Party and hoped it would resume power in the next presidential election. But he now preferred to call it the Republican Party, since to him the word "democracy" had a tinge of "mobocracy."

In his eye, the Whigs had exploited the doctrine of popular sovereignty to the benefit of the rich. The real mob, then, was not after all the "unwashed mob" in the streets or even less the misled majority at the polls, but the "well-clad mob of brokers, stock-jobbers, bankers, speculators, and ambitious and intriguing politicians."[67]

In order to protect the individual against this "well-clad mob" and the misled majority, Brownson had resort to "constitutional republicanism," and declared: "The real issue before the country between the Whigs and Republicans is, then, no longer bank or no bank, but *Constitution*, or no *Constitution*; the *Freedom* of law and order, or the *Tyranny* of an irresponsible majority."[68]

Since in more recent times political conservatism, rightly or wrongly, has often been linked with economic liberalism, it should be emphasized that Brownson's beginning conservatism was no defense of the business interests; rather, it was meant to be a defense against them and the allegedly deluded masses.

On the whole, despite his fears of "an irresponsible majority," Brownson still seemed to believe in the basic integrity of "the people." Consequently, he attacked more strongly the leaders of the masses than the masses themselves and was apt to excuse blunders and even crimes committed in the name of an allegedly deceived majority. To Brownson, in the United States of 1840 the commercial and manufacturing interests swayed public opinion, and in France of 1789 not the people, but the court and nobility were those really guilty of the crimes.[69]

Therefore, he leveled a scathing attack on Edmund Burke, who in his *Reflections on the Revolution in France* (1790) was supposedly disloyal to the cause of the people: "We forsake our dearest friend the moment we suspect him of being false, or capable of proving false to the sacred cause of popular enfranchisement, or social amelioration ... All we can say of him is, let his memory be forever execrated by the friends of truth, righteousness, and freedom."

Scarcely more lenient was his criticism of the popular novelist Edward Bulwer-Lytton, who also condemned the French Revolution and thereby the cause of the people: "Sir Edward's attack on the French

Revolution has resulted from despair of the popular cause. We can pardon something to feelings of despair; for there is something in the stupidity of the mass, in their readiness to follow their enemies and to desert their real friends, that may almost justify a momentary spleen, almost a momentary despair." But after all, Brownson continued, "this spleen, this despair can affect none but a sentimentalist. He who has risen ... from the sentimental to the ideal, can never be affected by either.... He is always calm, serene, hopeful, for he knows in whom he has believed, and his faith is equal to all emergencies, like that of the early Christians, overcoming the world."[70]

In the light of the decisive and lasting impact that the 1840 election had on his mind, Brownson himself, according to his own definition, seems to have been "a sentimentalist." Yet, striving to overcome his despair–momentary or not–of the masses, he now seemed to consider social reform as a slow and laborious process, which is evident from his following statement: "If the people were ready and able to respond to the first note of reform we sound, they would prove either that they need no reforming, or that they are already so nearly up with us, that the adoption of all we can propose would prove to be no advancement. He who has had faith in the progress of humanity, but has lost it, has lost it because it was with him only a sentiment, never an idea."[71]

But to this one might add that, whether regarded as sentiment or idea, faith in the progress of humanity is far more "safe" and indefinite than faith in specific social-political measures to improve the lot of certain portions of humanity today. Obviously, Brownson was now seeking for more long-range "measures" in religion, and apparently had lost to some extent his interest in social and political problems. Typically, he resumed his "labours as a Preacher of the Gospel" to his Society for Christian Union and Progress, and in his "Introductory Address" (first Sunday in April, 1842) he explained away, although wrongly, his political activity only as an "episode."

Also, from what one might gather from the same address, he seems to have come to better terms with the clergy, whose opposition to his social-radical views was, probably, the main reason of the three years' (1839–1842) interruption of his preaching to his society. Again, in harmony with his general emphasis on "the progress of humanity," he now expressed his intention of preaching for humanity or all classes and not particularly for the workingmen, which he had done earlier.[72]

His belief in "the progress of humanity" implied an increasing respect for tradition and made him re-emphasize his earlier expressed wish of combining "the Conservator" and "the Radical."[73] He stressed the view that, although man was made for progress, real progress did not mean a total rupture with tradition, but an organic growth of living, traditional elements. Strangely enough, Brownson did not even regard the French Revolution as a total breach with the past, and even less he considered the French philosophers of the eigtheenth century destructive. The reason was that they believed in the grand idea of the *Perfectibility of the Race.* Such a belief was in itself something positive and not at all destructive![74]

To Brownson, then, there was no basic difference between so-called radicals and conservatives. But even though all men, whether they were called reformers or conservatives, were making progress, Brownson was now shifting his emphasis on to another alleged difference. Until 1840 he had believed the masses to be mainly responsible for the progress of mankind. Partly as a result of the defeat of the Democratic Party in 1840, and partly owing to the influence of Pierre Leroux's writings, Brownson now seemed to transfer gradually his trust in the masses to a trust in "providential" or "*individual messengers.*"

These Providential men or agents, above all religious leaders, had inspired mankind and lifted it to constantly higher levels. God himself, in His wise and benevolent Providence, had raised such gifted individuals for the benefit of humanity. It was chiefly through these individuals that God had given to men "a positive supernatural revelation," which became natural religion when most of the elements of faith had been assimilated by mankind. The idea that the same religion or even one particular religious doctrine might be called supernatural and natural according to the intellectual and moral stage of mankind is interesting; but more important, it shows that Brownson, as yet, did not make any real distinction between revealed religion and natural religion.[75]

Clearly, Brownson's view of history as an organic growth was a dominant feature of Romantic thought. Thus Thomas Carlyle praised Napoleon's attempts to make the French Revolution "organic," although at the same time he condemned the French emperor for his tyranny.[76]

Also, Brownson's idea of Providential messengers reflected the general Romantic and Transcendentalist belief in particularly gifted individuals like poets and prophets: veritable depositories of divine inspiration. More especially, apart from the direct influence from Leroux, Brownson's Providential men had obvious parallels to Cousin's "le vrai représentant," Emerson's "Representative Men"[77] and Carlyle's "Heroes." But far more markedly than the others, Brownson considered these "individual messengers" primarily religious leaders and not poets, artists, and philosophers.

However, although there were "heights in the life of Jesus which no human imagination has scaled," Brownson did not yet regard Jesus as *the* Providential man, standing out from all other Providential men and essentially different from them. On the other hand, the conception of "the *special inspiration of individual messengers*" was a specification of his still retained idea of the general incarnation or the inspiration of all men. The doctrine of "the *special inspiration*" might lead to a more traditional conception of Jesus and finally even did lead Brownson to this conception; but so far he only expressed mankind's—and his own—general need of "Bibles and Messiahs."[78]

On another point, however, Brownson seemed to approach more definitely a genuine Christian idea. Quoting Emerson's famous verse: "Out of the heart of Nature roll'd/The burdens of the Bible old;"..., Brownson rejected the poet's idea of "the Litanies of nations" coming from "the burning core," or—as he interpreted Emerson—the human heart. To Brownson, nature or man himself did not produce the Bible and Christianity. On the contrary, they came from God! Thus Brownson was beginning to lay a more distinct emphasis on the objective side of religion than his fellow Transcendentalists, who, according to Brownson, thought the "transcendental truths to exist in the soul." Brownson, who already in 1838 in his comments on Emerson's and Bronson Alcott's works had suggested a similar criticism of Transcendentalist subjectivism,[79] now more firmly stated his position: "It is always out of us we are to look for the truth; never in us; for it is only as we are reflected from what we are not, as in a glass, that we learn what we are, or even that we are."[80]

Brownson, then, had become fully aware that truth must be sought outside man, or the subject. But the need of an object, or a *not-me*, was not only caused by his earnest desire to establish a firm basis of the truth of religious and philosophical doctrines. In order to justify his belief in man's progress, he came to realize that man's own internal powers were not enough: "No man can rise above himself, or lift himself by his own waistband." Something "which is not man" was necessary to enable him to make progress and erect the Church of the Future.[81]

As mentioned in another context, Brownson increasingly felt that Cousin's doctrine of Reason as something divine and at the same time a faculty of the human soul did not clearly state the objectivity of truth. But then Pierre Leroux drew Brownson's attention to a doctrine already formulated by Cousin, that thought consists of three elements, i.e. the subject or the thinker, the object or what is thought, and the relation between the two, or the form of thought. In the last analysis, the object is God, and without the object man is not able to think at all. Leroux developed this doctrine and, in Brownson's view, showed more clearly than Cousin that thought is a synthesis, resulting from two factors: the object and the subject, which are given simultaneously.

With the enthusiasm typical of Brownson when he had hit upon ideas that especially appealed to him, he confidently stated that this doctrine of the character of thought "stripped philosophy of its mystery" and "divested it of its endless abstractions." To a possible question of whether or to what extent the objective part of thought would be colored or influenced by its subjective part, Brownson would have his answer ready: "The object, then, is always real, and no thought ever is or ever can be totally false or purely subjective."[82]

More important, Leroux taught him that this synthesis of object and subject did not only concern the intellectual order, but all fields of human life and activity. In none of these fields can man exist without communion with an "object," whether this object be external nature or his fellow men. But the object does not only enable man quite simply to exist, it should also elevate him and lead him on to a still higher and nobler life.

Thus far Brownson followed his new "light." Strangely enough, the French philosopher who was in some circles even regarded as an atheist, really helped Brownson to form a less abstract, a more living image of God than he had done before. Even if he did not accept Leroux's pantheistic conception of God, he grasped the Frenchman's idea of God as the indispensable, underlying element of man's thoughts and the constitutive element of man's moral acts. In other words, the idea of God had been actualized in the concrete; the abstract God had become a living God. Leroux, then, furnished Brownson with the philosophical basis of the traditional Christian belief in God manifest in the flesh, or God revealed in His works.[83]

On the whole, Pierre Leroux's writings indicate a man of warm sentiments rather than cool reflections. His words about sentiments and the heart are almost like proverbs: "Voir, ... c'est sentir" and "Les grandes pensées viennent du cœur."[84] Also for this reason Brownson, consciously or unconsciously, must have felt a certain attachment to him.

Probably he had got a little tired of Cousin's elegant, refined style and beautiful rhetoric, which, moreover, did not and even could not hide certain alleged inconsistencies in his philosophy.[85] Nor could Brownson with his increasing demand for *the* truth find lasting satisfaction in Cousin's apparently bland, vast tolerance of almost all philosophical systems. However, Cousin's eclectic approach to philosophy had always a strong hold on him, chiefly because it seemed to correspond to his own favorite mode of reasoning.[86]

Anyhow, Brownson studied Leroux's book *Réfutation de l'Eclectisme* (1839) with great interest. In this book, which Brownson read in 1841 or 1842,[87] Leroux attacked above all the supposed philosophical and political indifference of the Eclectic philosophers: "l'éclectique est un homme indifférent par nature"–and even thought that Cousin was a skeptic at heart. In contrast to Cousin's "éclectisme-système," which he considered a sort of mechanical mixture or a "misérable syncrétisme," Leroux wanted a "véritable éclectisme" or a "véritable synthèse," i.e. a real organic fusion of two ideas through "un mystère de transformation." For the formation of such a higher, Hegel-inspired synthesis, Leroux stressed the great importance of "sentiment," which he thought that Cousin had neglected in his philosophy.[88]

Already in Brownson's essay on "Reform and Conservatism" in the January, 1842, issue of his review, the influence from Pierre Leroux was manifest: "Mere eclecticism, taken strictly, is impotent, ... rendering us indifferent... Eclecticism wants life, power to quicken men's souls..."[89] But first of all, it was Leroux's work *De l'Humanité* (1840) that deeply influenced Brownson's views and even induced him to take decisive steps toward traditional Christianity.[90]

In his essay "Leroux on Humanity" in the July, 1842, issue of his review, Brownson stressed Leroux's affiliation with the Saint-Simonian School, which, in contrast to the Eclectic School of Cousin with its marked *juste-milieu* or *bourgeois* tendencies, had a great social-radical ideal: "to effect in the speediest manner possible the moral, intellectual, and physical amelioration of the poorest and most numerous class." On the whole, Leroux's views were based on a strong belief in the progressiveness of man, society, and humanity. More particularly, this belief meant that future generations would not only benefit from an increased scientific and cultural heritage, but would also be born with "greater internal capacities." Brownson, too, seemed to share this Saint-Simonian view of progress.[91]

But the real benefit he got from the book was Leroux's doctrine that man cannot live, act, or think without an object, or a *not-me*. To Leroux there were three primary "objects:" nature or the world, humanity, and God. More specifically, Leroux pointed out certain "media" through which man established contact with his "objects." Through property (of all things!) man communed with nature, through family and country he communed with his fellowmen or, more generally, humanity. Again, through humanity he communed with God.[92]

Evidently, Leroux's doctrine of property, family, and country as necessary intermediaries between man and his "objects" could not fail to justify or strengthen Brownson's beginning tendencies toward political conservatism. But it should be added that both Leroux and Brownson regarded these three traditional, conservative cornerstones not as objects sufficient unto themselves, but as indispensable means to the constant improvement of man's condition.[93]

Leroux extended his idea of communion between individuals into the idea of an all-comprising solidarity among all men. Virtually, though not actually, the object of each man was all men. Both Leroux and Brownson maintained that the Christian church had not encouraged this solidarity or, in other words, the church had not managed to reconcile the love of self with the love of one's neighbor. Instead, the Christian had been compelled to abnegate his own self and turn to the "pure" or exclusive love of God. Yet in clear contrast to Leroux, Brownson held that Christianity as such was essentially the religion of reconciliation or real synthesis.[94]

More important, Brownson differed from Leroux concerning the views of God and creation. Leroux seemed to identify God with the universe, or, on other occasions, with humanity.[95] Leroux's doctrine of the synthesis of object and subject, which justified Brownson's belief in a living God manifest in the flesh–i.e. as the fundamental object of man's thoughts, acts, and life–did not, apparently, lead the French philosopher to similar conclusions. In *The Convert* (page 131) Brownson, with his almost typical cocksuredness, declared that Leroux "never fairly understood his own philosophy," because he "asserted God as the Void of the Buddhists, the infinite possibility of the universe" and not its immanent reality. But what really mattered to Brownson, was that the French philosopher "had asserted direct intuition of God, that we think God, and God must really be, or we could not think him." Also, Leroux's emphasis on life as "growth" and not only "development"[96] and, consequently, his belief in the organic character of the synthesis between object and subject tended to reinforce Brownson's idea of a living, real God.

Yet Brownson was careful to point out that synthesis of object and subject did not mean identity. Therefore, he now felt he had a clear, philosophical reason for rejecting the doctrine of the identity between the human and the divine, or the doctrine of "no God but the God in man." This conclusion filled him with "an inexpressible joy." For more than ten years he had taught his "religion of humanity," a kind of natural, rationalistic religion with more or less spiritualistic overtones. But now, for the first time, he felt he was headed in the direction of real Christian beliefs.[97]

Brownson had adopted Pierre Leroux's main philosophical doctrine and suggested a religious interpretation of it. But he developed Leroux's doctrine further in a long "letter" to William E. Channing, written in June, 1842, and afterward published as a booklet under the title of *The Mediatorial Life of Jesus.*

He opened his letter by praising Channing as his "spiritual father." Channing had always helped and encouraged him. Above all, Channing's sermon on "Likeness to God" (1828) had filled young Brownson with indescribable delight and made him aware that even he, from early age a fatherless child, was after all not left to himself: "I seemed suddenly to have found a Father."[98]

True, Brownson's attitude toward religion was made up of various components, but his search for a "father" seems to have been basic. Channing undoubtedly presented to him an even more living and distinct image of the heavenly father. Obviously, the idea of God as father implied the ideas of personality and Providence, and, in fact, except for his brief period of unbelief, Brownson had always seemed consciously anxious to avoid any impersonal or fatalistic conception of God.

However, it was Leroux who, through his doctrine of Providential men, provided him with a philosophical key to verify the idea of divine Providence. Yet the following quotation from *The Convert* (page 140) illustrates not only a logician searching for a philosophical basis for his idea of God's "freedom," but far more a "son" searching religiously for a "father:" "I was no longer fatherless, an orphan left to the tender mercies of inexorable general laws, and my heart bounded with joy, and I leaped to embrace the neck of my Father, and to rest my head on his bosom. I shall never forget the ecstasy of the moment, when I first realized that God is free."

Evidently, this sudden philosophical insight into a cherished, but not "legitimated" belief seems to have motivated his letter to Channing. In any case, he declared that those who identify God with nature or the so-called natural laws and deny His special intervention in the affairs of mankind, not only deny that God is free and, consequently, is our father, but "virtually deny his existence."[99]

Yet Brownson's search for a "father" did not only predispose him to accept the universal Christian belief in the fatherhood and Providence of God; his quest of a father figure was probably the main reason for his need of an authoritative religion: "I felt, as I had felt from my boyhood, that I had need of an authoritative religion; and that a religion which does not and cannot speak with divine authority, is simply no religion at all."[100] Most probably, only in the light of his intense craving for a "father" may the somewhat paradoxical combination of his beliefs in God's freedom and an authoritative religion be seen and understood. So according to this interpretation, it is perhaps not quite surprising that Brownson in 1871, remembering with joy the day when he realized that God is free, declared that his conversion to Catholicism really began from that day.[101]

But even if the mild, unauthoritative Channing had stimulated him in his search for the heavenly father, he had a growing feeling that Channing's conception of Christianity and, more particularly, of Christ was incomplete. From Channing's above-mentioned sermon he had gathered only two doctrines in addition to that of God as father—namely the divinity of humanity and the brotherhood of men. He said that so far he had been reluctant to go beyond these doctrines, partly from conviction and partly from the tactical reason of trying to win unbelievers for what he thought was "sufficient" Christianity. Yet he had now worked out a principle which he thought would throw light on the role of Jesus as mediator and even prepare the ground for unity between Trinitarians and Unitarians.[102]

In this connection it should be emphasized that Brownson, although he regarded Unitarianism of "the Old School" as dead, still declared himself loyal to "the Unitarian Party," to which he had belonged since 1831. Now, in 1842, he even found "the Unitarian movement" or "the Unitarian community" to be "the truest *Christian* church now on earth." To all intents and purposes, Brownson partly restated his earlier intention—already expressed in his *New Views*—of applying "the New School" Unitarianism as a vehicle for introducing his Church of the Future. But his positive reappraisal of church principles and orthodox dogma also reflected an increasing tendency in the 1840's among "the New School" Unitarian ministers to combine elements of Transcendentalist thought with orthodox, churchly symbols.[103]

The principle which Brownson referred to in his letter to Channing was the doctrine suggested by Cousin and elaborated by Leroux, that the object, the subject, and their relation are given simultaneously in thought. In his book *De l'Humanité* Leroux showed him the social application of this doctrine, but then one day, when preparing a sermon, Brownson suddenly devised a theological application of the principle.[104]

In order to explain this application, to which he claimed originality, he put forth three questions, all centering on the person of Christ. To the first question: "Whence comes the Mediator?" he answered that Jesus came from God as a "providential man," who "stands out alone, distinct, peculiar."[105] And even if Brownson, as yet, did not consider him essentially different from Moses, the prophets, and the apostles and not even great heathen philosophers like Socrates, Plato, and Confucius, he thought Jesus to be preëminent among them all and the one supplying all that was wanting in the others.[106] In any case, he wanted to signalize his distance from sheer rationalism by stating that Jesus was supernaturally inspired and not a man whose greatness was based on natural endowments.[107]

To the next question: "What is his work?" Brownson answered that Jesus redeems human nature from its inherent depravity and gives it a new and divine life. More interesting, however, were Brownson's premises for his answer. Strangely enough, he now criticized Channing for the very same statement that he had called a "sublime declaration" about eight years before: " 'In ourselves are the elements of the Divinity. God, then, does not sustain a figurative resemblance to man. It is the resemblance of a parent to a child, the likeness of a kindred nature.' "[108]

Brownson now argued that, according to these words of Channing, the human and the divine were at bottom identical. Among the Transcendentalists, this doctrine had led to the deification and worship of the human soul. Some of them had even drawn—and perhaps not quite illogically—the conclusion that they themselves were God; but Channing himself—as far as Brownson understood him—probably only meant that in ourselves we find the germs not of God, but of the idea of God.

But something more than unwarranted conclusions was at stake. Brownson maintained that Channing's statement in itself was untenable, because tradition, the Bible, and human experience all testified to the power of sin in man's life. To Brownson, therefore, the two terms "*naturally* divine" were contradictory. Evidently, Brownson, who in his *New Views* seemed largely to overlook the power of sin and evil, had now adopted a more dualistic conception of life.

Although he did not believe in the dogma of the Fall of man from an originally perfect state, he believed that man, being created imperfect, must have naturally, if not inevitably, sinned, and this sin necessarily corrupted human nature. Not by covenant or imputation as the church maintains, but by a "law of life" had all men become involved in Adam's sin.

According to this "law," man's life is—for good and for evil—bound closely together with that of mankind, both in time and space. Despite its element of necessity, which seemed to contrast Brownson's joyous belief in God's freedom and Providence, there is something grandiose about this Law of Life in its emphasis on the solidarity or even oneness of mankind: "It follows necessarily from this oneness of the life of all men, that no one member can be affected for good or evil, but the whole body, all humanity in space, time, and eternity must actually or virtually be affected with it." Sin, the reverse side of the Law of Life, propagates evil, and nothing but God's sovereign grace can stop the power of sin and introduce—through the same Law of Life—the power of goodness. This was the mission of Jesus.[109]

To the third question, which concerned the method or the character of his mission, Brownson replied that Jesus as "very God of very God, and very man of very man" is the true mediator between God and man. As partaker of divine life, he communed directly or immediately with God, and through Jesus, his disciples communed mediately with God. In accordance with the doctrine of the concurrent object and subject, the supernatural element, constituting the "object," was transmitted by the disciples to the succeeding generations.

Brownson particularly stressed that the Law of Life meant a plain, literal interpretation of the words of Jesus: "I am the way, the truth, and the life." He pointed out that this doctrine was a reaction both against "the Old School" Unitarians, who regarded Jesus only as a model man or a teacher of moral truths, and against the Transcendentalists, who considered Jesus only a philosophical conception or gave him only a kind of representative value. As for himself, he had belonged to the latter category. But his new conception of Jesus as literal mediator or "LIFE," providing the actual or virtual objective component of every man, laid a firm basis for Brownson's belief in the constant progress of the human race.[110]

Significantly, the Law of Life increased Brownson's respect for certain dogmas of "the catholic or universal church," such as infant baptism, the apostolic succession, and the Eucharist.[111] No less important for his approach to traditional Christianity was his strong emphasis on the power of sin. True, he admitted later that his application of Leroux's doctrine had not at all enabled him to grasp the real meaning or significance of Catholic dogma, but his Law of Life removed the obstacles of human reason to real belief in Christianity, and more particularly, Catholicism. For, as Brownson confidently stated: "To believe is normal."[112]

But even if this doctrine removed certain "prohibentia" to belief and even, according to Brownson, was "included in Catholic theology,"[113] it had nonetheless some aspects which made it difficult, to say the least, to reconcile it with the traditional conception of Christian dogmas.

First, Brownson seemed to interpret the Christian dogma of redemption as a gradual improvement of man's or humanity's moral standard, not as a special divine intervention to save a soul for heaven. Second, this "redemption" was not, apparently, the result of the free will of the individual. Instead, the Law of Life seemed to have a sort of magic power, operating out of necessity. Third, Brownson seemed still to be concerned primarily with God's kingdom on earth, which was to be realized by the common efforts of mankind. Typically, he expressed the hope that humanity and not the individual would or should "work out its own salvation."[114]

Yet on the whole, *The Mediatorial Life of Jesus* indicated a decisive step toward Christianity. Moreover, Brownson's earnest craving for life and unity in religion could scarcely fail to make impression on the readers. Some statements have a pathos which makes one think of Carlyle: "I feel too, that I can now go and utter the very word this age demands. That word is *Communion.* The age is waiting for it. It is sick of divisions, sick of mere forms, wearied and disgusted with mere cant; no better pleased with mere metaphysical speculations; impatient of dry disquisitions, and of cold, naked abstractions. It demands Life and Reality."[115]

Even if Brownson in his letter to Channing seemed to dissociate himself from both his "spiritual father" and the Transcendentalists, he nevertheless expressed thoughts and sentiments which more or less coincided with their own. Thus Brownson's ideas of life and communion had their more or less related parallels. Channing considered God not only "essentially goodness, holiness, justice, and virtue," but also "the life, motive, and sustainer of virtue in the human soul."[116] And in a discourse on "The Church" he stressed the ability of the church to illustrate the living continuity between the generations, and called for "a grander church than all particular ones, however extensive; the Church Catholic or Universal, spread over all lands, and one with the church in heaven."[117]

Similarly, a reviewer in the *Dial* wanted "a Church Universal, a Communion of Saints, a fellowship of good and true minds, reaching through all time and spread over all lands," manifesting itself "in great moral convictions;"[118] and in the same periodical Elizabeth P. Peabody exclaimed that Transcendentalism "is the common ground to which all sects may rise, and be purified of their narrowness."[119]

Further—and partly beyond Transcendentalist idealism—Brownson's emphasis on life as organic growth and on the living unity of mankind past and present was in the broad mainstream of Romantic thought. One might even suggest, though a bit timidly, that Carlyle's conscious intention of contrasting the "*tree* Igdrasil" with the "World-*Machine*" had a remote parallel in Brownson's unconscious desire of contrasting his Law of Life not only with his earlier deistic-mechanistic views of the universe, but also with the modern industrial system.[120] Anyhow, it is noteworthy that about the same time when stating his Law of Life or his doctrine of life and communion, he seemed to favor, without altogether endorsing Fourierism, its half-romantic idea of "attractive" or "associated" industry.[121]

But in addition to Transcendentalist and Romantic patterns, Brownson's Law of Life in its more distinct approach to traditional Christian beliefs had certain counterparts in the contemporary Unitarian movement. Thus in 1841 James Freeman Clarke voiced views and sentiments not very much unlike Brownson's Law of Life. Clarke declared that Christianity was something more than religion of nature and that God revealed himself both in nature and Providence, through "Inspired men," more particularly so through Jesus Christ, and finally through "Inward Influence." And to Clarke, this "Influence of the Holy Spirit" should not be identified with "the natural light," a fault committed by the Transcendentalists. Although apparently more optimistic than Brownson regarding the problem of sin, Clarke stated his general view of Christianity, a view not very dissimilar from Brownson's Law of Life: "Christianity lay at first in the mind of God as a necessary part of the great whole, and... neither sin nor redemption are [sic] casual, or unnecessary to the unity and harmony of creation."[122]

The response from Channing to Brownson's letter was sympathetic. True, he was somewhat skeptical as to the Law of Life, thinking that it "would lead an incautious reader to think you a thoroughgoing Universalist and as asserting the actual appropriation of the life of Christ to the whole human race, past and present, will they or nill they..." But he also felt sure that Brownson had "found new light; and I am disposed to look upon your changes, not as fluctuations, but as steps of rational progress, and to wish you joy in your consummation... Let us see you at the head of a really earnest and vital society of our own. God made you for something more than to scatter random shot, although those shot may sometimes be grand ideas and may hit old errors between wind and water."[123]

In the *Dial* Emerson, in a short review of Brownson's treatise, did not take direct issue with the author, but made the interesting observation that Brownson's doctrine was "the doctrine of John the Evangelist throughout, that the soul lives by the real presence of Jesus Christ, as literally as the body lives by bread."[124]

But in a letter of June 9, 1842, to Elizabeth P. Peabody he was more outspoken: "This matter of Christianity, for instance, is so managed in almost all conversations as instantly to paganize me... it is so here in Bronson's [sic] pamphlet at which I looked yesterday in obedience to your letter. With such questions I find myself unrelated. They are for those whom they concern. It is all positive, local, idolatrous."[125]

Yet whether Brownson's application of Leroux's "formule de la vie"[126] signalized "steps of rational progress" or only something "positive, local, idolatrous," he developed his Law of Life in a long review article on Theodore Parker's book *A Discourse of Matters Pertaining to Religion.*

Theodore Parker was perhaps the most radical minister of "the New School" Unitarians, and his sermon "On the Transient and Permanent in Christianity," delivered in the spring of 1841, made "the Old School" Unitarians regard him with lifted eyebrows, but his lectures on "Matters Pertaining to Religion," given in the autumn of the same year, made them stigmatize him as a heretic and brought "the confessional question" to a head.[127] One of the "oldtimers," Nathaniel Frothingham, declared Parker's views to be "subversive of Christianity." But no less important, even some of "the New School" Unitarians felt embarrassed, and James Freeman Clarke publicly called Parker's system a "shallow naturalism."[128]

Brownson, when he heard Parker's lectures on religion, which on the whole were a restatement of his own "religion of humanity," he immediately felt an instinctive repugnance to Parker's and his own formerly cherished doctrines. What he particularly reacted against was Parker's insistence on the religious sentiment in man as the real ground and origin of religion. Parker stated the doctrine in its very nakedness, thus making religion something purely subjective, whereas Brownson–logician though he was–said he had never maintained the doctrine in its absolute sense, but supplemented it with elements of traditional faith.[129]

Yet by now he realized that the doctrine was not tenable at all, unless religion should be reduced to sheer subjectivity or even soul-worship. Instead, he was now convinced that religion presupposed belief in and worship of God, and it presupposed intercommunion between God and man, i.e. between a distinct object and a distinct subject. Therefore, rejecting the doctrine of the religious sentiment in man as the origin and ground of religion, or, as he called it, the "natural-religious view" and "sheer naturalism," he "placed the origin and ground of religion in the relation of Creator and creature, of God and man, made known to man by God himself, and held it to be the infusion, through communion, of a supernatural life into natural human life."[130]

In the light of this leading principle he reviewed Parker's book, which convinced him of "the utter insufficiency, the nothingness, of the system to which I had been more or less attached for nearly twenty years, and which, I must say, had never satisfied my reason." What was more, he "caught glimpses of Christian truths which were to me both new and cheering," and he also began to understand that the Catholic conception of the church was profounder than the no-church system of Dr. Channing and other Unitarians.[131]

In reviewing Parker's book, Brownson stated five cardinal points on which he differed from the author. First, in contrast to Parker, who maintained that the religious element in man was an inherent idea, Brownson held that man had the power or faculty to perceive religious truths, which must be something objective, something outside of the *me* or the subject. Second, while Parker thought the religious sentiment to be identical with man's feeling of dependence on God, Brownson identified it with man's aspiration toward the highest, i.e. God.

Third, their views on "inspiration" were different. To Parker, inspiration simply meant man's obedience to the law of the so-called "absolute religion," which God had given every man as part of his nature. The great men in history, like the authors of the Bible, were great because they were more obedient to this law than others. Brownson, on the other hand, considered inspiration something supernatural, i.e. given directly by God to so-called Providential men, whom he had elected simply out of grace and not on the basis of merit.

Fourth, Brownson stressed the uniqueness and necessity of Christianity as a revealed religion. More strongly than before, he emphasized that only Christianity had—and could have—revealed the nature and character of God. He dissented sharply from Parker, whose "absolute religion" virtually denied the peculiar character of Christianity and the idea of the personality and special Providence of God.

Indeed, Parker's "natural-religious view" and his belief in stoical calm as the highest virtue made Brownson keenly aware of the impersonality of "absolute religion:" "O, leave the poor sinner, eating husks with the swine, the thought that he has yet a Father, and a Father's house to which he may return."[132]

Brownson's idea of Jesus as mediator between God and man gave him a more orthodox view of the biblical miracles. Now he was beginning to regard the miracles as "media" through which one could "rise to the perception of the truth." Thus the miraculous Resurrection of Jesus helped men to perceive his divinity and mission. Brownson no longer considered the miracles as myths representing general symbolical truths, and he even seemed to approach the position of "the Old School" Unitarianism with regard to the question of miracles.[133]

But even if Brownson more definitely than before gave to Jesus the first place among the Providential men, he was still only *primus inter pares*, possessing in "fulness" what the others only had in "degree." And even if Brownson did not wait for another Messiah, he envisaged the possibility of higher "revelations" in the future. Finally, stressing the significance of "the phenomenal Jesus; that is, his life," Brownson neglected his "being" or "the ontological Christ."[134]

However, Brownson's conception of Jesus determined his changed and changing view of the church, which he dealt with under the fifth point of his treatise. While Parker regarded "the church" only as a meeting place for a more or less loosely knit group of individuals, Brownson was now beginning to believe in the role of the church as "medium," keeping and transmitting the life of Jesus. He believed that the Holy Ghost represented the divine life of the church after the "personal Jesus departed to his Father," and that Jesus through the Holy Ghost had "embodied himself in the Church." Thus Jesus is only in the church, which consists of individuals who have divine life in them.

On the ground of this divine life constituting the church, Brownson concluded, albeit somewhat unexpectedly, the necessity of "a one Catholic Church, clothed with supreme authority over all matters pertaining to human life, whether spiritual or material." And for the same reason he rejected Protestantism, which wanted "organic power," causing "the multiplicity of its sects, the anachic life, which is but death." He concluded: "For ourselves, we are no Protestants. We believe the problem for our age is *Catholicism without Papacy*, on the one hand, and *Liberty without Individualism*, on the other."[135]

But even apart from his lack of belief in papacy, Brownson had not yet adopted Roman Catholicism or even common Christian beliefs. His "creed" for the "one Catholic Church," which he also called "the true Church" and the "Church of the Second Advent," re-echoed primarily the doctrines of the Saint-Simonian School, such as union and progress, the continual improvement of the conditions of mankind, especially of the poorest class, and salvation from sin and quest for a blissful hereafter "by doing the best to create a heaven for all mankind on earth."

This was his creed for his Church of the Future. He declared that he could not accept the articles of faith of the "so-called" churches, "whether Grecian, Roman, Anglican, or Protestant." As for the Roman Catholic Church, it had all since Pope Leo X been a church "in the wilderness."[136]

Only the Unitarian Church or rather "*movement*" seemed promising to him: 'But it is rapidly assuming a new form, and must inevitably assume a form that will combine the freedom it has asserted, with the rich spiritual truths heretofore expressed by Orthodox symbols." Complaining that Parker and others continued the Unitarian protest, which led to naturalism, Brownson declared that "Unitarianism must cease to be protestant, and become affirmative and catholic. It must advance in the direction of supernaturalism, and not in the direction of naturalism, but a supernaturalism freed from the superstition and metaphysical absurdities of the Orthodox School."

Interestingly, his desire for a reconciliation between the supernatural and the natural, a synthesis which he believed the Unitarian movement would soon bring about, was a restatement of his thesis in *New Views* concerning the union of the spiritual and the material.[137] Yet more important in the light of his later development was that his belief in the organic unity and supreme authority of "the church" and his increasing resentment to Protestant individualism would–in due time–make him more susceptible of the claims of the Roman Catholic Church.

According to William R. Hutchison, particularly in the 1840's, Unitarian or–as he prefers to call them–Transcendentalist ministers like Frederic Henry Hedge, James Freeman Clarke, Brownson, and William Henry Channing tried to combine Transcendentalist thought with traditional Christian faith and emphasized "the historical dimension of Christian experience." Clarke, for one, when founding "The Church of the Disciples," formulated as its creed the belief in "Jesus, as the Christ, the Son of God" and even declined the suggestion of the aging William E. Channing to change its creed into belief in Jesus as "the divinely appointed teacher of truth."

The Transcendentalist influence in these congregations was above all manifest in the democratic or unclerical, if not anticlerical, church organization. Thus Hedge stated his belief in a hierarchy of the wise and good, and Clarke bluntly declared that "the clergy-church must be changed into the Church of the People," and even to a large extent made use of lay preachers in his congregation.[138]

Most probably, the general skepticism among these "affirmative"

Unitarians as to an institutionalized clergy and Brownson's own comparatively recent outright denunciations of the priesthood motivated his desire for a "Catholicism without Papacy."

In the last number of the *Boston Quarterly Review* the editor wrote that it had been a "private Journal," mostly written by himself. He also re-emphasized the aim he had with his review: "the great Idea ... of man's moral, intellectual, and physical amelioration, on earth."[139] Yet his opinions of how to realize this "great Idea" were changing, and these changes or modifications of views represented his intellectual development during the five years when he was editing the *Boston Quarterly Review.*

Politically and socially, Brownson reached a radical climax in 1840 when in his essays on "The Laboring Classes" he advocated the abolition of hereditary descent of property. But the election campaign and the ensuing Whig victory the same year crushed his belief in the intelligence and instincts of the masses. For this reason he began to stress the need of a strong government, though only on the state and not on the Federal level, and expressed his belief in "constitutional republicanism." Yet in social matters he still advocated reform. But while he formerly meant to effect progress through changing or even abolishing certain institutions, he became increasingly aware that real progress, individual and collective, could only be effected by religious and moral influence.

Philosophically, Brownson described himself as an Eclectic, an adequate term for his double emphasis on phenomena like psychology and history, reason and tradition, individual and society. Yet he also allied himself with the Transcendentalists and defended powerfully "the New School," above all in 1840. Generally, he was a Transcendentalist in his emphasis on intuition and the inner light. On the other hand, already from 1838 he signalized his growing dissent from Transcendentalist subjectivism and idealism. Despairing of passing from the Subjective to the Objective, Brownson found the solution to his problem about the objective validity of thought in Pierre Leroux's "synthetic" approach.

Religiously, Brownson advanced from a "religion of humanity" or natural religion to a more positive appraisal of Christianity as a peculiar, revealed, or supernatural religion. From regarding Jesus as a model man or as a representative of certain abstract principles like love and truth, he gradually came to see him as the greatest one among the Providential men, as the God-Man who during his life communed directly and supernaturally with God and transmitted by a sort of magic or mystery this divine life to mankind.

The Law of Life or the doctrine of life and communion gave him a better understanding than before of certain agelong Christian dogmas and rites. No less important, his view of the church was changed. His former conception of "the church" as an internal principle or as a broad, vaguely defined system comprising Church and State was replaced by the view of the church as an organic unity in space and time, created and continued by the divine life of Jesus and for this very reason having supreme authority.

But although craving for "a one catholic church," he had not as yet become a Roman Catholic, not even a Christian in the traditional sense of the term. His creed was still a kind of "social gospel" along Saint-Simonian lines, although with one important addition: the progress of mankind was no longer supposed to depend on the capacities of human nature, but on the supernatural intervention of God through specially raised messengers or Providential men. Regarding himself still as a Unitarian, Brownson called for an "affirmative and catholic" Unitarianism.

Despite Brownson's change of emphasis from a social-radical Transcendentalism toward a more conservative position in politics and religion, there was nonetheless a basic consistency in his intellectual development, even from 1840 to 1842. After 1840, when he lost his faith in the masses as depositories or "media" of the divine wisdom and justice, he was seeking for more particular depositories or "media" for God's influence, and found them, on the political level, in the Constitution and a strong government and, on the religious level, in supernaturally inspired Providential men and in the church.

Finally, one may characterize Brownson's development during those five years (1838–1842) as a continual search for synthesis. Above all, the last year brought this tendency sharply into focus. In the political and social field, he wanted to combine "conservatism" and "radicalism," though, admittedly, he had little left of radicalism by 1842. In philosophy, he voiced a basic synthesis between a distinct object and a distinct subject as the ground for the validity of thought and the belief in a living God, and typically enough, his ideal was a synthetic philosophy.[140] Even in literature he demanded a "living synthesis" of "realism" and "idealism," although by twentieth-century standards his view of "realism," too, seems rather "idealized."[141] And in religion, he sought for "a one catholic, universal church," which was to combine tradition with progress, the natural with the supernatural.

1 *The Convert*, p. 112.
2 Schlesinger, *The Age of Jackson*, pp. 355–356.
3 "Charles Elwood," *Christian Review*, V (Sept. 1840), 435, 438.
4 "The Rich against the Poor," *Methodist Quarterly Review*, 3rd series, V (Jan. 1841), 116.
5 *The Age of Jackson*, p. 302.
6 Quoted in Schlesinger, *Orestes A. Brownson*, p. 101.
7 *The Age of Jackson*, p. 303.
8 *The Convert*, pp. 103, 119, 120.
9 *Daniel Webster*, II (Boston, 1930), pp. 80, 65.
10 Edward M. Shepard, *Martin Van Buren* in *American Statesmen, Standard Library Edition*, XVIII (Boston and New York, 1899), pp. 387–390; Claude Moore Fuess, *Daniel Webster*, 2 vols. (Boston), 1930), p. 84; C. R. Fish, *The Rise of the Common Man: 1830–1850*, p. 165.
11 *The Journals of Bronson Alcott*, ed. Odell Shepard (Boston, 1938), p. 123.
12 Shepard, *op.cit.*, p. 378.
13 Fuess, *op.cit.*, p. 80; Fish, *op.cit.*, p. 57.
14 *Daniel Webster* in *American Statesmen, Standard Library Edition*, XXI (Boston and New York, 1899), p. 233.
15 Shepard, *op.cit.*, pp. 378–379.
16 Quoted in Shepard, *op.cit.*, p. 382.
17 *Ibid.*, p. 379.
18 *Ibid.*, pp. 390–391.
19 "Democracy and Liberty" *(Democratic Review*, April 1843), *Works*, XV, 259.
20 "The Democratic Principle" *(BrQR*, April 1873), *Works*, XVIII, 223.
21 *Early Life*, p. 182; "Philosophy and Common Sense" *(BQR*, Jan. 1838), *Works*, 1, 17; *The Convert*, p. 101.
22 "Conversations with a Radical," *BQR*, IV (Jan. 1841), 1–41.
23 "Our Future Policy" *(BQR*, Jan. 1841), *Works*, XV, 123–124; "Social Evils and their Remedy," *BQR*, IV (July 1841), 273; *The Convert*, p. 121.
24 "Our Future Policy," pp. 127–128; *BQR*, IV (July 1841), 392.
25 "Our Future Policy," pp. 114–119, 122; *BQR*, IV (Jan. 1841), 112–127.
26 "Conversations with a Radical," *BQR*, IV (April 1841), 159.
27 *BQR*, IV (Jan. 1841), 30. See also "The Laboring Classes," *BQR*, III (July 1840), 369–370: "'She has worked in a Factory,' is almost enough to damn to infamy the most worthy and virtuous girl."
28 "Letter to the Editors of *The Lowell Offering*," *BQR*, IV (April 1841), 261–264.
29 *BQR*, IV (July 1841), 278–280.
30 *Ibid.*, pp. 284–287.
31 *Ibid.*, p. 289.
32 "Executive Patronage" *(BQR*, July 1841), *Works*, XV, 183–184.
33 In his *Dedham Address* (1834) he expressed the view that the authors of the Constitution, at least unconsciously, believed in "the great principle of equality, . . . that soul-kindling truth, man equals man, man measures man, the world

over" (p. 5), but now, in 1841, he objected to Van Buren's statement that the Constitution expressed the will of the majority *(BQR,* IV, 286–287).

[34] H. von Holst, *John C. Calhoun* in *American Statesmen, Standard Library Edition,* XXII (Boston and New York, 1899), p. 77. As for the principle of "concurrent majority," Herbert W. Schneider maintains that it originated with Jefferson, and not with Calhoun *(A History of American Philosophy* [New York], p. 104).

[35] *Early Life,* p. 326.

[36] *BQR,* I (Jan. 1838), *Works* I, 17.

[37] "The Secret of the Lord," *BQR,* IV (July 1841), 308–320, esp. 311, 312.

[38] *Ibid.,* p. 313.

[39] *Ibid.,* pp. 313–314.

[40] *Ibid.,* p. 314; *New Views,* pp. 17–24.

[41] *BQR,* IV (July 1841), 392.

[42] "Essays: By R. W. Emerson," *BQR,* IV (July 1841), 294.

[43] *Ibid.,* pp. 295–296.

[44] *Ibid.,* p. 297.

[45] *Ibid.*

[46] C. H. Faust, "The Background of the Unitarian Opposition to Transcendentalism," *Modern Philology,* XXXV (Feb. 1938), 297–324.

[47] "The Unitarian Movement in New England," *Dial,* I (April 1841), 414–415.

[48] *Ibid.,* pp. 430, 433.

[49] "Ernest the Seeker," *Dial,* I (July 1840), 52, 57.

[50] "The Religion of Beauty," *Dial,* I (July 1840), 21.

[51] *Nature* in *Complete Works, Concord Edition,* I (Boston and New York, 1903), 24, 34, 47.

[52] *BQR,* IV (Oct. 1841), 436–474, esp. 471.

[53] *Ibid.,* pp. 465–467.

[54] *Ibid.,* pp. 471–474; *The Convert,* pp. 151–152.

[55] *BQR,* IV (July 1841), 299–301.

[56] *Ibid.,* pp. 301–303.

[57] *Ibid.,* p. 304.

[58] *BQR,* IV (July 1841), 275.

[59] *BQR,* IV (April 1841), 173, 176.

[60] *BQR,* IV (July 1841), 319.

[61] See Emerson's essay on "Prudence" (1841) in *Essays, First and Second Series* (London and New York, 1947), pp. 131, 134.

[62] "Constitutional Government" *(BQR,* V, Jan. 1842), *Works,* XV, 234, 237, 239, 253–254.

[63] *Ibid.,* pp. 235, 248–252.

[64] *Ibid.,* pp. 231–232, 255.

[65] *Ibid.,* p. 221.

[66] *Early Life,* p. 362.

[67] *Works,* XV, 258, 241, 251, 205, 208.

[68] *Ibid.,* p. 208.

[69] *BQR,* V (July 1842), 353.

[70] *Ibid.,* pp. 357–358.

[71] *Ibid.,* p. 358.

[72] *BQR,* V (July 1842), 366–371.

[73] See Ch. IX, n. 13.

[74] "Reform and Conservatism" *(BQR,* V, Jan. 1842), *Works,* IV, 88–89.

75 *Ibid.*, p. 92.
76 *On Heroes, Hero Worship and the Heroic in History (The World's Classics,* 62; London, 1950), pp. 313, 318.
77 See Emerson R. Marks, "Victor Cousin and Emerson," *Transcendentalism and Its Legacy*, ed. Myron Simon and Thornton H. Parsons (Ann Arbor, 1966), p. 77.
78 *Works*, I,V 92, 94.
79 *BQR*, I (Oct. 1838), 417—432, 500—514.
80 *Works*, IV, 93, 97.
81 *The Convert*, pp. 121—132, esp. 123.
82 *Ibid.*, pp. 127—129.
83 *Ibid.*, pp. 128—131.
84 *Réfutation de l'Eclectisme* (Paris, 1839), pp. 50, 253.
85 "Charles Elwood Reviewed," *(BQR*, V, April 1842), *Works*, IV, 358—360.
86 Letter of Dec. 22, 1858 to Cousin: *Brownson Papers.*
87 *The Convert*, p. 124; Letter of Sept. 1, 1844, to Cousin: *Brownson Papers.*
88 Leroux, *op.cit.*, pp. 60, 70, 253, 263, 273, 275.
89 *Works*, IV, 86—87.
90 *Ibid.*, p. 144.
91 *Ibid.*, pp. 104, 112.
92 *Ibid.*, pp. 115—116; *The Convert*, pp. 130—131.
93 *Works*, IV, 117.
94 *Ibid.*, pp. 121—125.
95 *Ibid.*, p. 129; *The Convert*, pp. 130—131.
96 *Early Life*, p. 441.
97 *The Convert*, p. 132.
98 *Works*, IV, 141.
99 *Ibid.*, pp. 148—149.
100 *The Convert*, p. 134.
101 *Works*, VIII, 262.
102 *Works*, IV, 141—143.
103 *BQR*, V (April 1842), 198—201; William R. Hutchison, *The Transcendentalist Ministers* (New Haven, 1959), pp. 137—189.
104 *Works*, IV, 144.
105 *Ibid.*, pp. 146, 149.
106 *The Convert*, pp. 140—141.
107 *Works*, IV, 149.
108 *Ibid.*, p. 149; *New Views*, p. 46.
109 *Works*, IV, 149—156; *New Views*, p. 10.
110 *Works*, IV, 157—162.
111 *Ibid.*, pp. 157, 162—166.
112 *The Convert*, pp. 136, 148—149.
113 *Ibid.*, pp. 135, 149.
114 *Ibid.*, p. 167.
115 *Ibid.*, p. 170.
116 "Unitarian Christianity" (1819), *The Works of William E. Channing, Eighth Complete Edition*, III (Boston and New York, 1848), p. 94.
117 "The Church" (1841), *Channing's Works*, VI, 203, 206.
118 *Dial*, I (Oct. 1840), 268.
119 *Dial*, II (Oct. 1841), 371.
120 As for the principles of life, growth, and "dynamism" in European and American Romantic thought, see Howard Mumford Jones, "The Influence of

European Ideas in Nineteenth-Century America," *American Literature*, VII (Nov. 1935), 263–270; Carlyle, *On Heroes, etc.*, pp. 224 ff.

[121] *BQR*, IV (Jan. 1841), 127–129.

[122] *Dial*, II (Oct. 1841), 389–390. Consequently, Lapati seems too categorical when maintaining that Brownson's views at that time were unique among the Unitarians (*Orestes A. Brownson*, p. 37).

[123] *Early Life*, p. 444 (Letter of June 10, 1842).

[124] *Dial*, III (Oct. 1842), 277.

[125] *The Letters of Ralph Waldo Emerson*, III (New York, 1939), pp. 63–64.

[126] Leroux, *op.cit.*, préface, xviii.

[127] Hutchison, *op.cit.*, pp. 98–136.

[128] Henry Steele Commager, *Theodore Parker* (Boston, 1947), pp. 88, 86.

[129] *The Convert*, p. 152.

[130] *BQR*, V (Oct. 1842), 423, 426; *The Convert*, p. 154.

[131] *The Convert*, p. 155.

[132] *BQR*, V (Oct. 1842), 419–440, 462.

[133] *Ibid.*, p. 469; "Leroux on Humanity," *Works*, IV, 133.

[134] *BQR*, V (Oct. 1842), 450, 373, 475, 486; *The Convert*, pp. 145–150.

[135] *BQR*, V (Oct. 1842), 488, 499–501, 510.

[136] *Ibid.*, pp. 489, 508, 510, 511.

[137] *BQR*, V (April 1842), 198–201.

[138] Hutchison, *op.cit.*, pp. 139–149, 189.

[139] *BQR*, V (Oct. 1842), 513–514.

[140] *Works*, I, 58–129.

[141] *BQR*, V (July 1842), 342–366, esp. 366.

XIV
Conversion

Already in May, 1842, John O'Sullivan, the editor of the *United States' Magazine and Democratic Review* in New York, had suggested to Brownson the idea that the *Boston Quarterly Review* might be merged with his own periodical.[1]

O'Sullivan, whom Julian Hawthorne described as "a cosmopolitan of Irish parentage on his father's side, and one of the most charming companions in the world,"[2] started his review in 1837 at the age of 28. Obviously, his intention with his periodical was greatly similar to Brownson's aim with his *Boston Quarterly Review.* Thus in a letter of August 13, 1837, to Brownson, O'Sullivan wrote that his magazine would "be democratic, in the broad and historical signification of the word," but added that "to every measure of a particular and extended political party, it would be impossible to pledge such a work."[3] Similarly, Brownson, who praised the general "design" of O'Sullivan's magazine,[4] declared in a letter of April 2, 1838, to President Van Buren that his own review had been "established for the purpose of enlisting Literature, Religion, and Philosophy on the side of the Democracy."[5]

Most probably, economic reasons forced Brownson to stop the publication of his own review and to merge it with O'Sullivan's magazine. In June, 1842, the latter told Brownson: "It was evident that your work could not possibly stand with 500 subscribers,"[6] and in the *Democratic Review* for December, 1843, when their coöperation was drawing to a close, the editor mentioned Brownson's financial difficulties with his *Boston Quarterly Review.*[7]

Whether or not a magazine at that time could "stand with 500 subscribers," one might mention that each number of the *Dial* was, at most, sold only in 250 copies, while, on the other hand, the *North American* averaged 3000 and Edgar Allan Poe's *Southern Literary Messenger* no less than 5000 copies.[8] At any rate, Brownson, being promised three dollars for each page he wrote, accepted O'Sullivan's proposal, and according to the terms agreed upon, Brownson was to write an article per month for the *Democratic Review*.[9] His first article appeared in the October, 1842, issue of the review, and until the end of the next year he wrote a series of articles for O'Sullivan's periodical on philosophical, political, and social subjects, and also touched religious issues.

In April, 1842, Brownson had promised to lay "before the public at the earliest day possible" a philosophical system of his own, though, admittedly, not without assistance from different sources.[10] This system was presented in a long essay, called "Synthetic Philosophy," in the *Democratic Review* for December, 1842, and January and March, 1843. But he also treated and developed the same theme in other articles for the review, especially in his essays on "Schmucker's Psychology" (Oct. 1842) and "The Philosophy of History" (May and June 1843).

Brownson, starting with the problem of knowledge, its source and veracity, declared that in "the primitive fact of consciousness" the subject, the object, and their form or relation constituted an indissoluble synthesis: "The Form is the Notion, or what the subject notes, in the act of thinking, of both subject and object. The subject taking note of both subject and object, in the face of life, is called the fact of consciousness." Thus Brownson considered consciousness not a faculty or an act, but a kind of higher perception.[11]

This higher perception and the immediate participation of the object in thought were, in Brownson's view, *a priori* warrants of the objective validity of thought: "Whatever then I think exists, and independent of me. If I think an external world, then is there an external world; the finite, then is there the finite; God, then God is." True, the intelligence of man is limited. But thought, which contains *me* and *not-me*, subject and object, must contain the infinite and absolute.[12] Or as he stated even more strongly the previous year: "All reality is, then, under the form of every thought; all infinitude, God and man, are under every notion, and are indispensably necessary as the basis of the smallest, least significant thought. Of such grandeur is thought!"[13]

To the modern eye, Brownson seemed much too optimistic about the power of thought to grasp final truths. Apparently, he passed too easily from the realm of logic into that of ontology and even regarded them as identical. But in his own view, premising the synthesis of a distinct object and a distinct subject as the *a priori* basis of thought was the only means of justifying one's belief in the objective, absolute truth of ultimate ideas.[14]

Indeed, the real reason of Brownson's view was his strong desire to state final ideas with absolute certainty and authority: "All faith, if genuine, if deep, if earnest, if living, is, say what we will to the contrary, exclusive and intolerant. Nothing is so exclusive and intolerant as truth, which has no patience with error, but excludes the semblance even of falsehood... Every honest man does and cannot but hold his own faith to be the true faith; and therefore does and cannot but hold every opposing faith to be false."[15] Evidently, Brownson's earnest search for *the* truth had by now removed him from Eclecticism, i.e. understood as a broad toleration of all philosophical and religious systems. But he recognized his great debt to Cousin, who had provided him with the basic elements of his own synthetic philosophy.[16] For this very reason he generously stated that Cousin's philosophy, properly speaking, was "synthetic!"[17]

At least to modern minds, Brownson was more successful when applying his idea of synthesis to psychology. With a sharp sense of the close and continuous interplay of all human faculties, he rejected the thesis that some phenomena should be purely actions, some purely cognitions or some purely feelings: "The *me* acts always as the living and indestructible synthesis of all its faculties." He seemed to be keenly aware of the complexity and the essential unity of the operations of the human mind: "Since I am a unity, and therefore must act ever as a whole, in all my integrity, I must act in them all with my threefold power of acting, knowing, and feeling..."

Somewhat more dubious, however, were the metaphysical conclusions he drew from the operations of the three faculties of the human mind. Man, he declared, "is then a TRINITY, a living type of that sublime doctrine which lies as the bottom of all Christian theology, and not only the type, but in some sort the origin and basis."[18] It is a bit surprising, though, that Brownson, who criticized Cousin for making psychology the basis of ontology,[19] now made psychology "in some sort" the basis of the most fundamental Christian doctrine.

It is also noteworthy that Brownson emphasized sensibility as the central element of the *me* or the subject, and not intelligence, as might have been expected of a logician. Consequently, he maintained that man came nearest to truth in imagination, and that poets and artists, whose power of imagination was stronger than that of other men, were the only teachers of mankind.[20] Again, "the logick of the heart" above "the logick of the head!"

Despite his opposition to Transcendentalist subjectivism and his dislike of Transcendentalist tendencies to mysticism, he could himself still strike tones as the following: "The 'land of dreams,' in which the lover and the poet, in their intensest frenzy, rise free and delighted, is, if we did but know it, more substantial than this cold, dry, work-day world, in which for the most part of the time we merely vegetate, and call it living. In these moments the soul penetrates beyond the Actual to the Ideal, which is the basis of all reality, that in which we are all without seeming to know it, immersed as in a vast ocean of being."[21]

In harmony with his view of sensibility and imagination, Brownson stressed that philosophy itself should not only be a product of the Reflective Reason, as Cousin contended, but just as much a direct result of inspiration. Brownson even maintained that philosophy was a specific part of religion, and that "revelation" was necessary not only for religion, but also for philosophy. Rejecting Leibniz's theory that revelation belonged only to religion, while God gave men philosophical insight through nature, Brownson argued that philosophy was the form of religion "when subjected to the action of the human mind." No wonder, therefore, that he considered the New Testament the best manual of philosophy he was acquainted with. In fact, declaring his wish to "resolve philosophy into religion," he advocated a synthesis and not only a reconciliation between them. The principal reason for his argument was his insistence on the close relation between basic thinking and basic religious belief: "Mankind believe in God, in themselves, and in nature, for the best of all possible reasons, *because they think them, and cannot think without thinking them.* Humanity is never a sceptic."[22]

No doubt, Brownson's synthetic philosophy had traits in common with Hegelianism, especially as reflected in Pierre Leroux's philosophy: "Through the whole runs a never failing duality; all is bifold, or separated, as it were, into two sexes, without whose conjunction there is never a generation."[23] Such a statement might remind one of Hegel's theory of thesis, antithesis, and synthesis; but Brownson did not develop his philosophy further along those lines. Though believing in the principle of growth and development, he was anxious to point out that the subject and the object were distinct realities, which should not be destroyed to bring about a higher idea or reality.

On the whole, Brownson, in René Wellek's words, during thirty-five years showed a "remarkable consistency and uniformity of his criticism of Kant and Hegel," and rejected generally German philosophy "as subjectivism and pantheism, skepticism and atheism."[24] More particularly, in 1843 Brownson objected strongly to Hegel's philosophical point of departure in *Esse* or *Sein*. To Brownson, the real starting-point of philosophy was not *Esse*, but *Life*. He objected to the markedly ontological and pantheistic character of Hegelianism, and its insistence on the inevitability of the historical development. Hence Hegel's neglect of human, individual efforts, and his only too great willingness to defend the political *status quo*.[25]

However, as indicated earlier and later on in this dissertation, Brownson, through his knowledge of contemporary French philosophy, was subjected to more indirect and remote influences from Hegelianism and German Romantic philosophy in general.

Interestingly, Brownson's above-mentioned criticism of Hegel did not seem very much unlike that of Søren Kierkegaard (1813–1855). Kierkegaard's preference of *existence* to *essence* and his belief in individual exertions seem to reflect the same attitude as Brownson's. Yet Brownson would hardly have accepted Kierkegaard's emphasis on "the subjectivity" of truth ("Subjectiviteten er Sandheden") without some important additions, or at least definitions.

Brownson's almost "Existentialist" idea of philosophy as *Life* meant that the universal ideas or categories were no pure abstractions, but manifested themselves and were perceived in the concrete, or "the Ideal" manifested itself in "the Actual."[26] Also for this important element of his synthetic philosophy he expressed his gratitude to Cousin, who had stated the theory that "we never seize the category of being, or substance, save in the category of cause; that is, the subject in the phenomenon, the actor in the act. The rationalist assumes that we can seize being in itself; the empiricist, that we can seize in the phenomenon only the phenomenal; the synthetist, which Cousin should be, and is when he is himself, asserts that in the act we seize the actor, and have the power to perceive the spiritual in the material . . ."[27]

Brownson's conception of philosophy as *Life* was also based on his theory of growth resulting from the necessary communion of "the subject" with "the object," or of man with other men, nature and God. More immediately, his emphasis on "growth" and "sensibility" clearly indicated influences from Leroux.[28]

However, the finishing touch to, or even a sort of basis of his philosophy was furnished by Leibniz, who in his monadology emphasized that everything partakes of life, possessing more or less activity, sensibility, and intelligence. Already in a letter of September 6, 1839, to Cousin, Brownson wrote that "Leibnitz [sic] was a wonderful man," and in a letter of September 1, 1844, he thanked the French philosopher for having drawn his attention to Leibniz. And Brownson added: "I accept his definition of Substance, *vis activa*, and it becomes the basis of my own philosophy."[29]

Chiefly reflecting and combining the philosophies of Leibniz, Cousin, and Leroux, Brownson's synthetic philosophy could scarcely be regarded as an original contribution to philosophy. But his emphasis on life, "sensibility," and synthesis illustrates, on the one hand, his own temper and basic view of thought, and, on the other hand, the Romantic and even Transcendentalist skepticism as to everything "analytic" and the general predilection of the age for "the synthetic." Wordsworth complained of the scientific tendency to "murder to dissect;" and Emerson, in his " 'American Scholar' Address" of 1837, wanted a "philosophy of life," and contrasted the "blood-warm" writing of Goethe, Wordsworth, and Carlyle to the alleged "cold and pedantic" productions of Pope, Johnson, and Gibbon. To Emerson, this "blood-warm" writing showed to man that "things near are not less beautiful and wondrous than things remote. The near explains the far. The drop is a small ocean. A man is related to all nature."[30] Perhaps an even closer parallel to Brownson's synthetic philosophy was A. Bronson Alcott's "orphic saying:" "Life, in its initial stage, is synthetic; then feeling, thought, action are one and indivisible."[31]

Significantly, Emerson, when later looking back on the hectic 1830's and 1840's, remarked that the young restive seekers of that time put their trust in typically organic and synthetic conceptions of nature and history.[32] No wonder, therefore, that Leibniz with his belief in dynamic life and synthesis and, on the other hand, his rejection of the atomistic theory fitted well into this broad Romantic and Transcendentalist pattern. Accordingly, Leibniz also fitted well into Brownson's synthetic philosophy, and, as René Wellek also points out, was the only German philosopher who directly appealed to him.[33]

But like Cousin, who tried to verify his psychology through history or the psychology of humanity,[34] Brownson in a long essay on "The Philosophy of History" tested his synthetic philosophy in the light of the "Universal History" of mankind. By "Universal History" he meant the general laws and principles that, in his view, determined historical facts, and not the simple narration of these facts themselves. Discarding Michelet's "war-theory," which presented the relation between spirit and matter as an eternal conflict, Jouffroy's "humanitarian theory," which excluded the special divine intervention, and Hegel's and Cousin's "rationalistic theory," which gave human history a too impersonal character, he postulated his own "providential theory," which signalized his belief in a synthesis of God's Providence in the life of mankind and human, even individual freedom and action. Moreover, he restated his belief in Providential men and their great influence on their contemporaries and on later generations.[35]

On the whole, Brownson's view of history was teleological and moderately optimistic, but he was also keenly aware of the tragic element of human life and history. More particularly, he raged against the factory system or industrialism with its recurrent and unpredictable crises. Yet he had no economic or social solution to this aching problem, but stressed in general terms the need of a strong government (on the state level) and the revival of Christianity and the Christian church, although not the old Catholic Church.[36] At least, not yet.

Brownson's increasing emphasis on the Constitution and a strong government was motivated by the election of 1840. This election had taught him that the manufacturing and commercial interests dominated the workers or the majority. Consequently, instead of predicting a coming class war as he had done in the late 1830's and particularly in 1840, he now advocated a more organic approach to the social problem, finding its solution in a peaceful coöperation between the classes. Thus Brownson now resumed his attitude toward the social problem from the early 1830's.

Another lesson that the election of 1840 taught him was the alleged futility of believing in "good" ideas as such, and their inherent potency to convince and almost automatically materialize themselves. Brownson now realized that such a belief tended strongly toward "no-governmentism" and actually left the rule of the country in the hands of the capitalists. Therefore, he increasingly felt the need of replacing any tendency to "no-governmentism" and even the notion of government as the agent of society by the conception of government as "an authority having the right and the power to govern society." Only in this way—so Brownson seemed to think—could the business interests and the more or less deceived majorities be efficiently counteracted.[37]

True, the Whig Party was rapidly losing influence, especially because Vice-President John Tyler, who succeeded to the presidency on the death of William H. Harrison (April 4, 1841), was to some extent a disguised Democrat.[38] Yet Whig difficulties did not alter essentially Brownson's general fear of majority rule; instead, he pointed at similar tendencies having manifested themselves during the Jacksonian administrations.[39]

In order to check these tendencies to an unrestrained majority rule, Brownson had resort to an imposing list of "remedies:" the American Constitution, strong state governments with a certain control of industry, individual statesmen, and, without any definition, the church.[40]

The very titles of his political articles for the *Democratic Review* indicated his great interest in the discussion of first principles, especially "government," its origin and purpose: "Democracy and Liberty" (April 1843), "Popular Government" (May 1843) and "Origin and Ground of Government" (end of 1843).

But one has the impression that Brownson's love of first principles here carried him a bit too far, making the exposition of his views rather abstract and theoretical, above all as compared with his "blood-warm" essays on "The Laboring Classes" of 1840. His theories of government, its origin and purpose, were theologico-political philosophy rather than political science. Despairing of finding any real historical origin of government, he confidently declared that government had its philosophical origin in God. The divine authority was represented in one visible institution, which consisted of two departments, i.e. the State and the Church. Thus Brownson reaffirmed his cherished doctrine of the unity, though not union, of Church and State. But in contrast to 1840, when he wanted only an invisible "church" and only one outward organization, i.e. the State, he now called for the church as a visible, though still undefined, institution.[41]

Since, according to his present belief, God's sovereignty was more distinctly embodied in the church than in the State, Brownson concluded that the church had a higher authority than civil government. At least indirectly, Brownson now admitted the supremacy of the church above the State. As Samuel anointed Saul, the task of the church should be to "commission" the State, and if this did not actually mean to lead or dominate the State, in any case it meant to infuse it with religious ideals. Partly echoing old Puritan sentiments and partly reflecting his increasing interest in medieval culture, Brownson now expressed his belief in a "uniform theocratico-democratic commonwealth."[42]

With its curious mixture of politics and theology it is difficult to understand fully what Brownson really wanted to obtain—or to retain—with his conception of government. But his openly avowed sympathy for John Calhoun and even his approval of Hayne's arguments against Webster in the famous debate on the Union in 1830 indicated his predilection for a pre-industrial, essentially agrarian society along Jeffersonian lines. Therefore, one might suggest a deeper consistency in Brownson's views from 1840 to 1843. If wage labor and the factory system could not be abolished through direct social-political legislation, as he proposed in 1840, he now instead had resort to "constitutional republicanism" and states' rights in order to halt the progress of industrialism and the increasing influence of the manufacturing and commercial classes.[43]

As a result of his more recent thought, his idea of government as a providential "medium" which not only ruled the individuals, but also helped them realize their capabilities, clearly reflected his doctrine of life and communion, and his belief in individual statesmen, like Calhoun, was another version of his trust in Providential men.

On the whole, Brownson's increasing emphasis on the Constitution as a check on the will of numerical majorities, his growing skepticism of the doctrine of social equality, his general distrust of democracy as a form, though not as the end, of government and, finally, an increasing tendency to emphasize ancient and medieval times at the expense of the present strongly indicated his conservative leanings.[44] Apart from the distinctly religious overtones of Brownson's conservatism, it is perhaps not too wide of the mark to compare it with J. F. Cooper's agrarian republicanism and also with the views of Francis Lieber, who advocated "institutional liberty" and rejected the doctrine of popular sovereignty.[45] A third contemporary parallel to Brownson's conservatism might, as also indicated earlier, be found in Alexis de Tocqueville's skepticism as to the democratic form of government and majority rule. More distant sources of influence on or confirmation of Brownson's political views were Jefferson's distrust of the passing whims of majorities,[46] and perhaps even more Aristotle's negative conception of the democratic form of government.[47]

However, Brownson's conservatism was hardly shared by most of his compatriots, and the editor O'Sullivan's objections to Brownson's views of democracy and government were undoubtedly representative of public opinion. O'Sullivan believed that after all the instincts of the people were in the long run more right than the shortsighted speculations of the politicians. And even if the people were sometimes mistaken, he firmly believed that "self-government" or democracy as a form of government would be preferable to any other sort of government, even if the archangel Gabriel himself should be its leader.[48] Somewhat later O'Sullivan was more blunt, characterizing Brownson's views as downright ultraistic and antidemocratic. The editor of the *Democratic Review* wanted to make clear that the people or the nation stood above the Constitution and were completely entitled to change it if they wanted. With some apparent inconsistency he accepted Brownson's and Calhoun's view of checks and balances and the rights of the minorities, although at the same time advocating the "absolute and unchecked government" of the majority.[49]

More to the point, however, was O'Sullivan's criticism of Brownson's loose and ill-defined views of the church and its relation to the State. With some right, the editor maintained that Brownson's conception of the church as having higher authority than the State might easily lead to ecclesiastical domination in State affairs. He thought that Brownson's ideas were nothing than a revival—or an attempt at a revival—of the old feudal doctrines of the divine right of kings and the supremacy of the church. Anyhow, O'Sullivan, for one, did not believe that the church as an institution could support the State any more than a tortoise could carry an elephant![50]

As for Brownson himself, his Law of Life had led him to regard "the church" as a "medium" or depository of divine life and power, and he concluded that, as a medium or depository, the church had to be an institution. But paradoxically, at least so far, his ideas about this concrete institution were rather abstract. Yet his desire for a "theocratico-democratic commonwealth" reflected, as a result of his Law of Life, his positive reappraisal of the clergy; and this desire also indicated his increasing sympathy for the Saint-Simonian emphasis on institutions. Not unlike the Saint-Simonians, he now considered the churchly institution a "medium" or an instrumental cause of love in men; this would, supposedly, make the church a lever for social reform, which, again, would enable the individuals to live the real Christian life.[51]

Moreover, Brownson's idea of the church as a "medium" might be more easily understood if seen in the light of his synthetic philosophy. His belief that "the Ideal" manifested itself in "the Actual," being in the phenomenon or—recalling his *New Views*—"the spiritual in the material," strengthened his belief in the church as an organism or an institution.

In fact, similar ideas of a churchly institution were not altogether strange even to Transcendentalists, who, however, generally considered "the church" as universal moral and religious principles and were skeptical about priesthoods. Already in 1840 an above-quoted writer in the *Dial*, calling for "a Church Catholic or Universal," also suggested that this "Church" should be "with or without what is called 'ecclesiastical polity.' "[52]

A more indirect, contemporary parallel to Brownson's belief in an institutional church was the belief of many Transcendentalists in the so-called "community system," which materialized in Brook Farm and other similar institutions. Although historians have characterized this system as a conscious or unconscious attempt at escaping from the urging problems of society,[53] there can be no doubt that the members themselves earnestly wanted to carry out their ideas and ideals in practice and even—like George Ripley—made great personal economic sacrifices. And not quite unexpectedly, Sophia Ripley, in justifying Brook Farm as an expression of "the Ideal" in "the Actual," spoke warningly to Theodore Parker "of the danger of losing our humanity in abstractions," and her almost religious interest in the institution and her corresponding disappointment with "the associative experiment" partly explained her later conversion to Catholicism.[54]

Also other contemporaries looked upon Brook Farm almost with religious enthusiasm. Thus the ubiquitous Elizabeth P. Peabody hailed the community as "a pearl *hidden in a field*" and considered it a model of "a reörganization of society itself, on those very principles of love to God and love to man, which Jesus Christ realized in his own daily life."[55] And Nathaniel Hawthorne, who had sunk most of his Custom House savings in Brook Farm, wanted to show "mankind the example of a life governed by other than the false and cruel principles on which human society has all along been based."[56] At least during the first part of his stay at Brook Farm he declared almost religiously that "such a delectable way of life has never been seen on earth since the days of the early Christians,"[57] and he felt "engaged in a righteous and heaven-blessed way of life."[58]

However, only a couple of months later Hawthorne wrote that his life at Brook Farm had been "an unnatural and unsuitable, and therefore an unreal, one,"[59] and in 1852 appeared his novel *The Blithedale Romance,* in which he particularly attacked the alleged intolerance of the philanthropic spirit.

To Emerson, who refused to join the community experiment, though "very slowly and almost with penitence," Brook Farm "was a perpetual picnic, a French Revolution in small, an Age of Reason in a patty-pan," but he, too, emphasized the religious fervor of the members, especially of their leader: "What a brave thing Mr. Ripley has done! He stands now at the head of the Church Militant, and his step cannot be without an important sequel."[60]

When after three years' existence Brook Farm Community in 1844 was turned into a Fourierite Brook Farm Association, at least Elizabeth P. Peabody expressed some misgivings: "Fourier does homage to Christianity with many words. But this may be cant, though it thinks itself sincere."[61]

On the other hand, young Isaac T. Hecker in a letter of April 6, 1844, to Brownson wondered if "the doctrine of unity and diversity of action in the industrial world as held out by these men [i.e. George Ripley and other Fourierites] what is it but Catholicity in the industrial world?"[62] And to the leading Fourierite and Unitarian minister William Henry Channing there was even a closer parallelism between Fourierite associations and churchly institutions. Channing, whose sympathies for churchly tradition had almost made him a convert to Catholicism in 1835,[63] expressed in a speech on May 27, 1846, at a Fourierite convention in Boston his longing "for churches which may be really houses of God, glorified with an indwelling spirit of holiness, and filled to overflowing with heavenly charity."[64]

Thus Brownson's belief in the church as an institution seems to resemble the Unitarian-Transcendentalist belief of the 1840's in communities or associations with a more or less religious basis. Further, his belief in the church as a means of social reform was a parallel to the belief of the Brook Farmers and other utopian socialists in their communities as models of "a reörganization of society itself."

Even if Brownson was no member of Brook Farm or any other similar community, he seems—as already mentioned—to have encouraged his friend Ripley to undertake the experiment,[65] and in the *Democratic Review* for November, 1842, he wrote a laudatory essay on Brook Farm. In harmony with his conservative outlook, he praised Brook

Farm as an experiment that required "no rupture with society as it is" nor broke "the law of continuity," but let both the State and the Church remain in "all their necessity and force." Yet he believed that in the long run the atmosphere of such communities would influence the large society outside. And, as an interesting illustration to the above-mentioned parallelism between churchly and community institutions, Brownson maintained that "these communities are models of what must hereafter be the social element of the Christian Church."[66]

Brownson's dislike of competition in industry made him a staunch advocate of so-called associated and attractive labor, as generally stated by Owen, Fourier, and Albert Brisbane.[67] In fact, already before 1829 Brownson had espoused similar principles.[68] Yet Fourier's scheme for organizing his associated and attractive industry was, in Brownson's eyes, "too mechanical, making of the phalanx not a living organism, but a huge machine."[69] Or, as Emerson more briefly put it: Fourier skipped no fact but life.[70]

For some time, Brownson's eldest son, Orestes, stayed at Brook Farm and attended the school there. His father sometimes visited the place, telling his friends and others who wanted or cared to listen, about his doctrine of life and other subjects which occupied him. But according to Lindsay Swift, "the occasional appearance of the contentious Brownson was no signal of mirth," and his "heavy polemics" soon exhausted the patience of his listeners.[71]

However, Brownson, at least to some extent, must have found a positive response to his Catholizing tendencies at Brook Farm. According to Georgiana Bruce Kirby, "the subject of Catholicism was quietly discussed among a few of us, and a mild sort of Catholic literature circulated. We heard of Pascal and the Jansenists, the nuns of Port Royal, and the exiles of Arcadia." But, she continues, "it was easy for me to indulge in a little sentiment about crosses, rosaries, cathedrals, and madonnas. It was quite another thing to give up my right of private judgment, my right to think *at all*, in fact, on matters of any moment, and walk backwards into the mental inaction and spiritual tyranny of the Church."[72]

Whether Brownson's road to Catholicism was a walk forward, or a walk backward, as G. B. Kirby contended,[73] in any case his conversion was not motivated by esthetics or sentimentality. Instead, as Lindsay Swift points out, the Catholic Church at last became to him "a crying necessity."[74]

We have seen that Brownson's philosophical and political views in 1843 were, as often before, closely related to religious questions. As for his synthetic philosophy, it had definite religious implications, above all reflected in his wish to "resolve philosophy into religion." Further, his desire for a strong government to counteract arbitrary majority rule and the evils of industrialism made him conclude the necessity of a Christian revival and a unified, authoritative church, which should give moral and religious support to civil government.

But more particularly, he developed his modified views of Christianity and the church in a series of articles in the *Christian World*, a new—or at least remodeled—weekly paper, published by George G. Channing, a brother of the late William Ellery Channing.[75] According to the "prospectus" in its first number (Jan. 7, 1843), the purpose of the journal was to stimulate to spiritual life, especially among the Unitarians.

Brownson's contributions were a series of "letters" on "The Mission of Jesus." Without knowing exactly where his thoughts would lead him, he intended to apply and develop his doctrine of life and communion and, more generally, revive the belief in the church as an "organism" and not only as a loose association of individuals.[76]

Yet if he did not himself see where he would arrive, others were not even sure of his present position in the religious world. Thus a writer in the *Christian World*, although certain that Brownson by now was a Christian, wondered what sort of Christianity he really stood for. But the interested writer concluded that Brownson's Christianity probably was a medley of Evangelical and Catholic elements, spiced with some Unitarian ingredients.[77]

No wonder, therefore, that Brownson's essays in the journal pleased —alternately—Unitarians, Evangelicals, High Church Episcopalians, and Catholics. His rejection of the doctrine of the vicarious atonement of Christ and, likewise, his distrust of Luther's and Calvin's doctrine of justification by faith alone made him agreeable to the Unitarians. On the other hand, his insistence on man's inherent depravity and complete dependence on God favorably aroused the interest of the Calvinists and the Evangelicals. Assuredly, Brownson's expressed confidence in God's help when the individual cried to him "out from the very depths of despair" sounded genuinely Christian and indicated his growing desire of saving his own soul.[78]

Again, his emphasis on the Eucharist or the Holy Communion was duly praised in Episcopalian quarters. But when he began to develop his views of the church, the Catholics became really interested, and for good reason: actually, it became more and more evident that Brownson was heading toward the Catholic Church.[79]

In accordance with his Law of Life and his synthetic philosophy, he stressed the necessity of the church as a medium, or as the Body of Christ. Jesus as pure spirit or Logos would not avail us at all: "Can the human mind know pure Spirit, seize it in any sense whatever?" Interestingly, Brownson, who both in his *New Views* of 1836 and in his essays on "The Laboring Classes" of 1840 had distinguished between "the Christianity of Christ" and "the Christianity of the Church," now stated as his conviction that the very first "church" was Christ himself, who communicated his divine life to the apostles, who, again, transmitted the divine life to successive generations of believers. Accordingly, the continuous presence of Jesus through the Holy Ghost made the church "one, catholic, inspired and authoritative." Since life was only in the body as such or in the whole "organism" and not in the limbs separately, sectarianism had to be condemned as unchristian. Indeed, Brownson seemed already very close to accepting the claims of the Roman Catholic Church: "All we say is, that the true Church of Christ is an outward body, formed by the indwelling of his Spirit, and that it still exists in time and space, unchanged in spirit, capacity, disposition, or authority, from what it was in the Apostolic age."[80]

In his next "letter" he was even more distinct: "This outward visible body is the HOLY CATHOLIC APOSTOLIC CHURCH, which remains unchanged in character, disposition, ability, or authority, from what it was in its origin, and which ever will so remain till the end of the world." Brownson accepted already wholeheartedly, and in its strictest sense, the Catholic doctrine: "Out of the pale of the Church, no salvation."[81]

For his own part, being convinced of the supreme authority of this church, not only in spiritual, but also in temporal matters, he declared himself willing to submit completely to her decisions. With a strange mixture of humility and self-confidence, he stated his distrust of his individual reason, while in the same breath maintaining that his present views of Christ and the church were not his personal opinions, "but the views which Christ, through his Church, has taught me."[82]

Thus Brownson once again was dead sure of the validity of his premises and his conclusions—indeed, even more so than ever before, judging from his authoritative mode of utterance. In a polemic in the *Christian World*, the Unitarian minister and publicist James Freeman Clarke gave the following comment on Brownson's manner of reasoning: "No sooner does he come upon a new truth, than with uncontrollable ardor he runs it out as far as it can possibly go, refusing for the time to look at any of its practical limitations, or at any antagonist principles. No result to which he may come, however unexpected or extraordinary, ever appears to make him doubt the correctness of the reasoning which led to it, or the soundness of the principle on which it depends. This fiery intellectual impetus, while it gives perpetual freshness and charm to his writings, appears to me to be the source of frequent error."[83]

Obviously, despite its exaggerated form, there was much truth in Clarke's statement, especially as seen on the background of Brownson's own words in the same journal only two weeks before:

For years, up to 1841, . . . I believed the Church wholly internal, transcendental, and that no outward organism but the state was needed or admissible. Hence, I decried all outward visible organism; and believing that the one sacrifice of Christ on the cross, offered once, was all-sufficient, and needed not to be repeated in the case of every individual sinner, I rejected and denounced, as I needs must, all outward priesthoods, as an impertinence, declaring the 'word of God never drops from the priest's lips.' This I did, not, as was supposed, in the interests of infidelity, but, as I verily believed, in the interests of true piety. I have since learned that I was wrong, that the spiritual is found only in the material, the Spirit of Christ only as embodied in the Church. Therefore, conferring not with flesh and blood, I have not hesitated to renounce my errors, and to contend earnestly for the faith once delivered to the saints, . . . as explained by the Universal Church, the Congregation of the Faithful.[84]

But despite his expressed lifelong desire of an authoritative religion,[85] and his recently expressed contempt for his own, individual reason, he was very anxious to point out the alleged harmony or correspondence between the natural and the supernatural, reason—in the sense of "the universal belief of the race"—and revelation.[86] Accordingly, the Catholic Church was not beyond the realm of human logic, only to be grasped through an intellectual *tour de force*. On the contrary:

Start with a true philosophy of human nature as your data, and you may logically reproduce the whole Catholic Church, even to the apparently least significant article of its faith or dicipline.—It has been in this way that we ourselves have come to our present understanding of the Church; . . . We have stood in awe of the Miracle before us, the perpetual miracle, and exclaimed, He who made the reason of man, He also has made the Church; and we have bowed down to it, as a visible manifestation of the wonderful wisdom, and power, and love, of the Invisible God. To strike out any article of its faith or discipline, is like striking out the key-stone of the arch. We must accept it as a whole, or not at all.[87]

In *The Convert* (pages 156 ff.) Brownson said that when beginning to write his articles for the *Christian World*, he had no idea of becoming a Catholic, but his arguments led him "by an invincible logic" to accept the Catholic Church as *the* Church. On the spur of the moment he even wanted to declare immediately his willingness to convert to Catholicism after getting the necessary instruction. But even though logical consistency might have required such a step, he hesitated for one year, and for different reasons, before he took this decisive step.

First, he had considered Catholicism and the Catholic Church mostly in the abstract and had little knowledge of and little sympathy for contemporary Catholicism. His respect for this church was, properly speaking, a respect for medieval Catholicism. True, his suggestion of a "continuous Inspiration" within the church might indicate a reappraisal of modern Catholicism,[88] but the dry and unattractive style of some modern Catholic treatises which he had read, hardly strengthened his idea of such a "continuous Inspiration." Moreover, although skeptical as to Protestant sectarianism and individualism, he was unwilling to condemn as false and mischievous the whole Protestant world, so much the more because "the great, energetic nations of the day were the non-Catholic nations, Great Britain, Russia, and the United States," and because even in so-called Catholic countries the intellectual *élite* was predominantly non-Catholic.

Second, his statements in the *Christian World* notwithstanding, he doubted that the divine-human life of the church was lived only within the pale of the Catholic Church. After all, the Christian church as such no longer existed in its unity and integrity, and although the Roman Catholic Church was the largest fragment and, undoubtedly, had the greatest share of the divine-human life, this life also existed in the smaller fragments, i.e. in the different Protestant churches. And in a broader sense, this divine-human life manifested itself in what was generally called Christian culture and civilization. Further, he did not feel quite sure that this divine-human life was completely unimpaired by human error even in the Catholic Church itself.

Third, he hesitated out of a natural "fear" for the unknown. For one born and reared in a Protestant community, the passing from one Protestant church to another was like passing from one apartment to the other in the same house, a practice which Brownson was not quite unacquainted with; but the passing from Protestantism to Catholicism was something more than internal house walks. He felt it was like entering into "a new and untried region, and we fear the discoveries we may make there, when it is too late to draw back."[89]

Mainly for these reasons he hesitated to take the decisive step which would bring him into the Roman Catholic Church. Instead he resolved to continue his labor for Christian unity by trying to combine the different "fragments" and thus restore "the body of Christ to its original unity and integrity."[90] Also, from Brownson's writings in 1843 one has the definite impression that he was primarily concerned with the idea of a universal or catholic institutionalized church, and not yet with the question of whether his church was already represented by one particular denomination. He was still dreaming of his Church of the Future, although by now he realized much more clearly than before that he had to build on existing foundations.[91]

Throughout the year 1843 Brownson grew more and more convinced that someone or something above man or the individual was needed to guide him and secure his "progress," whether a strong government (on the state level), Providential men or an authoritative church. Instead of abstract notions like the instincts of the masses, no-government tendencies, and an internal, invisible "church," he increasingly realized the need for concrete, "actual" or "material" means like the government and a visible church—means that would help man to find outlets for his capabilities and provide for his material and spiritual progress.

The underlying philosophical principle which motivated his changed views of Christianity and the church was "that the spiritual is found only in the material." Yet interestingly enough, this principle was after all a version or an application of his idea advanced already in his *New Views* about "the union of spirit and matter."[92] Consequently, despite his shifts of emphasis and even changed views, his quest in 1836 for "a new synthesis of the elements of the life of humanity"[93] and his presentation in 1843 of his synthetic philosophy indicated a deeper consistency in Brownson's thought.

From a broader point of view, Brownson's ideas by 1843 reflected the Transcendentalist emphasis on the synthetic-dynamic character of life, and the general Romantic belief in the value of past ages and in history as a more or less organic, teleological process. By consequence, not only institutions like the State and the Church, but also humanity in space and time were considered living organisms. And as humanity or a human society was more than an "association of equals,"[94] civil government should be more than the mere agent of society, and the church more than a loose conglomeration of sects.

Brownson's theories of the church amazed and almost bewildered the editors of the *Christian World* and the *Democratic Review.* True, they did not expressly ask him to stop writing for their publications, but to all intents and purposes both of them drew a sigh of relief when the "troublemaker" left the arena.

Already in February, 1843, George G. Channing had observed the unexpected trend of Brownson's essays, and felt the need to state that the journal was after all a Protestant publication. According to Brownson, the editor "disclaimed... peremptorily" his views of the church, and later even refused to insert a brief reply from Brownson to James Freeman Clarke, finding the debate "subversive" of the original plan of the journal. This refusal made Brownson unwilling to write his last article of his series for the *Christian World.*[95] Yet Brownson seemed to dramatize matters a little when at a later date stating that the publisher simply refused to insert his last article, which was to give his answer to the question: Which is the true Church or Body of Christ?[96] However, in the *Christian World* the editor declared that he had nothing against printing Brownson's intended last essay.[97]

The leave-taking from O'Sullivan, though, seems to have been less cool. Though admitting a widespread criticism of Brownson's articles among the readers, the editor of the *Democratic Review* made it clear that Brownson himself had decided to leave the magazine in order to start his own review. Yet, according to the agreement made between them, Brownson was not allowed to call it by the old name: the *Boston Quarterly Review.*[98] The solution adopted was *Brownson's Quarterly Review.*

Although indicating a bit too much pride and self-assertion, the name of the review signalized the plain fact: already from the start Brownson declared his intention to write his review singlehandedly. He wanted to make it exclusively his own organ or mouthpiece, not only for the sake of coherence, but also because he had come to consider himself more a teacher or instructor than a learner.[99]

In the "Introduction" to his new or revived review he gave due credit to O'Sullivan, but added, significantly, that he did not feel at home in the *Democratic Review.* Anyhow, there could be no doubt as to his present position: "No radicalism in church, state, philosophy, or morals, but should be formally and solemnly eschewed. No efforts to create an entirely new order, instead of carrying forward, to its perfection, the old, can be wisely, or safely, countenanced."[100]

However, politically conservative though he was, he still considered the great aim of society "the moral, intellectual, and physical amelioration of the poorer and more numerous classes." But more distinctly than before Brownson now stressed religious faith as the only real means of bringing about this amelioration. And more particularly, he reëmphasized his belief in the church or "the Body of our Lord, as the divinely appointed medium of individual and social regeneration and progress."[101]

Yet in the "summing-up" of his position at the beginning of 1844, he declared that he had not joined nor was intending to join the Roman Catholic Church, even though he had by now come to "accept the general theory of that Church, as the true theory of the Church of Christ." Why, then, did he still hesitate?

He gave a strange reason, indeed. He had found out that not even the Roman Catholic Church was catholic enough for him! With a really Transcendentalist distrust of bygone inspiration, he declared that "the vital principle, the organic force, of the Church, is the *indwelling Life, or Spirit, of Christ*, not the mere fact that she is the depository of *past* revelations and inspirations." On the contrary, "*its mission is the continued evolution*" through "*continuous inspiration.*" Since a Catholic doctor had written that Brownson, in claiming continuous divine inspiration for the church, actually went farther than the Catholics themselves, Brownson concluded that the Roman Catholic Church was not catholic enough. But since he now believed that the Church of the Future was already, in theory, present in the Old Church, he stated that the coming church organization would only be "the old transformed."[102]

During the following months, Brownson's political conservatism became more and more manifest, and more than ever before his view of politics was closely related to that of religion: "We all of us, from the highest to the lowest, owe obedience to authority," he firmly declared, "to the state in civil matters, and to the church, authorized to speak in the name of Christ, in spiritual matters; and we have no *right* to use any methods or means of redressing wrongs, to labor for any ameliorations, but in submission to these."

Contemptuous of all "*via-media* folks," those who did not dare to push their doctrines to extremes, Brownson now recognized only two principles in their theoretical nakedness: "Either we must accept the conservative doctrine, and give to authority the sole right to take the initiative in all reforms, and suffer the individual to work only under and through law; or else we must accept pure and absolute individualism, proclaim the absolute freedom and independence of individual reason, individual conscience, individual whim or caprice, and individual action, leaving each individual to answer to his God for his entire life, as best he may,— . . . " The stern logician, now obviously scorning any middle course and any attempt at "eclectic" or "synthetic" reasoning, rejected any compromise: "There is no such thing as pushing a sound principle too far. If your principle will not bear pushing to its extreme, you may know that it is false, and that the error is, not in pushing it too far, but in adopting it at all."[103]

A similar extreme attitude might seem strange and even terrifying, but it expressed the deep, all-absorbing feelings of a man completely disgusted with the supposed trend of contemporary society toward an increasing individualism and subjectivism in politics, philosophy, and religion. Right or wrong, there is something pathetic about a man who so stubbornly defies "public opinion" and takes such a definitely "unpopular" position: "Change our ground, take the conservative side, and he, who yesterday was the master spirit of his age and country, speaks only to listless ears; his power is gone; there is no eloquence in his voice, no magic in his words. The few who may applaud, who may hope to use him for their own purposes, half despise him, and he sinks into insignificance."[104]

Doubtless, as for Brownson himself, his eloquence was still there, as evidenced by his characterization of what he thought to be Transcendentalist subjectivism: it "spins Truth, Good, Beauty, even God himself, out of the human soul, as the spider spins its web out of its own bowels."[105] Yet the import and presentation of his extremism, radiating incandescent light but no genial warmth, could not fail to alienate him from other people. The fact that his extremism was marred by bitterness did not improve matters. Thus, for example, he declared Margaret Fuller to be "wholly deficient in a pure, correct taste, and especially in that tidiness we always look for in woman." And as if this were not enough, he added that he knew "nothing more abominable" than the doctrines of that "heathen priestess."[106] Worse still, he wrote indignantly that both the late William Ellery Channing and Emerson, whom he had formerly treated with great respect and, as for Channing, even with reverence, had such an unsound and meager philosophy and theology that their memory would be "shortlived."[107] Indeed, before entering the "new and untried region," Brownson seemed anxious to burn all bridges behind him...

In religion, he found the great question to be Catholicism or individualism, religion or infidelity.[108] During the first months of 1844 Catholicism still meant to him a higher form of Christian unity, comprising all or most churches. He hoped that each denomination should finally cease to exist as a particular communion, and that no single existing church organization should absorb the others. Pointing to the widespread desire for Christian unity in many Protestant churches of the time, he stressed particularly the so-called Oxford Movement within the Anglican or Episcopal Church.[109]

If he never "seriously contemplated" joining the Episcopal Church,[110] the thought of so doing must have crossed his mind. At least he wrote the following in the July, 1844, issue of his review: "Feeling our own sad condition, we naturally turn towards the Episcopal church. It is professedly the church of our ancestors; it speaks our mother tongue; and to enter it is not to go among strangers, to desert one's friends and kindred."[111] But his final conviction that only the Roman Catholic Church had the truly apostolic ministry was the decisive reason for his conversion to Catholicism.[112]

Undoubtedly, Brownson's Unitarian and Transcendentalist "brethren" witnessed with great interest and surprise their Romeward-bound colleague. Above all, the Rev. Convers Francis seems to have observed a fair share of Brownson's development during the months before his conversion, and Francis communicated his impressions to Theodore Parker. Already in a letter of December 30, 1843, Francis remarked Brownson's Catholic trend: "Brownson is trying to ride with all his might the hobby of the Old Church, and gives us a mawkish, mongrel mixture of Leroux and Romanism. He says that whatever the Catholic Church has decided must be true, and that that Church (meaning literally the Roman Church) never has contradicted itself! ... Whether this will atone with the Boston aristocracy for past sins of radicalism, I know not ..."

Yet in a letter of April 20, 1844, Convers Francis was not quite sure where Brownson would finally land: "Thus nothing can be more strong and peremptory than the claims he sets up for *the Church*, and yet to this day, nobody can tell what he means by the Church ..." However, already on April 28, 1844, Francis, apparently, had become quite certain of Brownson's Romeward drift: "I have just heard that Brownson says, he is ready to swallow the Pope's infallibility now." And he also reported that "they hooted him at a democratic meeting the other day."[113]

Brownson's tendency to extremism and his personal bitterness, which were particularly manifest during the last months before his conversion, partly explain the sarcastic tone of the above-quoted letters. On the other hand, an increasing opposition, whether in the form of hooting or in more suave forms of derision, to his Romanizing views hardly reduced his extremism and bitterness.

However, it is only just to mention that Brownson at that time, in his letters to his young friend Isaac T. Hecker, who was also approaching Catholicism, also revealed sympathetic features of his character. In his letter of March 11, 1844, the "extremist" who at that time loved to present clear-cut alternatives, admitted his internal struggles: "My own feelings and convictions, in spite of my struggles to the contrary, convey [?] me to the Catholic Church, and I foresee ..., that I must sooner or later become a member of it. There is no help for it."[114]

During the months before his conversion to Catholicism, Brownson's idea of the church as a lever of social progress and as a means of introducing God's kingdom on earth[115] was gradually overshadowed by his all-absorbing thought of his own salvation for heaven. Finally, " 'one thing only' " was " 'needful' " to him.[116]

In the last week of May, 1844, he expressed to the Right Reverend Benedict Joseph Fenwick, the Bishop of Boston, his wish to become a Catholic, and Bishop Fenwick introduced him to his successor, the Right Reverend John Bernard Fitzpatrick, who was to give Brownson the necessary instruction. On October 20, 1844, at the age of 42, and 22 years after he had joined Presbyterianism, he became a convert to Catholicism.[117]

On June 1, 1844, Brownson wrote to Isaac T. Hecker a warm and touching letter, which revealed a basic tenderness and even humility in a man who often gave the impression of being extremely proud and self-assertive:

But my dear Isaac, you cannot gain this victory alone, nor by new . . . meditations, and prayer, you can obtain it only through the grace of God, and the grace of God only through its appointed channels. . . . Do you really believe the Gospel? Do you really believe the Holy Catholic Church? If so, you must feel yourself under the direction of the Church. I have commenced my preparation for uniting myself with the Catholic Church. I do not as yet belong to the family of Christ. I feel it, I can be an alien no longer, and without the church I know by my past experience, that I cannot attain to purity and sanctity of life. I need the counsels, the aids, . . . and the constitutions of the Church. It is the appointed medium of salvation, and how can we hope for any grace except through it? . . . I have made up my mind, and I shall enter the Church if she will receive me.[118]

1 *Early Life*, pp. 344–345.
2 *Nathaniel Hawthorne and His Wife*, I (Boston and New York, 1884), p. 160.
3 *The Brownson Papers*, Notre Dame University.
4 *BQR*, I (Jan. 1838), 125–126.
5 *The Brownson Papers.*
6 Letter of June 29, 1842: *The Brownson Papers.*
7 New Series, XIII, 653–660.
8 Mason Wade, *Margaret Fuller: Whetstone of Genius* (New York, 1940), p. 88.
9 Letter of July 5, 1842, from O'Sullivan to Brownson: *The Brownson Papers. Early Life*, pp. 344–348.
10 "Charles Elwood Reviewed" *(BQR*, V, April 1842), *Works*, IV, 360.
11 "Schmucker's Psychology," *Works*, I, 52; "Synthetic Philosophy," *Works*, I, 68, 61.
12 *Works*, I, 63, 70.
13 *BQR*, V (Oct. 1842), 417.
14 *Works*, I, 62–63, 118, 128.
15 *Ibid.*, pp. 26–27.
16 "The Philosophy of History" *(Dem. Rev.*, May and June 1843), *Works*, IV, 389–390.
17 *Works*, I, 53–54.
18 *Ibid.* pp. 52, 73.
19 *Works*, IV, 381. Most probably, however, Brownson would have defended himself by stating that ontology or "the object" formed part of every primitive fact of consciousness.
20 *Works*, I, 99, 105–106.
21 *Ibid.*, p. 105.
22 *Ibid.*, pp. 20, 22, 23, 56, 66.
23 *Ibid.*, p. 79. See also Leroux, *Réfutation de l'Eclectisme*, p. 275.
24 "The Minor Transcendentalists and German Philosophy," *New England Quarterly*, XV (Dec. 1942), 669–677.
25 *Works*, I, 64; IV, 378–392, esp. 380, 384.
26 *Works*, I, 32, 101.

27 *Works*, IV, 392.

28 *Works*, I, 29–30; *The Convert*, p. 123; *Early Life*, p. 441. More particularly, see *Réfutation de l'Eclectisme:* "C'est avec le sentiment caché sous les idées qu'on peut réellement faire de l'éclectisme, c'est-à-dire de la synthèse. . . . Il faut donc le coeur, l'amour, la charité, le sentiment, pour une pareille oeuvre, la synthèse" (p. 275).

29 *Works*, I, 54; *The Brownson Papers.*

30 Wordsworth's poem "The Tables Turned," last stanza but one (quoted in *The College Survey of English Literature*, II [New York, 1947], 52); Emerson's "'American Scholar' Address" (quoted in *American Literature: A Representative Anthology of American Writing from Colonial Times to the Present*, ed. Geoffrey Moore [London, 1964], p. 240).

31 *Dial*, I (July 1840), 96.

32 "Historic Notes of Life and Letters in New England," *The Complete Works of Ralph Waldo Emerson*, X (Boston and New York, 1904), 338.

33 "The Minor Transcendentalists and German Philosophy," p. 677.

34 *Works*, I, 44.

35 *Works*, IV, 361–423.

36 "The Present State of Society" *(Dem. Rev.*, July 1843), *Works*, IV, 423–460.

37 "Democracy and Liberty" *(Dem. Rev.*, April 1843), *Works*, XV, 269; "Popular Government" *(Dem. Rev.*, May 1843), *Works*, XV, 286, 287, 294; *The Convert*, p. 121.

38 A Virginian exponent of states' rights, President John Tyler rejected cherished Whig beliefs in internal improvements, a U.S. Bank, and protective tariffs (See Claude Moore Fuess, *Daniel Webster*, II, pp. 82, 95); "The Distribution Bill" *(BQR*, V, Jan. 1842), *Works*, XV, 229–230.

39 "Constitutional Government" *BQR*, V, Jan. 1842), *Works*, XV, 254; "Origin and Ground of Government" *(Dem. Rev.*, 1843), *Works*, XV, 333–334, 340.

40 "Democracy and Liberty," p. 279; "Origin and Ground of Government," p. 384; "Our Future Policy" *(BQR*, IV, Jan. 1841), *Works*, XV, 126–128; "Brook Farm," *Democratic Review*, New Series, XI (Nov. 1842), 486.

41 *Works*, XV, 325–327, 353, 392.

42 *Ibid.*, pp. 348–350, 353, 355, 361, 398.

43 *Ibid.*, pp. 209, 285, 296, 375, 379–389, 402.

44 *Ibid.*, pp. 279, 326, 330, 372–373, 384, 391, 396–397, 400. See also "The Scholar's Mission: An Oration Pronounced before the Gamma Sigma Society, of Dartmouth College, Hanover, N. H., July 26, 1843," *Works*, XIX, 70–73; *Early Life*, pp. 382–385.

45 Walter Fuller Taylor, *A History of American Letters* (New York, 1947), p. 107; Herbert W. Schneider, *A History of American Philosophy* (New York, 1947), pp. 165–166.

46 Max Beloff, *Thomas Jefferson and American Democracy* in *Teach Yourself History Library*, ed. A. B. Rowse (London, 1948), pp. 122–123.

47 According to *The Convert* (pp. 120–121), Brownson read Aristotle's *Politics*, in which democracy (demokratía) mostly signifies the perverted majority rule or even the dictatorship of the masses.

48 "Note to 'Democracy and Liberty,'" *Dem. Rev.*, New Series, XII (April 1843), 387–391.

49 "Note to 'Popular Government,'" *Dem. Rev.*, New Series, XII (May 1843), 537–544.

50 "Mr. Brownson's Recent Articles in the *Democratic Review*," New Series, XIII (Dec. 1843), 653–660.

[51] *The Convert*, pp. 97–98, 163; *Early Life*, pp. 451–453.
[52] *Dial*, I (Oct. 1840), 269.
[53] See, for example, Ch. XXVII: "Jacksonian Democracy and Utopia" in Arthur M. Schlesinger, Jr., *The Age of Jackson*, pp. 361–368.
[54] O. B. Frothingham, *George Ripley*, pp. 111, 199.
[55] "Plan of the West Roxbury Community," *Dial*, II (Jan. 1842), 365; "A Glimpse of Christ's Idea of Society," *Dial*, II (Oct. 1841), 214–228 (quoted in John Humphrey Noyes, *History of American Socialisms* [1869; reprinted in New York, 1961], p. 110).
[56] Julian Hawthorne, *Nathaniel Hawthorne and His Wife*, I, p. 201; *The Blithedale Romance* in *The Works of Nathaniel Hawthorne, Standard Library Edition*, V (Boston and New York, 1883), p. 342.
[57] *Nathaniel Hawthorne and His Wife*, I, p. 228 (letter from Brook Farm, May 3, 1841, to his sister Louisa).
[58] *Passages from the American Note-Books* (Entry of May 4, 1841) in *The Works of Nathaniel Hawthorne, Standard Library Edition*, IX (Boston and New York, 1896), p. 234.
[59] *Ibid.* (Entry of Sept. 3, 1841, at Salem), p. 237.
[60] "Historic Notes of Life and Letters in New England," *The Complete Works of Ralph Waldo Emerson*, X, pp. 364, 571 n.
[61] J. H. Noyes, *History of American Socialisms*, p. 518.
[62] *Early Life*, p. 525.
[63] William R. Hutchison, *The Transcendentalist Ministers*, p. 196.
[64] Noyes, *op.cit.*, p. 531.
[65] *Early Life*, p. 313.
[66] *Dem. Rev.*, New Series, XI (Nov. 1842), 489–490. Interestingly, in an inserted letter from a lady to Brownson, the writer in question wondered if Brook Farm did not realize in miniature the identity between Church and State, "which you [i.e. Brownson] think is the deepest idea of our American government?" (p. 495).
[67] *Ibid.*, p. 490; "The Community System," *Dem. Rev.*, New Series, XII (Feb. 1843), 143–144.
[68] *Early Life*, p. 448; *G. A.*, VII (Sept. 5, 1829), 282–283: "In those branches which the individual can not master, the principle of co operation may be introduced. But there should be no such thing as a laboring class, and consuming class, one separate from the other."
[69] "Brook Farm," *Dem. Rev.*, New Series, XI (Nov. 1842), 488.
[70] "Historic Notes of Life and Letters in New England," p. 352.
[71] *Brook Farm: Its Members, Scholars, and Visitors* (New York, 1900), pp. 54, 56, 75, 245.
[72] *Years of Experience* (New York and London, 1887), p. 182.
[73] *Ibid.*, pp. 146–147.
[74] Lindsay Swift, *op.cit.*, p. 245.
[75] *The Convert*, p. 155. The *Christian World* (Boston), Jan. 7, 1843: Formerly, the name of the journal had been the *Gospel Quickener*.
[76] *The Convert*, p. 155.
[77] *Christian World*, Jan. 14, 1843.
[78] *The Convert*, pp. 155–156; *Christian World*, Jan. 7, 14, 21, 28, 1843.
[79] *Christian World*, Jan. 21, 28, Feb. 4, 11, 18, 25, April 15, 1843.
[80] *Ibid.*, Jan. 28, Feb. 4, 1843.
[81] *Ibid.*, Feb. 11, 1843.
[82] *Ibid.*, April 1, 8, 1843.

[83] *Ibid.*, April 15, 1843.
[84] *Ibid.*, April 1, 1843.
[85] *The Convert*, p. 134.
[86] *Ibid.*, p. 133.
[87] *Christian World*, April 15, 1843.
[88] *The Convert*, pp. 156–157; *Christian World*, April 8, 1843.
[89] *The Convert*, pp. 157–160; "The Philosophy of History," *Works*, IV, 410.
[90] *The Convert*, p. 160.
[91] *Christian World*, Feb. 4, 1843.
[92] *Works*, IV, 33.
[93] *Ibid.*, p. 43.
[94] *Christian World*, Feb. 25, 1843; *Works*, XV, 372.
[95] *Christian World*, Feb. 18, 25, April 22, 1843.
[96] *The Convert*, p. 156: But in any case, in the draft of this intended essay he "evaded a direct answer to the question raised."
[97] *Christian World*, April 22, 1843.
[98] *Dem. Rev.*, New Series, XIII (Dec. 1843), 653–660; *Early Life*, p. 349.
[99] *BrQR*, I (Jan. 1844), 6, 136.
[100] *Ibid.*, pp. 1–2, 18–19.
[101] *Ibid.*, pp. 23, 25–27.
[102] *Ibid.*, pp. 11, 14–16, 17, 18; *The Christian World*, April 8, 1843.
[103] "Come outerism: or the Radical Tendency of the Day" *(BrQR*, July 1844), *Works*, IV, 551, 553, 554.
[104] *Ibid.*, p. 556.
[105] *BrQR*, I (Jan. 1844), 136.
[106] *BrQR*, I (Oct. 1844), 546–547. Yet he admitted that times and circumstances were largely responsible: "We see in her a melancholy instance of the fate which awaits a gifted woman in an age of infidelity."
[107] *BrQR*, I (April 1844), 271.
[108] "The Church Question" *(BrQR*, Jan. 1844), *Works*, IV, 483.
[109] *The Convert*, pp. 160–161.
[110] *Ibid.*, p. 160.
[111] "Bishop Hopkins on Novelties" *(BrQR*, July 1844), *Works*, IV, 531.
[112] "Sparks on Episcopacy" *(BrQR*, July 1844), *Works*, IV, 559; "The Anglican Church Schismatic" *(BrQR*, Oct. 1844), *Works*, IV, 567–589.
[113] *Brownson Papers*, Notre Dame University (Copies of *Parker Papers*, Massachusetts Historical Society).
[114] *Brownson Papers.*
[115] "No Church, No Reform" *(BrQR*, April 1844), *Works*, IV, 496–512, esp. 511; "Church Unity and Social Amelioration" *(BrQR*, July 1844), *Works*, IV, 512–526, esp. 521.
[116] *Works*, IV, 525. See also *Works*, IV, 562–563; *The Convert*, p. 162.
[117] *The Convert*, pp. 164, 167–168.
[118] *Brownson Papers.*

XV

Concluding Thoughts on the Conversion and the Convert

In the preceding pages I have tried to trace Brownson's long and winding road to Catholicism and have pointed to different factors that motivated his final decision. Brownson himself was convinced that "conversion is, of course, the work of grace, and without grace no man can come into the church any more than he can enter heaven." But he was no less convinced that his own intellectual development led him, as it were, to the very threshold of the Catholic Church.[1] Let us, then, sum up and analyze those thoughts of his which removed the obstacles of human reason, i.e. *his* reason, and made him accept the claims of the Roman Church. Moreover, since–in the words of John Henry Newman, another well-known contemporary convert to Catholicism–"the whole man moves"[2] and not only his intellect, I will suggest some general or deeper motives for Brownson's conversion. Finally, I will give a short treatment of his Catholic period, especially in relation to his pre-Catholic phase.

Brownson himself regarded the so-called doctrine of life and communion or the Law of Life as the most important intellectual motive for his conversion. This doctrine or "law" was his theological or religious application of Pierre Leroux's "formule de la vie," i.e. his theory of the synthesis of object and subject in thought and life. Moreover, Leroux's doctrine meant the actualization of being in life, the spiritual in the material, or, in Brownson's theological interpretation, God manifest in the flesh. Thus, except for its specific theological import, Brownson's doctrine of life and communion was basically identical with his synthetic philosophy.

Brownson's immediate reason for adopting and developing Leroux's doctrine was his need to motivate and assure man's individual and social progress on earth. Increasingly skeptical as to man's own capacities to achieve this, he felt the urgent need of supernatural intervention through Providential men, above all the God-Man Jesus and his "medium," i.e. the church. As the church since the time of her founder and the apostles was the depository of his divine-human life, Brownson's former distinction between "the Christianity of Christ" and "the Christianity of the Church" had to give way to a synthetic conception which might be termed as follows: The Christianity of Christ is the Christianity of the church. As "the Body of our Lord" the church was considered continuing the Incarnation.

This view of the church as a living organism in space and time, containing and actualizing the divine life, meant a positive appraisal of the church as such, or High Church principles. Indeed, Brownson's application of Leroux's doctrine largely coincided with the so-called "Sacramental system," above all espoused by the Catholizing Oxford Movement within the Anglican Church. It is worthy of note that already in 1827, six years before this movement took its real, official beginning, John H. Newman, who became a convert to Catholicism in 1845 and was made a cardinal in 1879, enthusiastically accepted a greatly similar doctrine about being and phenomena as a philosophical explanation of the church: "The Sacramental system ... is the doctrine that material phenomena are both the types and the instruments of real things unseen,–a doctrine, which embraces, not only what Anglicans, as well as Catholics, believe about Sacraments properly so called; but also the article of 'the Communion of Saints' in its fulness; and likewise the Mysteries of the faith ..."[3]

In the United States, John Henry Hobart (1775–1830), the Episcopal Bishop of New York, had strongly emphasized the importance of the apostolic succession, the ministry, and the sacraments as signifying the visible "Catholic" Church. In the 1840's and 1850's these High Church tendencies were intensified through the influence of the Oxford Movement or the so-called Puseyism. By the mid-1850's no less than half of the Episcopal bishops in the United States were reported to be Puseyites, and between twenty and thirty Episcopal clergymen had even converted to Catholicism.[4]

Yet these churchly tendencies made themselves more or less manifest at that time in many denominations. Thus, many Evangelicals–Puritans and Methodists–became Episcopalians, and some of them even ended up in the Catholic Church.[5]

Interestingly enough, the High Church principles were most clearly and brilliantly articulated by the learned Mercersburg theologians, who represented the German Reformed Church and, thereby, a modified Calvinism.[6] Influenced by the German church historian J. A. W. Neander (1789–1850) and the theologian-philosopher Schleiermacher, who both stressed Christianity as life more than as a fixed dogmatic system, John W. Nevin (1803–1886), who was attached to the Mercersburg Theological Seminary, Pa., from 1840 to 1853, attacked religious sectarianism, subjectivism, and individualism, and stressed the objective, lifegiving character of the Lord's Supper (the "spiritual presence" of Christ). Even if he wanted, primarily, to revive Calvin's and even Luther's alleged emphasis on church principles, Nevin underscored the importance of Christian ecumenics and "evangelical Catholicism." Premising that the universal preceded the particular, he concluded that the church was before the individual.[7]

His colleague, the German scholar Philip Schaff (1819–1893), who taught at the same seminary from 1843 to 1863, in his inaugural address of 1844 on "The Principle of Protestantism" gave a rather favorable interpretation of medieval Catholicism and even of the Roman Catholicism of his day.[8] In his representative and highly interesting book on *America* (1855), Schaff, regarding "the colossal theocratic organism of Church and State in the Middle Ages" as the "anticipation of the *regnum gloriae*," pointed to contemporary tendencies toward Roman Catholicism, like the beliefs in the "outward visible unity" and the "historical unity of the church" and the Roman Catholic "idea of sacrifice." Although not wanting any "retrograde movement to Romanism," he hoped "for a new reformation, which should save all the positive elements of truth and piety in Protestantism, and unite them with the excellences of Catholicism."[9]

Apart from the word "evangelical" and its import, Brownson's views of the church from 1842 to 1844 were surprisingly similar to those of the Mercersburg School. Yet it should be mentioned that even if Brownson rejected the specific Calvinist dogmas of predestination and reprobation, he generally shared the Calvinist or Puritan idea of the unity of Church and State or of a Christian commonwealth. For this reason, the Calvinist-Puritan idea of Church and State made both Brownson and the Mercersburg theologians open to the Catholic idea of theocratic government as practiced in the Middle Ages. On the other hand, there is little reason to believe that Brownson's desire in the early 1840's for a "unified theocratico-democratic commonwealth" would mean the actual political domination of the State by the clergy. Most probably, in 1843–1844 and not only in 1836 and 1840, Brownson wanted the Church to give to the State, society, and individuals religious and moral support, and act as a kind of "public conscience." In any case, the system of "established" or State churches had been abolished in the United States, and there is no indication to believe that Brownson wanted this system re-introduced.

Also in Lutheran churches, both in the United States and in Europe, High Church principles were in vogue. In the United States the Lutheran Seminary Professor and President Samuel S. Schmucker (1799–1873) in 1838 published his *Fraternal Appeal to the American Churches: With a Plan for Catholic Union, on Apostolic Principles.* To a Scandinavian it is interesting to observe that the influential Danish author and clergyman N. F. S. Grundtvig (1783–1872) presented, with his so-called "Churchly Conception" ("den kirkelige Anskuelse") and more particularly with his emphasis on "the Living Word" ("det levende Ord") as expressed in the Apostles' Creed and in the formulas applied and mystically related to the sacraments, an interesting parallel to the Puseyites, the Mercersburg theologians, and Brownson.

In 1858, Brownson, defending himself against the charge of a Presbyterian reviewer–probably Charles Hodge–who had written that Brownson's application of Leroux's doctrine was "exactly the method of transcendental ritualism" of Mercersburg and Oxford, firmly declared that "the author is entitled to all the originality he claims, whether his views had previously been set forth by others or not."[10] Interestingly enough, in *The Convert* (page 26) Brownson had described Hosea Ballou's views in *A Treatise on Atonement* as "old, but . . . nearly all original with the author."

Obviously, Brownson had not consciously–or even hardly unconsciously–borrowed his "method" from the Oxford Movement or the Mercersburg School, although he admitted that his doctrine "undoubtedly favors the views of both Mercersburg and Oxford, touching what they call the sacramental system."[11] In fact, the Puseyites, the Mercersburg theologians, and Brownson were all subjected to the more or less remote or mediate influences from Hegelianism, which postulated the actualization of the Absolute Spirit in concrete realities, and generally stressed, in accordance with "philosophical Romanticism," the " 'whole' and the 'concrete' as opposed to the abstract, the schematized, the limited, the dead, the dismembered, and the lifeless."[12]

Brownson, who in 1844 wrote that he had derived only little benefit from German philosophy,[13] in the earlier cited letter of November 15, 1836, to Cousin declared that he liked German philosophy so much the better when it had been "filtered" through the mind of France.[14] Apart from the fact that the term "diluted" might be no less appropriate than "filtered," it should be added in this connection that Brownson hardly ever undertook any serious study of German philosophy at first hand. It was through the philosophies of Cousin and Leroux, who were both influenced by Hegel,[15] that Brownson derived the above-mentioned Hegelian and broadly Romantic conceptions, which were basic to his Law of Life, his synthetic philosophy, and his general views of civil government and the church.

After establishing the doctrine of Christ in the church, Brownson's philosophy eventually led him to accept the claims of the Roman Catholic Church as *the* true Church, on the basis of apostolic succession. On his own principle, he could not avoid the conclusion that this church contained by far the largest stream of the divine life, and that the other churches only possessed small streams of this life and in a rather incomplete manner.

Moreover, his doctrine of life and communion, giving him the idea of Christianity "as a divine scheme of mediatorial grace,"[16] also made him open to Catholic dogma and ritual, and its emphasis on the sacraments, above all the Eucharist or the Holy Communion. Again, his belief in the divine life both as a process and as a *Real Presence*[17] in the church made him consider the Protestant dogma of a merely imputed or forensic righteousness as something artificial or, at best, very one-sided. Replacing "*imputed*" by "*imparted*" righteousness,[18] he was brought more closely to Catholic dogma, which holds salvation to be the result of a process rather than the result of "faith as an inward act or persuasion of the creature, whether naturally or supernaturally produced."[19]

Basic to his doctrine of life and communion was his belief in a correspondence or parallelism between the natural and the supernatural, reason and revelation. As man, in the natural sphere, communes with his "object," i.e. nature and other men—he communes with God in the supernatural sphere.[20] Undoubtedly, his belief in such a "correspondence" tended to bring him in harmony with general Catholic thought, which—unlike orthodox Protestantism or, at least, Brownson's conception of it—stresses the harmony between nature and grace.[21] As Thomas Aquinas expressed it: "Gratia non tollit naturam, sed perfecit" (Grace does not supersede nature, but completes it).

Yet his view of a kind of parallelism between different spheres of life also had Transcendentalist counterparts, a fact which Brownson's young friend and fellow convert Isaac T. Hecker seemed anxious to point out.[22] In fact, Hecker had gone through an intense Transcendentalist phase, which included stays not only at Ripley's Brook Farm, but also at Bronson Alcott's Fruitlands. He and Thoreau had even made plans for a trip to Europe, but their youthful plans did not materialize.

At any rate, from a general point of view, the conception of correspondence, coincidence, or symmetry between different spheres of life is rather frequent in Emerson's writings. Already in *Nature* (1836) he declared that "particular natural facts are symbols of particular spiritual facts," "the use of natural history is to give us aid in supernatural history" and "the laws of moral nature answer to those of matter as face to face in a glass."[23] And in his essay "Prudence" (1841) he expressed the belief that "human nature loves no contradictions, but is symmetrical," and that "every fact hath its roots in the soul."[24]

While "the Old School" Unitarianism, at least according to Cameron Thompson, thought reason and faith to be "innately hostile to one another,"[25] the belief of the Transcendentalists, on the other hand, in divine immanence tended to deny any sharp antithesis between the natural and the supernatural, between natural and revealed religion.[26] Indeed, the strong tendency of the Transcendentalists to consider mind "the only reality" and to reckon "the world as an appearance," though not denying "the sensuous fact,"[27] might easily reduce the idea of correspondence between two distinct realities to an "ideal identity," albeit not "absolute identity," between one reality and its "appearance."[28]

Along these lines, a writer in the *Dial* confidently declared that "Revealed Religion does not differ in its nature from Natural Religion. They are only different flowers from the same root."[29] And another writer in the same review stated in similar terms that "Nature and Revelation are parts of the same system, and proceed from one source."[30] Yet a third writer for the *Dial*, obviously from a more dualistic point of departure, would have welcomed "a philosophy which maintains a sublime harmony with the teachings of revelation."[31]

But even if Brownson rejected Transcendentalist idealism and instead stated his belief in the *real* existence of mind *and* matter, the supernatural *and* the natural, he was at least still so much of a Transcendentalist that he did not believe these distinct realities to be antithetic.

Also, Brownson's very emphasis on "life" sounded particularly Transcendentalist and not only broadly or vaguely Romantic. Both to Emerson and Brownson, "a thread runs through all things." To Emerson, this "thread," or "a mysterious principle of life," made nature, whether regarded as "symbol" or "sensuous fact," an organic whole, and to Brownson, his Law of Life was the "thread" that ran through all human history and infused it with the supernatural.[32]

Consequently, owing to these similarities between Transcendentalism with its reliance on "Life-Power,"[33] and Brownson's Law of Life, the Presbyterian reviewer was not wholly in the wrong when calling Brownson's principle "transcendental ritualism;" and Lindsay Swift, evidently viewing Brownson's doctrine in a more favorable light, thought it to be "not so wide a digression, after all, from the upward path of his friends the Transcendentalists."[34]

Yet, wide or not, it was a digression at least from Transcendentalist idealism and subjectivism. We have seen that while Emerson believed in the almost exclusive reality of mind, Brownson's attitude was "eclectic" or "synthetic," stressing both spiritualism and materialism, "speculation" and "experience,"[35] the world of ideas and the world of the senses, identity and diversity, unity and multiplicity, psychology and history, even "the psychological Christ" and "the historical Christ."

Moreover, while to Emerson "all men, all things, the state, the church, yea the friends of the heart are phantasms and unreal beside the sanctuary of the heart,"[36] and "nature, literature, history, are only subjective phenomena,"[37] Brownson regarded them as objective realities. In consequence, while Emerson rejected any idea of "helps" between the soul and the divine spirit,[38] and Bronson Alcott denied that the soul was saved or judged by "proxy,"[39] Brownson developed his idea of objective "media" through which the divine spirit manifested itself.

As mentioned earlier, the typical Transcendentalist idea of nature and the world as "symbols" offers a kind of remote parallel to Brownson's conception of the Ideal in the Actual, but in this connection it is interesting to see how Brownson himself reasoned on this subject. In 1843 he wrote as follows: "The material fact is not as some say the symbol of the spiritual, serving merely to direct us to its whereabout, but is the medium which contains it, and transmits it, so to speak, to the mind,–the medium in which the soul grasps the spiritual, however far into the transcendental world it may send its piercing glance." Brownson based his conception of "media" on his old cherished idea of combining materialism and spiritualism, thus creating a synthesis, which to him was basic to Christianity as well as to every sound philosophy.[40]

Even if the difference between the Transcendentalist idea of "symbol" and Brownson's view of "media" may be difficult to grasp, at least Brownson's underlying and consistent thought of a synthesis of spirit and matter reflected the traditional Christian beliefs in the Incarnation and the Resurrection.

Moreover, Douglas Clyde Mackintosh, in an essay on "Theology and Metaphysics," throws some light on the relations between idealistic philosophy and Christianity. Reflecting on Kantian influence on Ritschlianism, he asks "how an independently existing divine Reality can possibly be revealed in either human history or human experience, if experience always is and has been of the phenomenal only."[41]

Even Saint Augustine's relation to Platonism or Neo-Platonism offers some striking parallels to Brownson's relation to Transcendental idealism. The Platonists taught Saint Augustine "to search for incorporeal truth" and "invisible things." Also, they taught him about God and Logos, "that true light that lighteth every man that cometh into the world." But what they did not teach him was that "the Word was made flesh, and dwelt among us."[42]

Similarly, American Transcendentalists emphasized the existence of an extrasensory world and believed in Logos or Reason as the "true light that lighteth every man." But they did not generally believe in the Word being made flesh, or in other words: they did not believe in Christ Jesus as *the* God-Man or *the* Providential man, but in Jesus as *the* Representative man, or he who was "true to what is in you and me."

After all, Frederic J. Carpenter may have a point when stating that Transcendentalism was "the worship of the unknown God,"[43] or in Emerson's phrase, the "Unknown Centre."[44] On the other hand, just as Saint Augustine's Platonism, according to Jacques Maritain, was "transfigured by the wisdom of grace,"[45] one might be entitled to say that Brownson's conversion was conditioned by Transcendentalism, "transfigured" or at least supplemented by a belief in "the wisdom" of tradition, above all the Christian and churchly tradition.

In any case, Brownson's Law of Life really meant "Life" to him and was indeed something infinitely more to him than a bleak, theoretical abstraction. Joseph Henry Allen observed the impact of this doctrine on Brownson's mind: "The hard, restless, implacably honest, and domineering temper of Orestes Brownson had just been greatly softened, at the time I first knew him, by a sudden flow of religious feeling in channels which he had thought dried up. A mere accident, as it were, had turned him from a very positive disciple of the French Eclectics to an equally positive and unsparing critic of them in the name of a new teacher (Pierre Leroux), whose phrases he recently took for the key to a new rendering of the Christian revelation,–a reading of it which, with a certain pious and grateful fervor, he detailed in a letter to Dr. Channing on 'The Mediatorial Life of Jesus.' "[46]

Isaac T. Hecker even more strongly stressed Brownson's "devotion to principle:" "What native trait of Dr. Brownson marks him off from other men? I answer, Love of truth, devotion to principle. Oh! how many hours did he spend agonizing for the truth! How coolly he touches on it in *The Convert*! How lightly he passes over the great conflicts of his soul!" Indeed, his doctrine of life and communion made it an imperious necessity for him to know the whole truth.[47] And at least in his "disciple" Hecker's view, Brownson sufficiently proved that the supernatural is "the most sublime assertion of the natural."[48]

Brownson's principle, then, which made him accept the Roman Catholic Church as the true Church, was based both on an argument from philosophy or human reason and on an argument from history. The latter argument was the proper one to decide *which* church was the real apostolic Church when the essential question as to *what* the church was had been settled.[49]

While John Henry Newman in his pre-Catholic phase was particularly impressed by the church in its first centuries,[50] Brownson in his pre-Catholic period was above all fascinated by medieval Catholicism. Already in his *New Views* he had contrasted the constructive work of medieval Catholicism with the disintegrating character of Protestantism. Yet with his growing desire for a strong government, medieval Catholicism with its theocratic theories and practice appealed even more to him.

On the whole, his positive appreciation of historical Catholicism should not be underrated. Thus the author of the obituary in the *American Catholic Quarterly Review* maintained that Brownson through his reading of history "was compelled to recognize, especially in the Church of mediaeval Europe, what not only realized but fully completed his own imperfect ideal."[51] The Englishman William L. Gildea also emphasized Brownson's positive attitude toward medieval Catholicism, above all for its alleged defense of the people against the princes, of the poor against the rich.[52]

Generally speaking, Brownson was struck by the supposed or real unity and harmony of medieval cultural and social life brought about by the guiding and commanding Universal Church, while regarding with skepticism the individualistic and pluralistic tendencies of contemporary society. And more than before he considered the advent of Protestantism the deplorable finish of the very authority which so far had counteracted the selfishness and power of the rising capitalist class.[53]

In the light of Brownson's general skepticism about the factory system and the business civilization, Helen S. Mims seems to point out an important motive for Brownson's conversion to Catholicism: "Linked historically with a stage of society and a social class anterior to capitalism, bearing no very visible relationships with the dominant bourgeoisie, it [Catholicism] could furnish comfort to an Adam Müller and a de Maistre, who yearned for a return to the past, or to a Brownson, who wanted a higher law for the future."[54]

Thus, in consistent accordance with his general "double" approach, Brownson applied a doctrine which contained arguments both from reason and history. Yet he had a distinct predilection for the former, and was disappointed with Bishop Fitzpatrick, who ignored his philosophy and instead instructed him only according to the ordinary method, i.e. "arguments drawn from the wants of nature, the insufficiency of reason, prophesies, miracles, and historical monuments."[55] Yet for the time being he abandoned his cherished doctrine, and was received into the Church "on the strength of another, and, perhaps, a more convincing process."[56]

But later, when adopting the purely historical method in his controversies with non-Catholics, he had a growing disagreeable feeling of being inconsistent both in his own eyes and in theirs. He felt that modern disbelievers wanted first principles of reason before ever thinking the idea of becoming Catholics. Consequently, his doctrine of life and communion was perhaps after all better suited to lead unbelievers to the Catholic Church than the ordinary method! And thirteen years after his conversion he was assured that his doctrine by no means was incompatible with Catholic theology. Indeed, *The Convert* was written expressly for the justification of this doctrine and, implicitly, for the refutation of Bishop Fitzpatrick's method as the most expedient method of converting non-Catholics.[57]

Hecker could never forgive Bishop Fitzpatrick, who to him was more intent on finding errors than truths in the views of those who sought for admission into the Church, like Brownson and himself. Not even the lapse of about forty years seemed to have softened his antipathy for the Bishop, whom he described as "the hierarchical exponent of all that was traditional and commonplace in Catholic public life."[58]

Brownson himself, however, was both grateful and generous to the Bishop, at least in *The Convert* (pages 164, 169, 167), where he declared that the owed him more than it was possible for him to owe to any other man. "I have met men," he continued, "of more various erudition and higher scientific attainments; I have met men of bolder fancy and more creative imaginations; but I have never met a man of a clearer head, a firmer intellectual grasp, a sounder judgment, or a warmer heart." But just as bluntly he declared that it was his own doctrine which "did legitimately lead me to the Catholic Church," whereas he "wanted the internal or subjective disposition to understand and receive" Bishop Fitzpatrick's method. Graciously, but with a clear intention Brownson dedicated his autobiography, *The Convert*, to the Bishop of Boston.

In his *Apologia* (1864) Newman exclaimed: "For who can know himself, and the multitude of subtle influences which act upon him?"[59] And there is reason to add: "Who can know" others? Yet some deeper motives for Brownson's conversion to Catholicism may be suggested.

First, a never failing quest for unity or synthesis dominated his thinking. Whether this search for unity found its expression in the very name of his Society for Christian Union and Progress, his views of a "Church of the Future" based on the union of the "affirmative" portions of spiritualism and materialism, his desire of combining "the psychological Christ" and "the historical Christ," his idea of a "catholic" Unitarianism, his ecumenical vision of a higher Christian unity in an all-comprising, really universal church, his espousal of Eclecticism, his synthetic philosophy, and, finally, his doctrine of life and communion, there was all the way an intense, consistent striving for unity, for the reconciliation of different principles in a real synthesis. When, at last, he became a convert to the Roman Catholic Church, it was greatly due to his firm conviction that this church represented or possessed the whole Christian truth and life.[60] And significantly, he preferred the term "Catholicity" to Catholicism.[61]

Even more important, his way to traditional Christianity and, more particularly, to Catholicism was his fervent search for a FATHER. The tragic loss of his father in childhood seemed to motivate to a great extent his desire of believing in a heavenly father.[62]

In fact, during most of his pre-Catholic phase, Brownson believed in God's personality and Providence. Recollections from his childhood and, later, the strong and decisive influence of William E. Channing prevented him from ever falling into real pantheism or religious subjectivism. His basic, consistent belief in God as father and not only as an abstract philosophical idea seems to have motivated his increasing desire to distinguish philosophically between the object and the subject, and above all between the supernatural and the natural. In any case, it seems unreasonable that a belief in God as father would be identical with the more typical Transcendentalist belief in an "Unknown Centre" of oneself.[63]

The argument that Brownson's search for a father strongly motivated his philosophical speculations on the problem of God is confirmed in an article of 1836 on Cousin's philosophy. Brownson, after marshaling a stunning array of philosophical terms signifying ultimate reality, finally revealed what all these more or less abstract notions really meant to him: "Hence, from the absolute principles of Causality, Substance, Unity, Intentionality, the Just, and the Beautiful, we obtain the absolute God, Cause of causes, Being of beings, Substance of substances, Unity of unities, Intentionality of intentionalities, morally just, beautiful, righteous,–our Father."[64]

However, his philosophical studies, perhaps above all Cousin's idea of the necessity of creation, for some time marred Brownson's belief in God's freedom and Providence. But when–as pointed out in another context–Brownson asserted, philosophically, the freedom of God, he at once also asserted, and with religious fervor, the fatherhood of God.[65]

Further, his doctrine of life and communion made God as father even more real to him, manifesting Himself in the God-Man Jesus and the church. More particularly, God as father manifested Himself in papacy, which he regarded as "the especial providence of God,"[66] and whose spiritual authority he was always happy to acknowledge.

Obviously, Brownson's emphasis in his pre-Catholic period on the fatherhood of God partly reflected Universalist and Unitarian beliefs, which were a reaction to the Calvinist conception of a stern and implacable Jehovah. One might even suggest that Brownson's belief in God as father reflected broad, though elusive, Romantic influences. In any case, Schiller's famous lines in "An die Freude:"

> Brüder–überm Sternenzelt
> Muss ein lieber Vater wohnen

have an interesting parallel in Brownson's emotional reaction to Channing's sermon on "Likeness to God:" "I too had become a son, and could look up and say, 'my father'–around and say, 'my brothers.' "[67]

But despite immediate and remote influences, Brownson's belief in God as father seems to have had its primary cause in personal experience, and probably for this very reason this belief of his was a recurrent theme in his writings and formed, as it were, the basis of his religious outlook. According to Theodore Maynard, Brownson "was concerned that men should have right ideas about God; that they should love God he regarded as something outside his province."[68] Perhaps. But Brownson's intense concern with his idea of God as a living reality, as father or "moral governor" of the world, could not avoid having some influence on readers and audiences and even inspire some of them to "love God."

In a larger perspective, Brownson with his more or less distinct sense of loneliness, his ardent belief in human fellowship or "communion" and his search for a "father" reflect certain marked tendencies in American intellectual and literary tradition. In philosophy, men like Charles S. Peirce and Josiah Royce urged the reconciliation between the individual and society with the view of creating "the Beloved Community." And Peirce's belief in "agapaticism" and Royce's idea of a "city out of sight" (a divine, invisible kingdom) seem to imply a belief in the Providence of God.[69]

Yet in fiction similar tendencies are even more manifest. In an essay on "Ishmael–or the Theme of Solitude in American Literature," Roger Asselineau points out that authors from Melville to Hemingway have been "lonely Ishmaels craving for the love of their brothers." And it may be added that in "the search for a father" Thomas Wolfe is even a kind of direct parallel to Brownson. Characteristically, Asselineau suggests two main reasons–one particular, another general–for this attitude of many American authors: the early loss of or disappointment with the earthly father, and the very geographical character of the country.[70]

In a still larger perspective, a modern reader cannot but be struck by a certain similarity between Brownson and the twentieth-century German-Jewish philosopher Martin Buber. In his book *Ich und Du* (Jerusalem, 1964) Buber stresses the essential difference as well as the close relation between *ich* and *du*, or the subject and the object, but also—like Brownson—finds that the object in the last analysis is God as father: "das ewige Du." Both Ishmaels and Isaacs, then, are searching for their "father."

But as already suggested, Brownson's belief in God as father also motivated to a great extent his need of an authoritative, albeit "reasonable," religion. At the beginning of 1844, having found out after a supposed "thorough investigation of the Catholic Church" that it was "at bottom ... favorable to freedom and progress," he confidently stated that "submission to the Church is the condition of mental liberty."[71]

To the modern mind, submission to an institution as the condition of mental liberty sounds strange, indeed. After all, then, there may be some grain of truth in Herbert W. Schneider's sweeping statement on Brownson's conversion: "For him conversion to the Church of Rome was not a return home, but a new adventure, conceived in a thoroughly romantic spirit."[72]

Evidently, a similar attitude reflected the Romantic reliance on the church as an organism and also the Romantic nostalgic sentiment for a more or less intense, self-denying identification with and subjection to higher, collective unities. Thus Hecker, for one, wrote as follows in a letter of July 23, 1844, to Brownson: "I want her [the church] to crush me, so that she may be all in me, which she now is not. There is no use of compromise. There can be no looking back. I want a discipline that sinks deeper than what I have yet experienced. I have too much liberty. This liberty abridges my freedom."[73] Yet even more interesting is the utterance of the non-Catholic author Ernest Renan, who in 1854 declared that he had rather submit to the church than to the Bible, because the church was more humane and living than a mere book possibly could be.[74]

Yet in the light of Brownson's reliance on the fatherhood of God and, more particularly, his more recent belief in the Catholic Church as the "medium" of divine life and the especial Providence of God, his conversion to Catholicism was also a kind of "a return home" to his father's house. Even though Brownson later found this "house" sometimes to be an "uneasy haven,"[75] he never changed his essential belief in the Catholic Church as his spiritual parental home.

In addition to his quest of synthesis and a father, his increasing belief in the church as a "means" of individual salvation, i.e. his own salvation, became a strong motivation for his conversion. While, apparently, ignoring the power of evil when writing his *New Views*, he had a growing sense of the influence of sin and evil in social and individual life. His general predilection for synthesis could not blot out his sense of a basic dualism between good and evil. Thus, he reacted increasingly against the pervading optimism of an Emerson, a Parker, and a Cousin. On the other hand, Brownson never reached the deep and sinister insight into the problem of evil as did Hawthorne or Melville.

At last, the problem of sin and salvation, heaven and hell became "existential," and there is no reason to believe that the following statement in *The Convert* (page 166) was simply rhetoric: "I had made up my mind that the church was my last plank of safety, that it was communion with the church or death." But even Brownson seems to have exaggerated intentionally when "instantly and grimly" he told Joseph Henry Allen that he would have gone to hell if he had died the day before his official conversion to Catholicism on October 20, 1844. Anyhow, as Allen correctly observed, Brownson had "a religious need craving and imperious as in any zealot of any period."[76] Interestingly, John Henry Newman, the other great convert to Catholicism of that period, seemed to consider the necessity of his own immediate salvation as no less crucial: "The simple question is, Can *I* (it is personal, not whether another, but can *I*) be saved in the English Church? am *I* in safety, were I to die to-night?"[77]

"After years of wandering, doubt, and perplexity," Brownson had finally "found a resting-place, and the heart the repose" it had sought.[78]

I hope I have been able to show a basic consistency in Brownson's intellectual development from the early 1820's to the middle 1840's. Obviously, his consistency was not fixed or static–in Emerson's words: "the hobgoblin of little minds"[79]–but rather–as William E. Channing characterized Brownson's development–"steps of rational progress."[80]

On the other hand, in order to prove a thesis, one may, at least unconsciously, leave out of account or explain away things less favorable to it. Above all, what complicated matters in our case where the often mentioned opposed tendencies in Brownson's mental make-up: a predilection for synthesis and a love for extremes, an independence of spirit and a craving for an authoritative religion. Evidently, these opposed tendencies often led to strong shifts of emphasis, which at least to contemporary observers, lacking the necessary perspective, might indicate real inconsistencies.

From the viewpoint of intellectual history, Brownson's development until his conversion reflected in the 1820's–with the exception of his spasmodic Presbyterian prelude–ideas of the Enlightenment, in the 1830's Transcendentalism with its spiritual emphasis and strong reliance on the inherent power of ideas, and from the early 1840's Romanticism in a broader sense with its marked belief in growth and tradition: the Ideal in the Actual. But although increasingly skeptical of the "pantheistic idealism"[81] and subjectivism of Transcendentalist thought, he retained the general belief of the Transcendentalists in intuition and their dynamic conception of life. Yet clearly enough, Brownson's general "double" or "eclectic" aproach, manifest already in the 1830's in his desire for combining "spiritualism" and "materialism," psychology and history, never made him a "pure" Transcendentalist.

Just before his conversion and during the following years till about 1850 he showed an extreme zeal more or less typical of recent converts, and presented Catholicism in its exclusive more than in its universal character. J. R. Lowell was perhaps not wholly wrong when in *A Fable for Critics* of 1848 he humorously described the convert Brownson as having "his mouth very full / With attempting to gulp a Gregorian bull."[82]

However, generally speaking, Brownson, at least theoretically, seemed to prefer the "double" or "synthetic" approach. In fact, already in the just mentioned year 1848, he complained that modern Catholics–and himself included–were too polemical, considering, partly because compelled to do so, the distinctive instead of the universal character of Catholicism.[83]

Then, from the beginning of the 1850's, under the influence of the Italian philosopher Vincenzo Gioberti, he gradually resumed his former broad Transcendentalist and "synthetic" positions. He praised Gioberti for his "ideal formula:" *Ens creat existentias*, his indispensable "synthetic method," which, to Brownson, confirmed his own intuitionist beliefs and his synthetic philosophy. And significantly, he joined hands with old friends: "As our old Transcendentalist friends were accustomed to say, 'In analysis we murder to dissect.' " Obviously, like these old friends of his, the Catholic Brownson was still in quest of the thread of life running through all things.[84]

Moreover, Gioberti and perhaps no less Comte de Montalembert, the leader of the "liberal" French Catholics, and with whom Brownson frequently corresponded, reawakened his former belief, originally inspired by Lamennais and Lacordaire, in the reconciliation between religion and modern society.[85]

No longer under Bishop Fitzpatrick's control and censorship, which had become increasingly irksome, Brownson resumed, with apparent relief and satisfaction, the link with his pre-Catholic past, and thus regained his "personal identity."[86] The first coherent statement of this change of front, which after all signalized a return to and development of old standards, was *The Convert*, published in 1857, two years after he had moved from Boston to New York.

Yet the period 1860–1864 marked the culmination of his liberal tendencies, highlighted by his objections to the expediency of the temporal power of the Pope, his critical attitude to Scholastic philosophy, his surprisingly balanced view of the Protestant Reformation, his opposition to Catholic servility to temporal and spiritual leaders at home and abroad, and finally, his fervent espousal of the Union cause.

Many contemporary Catholics looked on their *enfant terrible* with suspicion and alarm and even feared—or perhaps some of them hoped for—his return to Protestantism. In fact, already in the mid-1850's the learned Professor Philip Schaff of the Mercersburg Theological Seminary declared that "in spite of all his asseverations (noticeably repeated, and for this reason rather suspicious) of absolute submission to the infallible authority of the pope and even of his diocesan bishop, Brownson has still in the bottom of his heart a whole mass of Protestant principles and impulses of independence and private judgment, and remains a restless agitator and democrat."[87]

In addition to the repeated charges of ontologism leveled against him, Brownson was reported twice to Rome under charge of heresy: the first time above all for his views on the temporal power of the Pope, and the second time—somewhat later in the 1860's—for a supposedly wrong rendering of the Trinitarian dogma. Yet both times Brownson was acquitted.

Theodore Maynard seems ill at ease about Brownson's liberal Catholicism, which he labels a "lapse into liberalism." Though more critical of Brownson's general tendency than his particular views, Maynard even thinks Brownson took extreme stands, and feels sure that he did not convince either Catholics or non-Catholics of the excellences of his religion and his church.[88]

However, in the *aggiornamento* atmosphere of the 1950's and 1960's, American Catholics seem to take a more positive attitude to Brownson's phase of "liberal" Catholicism. Thus Henry F. Browne emphasizes Brownson's role in trying to combine American democracy and Catholicism,[89] and John Courtney Murray voices ideas similar to Brownson's on the relations between American ideals and Catholic thought, more particularly on the relations between Church and State.[90] Robert Ludlow even regrets that Brownson after Pius IX's *Syllabus of Errors* (1864) too fast concluded that it condemned his "American position."[91]

Closely related to Brownson's "American position" were his provocative ideas about Catholic higher education, which, to him, ought to stress the importance of bold thinking, secular and not only purely theological learning. These ideas of his seem to appeal to modern Catholics,[92] and Robert Ludlow compliments Brownson for having "performed a needed (and still needed) service in subjecting Catholic institutions of learning to intelligent criticism."[93]

It is also noteworthy that prominent non-Catholics like the historians Charles and Mary Beard and the British socialist Harold J. Laski make favorable comments on Brownson's attempts to bridge the gap between Catholics or Catholicism and American civilization or society.[94]

On the whole, far from pushing his principles to extremes, Brownson during this period, which may roughly be set to between 1855 and 1865, illustrated in his writings his idea or ideal of Catholicism—or better: Catholicity—as being "never exclusive, but always conciliative, mediative between extremes, and harmonizing all opposites."[95] Obviously proceeding from his old cherished Transcendentalist and Eclectic beliefs, he declared that "the human mind is constituted for truth and is never able to operate without truth as its object,"[96] and that "to present truth in such a way to be understood by those whom we address, is to present it in such a way that it shall be seen to be consistent with, and to include the truth they already hold."[97]

And during the last years of his life, even though he rejected any synthesis between Catholicism and modern civilization, he still kept his belief in intuition and his synthetic philosophy.

Symptomatically, Brownson's very last article was an attempt at formulating a synthesis and not only a correspondence or parallelism between the natural and the supernatural—a synthesis he considered in the light of the Incarnation. But basic to this idea of synthesis were also the Transcendentalist emphasis on "a uniform and indissoluble whole" and his lifelong, strongly emotional belief in God as father: "The Father through Christ" elevates "the creature to oneness with the Creator."[98] Indeed, to the aging Brownson his Law of Life was still operating; to the very end his Christianity, his Catholicity, was a "transfigured" Transcendentalism.

In the same essay, characteristically called "Philosophy of the Supernatural," which showed his primary concern, Brownson regretted not having finished his treatment of the Incarnation, more particularly in its relation to all Christian doctrines.[99] This, too, was symptomatic of a man who never felt being "finished," but as a seeker for ever greater truths and syntheses was always on his pilgrim's road toward his—and our—"church of the ideal,"[100] the *real* Church of the Future.

But on our road to the Church of the Future, this nineteenth-century American pilgrim may have something to teach modern man, who seems apt to believe either in a vague, subjective spiritualism, a narrow, almost mechanical class or race solidarity, or a hardboiled materialism. To this—according to Herbert Marcuse—"one-dimensional" modern man Brownson suggests his "synthetic" approach: as the spiritual manifests itself in the material, "the Father," incarnated in Christ, *the* Providential man, elevates "the creature to oneness with the Creator" and with the whole creation.

1 *The Convert*, pp. 162, 165.

2 John Henry (Cardinal) Newman, *Apologia pro vita sua* (London and New York, 1955), p. 164.

3 *Ibid.*, p. 42.

4 Philip Schaff, *America. A Sketch of Its Political, Social, and Religious Character*, ed. Perry Miller (Cambridge, Mass., 1961), pp. 131, 188. The title of the original in translation: *America. A Sketch of the Political, Social, and Religious Character of the United States of North America, in two Lectures, Delivered at Berlin, with a Report Read before the German Church Diet at Frankfort-on-the-Maine, Sept., 1854.* By Dr. Philip Schaff. Translated from the German. New York, 1855 (Philip Schaff was Professor of Theology at the German Reformed Church Seminary [the Mercersburg Theological Seminary], Pa.).

5 *Ibid.*, p. 128.

6 In his book on *America* Schaff distinguished between Calvinism proper or "Roman Calvinism," the German Reformed Church, which he considered "Melanchtonian," and Lutheranism or "Germanic Protestantism" *(Ibid.*, p. 95).

7 See Sidney E. Ahlstrom, "John Williamson Nevin and the Mercersburg Movement," *Religion in American Life: The Shaping of American Religion*, ed. J. W. Smith and A. L. Jamison, I (Princeton University Press, 1961), pp. 267–271; "Ch. XIII: Resurgent Churchly Traditions," *American Christianity. An Historical Interpretation with Representative Documents*, ed. H. S. Smith et al., II (New York, 1963), pp. 66–115, esp. 68, 94.

8 See "Resurgent Churchly Traditions," *American Christianity*, II, 66–115; and Perry Miller's preface to Philip Schaff's book on *America* (ed. Perry Miller; 1961 edition).

9 Schaff, *America* (1961 edition), pp. 212, 188, 164.

10 "The Princeton Review and the Convert" (*BrQR*, April 1858), *Works*, V, 229.

11 *Ibid.*, pp. 229–230.

12 Richard Hoenigswald, "Philosophy of Hegelianism," *Twentieth Century Philosophy*, ed. Dagobert D. Runes (New York, 1947), pp. 267–268, 271, 273.

13 *BrQR*, I (Jan. 1844), 8.

14 *Brownson Papers*.

15 Bernhard Knoop, *Victor Cousin, Hegel und die französische Romantik* (Dissertation; Oberviechtach, 1932).

16 "The Church Question" (*BrQR*, Jan. 1844), *Works*, IV, 464–465.

17 "Nature and Office of the Church" (*BrQR*, April 1844), *Works*, IV, 492, 494; "No Church, No Reform" (*BrQR*, April 1844), *Works*, IV, 505.

18 *Christian World*, Feb. 11, 1843.

19 *Christian World*, April 15, 1843.

20 *The Convert*, pp. 132–133.

21 *Ibid.*, pp. 16–17, 133. However, modern scholars like Samuel Eliot Morison and Perry Miller have shown that the New England Puritans gave even "a respectable place" to "natural reason" (See Miller and Johnson, *The Puritans*, p. 23); and more generally, Calvinism seems to be less skeptical as to natural reason and philosophy than Lutheranism (See Etienne Gilson, *Christianisme et philosophie* [Paris, 1949], p. 28 ff., or A. H. Winsnes, *Jacques Maritain* [Oslo, 1957], pp. 18–19).

22 "The Transcendental Movement in New England," *Catholic World*, XXIII (July 1876), 528–537.

23 *The Complete Works of Ralph Waldo Emerson*, I, pp. 24, 32–33.

24 Quoted in *Essays, First and Second Series* (London and New York, 1947), p. 134.

25 "John Locke and New England Transcendentalism," *New England Quarterly*, XXXV (Dec. 1962), 439.

26 "Ch. XIV: The Transcendental Pattern of Religious Liberalism," *American Christianity*, ed. H. S. Smith et al., II, pp. 123–124.

27 Emerson, "The Transcendentalist," *Dial*, III (Jan. 1843), 298.

28 See Joel Porte, "Nature as Symbol: Emerson's Noble Doubt," *New England Quarterly*, XXXVII (Dec. 1964), 453–476; "Ralph Waldo Emerson," *Literary History of the United States*, I (ed. R. E. Spiller et al.; New York, 1948), pp. 369, 387.

29 "A Sign from the West," *Dial*, I (Oct. 1840), 171. The article was signed [C], which might indicate William Henry Channing as the author.

30 *Dial*, II (Jan. 1842), 388.

31 *Dial*, I (Oct. 1840), 259.

32 *The Complete Works of Ralph Waldo Emerson*, IV, p. 170; I, p. 200. By way of comparison, remark the striking similarity between Emerson's well-known phrase and Brownson's statement in "Primeval Man" (*Catholic World*, Sept.

1869), *Works,* IX, 332: "One divine thought runs through the whole, and nothing does or can stand alone. We study things too much in their analysis, not enough in their synthesis."

33 *Dial,* III (Jan. 1843), 411. The anonymous writer even defined Transcendentalism as "Life-Power."

34 *Brook Farm,* p. 245.

35 *Christian Examiner,* XXII, 3rd Series, IV (May 1837), 188, 195–196.

36 "Lectures on the Times," *Dial,* III (July 1842), 12.

37 "The Transcendentalist," *Dial,* III (Jan. 1843), 299.

38 "Self-Reliance" (quoted in *American Literature,* sel. Geoffrey Moore [London, 1964], p. 249).

39 *Dial,* II (April 1842), 425.

40 *Christian World,* Feb. 25, 1843.

41 "Theology and Metaphysics," *Twentieth Century Philosophy,* pp. 208–209 (Ritschlianism: a theology initiated by Albrecht Ritschl [1822–1889]).

42 Saint Augustine, *Confessions.* Translated with a preface by E. B. Pusey. *Everyman's Library,* ed. Ernest Rhys (London and New York, 1946), pp. 142, 130–131.

43 "The Genteel Tradition: A Re-Interpretation," *New England Quarterly,* XV (Sept. 1942), 433.

44 "The Transcendentalist," *Dial,* III (Jan. 1843), 299.

45 "The Humanism of St. Thomas Aquinas," *Twentieth Century Philosophy,* p. 301.

46 *Our Liberal Movement in Theology,* pp. 86–87.

47 "Dr. Brownson and Catholicity," *Catholic World,* XLVI (Nov. 1887), 234, 225–226.

48 *Ibid.,* p. 235; "Dr. Brownson's Road to the Church," *Catholic World,* XLVI (Oct. 1887), 4.

49 "Nature and Office of the Church" *(BrQR,* April 1844), *Works,* IV, 487.

50 *Apologia pro vita sua,* p. 94.

51 "In Memoriam: Orestes A. Brownson," *American Catholic Quarterly Review,* I (1876), 561.

52 "An English View of Brownson's Conversion," *Catholic World,* LXIX (April 1899), 24–31.

53 *BrQR,* I (April 1844), 279.

54 "Early American Democratic Theory and Orestes Brownson," *Science and Society,* III (Spring 1939), 197.

55 *The Convert,* pp. 174–175.

56 *Ibid.,* p. 166.

57 *Ibid.,* pp. 168–169.

58 "Dr. Brownson and Bishop Fitzpatrick," *Catholic World,* XLV (April 1887), 7.

59 *Apologia pro vita sua,* p. 101.

60 *BrQR,* I (July 1844), 408–410.

61 *BrQR,* II (Oct. 1845), 540–544.

62 "The Mediatorial Life of Jesus," *Works,* IV, 141.

63 Emerson, "The Transcendentalist," *Dial,* III (Jan. 1843), 299 ("Unknown Centre of him").

64 *Christian Examiner,* XXI, 3rd series, III (Sept. 1836), 50.

65 *The Convert,* pp. 139–140.

66 "The Anglican Church Schismatic" *(BrQR,* Oct. 1844), *Works,* IV, 589.

67 *Works,* IV, 141.

68 *Orestes Brownson,* p. 359.

69 See John E. Smith, *The Spirit of American Philosophy* (New York, 1963), pp. 32, 84, 91, 100, 107.

70 *USA in Focus* (ed. Sigmund Skard; Oslo, 1966), pp. 107–119, esp. 119.

71 *BrQR*, I (Jan. 1844), 14.

72 *A History of American Philosophy*, p. 261.

73 *Early Life*, p. 540.

74 Warner Berthoff, "Renan on W. E. Channing and American Unitarianism," *New England Quarterly*, XXXV (March 1962), 84.

75 The felicitous title of Chapter XII of Maynard's biography (pp. 244–279).

76 *Our Liberal Movement in Theology*, pp. 87–88.

77 *Apologia pro vita sua*, p. 210.

78 "Close of the Volume," *BrQR*, I (Oct. 1844), 548.

79 "Self-Reliance" (quoted in *Essays, First and Second Series* [London and New York, 1947], p. 37).

80 *Early Life*, p. 444 (Letter of June 10, 1842 to Brownson).

81 "The Church a Historical Fact" *(BrQR*, April 1846), *Works*, V, 471. See also Brownson's review of Emerson's *Essays* (1841) in *BQR*, IV (July 1841), where he criticized Emerson for his "ideal Pantheism" (p. 302).

82 *The Complete Writings of James Russell Lowell, Elmwood Edition*, XII (Boston and New York, 1904), p. 42.

83 *Works*, XIX, 255.

84 "Vincenzo Gioberti" *(BrQR*, Oct. 1850), *Works*, II, 126–127, and "Gioberti's Philosophy of Revelation" *(BrQR*, July 1861), *Works*, II, 146 ff.

85 "Lacordaire and Catholic Progress" *(BrQR*, July 1862), *Works*, XX, 258.

86 *Ibid.*, p. 253. During the period 1845–1855 Brownson's writings, except for literary notices and criticisms, were censured by Bishop Fitzpatrick or his representatives. Nonetheless, Brownson's coreligionists seemed to expect that he himself should take the whole responsibility for his writings, a fact which caused this exasperating comment from the increasingly more self-reliant convert: "What then is in my Review that is good is due, directly or indirectly, to the Bishop of Boston and his theologians; what there is erroneous or objectionable is due to myself" *(Middle Life*, pp. 4, 493–494, 503, 593, 636).

87 *America*, ed. Perry Miller (1961), pp. 189–190. Only the very last words should be somewhat modified. Brownson remained an adherent of "constitutional republicanism," and from 1840 he consistently regarded "democracy" primarily as the end and not as the form of government *(The Convert*, pp. 101, 120). However, much owing to political developments in France, he came to realize about 1850 the necessity of warring "against excesses of power" more than "against excesses of liberty" *(Works*, XVI, 525). Typically, in a letter of Dec. 27, 1857, to Montalembert, Brownson, eschewing the extremes of "caesarism" and radicalism, declared his preference for a constitutional monarchy in France, but added that Catholicism had "far more to fear from despotism than from liberty" *(Brownson Papers)*.

88 *Orestes Brownson*, pp. 280–317, esp. 281, 289. Yet it should be added that Maynard elsewhere more distinctly points out and approves Brownson's emphasis on the spiritual and not the temporal power of the Pope ("Orestes Brownson, Journalist. A Fighter for Truth," *Commonweal*, XXXVII [1943], 392).

89 "Catholicism in the United States," *Religion in American Life: The Shaping of American Religion*, ed. J. W. Smith and A. L. Jamison, I (Princeton, N. J., 1961), p. 79.

[90] *Ibid.*, p. 115; *American Christianity*, ed. H. S. Smith et al. (New York, 1963), II, pp. 514, 536–542.

[91] Book review of *The Brownson Reader*, ed. Alvan S. Ryan, in *The Catholic Worker* (Oct. 1955), reproduced in facsimile in *Emerson Society Quarterly* (1963/no. 32, part 3), 37.

[92] Excerpts from Brownson's essay on "Present Catholic Dangers" (*BrQR*, July 1857) are printed in *American Catholicism and the Intellectual Ideal*, ed. Frank L. Christ and Gerard E. Sherry (New York, 1961), pp. 17–19.

[93] See n. 91.

[94] Charles A. and Mary R. Beard, *The Rise of American Civilization*, IV (New York, 1948), pp. 232–233, 256–263. Harold J. Laski, *The American Democracy* (New York, 1948), pp. 269–270.

[95] "The Reunion of All Christians" (*BrQR*, Jan. 1862), *Works*, XII, 475–476. See also *The American Republic*, *Works*, XVIII, 193: "The law is the same: extremes must be resisted, because each is *exclusive* and therefore *uncatholic*."

[96] "Père Félix on Progress" (*BrQR*, April 1859), *Works*, XII, 191.

[97] "Various Objections Answered" (*BrQR*, Oct. 1861), *Works*, XX, 143.

[98] "Philosophy of the Supernatural" (*American Catholic Review*, Jan. 1876), *Works*, II, 273, 281.

[99] *Ibid.*, p. 281.

[100] See "Church of the Future" (*BQR*, Jan. 1842), *Works*, IV, 76.

Bibliography

List of consulted works

Adam, Ch. *Cousin, Jouffroy et la métaphysique individualiste*. Dijon, 1893.

Alcott, Amos Bronson. *Journals* (ed. Odell Shepard). Boston, 1938.

Allen, Joseph Henry. *Our Liberal Movement in Theology*. Boston, 1882.

American Catholic Quarterly Review. "In Memoriam: Orestes A. Brownson. " I (1876), 560–566.

American Quarterly Church Review. "Orestes A. Brownson as a Philosopher." XIX (Jan. 1868), 532–547.

Ballou, Hosea. *A Treatise on Atonement*. 6th ed. Utica, N. Y., 1839.

Beard, Charles A. and Mary R. *The Rise of American Civilization*. New York, 1927.

Beard, Mary R. *The American Labor Movement*. New York, 1928.

Beloff, Max. *Thomas Jefferson and American Democracy*. In *Teach Yourself History Library*, ed. A. L. Rowse. London, 1948.

Berthoff, Warner. "Renan on W. E. Channing and American Unitarianism," *New England Quarterly*, XXXV (March 1962), 71–92.

Blau, Joseph L. *Men and Movements in American Philosophy*. New York, 1953.

B[owen], F[rancis]. "Locke and the Transcendentalists," *Christian Examiner*, XXIII (Nov. 1837), 170–194.

Brinton, Crane. *The Shaping of the Modern Mind* (the concluding half of *Ideas and Men)*. A Mentor Book. New York, 1953.

Brooks, Van Wyck. *The Flowering of New England*. New York, 1941.

Brownson, Henry F. *Orestes A. Brownson's Early Life: from 1803 to 1844*. Detroit, 1898.

. *Orestes A. Brownson's Middle Life: from 1845 to 1855*. Detroit, 1899.

. *Orestes A. Brownson's Latter Life: from 1855 to 1876*. Detroit, 1900.

(ed.). *The Works of Orestes A. Brownson*. 20 vols. Detroit, 1882–1887.

Brownson, Orestes A. *Works* (collected and arranged by Henry F. Brownson). 20 vols. Detroit, 1882–1887.

. *An Address on the Fifty-Fifth Anniversary of American Independence, Delivered at Ovid, Seneca Co., New York, July 4, 1831*. Ithaca, N.Y., 1831.

. *An Address, Prepared at the Request of Guy C. Clark, with the Intention of Having It Delivered on the Day of His Execution, Feb. 3, 1832.* Ithaca, N.Y., 1832.

. *An Address on Intemperance, Delivered in Walpole, N. H., February 26, 1833.* Keene, N. H., 1833.

. *An Address, Delivered at Dedham, on the Fifty-Eighth Anniversary of American Independence, July 4, 1834.* Dedham, Mass., 1834.

. "Benjamin Constant on Religion," *Christian Examiner*, XVII (Sept. 1834), 63–77.

. "Principles of Morality," *Christian Examiner*, XVII (Jan. 1835), 283–301.

. *Sermon Delivered to the Young People of the First Congregational Society in Canton, on Sunday, March 24th, 1835.* Dedham, Mass., 1835.

. "Progress of Society," *Christian Examiner*, XVIII (July 1835), 345–368.

. "Education of the People," *Christian Examiner*, XX (May 1836), 153–169.

. *A Discourse on the Wants of the Times, Delivered in Lyceum Hall, Hanover Street, Boston, Sunday, May 29, 1836.* Boston, 1836.

. "Cousin's Philosophy," *Christian Examiner*, XXI (Sept. 1836), 33–64.

. "Book Review of Théodore Jouffroy's *Cours de droit naturel* and *Prolégomènes au droit naturel*," *Christian Examiner*, XXII (May 1837), 181–217.

. *Babylon Is Falling. A Discourse Preached in the Masonic Temple, to the Society for Christian Union and Progress, on Sunday Morning, May 28, 1837.* 2nd ed. Boston, 1837.

. *An Address on Popular Education. Delivered in Winnsimmet Village, July 23, 1837.* Boston, 1837.

. *Boston Quarterly Review.* Boston, 1838–1842.

. *Oration Delivered at Washington Hall, July 5th, 1841.* Boston, 1841.

. "Brook Farm," *Democratic Review*, New Series, XI (Nov. 1842), 481–496.

. "The Community System," *Democratic Review*, New Series, XII, 129–144.

. *Brownson's Quarterly Review.* 1844–1855, Boston; 1856–1864, 1873–1875, New York.

Brownson Papers, University of Notre Dame, Ind.

Buber, Martin. *Ich und Du.* Jerusalem, 1964.

Canby, Henry Seidel. *Thoreau.* Boston, 1939.

Caponigri, A. Robert. "Brownson and Emerson: Nature and History," *New England Quarterly*, XVIII (Sept. 1945), 368–390.

Carlyle, Thomas. *On Heroes, Hero-Worship and the Heroic in History. The World's Classics*, Vol. LXII. London, 1950.

. *The Correspondence of Emerson and Carlyle* (ed. Joseph Slater). New York and London, 1965.

Carpenter, Frederic I. "The Genteel Tradition: A Re-Interpretation," *New England Quarterly*, XV (Sept. 1942), 427–443.

Channing, William E., D. D. *Works. Eighth Complete Edition.* Boston and New York, 1848.

. *A Discourse on the Evidences of Revealed Religion.* American Unitarian Association Tract. 3rd ed., No. 8, I. Boston, 1826.

Christ, Frank L. and Sherry, Gerard E. (eds.). *American Catholicism and the Intellectual Ideal.* New York, 1961.

Christian Examiner. "New Views of Christianity, Society, and the Church." XXII (March 1837), 127–130.

Christian Register. Boston, 1831–1836.

Christian World. Boston, 1843.

Clarke, James Freeman. *False Witnesses Answered.* American Unitarian Association Tract. 1st Series, No. 97, IX. Boston, 1835.

C[larke], J[ames] F[reeman]. "Orestes A. Brownson's Argument for the Roman Church *(Brownson's Quarterly Review* 1844–1850)," *Christian Examiner*, XLVIII (March 1850), 227–247.

Clauss, Walter. *Deutsche Literatur.* 5. Auflage. Zurich, 1948.

Commager, Henry Steele (ed.). *Living Ideas in America*, New York, 1951.

. *Theodore Parker.* Boston, 1947.

and Nevins, Allan (eds.). *The Heritage of America.* Boston, 1951.

Commons, John R. and Colleagues. *History of Labour in the United States*, I of 2 vols. New York, 1926.

Cook, Thomas I. and Leavelle, Arnaud B. "Orestes A. Brownson's *The American Republic*," *Review of Politics*, IV (Jan. and April, 1942), 77–90, 173–193.

Cooke, George Willis. *Unitarianism in America.* Boston, 1902.

Cousin, Victor. *Nouveaux fragmen[t]s philosophiques.* Paris, 1828.

. *Philosophie populaire.* Petits Traits publiés par l'Académie des Sciences morales et politiques. 9e livraison. Paris, 1848.

. *Justice et charité.* Petits Traits publiés par l'Académie des Sciences morales et politiques. Paris, 1849.

. *Philosophie écossaise.* 3e éd. Paris, 1857.

. *Fragments philosophiques*, III. 5e éd. Paris, 1866.

. *Fragments philosophiques*, V. 5e éd. Paris, 1866.

. *Premiers essais de philosophie.* 6e éd. Paris, 1873.

. *Histoire générale de la philosophie.* 11e éd. Paris, 1884.

. *Introduction to the History of Philosophy.* Trans. Henning Gotfried Linberg. Boston, 1832.

. *Elements of Psychology.* 2nd, 3rd, and 4th eds. Trans. C. S. Henry, D. D. New York, 1838, 1842, 1856.

. *The Philosophy of the Beautiful.* Trans. Jesse Cato Daniel. London, 1848.

. *Course of the History of Modern Philosophy.* Trans. O. W. Wight. 2 vols. New York, 1852.

Curti, Merle. *The Growth of American Thought.* 2nd ed. New York, 1951.

D'Arusmont, Frances Wright. *Fanny Wright Unmasked, by Her Own Pen* (pamphlet). New York, 1830.

. *Political Letters.* New York, 1844.

Demos, John. "The Antislavery Movement and the Problem of Violent 'Means,'" *New England Quarterly,* XXXVII (Dec. 1964), 501–526.

Derleth, August. *Concord Rebel: A Life of Henry D. Thoreau.* New York, 1962.

Dial. Boston, 1840–1844. Reprinted edition. New York, 1961.

Dublin Review. "Orestes A. Brownson's Early Life." CXXIII (1898), 460–462.

. "Orestes A. Brownson's Middle Life." CXXVII (1900), 196–198.

. "Brownson's Latter Life." CXXIX (1901), 189–190.

Eliot, Samuel A. *The Results of an Inquiry into the Aims and Characteristics of Unitarian Preaching* (discourse). Boston, 1902.

Emerson, Ralph Waldo. *Complete Works. Concord Edition.* 12 vols. Boston and New York, 1903–1904.

. *Letters* (ed. Ralph L. Rusk). New York, 1939.

. *Journals and Miscellaneous Notebooks* (ed. William H. Gilman et al. Cambridge, Mass., 1965.

. *The Correspondence of Emerson and Carlyle* (ed. Joseph Slater). New York and London, 1965.

Emerton, Ephraim. *Unitarian Thought.* New York, 1911.

Evans, B. Ifor. *A Short History of English Literature,* Middlesex, 1944.

Faguet, Emile. *Politiques et moralistes du dix-neuvième siècle.* 2e série, 5e éd. Paris, 1903.

Farrell, Bertin, C. P., S. T. L. *Orestes Brownson's Approach to the Problem of God: A Critical Examination in the Light of the Principles of St. Thomas Aquinas.* Washington, D. C., 1950.

Faust, Clarence F. "The Background of the Unitarian Opposition to Transcendentalism," *Modern Philology,* XXXV (Feb. 1938), 297–324.

Fish, Carl Russell. *The Rise of the Common Man: 1830–1850.* In *A History of American Life,* VI of 12 vols., ed. Arthur M. Schlesinger and Dixon Ryan Fox. New York, 1927.

Fitzimons, M. A. "Brownson's Search for the Kingdom of God: The Social Thought of an American Radical," *Review of Politics,* XVI (Jan. 1954), 22–36.

Francis, Convers. *On Experimental Religion.* American Unitarian Association Tract. No. 14, II. Boston, 1827.

. "Natural Theology," *Christian Examiner,* XII (May 1832), 193–220.

. *Christianity as a Purely Internal Principle.* American Unitarian Association Tract. 1st series, No. 105, IX. Boston, 1836.

Free Enquirer. New York, 1829–1830.

Frese, Joseph R., S. J. "Brownson on Know Nothingism," *Historical Records and Studies,* XXVII (1937), 52–74.

Frothingham, Nathaniel L. "Sartor Resartus," *Christian Examiner,* XXI (Sept. 1836), 74–84.

Frothingham, Octavius Brooks. *Transcendentalism in New England.* New York, 1876.

. *George Ripley.* In *American Men of Letters.* Boston, 1883.

. *Recollections and Impressions: 1822–1890.* New York, 1891.

Frothingham, Paul R. *Our Heritage of Faith. A Sermon Preached at Sanders Theatre, Cambridge, Mass., May 10, 1925, in Celebration of the One Hundredth Anniversary of the Foundation of the American Unitarian Association.* Boston, 1925.

Fuess, Claude Moore. *Daniel Webster.* 2 vols. Boston, 1930.

Gannett, William C. *A Hundred Years of the Unitarian Movement in America: 1815–1915* (sermon). Germantown, Pa., 1915.

Gildea, William G., D. D. "An English View of Brownson's Conversion," *Catholic World,* LXIX (April 1899), 24–31.

Goddard, Harold Clarke. *Studies in New England Transcendentalism.* New York, 1960.

Gohdes, Clarence L. F. *The Periodicals of American Transcendentalism.* Durham, N. C., 1931.

Gospel Advocate. Buffalo and Auburn, N. Y., 1826–1829.

Grundtvig, N. F. S. *Kirkens Gienmæle.* Copenhagen, 1825.

Harding, Walter and Bode, Carl (eds.). *The Correspondence of Henry David Thoreau.* New York, 1962.

Harson, M. J. "Orestes A. Brownson, LL. D., 'A Man of Courage and a Great American,'" *Catholic World,* LXXIX (April 1904), 1–21.

Hawthorne, Julian. *Nathaniel Hawthorne and His Wife.* 2 vols. Boston and New York, 1884.

Hawthorne, Nathaniel. *Works. Standard Library Edition.* 12 vols. Boston, 1883.

[Hecker, Isaac T.] "The Transcendental Movement in New England," *Catholic World,* XXIII (July 1876), 528–537.

. "Dr. Brownson and Bishop Fitzpatrick," *Catholic World,* XLV (April 1887), 1–7.

. "Dr. Brownson and the Workingmen's Party Fifty Years Ago," *Catholic World,* XLV (May 1887), 200–208.

. "Dr. Brownson in Boston," *Catholic World,* XLV (July 1887), 466–472.

. "Dr. Brownson's Road to the Church," *Catholic World,* XLVI (Oct. 1887), 1–11.

. "Dr. Brownson and Catholicity," *Catholic World,* XLVI (Nov. 1887), 222–235.

Hedge, Frederic H. "Essay on Coleridge, Kant, Fichte, and Schelling," *Christian Examiner,* XIV (March 1833), 108–129.

. "Essay on the Influence of Christianity," *Christian Examiner,* XVI (March 1834), 1–21.

. "The Life of Friedrich Schiller," *Christian Examiner,* XVI (July 1834), 365–392.

. *Practical Goodness: The True Religion.* American Unitarian Association Tract. 1st Series, No. 154, XIII. Boston, 1840.

. *Theological Progress during the Last Half Century* (sermon). Providence, R.I., 1878.

Heine, Heinrich. *Zur Geschichte der Religion und Philosophie in Deutschland, Gesammelte Werke* (hg. G. Karpeles), 3. Ausg., V. Berlin, 1909.

Hewit, Augustine F. "Dr. Brownson," *Catholic World*, XXIII (June 1876), 366–377.

Hildreth, Richard. *A Joint Letter to Orestes A. Brownson and the Editor of the North American Review.* Boston, 1844.

Hoagland, Henry E. "Humanitarianism (1840–1860)," Common's *History of Labour in the United States*, I, 485–623. New York, 1926.

Holst, H. Von. *John C. Calhoun.* In *American Statesmen.* Boston and New York, 1899.

Hutchison, William R. *The Transcendentalist Ministers.* New Haven, 1959.

Janet, Paul *Victor Cousin et son œuvre.* 3e éd. Paris, 1893.

Jones, Howard Mumford, "The Influence of European Ideas in Nineteenth-Century America," *American Literature*, VII (Nov. 1935), 241–273.

Kirby, Georgiana B. *Years of Experience.* New York, 1887.

Knoop, Bernhard. *Victor Cousin, Hegel und die französische Romantik.* Oberviechtach, 1932.

Ladu, Arthur I. "Political Ideas of Orestes A. Brownson, Transcendentalist," *Philological Quarterly*, XII (Jan. 1933), 280–289.

Lapati, Americo D. *Orestes A. Brownson.* New York, 1965.

Laski, Harold J. *The American Democracy.* New York, 1948.

Lasserre, Pierre. *Le Romantisme français.* Paris, 1907.

Lathrop, George Parsons. "Orestes A. Brownson," *Atlantic Monthly*, LXXVII (1896), 770–780.

Le Breton, Dagmar Renshaw. "Orestes Brownson's Visit to New Orleans in 1855," *American Literature*, XVI (May 1944), 110–114.

Leroux, Pierre. *Réfutation de l'Eclectisme.* Paris, 1839.

Liebman, Sheldon W. "Emerson's Transformation in the 1820's," *American Literature*, XL (May 1968), 133–154.

Lodge, Henry Cabot. *Daniel Webster.* In *American Statesmen.* Boston and New York, 1899.

Lowell, James Russell. *Complete Writings. Elmwood Edition.* 16 vols. Boston and New York, 1904.

Ludlow, Robert. "Book Reviews," *Catholic Worker*, Oct. 1855. Facsimile in *Emerson Society Quarterly*. No. 32, pt. 3 (1963).

Martin, Michael and Gelber, Leonard. *The New Dictionary of American History*. New York, 1952.

Matthiessen, F. O. *American Renaissance.* New York, 1941.

May, Samuel J. *What do Unitarians Believe?* (pamphlet). 2nd ed. Syracuse, N. Y., 1865.

Maynard, Theodore. *Orestes Brownson: Yankee, Radical, Catholic.* New York, 1943.

. "Orestes Brownson, Journalist: A Fighter for Truth," *Commonweal,* XXXVII (1943), 390–393.

McAvoy, Thomas T., C. S. C. "Orestes A. Brownson and American History," *Catholic Historical Review,* XV (Oct. 1954), 257–268.

McLoughlin, J. Fairfax, LL. D. "A Study of Dr. Brownson," *Catholic World,* LXXVII (June 1903), 310–319.

Methodist Quarterly. "The Rich against the Poor. The Laboring Classes. By O. A. Brownson." XXIII (Jan. 1841), 92–122.

. "Brownson's Quarterly Review." XXVII (July 1845), 454–478.

Michel, Virgil, O. S. B. *The Critical Principles of Orestes A. Brownson.* Washington, D. C., 1918.

. "Brownson's Political Philosophy and To-day," *American Catholic Quarterly Review,* XLIV (April 1919), 193–202.

. "Orestes A. Brownson," *Catholic World,* CXXV (July 1927), 499–505.

. "Brownson: A Man of Men," *Catholic World,* CXXV (Sept. 1927), 755–762.

Miller, Perry. *The New England Mind: The Seventeenth Century.* New York, 1939.

. "From Jonathan Edwards to Emerson," *New England Quarterly,* XIII (Dec. 1940), 589–617.

. "Individualism and the New England Tradition," *Journal of Liberal Religion,* IV (Summer 1942), 3–21.

(ed.). *The Transcendentalists: An Anthology.* Cambridge, Mass., 1950.

and Johnson, Thomas H. *The Puritans.* Boston, 1938.

Mims, Helen S. "Early American Democratic Theory and Orestes Brownson," *Science and Society,* III (Spring 1939), 166–198.

Mittelman, Edward B. "Trade Unionism (1833–1839)," Common's *History of Labour in the United States,* I, 333–484. Boston, 1926.

Molland, Einar. *Fra Hans Nielsen Hauge til Eivind Berggrav: Hovedlinjer i Norges kirkehistorie i det 19. og 20. århundre.* Oslo, 1951.

. *Konfesjonskunnskap: Kristenhetens trosbekjennelser og kirkesamfunn.* 2. rev. utg. Oslo, 1961.

Month. "Brownson's Works." XLVII (March 1883), 429–431.

. "The Works of Orestes A. Brownson." XLVIII (July 1883), 439–442.

. "Brownson's Works." LIII (March 1885), 444–448.

. "Brownson's Political and Literary Essays." LV (Nov. 1885), 439–443.

Moore, Geoffry (ed.). *American Literature.* London, 1964.

Morais, Herbert M. "Marx and Engels on America," *Science and Society,* XII (Winter 1948), 3–21.

Morris, Max. "Chartism and the British Working-Class Movement," *Science and Society*, XII (1948), 400–417.

Murdock, Kenneth B. *Literature & Theology in Colonial New England.* Cambridge, Mass., 1949.

Nation. "Orestes A. Brownson's Early Life." LXVII (Sept. 15, 1898), 205–206.

. "Orestes A. Brownson's Middle Life." LXXI (July 26, 1900), 77.

. "Orestes A. Brownson's Latter Life." LXXIII (July 4, 1901), 16–17.

Nevins, Allan and Commager, Henry Steele. *The Pocket History of the United States.* Overseas Editions. New York, 1942.

Nevins, Allan (ed.). *America through British Eyes.* New York, 1948.

Newman, John Henry (Cardinal). *Apologia pro vita sua.* London and New York, 1955. First ed. 1864.

Norton, Andrews. *Statement of Reasons for Not Believing the Doctrines of Trinitarians, Concerning the Nature of God, and the Person of Christ.* Boston, 1819 (1833 ed. consulted).

. *A Discourse on the Latest Form of Infidelity.* Cambridge, Mass., 1839.

Noyes, John Humphrey. *History of American Socialisms.* Reprinted 1961, New York. First ed. 1869.

O'Callaghan, Jeremiah. *Atheism of Brownson's Review: Unity and Trinity of God. Divinity and Humanity of Christ Jesus.* Burlington, Vt., 1852.

O'Sullivan, John L. "Mr. Brownson's Recent Articles in the Democratic Review," *Democratic Review*, XIII (Dec. 1843), 653–660.

Parker, Theodore. *Works. Centenary Edition.* Boston, 1910.

Parry, Stanley J., C. S. C. "The Premises of Brownson's Political Theory," *Review of Politics*, XVI (April 1954), 194–211.

Parsons, Wilfred, S. J. "Brownson, Hecker and Hewit," *Catholic World*, CLIII (July 1941), 396–408.

Perkins, Alice J. G. and Wolfson, Theresa. *Frances Wright: Free Enquirer. The study of a Temperament.* New York and London, 1939.

Philanthropist. Ithaca, N. Y., 1831–1832.

Pierpont, John. *On Substitutes for Religion.* American Unitarian Association Tract. 1st Series, No. 56, V. Boston, 1832.

. *Jesus Christ Not a Literal Sacrifice.* American Unitarian Association Tract. 1st Series, No. 81, VII. Boston, 1834.

Platner, John Winthrop et al. *The Religious History of New England.* King Chapel Lectures. Cambridge, Mass., and London, 1917.

Porte, Joel. "Nature as Symbol: Emerson's Noble Doubt," *New England Quarterly*, XXXVII (Dec. 1964), 453–476.

Porter, Lawrence C. "Transcendentalism: A Self-Portrait," *New England Quarterly*, XXXV (March 1962), 27–47.

Post, Albert. *Popular Freethought in America: 1825–1850.* New York, 1943.

Princeton Review. "Brownson's Exposition of Himself." XXX (Jan. 1858), 117–150.

. "Brownson's Development of Himself" (letter from the Rev. Reuben Smith). XXX (Jan. 1858), 390–392.

Renan, Ernest. *Cahiers de jeunesse: 1845–1846*. Paris, 1906.

Ripley, George. "Sir James Mackintosh's Ethical Philosophy," *Christian Examiner*, XIII (Jan. 1833), 311–332.

. "Herder's Theological Opinions and Services," *Christian Examiner*, XIX (Nov. 1835), 172–204.

. "Schleiermacher as a Theologian," *Christian Examiner*, XX (March 1836), 1–46.

. "The Rationale of Religious Enquiry," *Christian Examiner*, XXI (Nov. 1836), 225–254.

(ed.). *Specimens of Foreign Standard Literature*. Vols. I–II. Boston, 1838.

. "Brownson's Writings," *Dial*, I (July 1840), 22–46.

and Bradford, George P. "Philosophic Thought in Boston." Justin Winsor's *Memorial History of Boston*, IV. Boston, 1881.

Roemer, Lawrence. *Brownson on Democracy and the Trend toward Socialism*. New York, 1953.

Rowland, P. James. "Brownson and the American Republic Today," *Catholic World*, CLII (Feb. 1941), 536–541.

Runes, Dagobert D. (ed.). *The Dictionary of Philosophy*. New York, s. a.

(ed.). *Twentieth Century Philosophy: Living Schools of Thought*. New York, 1947.

Ryan, Thomas, C. P P. S. "Brownson Speaks on England," *Catholic World*, CLIV (Jan. 1942), 426–429.

Saint Augustine. *Confessions*. Trans. E. P. Pusey. In *Everyman's Library*, ed. Ernest Rhys. London and New York, 1946.

Schaff, Philip. *America: A Sketch of Its Political, Social, and Religious Character* (ed. Perry Miller). Cambridge, Mass., 1961. First published: New York, 1855.

Schlesinger, Arthur M., Jr. *Orestes A. Brownson: A Pilgrim's Progress*. Boston, 1939.

. *The Age of Jackson*. Boston, 1946. 1950 ed. consulted.

Schneider, Herbert W. *A History of American Philosophy*. New York, 1947.

Schultz, Arthur R. and Pochmann, Henry A. "George Ripley: Unitarian, Transcendentalist, or Infidel?" *American Literature*, XIV (March 1942), 1–19.

Shepard, Edward M. *Martin Van Buren*. In *American Statesmen*. Boston and New York, 1899.

Shepard, Odell. *Pedlar's Progress: The Life of Bronson Alcott*. Boston, 1937.

Simon Myron and Parsons, Thornton H. (eds.). *Transcendentalism and Its Legacy*. Ann Arbor, Mich., 1966.

Skard, Sigmund (ed.). *USA in Focus: Recent Re-Interpretations*. Publications of the Nordic Association for American Studies, II. Oslo, 1966.

Skotheim, Robert Allen. *American Intellectual Histories and Historians*. Princeton, N. J., 1966.

Smith, H. Shelton, Handy, Robert T. and Loetscher, Lefferts A. (eds.). *American Christianity: An Historical Interpretation with Representative Documents*. 2 vols. New York, 1960, 1963.

Smith, James Ward and Jamison, A. Leland (eds.). *Religion in American Life: The Shaping of American Religion*. 4 vols. Princeton, N. J., 1961.

Smith, John E. *The Spirit of American Philosophy*. New York, 1963.

Smithline, Arnold. *Natural Religion in American Literature*. New Haven, 1966.

Souriau, Maurice. *Histoire du romantisme en France*. Paris, 1927.

Spiller, R. E., Thorp, W., Johnson, T. H. and Canby, H. S. (eds.). *Literary History of the United States*. 3 vols. New York, 1948.

Sumner, Helen L. "Citizenship (1827–1833)." Common's *History of Labour in the United States*, I, 167–335. New York, 1926.

Sumner, William G. *Andrew Jackson*. In *American Statesmen*. Boston and New York, 1899.

Sweet, William W. *Religion in the Development of American Culture: 1765–1840*. New York, 1952.

Swift, Lindsay. *Brook Farms: Its Members, Scholars, and Visitors*. New York, 1900.

Taine, H. *Les philosophes classiques du XIX siècle en France*. 5e éd. Paris, 1882.

Taylor, Walter F. *A History of American Letters*. Boston, 1947.

Thompson, Cameron. "John Locke and New England Transcendentalism," *New England Quarterly*, XXXV (Dec. 1962), 435–457.

Tocqueville, Alexis de. *Democracy in America* (ed. Richard D. Haffner). A Mentor Book. New York, 1956.

Todd, Edgeley Woodman. "Philosophical Ideas at Harvard College: 1817 to 1837," *New England Quarterly*, XVI (Dec. 1943), 63–90.

Unitarian. Cambridge and Boston, 1834.

Unitarian Affirmations: Seven Discourses Given in Washington, D. C. By Unitarian ministers. Boston, 1886.

Wade, Mason. *Margaret Fuller: Whetstone of Genius*. New York, 1940.

Ware, Henry, Jr. *Three Important Questions Answered*. American Unitarian Association Tract. 1st Series, No. 82, VII. Boston, 1834.

[Wayland, Francis]. "Charles Elwood," *Christian Review*, V (Sept. 1840), 419–442.

Wellek, René. "The Minor Transcendentalists," *New England Quarterly*, XV (Dec. 1942), 652–680.

———. "Emerson and German Philosophy," *New England Quarterly*, XVI (March 1943), 41–62.

W[ilson], D[exter] W[illiam]. "Charles Elwood; or, The Infidel Converted," *Christian Examiner*, XXVIII (May 1840), 180–198.

Wilson, J. B. "The Antecedents of Brook Farm," *New England Quarterly*, XV (June 1942), 320–331.

Winsnes, A. H. *Jacques Maritain: En studie i kristen filosofi.* Oslo, 1957.

Index

PUBLICATIONS OF
THE AMERICAN INSTITUTE
UNIVERSITY OF OSLO

Halvdan Koht: *The American Spirit in Europe. Survey of Transatlantic Influences.* IX, 289 pp. Out of print. (Philadelphia, Pa. 1949).

Einar Haugen: *The Norwegian Language in America. A Study in Bilingual Behavior.* Out of print.
Vol. I: The Bilingual Community. XIV, 317 pp.
Vol. II: The American Dialects of Norwegian. VII, 377 pp. (Philadelphia, Pa. 1953).

Sigmund Skard: *American Studies in Europe. Their History and Present Organization.*
Vol. I: The General Background, The United Kingdom, France, and Germany. Pp. 1–358.
Vol. II: The Smaller Western Countries, The Scandinavian Countries, The Mediterranean Nations, Eastern Europe, International Organization, and Conclusion. Pp. 359–736.
(Philadelphia, Pa. 1958.)

Americana Norvegica. Norwegian Contributions to American Studies.
Vol. I. Editors: Sigmund Skard and Henry H. Wasser. 340 pp. (Philadelphia, Pa. 1966).
Vol. II – Editor: Sigmund Skard. Editorial Committee: Ingvald Raknem, Georg Roppen, Ingrid Semmingsen. 357 pp. (Philadelphia, Pa. 1968).

Jan W. Dietrichson: *The Image of Money in the American Novel of the Gilded Age.* 417 pp. (Oslo and New York. 1969).

Per Seyersted: *Kate Chopin. A Critical Biography.* 247 pp. (Oslo and Baton Rouge, La. 1969).

Per Sveino: *Orestes A. Brownson's Road to Catholicism,* 340 pp. (Oslo and New York. 1970).